INCUBATION IN EARLY BYZANTIUM

CULTURAL ENCOUNTERS IN LATE ANTIQUITY AND THE MIDDLE AGES

VOLUME 41

General Editor
Yitzhak Hen, *The Hebrew University of Jerusalem*

Editorial Board
Barbara Bombi, *University of Kent*
Paul M. Cobb, *University of Pennsylvania*
Adam S. Cohen, *University of Toronto*
Kate Cooper, *Royal Holloway, University of London*
Maria Mavroudi, *University of California*
Judith Olszowy-Schlanger, *University of Oxford*
and *École Pratique des Hautes Études, Paris*
Carine van Rhijn, *Universiteit Utrecht*
Peter Sarris, *University of Cambridge*
Daniel Lord Smail, *Harvard University*

Incubation in Early Byzantium

The Formation of Christian Incubation Cults and Miracle Collections

ILDIKÓ CSEPREGI

BREPOLS

British Library Cataloguing in Publication Data

A catalogue record for this book is available from the British Library.

© 2024, Brepols Publishers n.v., Turnhout, Belgium.

All rights reserved. No part of this publication may be reproduced, stored in a retrieval system, or transmitted, in any form or by any means, electronic, mechanical, photocopying, recording, or otherwise without the prior permission of the publisher.

ISBN: 978-2-503-60660-6
e-ISBN: 978-2-503-60661-3
DOI: 10.1484/M.CELAMA-EB.5.134035

ISSN: 1378-8779
e-ISSN: 2294-8511

Printed in the EU on acid-free paper.

D/2024/0095/12

Table of Contents

Acknowledgements — 7

Note on Editorial Choices and Abbreviations — 9

Introduction — 11

Part I
Cults and Records

Chapter 1
Greek Incubation — 21

Chapter 2
The Literary Background of the Collections — 43

Chapter 3
The Christian Incubation Saints:
Their Cult Sites and their Miracle Records — 57

Part II
Sources

Chapter 4
Material Sources — 107

Chapter 5
The Oral Tradition in the Miracles — 137

Chapter 6
The Hagiographers: Who Makes the Incubation Stories? — 175

Part III
Stories

Chapter 7
Compositional Structure in the Miracle Collections — 193

Chapter 8
Narrative Techniques and Variants of the Dream Stories — 219

Chapter 9
Doctors and Miracles: Doctors and Medicine in Early Christianity and Byzantium — 245

Chapter 10
Mirroring Society and its Beliefs: Sinners, Pagans, Jews, Heretics, Non-Christians in Terms of Illness and Cure — 263

Conclusion — 289

Works Cited — 295

Index — 325

Acknowledgements

I am indebted to numerous people for their help, which came in the various forms of advice, critique, talks, or encouragement and friendship. I started to work on this topic in 2000, and since then I owe special thanks to Gábor Klaniczay for his immense help, guidance, and encouragement, to Evelyne Patlagean and Stephanos Efthymiadis, who were the first readers of my work, to Sarolta Takács, Vincent Déroche, and David Movrin, who wisely criticized great parts of it, and to Péter Agócs, Charles Burnett, Gábor Buzási, Averil Cameron, Felicity Harley, Judith Herrin, Michel Kaplan, Helen King, Vivian Nutton. I thank several scholars for letting me read their works in manuscript and for the friendly exchange of views: Charles Stewart, Gary Ferngren, Vincent Déroche, Phil Booths, William A. Christian Jr., Robert Wiśniewski. I cannot express enough my gratitude to Jordan Voltz and Frank Schaer, who corrected the English text with the patience of Byzantine saints. I thank the British Library for allowing me to have in hand and page through the tenth-century manuscript of the London Codex.

The completion of the book was financed by the Spanish Ministry of Universities under application 33.50.460A.752 and by the European Union NextGenerationEU/PRTR through a María Zambrano contract of the University of Vigo. I am also grateful for the research fellowship and the amazing working conditions at Dumbarton Oaks, given by Harvard University. And most warmly, for all the help and trust over the years, to the Warburg Institute.

Note on Editorial Choices and Abbreviations

For reasons of internal consistency across the book, English spelling is used for names of places, persons, and literary works where common. If there is no common English spelling, Latinized spelling or Greek transcriptions are used in my own text (e.g. Asclepius, Thecla) but in references, titles, and citations I kept the form their respective authors used (Asklepios, Thekla, etc.). An important note on translations and citations of Greek and Latin sources: Wherever I do not mention the name of the translators, or cite the work from which I am quoting, all translations are mine. Almost all the sources to which I make frequent references are bilingual. T stands for the Edelsteins' Testimonies, which give both the original Greek or Latin text side by side with the English translation. Similarly, the source editions of the miracle collections I use are bilingual. For most ancient quotations whenever possible I use the Loeb editions or other bilingual editions; therefore readers can easily find my references in the original.

AASS	*Acta Sanctorum*, ed. by Socii Bollandiani (Brussels: Société des Bollandistes, 1643–1940)
ANRW	*Aufstieg und Niedergang der römischen Welt: Geschichte und Kultur Roms im Spiegel der neueren Forschung*, ed. by Hildegard Temporini and Wolfgang Haase, Part I (vols I–IV) and Part II (vols I–XXXVII.3) (Berlin: de Gruyter, 1972–)
BHG	*Bibliotheca Hagiographica Graeca*, ed. by François Halkin, Subsidia hagiographica, 8, 3rd edn (Brussels: Société des Bollandistes, 1957 [1895])
BHO	*Bibliotheca Hagiographica Orientalis*, ed. by Socii Bollandiani, Subsidia hagiographica, 10 (Brussels: Société des Bollandistes, 1910)
CIA / CIG / IG	Corpus Inscriptionum Atticarum / Corpus Inscriptionum Graecarum / Inscriptiones Graecae, online: 'Searchable Greek Inscriptions', Packard Humanities Institute, <https://epigraphy.packhum.org/allregions>
PG	Patrologiae cursus completus, series Graeca, ed. by Jacques Paul Migne, 167 vols (Paris: Garnier, 1857–1886)
PL	Patrologiae cursus completus, series Latina, ed. by Jacques-Paul Migne, 221 vols (Paris: Imprimerie Catholique, 1841–1865)
T	*Asclepius: A Collection of the Testimonies*, ed. and trans. by Emma J. Edelstein and Ludwig Edelstein, 2 vols, 2nd edn (Baltimore: Johns Hopkins University Press, 1998)

Numbering of the miracles is consistent, and all editors, translators, and scholars have been using the same numbering over the last one hundred years; there are no variants according to different editions.

CL	Codex Londoniensis: *Cosmae et Damiani sanctorum medicorum vita et miracula e codice Londoniensi*, ed. by Ernst Rupprecht, Neue Deutsche Forschungen, 20 (Berlin: Junker und Dünnhaupt, 1935); my English translation is forthcoming in *Classica and Medievalia* (2024)
KDM	Kosmae et Damiani Miracula: *St Kosmas und Damian: Texte und Einleitung*, ed. by Ludwig Deubner (Leipzig: L. Deubner, 1907)
MA	Miracula Artemii: 1 (Greek–English), *The Miracles of St Artemius: A Collection of Miracle Stories by an Anonymous Author of Seventh-Century Byzantium* ed. and trans. by Virgil S. Crisafulli and John W. Nesbitt (Leiden: Brill, 1997); 2 (Greek–French), *Les Miracles d'Artémios*, ed. and trans. by Vincent Déroche, Le monde Byzantin (Paris: CNRS, forthcoming)
MCJ	Miracula Cyri et Johanni: 1 (Greek–Spanish), ed. and trans. by Natalio Fernandez Marcos, *Los Thaumata de Sofronio: Contribucion al estudio de la incubatio cristiana* (Madrid: Instituto Antonio de Nebrija, 1975), pp. 241–400; 2 (Greek–French), *Sophrone de Jerusalem: Miracles des Saints Cyr et Jean (BHG I 477–79)*, ed. and trans. by Jean Gascou (Paris: De Boccard, 2006)
MT	Miracula Theclae: 1 (Greek–French), *Vie et miracles de sainte Thècle: Texte grec, traduction et commentaire*, ed. and trans. by Gilbert Dagron (Brussels: Société des Bollandistes, 1978); 2 (English), Linda Honey, 'Thekla: Text and Context with a First English Translation of the Miracles' (unpublished doctoral dissertation, University of Calgary, 2011); 3 (English), *Miracle Tales from Byzantium*, trans. by Alice-Mary Talbot and Scott F. Johnson (Cambridge, MA: Harvard University Press, 2012)

The same numbering is observed in the collected volume *Sainte Thècle, Saints Côme et Damien, Saints Cyr et Jean (extraits), Saint Georges*, ed. and trans. by André-Jean Festugière (Paris: Edition A. et J. Picard, 1971)

Introduction

The place is deserted and no one near me will hear the words which I speak. Believe me, men, I had been dead during all the years of life that I was alive. The beautiful, the good, the holy, the evil were all the same to me; such, it seems, was the darkness that formerly enveloped my understanding and concealed and hid from me all these things. But now that I have come here, I have become alive again for all the rest of my life, as if I had lain down in the temple of Asclepius and had been saved. I walk, I talk, I think. This sun, so great, so beautiful I have now discovered, men, for the first time; now today I see under the clear sky you, the air, the acropolis, the theatre.[1]

These words were pronounced by a character from a lost comedy of Menander and in a powerful image describe how sleeping in the Temple of Asclepius might have been a life-changing experience. From this sleep, the individual not only awoke healed but saw the world around as never before. Temple sleep or incubation was a religious practice with a long past and an even longer future.[2] In many respects, it reached across the borders of religions and healing methods. It was practiced in ancient Mesopotamia and Asia Minor; in Greece and Rome as well as in pre-Christian Gaul; and it found its way into Judaism, Christianity, and Islam.[3] Islamic incubation was on the margins as well, since it is not found in the Qur'ān or the *hadīth*, and was never approved but always remained tolerated. Incubation was practised around the saints' tombs and involved various rituals, before and during the pilgrimage, such as purification, almsgiving, sacrifice, bathing in or drinking from the sacred spring, and the characteristic *ex voto* rags tied to sacred trees as proof of the

---

1 Menander, Papyrus Didotiana b, 1–15 = T419.
2 Thorough introduction of the practice, both pagan and Christian, is by Deubner, *De incubatione* and Hamilton, *Incubation*. More recently two major volumes were published, without knowing about each other, which address Greek incubation: Ehrenheim, *Greek Incubation Rituals* and the monumental work of Renberg, *Where Dreams May Come*; they are currently the two utmost authorities on the subject of ancient incubation, yet their appearance did not make superfluous the works of earlier scholars, often cited here, with whose ideas I often engage in discussion especially over details. Several aspects of incubation were addressed by the research group at the Humboldt University, under the direction of Christoph Markschies as well as by their conference 'Inkubation – Heilung im Schlaf: Heidnischer Kult und christliche Praxis' (Berlin, October 2007) (with some publications on their website, <http://www.antikes-christentum.de/heilung>, and more forthcoming).
3 On incubation in the Near East and the Bible, see Husser, *Dreams and Dream Narratives*, pp. 46–50, 69–70; Gil, *Therapeia*, fol. 358; and Renberg, *Where Dreams May Come*, pp. 36–73; in Egypt, Renberg, *Where Dreams May Come*, pp. 74–99; on incubation in Islam (*istikhāra*), see Dols, *Majnūn*, esp. pp. 234–35, 287; and T. Fahd, 'Istikhāra', in Bearman and others, eds, *The Encyclopaedia of Islam*, IV, pp. 259–60.

visit. Healing in the dream was represented in the forms of direct treatment or prescriptions, and it was common for healing sites to be specialized.[4]

In parts of the Mediterranean world, especially rural ones, Catholic, Orthodox, or Muslim, it has survived to the present day. I do not intend to suggest that we are dealing with a continuity of ritual, since the theological framework of each cult differed extremely, yet the practice itself was ubiquitous. One of the reasons for its tenacity and popularity was that in every period and geographical zone, it answered a fundamental demand for healing through communication with the divine, and yet it required so little: a sacred place and an individual who went there intending to sleep.

From these basic requirements for incubation, there was plenty of iteration and differentiation. The core element of the practice was that the worshipper voluntarily went to the sacred site (a cave, a tomb, a temple, a place with relics) with the intention of sleeping there (often in special circumstances, having performed specific rites, for example purification or abstinence, and wearing specific robes or waiting in specific circumstances for the appearance of a dream). During their encounter with the divine being of the place, pilgrims sought a cure or an oracle; this being might have been a deity, an animal-epiphany, a lesser-grade divinity, a hero, a nymph, a living holy man, or a martyr honoured after death. Although the oracular and healing activities of the incubation cult sites often ran parallel, the present study is concerned only with healing, and accordingly will use the term 'dream healing' as an equivalent of incubation / temple sleep.

The emerging Christian Church had to face the challenge presented by this practice: it was ubiquitous, it was immensely popular, and it concerned important life situations. It had been so deeply rooted and efficacious that the Church could not simply ban it. It was, however, an undeniably pagan practice. The Christianization of the incubation ritual is a lengthy and many-faceted success story. This long process involved so many aspects of the Church's self-definition, including the social and theological issues of that era, which would alone render incubation to be a fascinating subject with a plethora of information to impart upon the interested scholar. The list of such topics is long: from deciding the fate of Greek temples and artistic representations to confronting Hippocratic medicine and the learned Greek intelligentsia that remained faithful to the old gods for the longest; accounting for the miracles happening among the pagans; embracing the healing ministry by the Church both in secular terms as well as in ritual healing; creating Christian theories on dreams; and confronting the notions of magic and divination.

We have here a ritual inherited from Antiquity, the core of which is the healers' appearance in the dream of those who seek their help by sleeping in

---

4   For case studies on Muslim practices of visiting the saints' tomb for incubation, see Crapanzano, 'Saints, Jnūn, and Dreams', and Doutté, *Magie et religion dans l'Afrique du Nord*, pp. 410–14; for contemporary cases: Mittermaier, *Dreams that Matter*, pp. 95–100.

the temple/church. The healers then miraculously cure their patients, either with an immediate intervention or by giving some miraculous prescriptions. The ritual, however, is linked to the place; at the heart of the practice lies the patient's presence at the sacred spot. When it undergoes Christianization, this paradigm changes because of three critical problems it presents within a Christian framework: (1) the healer's being bound to a place (like the gods of Antiquity) was something definitely pagan and contradicts the fundamental Christian idea about God's omnipotence and omnipresence; (2) the emerging cult of the saints presents a different paradigm, into which the figure of the incubation healer does not fit; and (3) the cult of images and other portable holy objects that could transfer thaumaturgic power also affected the incubation paradigm.

To some extent, Christian incubation saints differ from other saints endowed with thaumaturgic gifts (popular living saints, ascetics, martyr saints venerated at their shrines, and saints in the form of relics — though these categories are not exclusive). In non-incubation healing, the most common types of miracles were modelled after the gestures of Christ and provided cures through words, touch, the sign of the cross, eulogies, and sanctified objects in various contexts, but there was little differentiation for person or ailment. However, in incubation miracles where the dream functioned as medium, the impact of medical learning and of doctors and the reflection of scientific achievements in miraculous cures allow us to indicate some changes within the format that may have been paradigmatic. These insights into the mentality, the inner consciousness of the community or individuals may represent, in some cases, only a personal point of view, but in others, it may provide an insight into the thought-world of a spiritually and socially turbulent period of early Byzantine society.

For the most part, I shall draw on the Christian incubation records as narrative sources. In order to fully explore cult practices in both their ancient and Christian forms, other types of sources need to be analysed as well, including the archaeological remains of cults and their artistic representations. Being neither an archaeologist nor an art historian, I have chosen to stick to the textual sources, focusing on the factors surrounding the emergence of the stories and compositional intentions that formed the narrative records of early Christian incubation healing into compositionally structured miracle collections.

My survey focuses mainly on the miracles of Saint Thecla, the two versions of the miraculous cures of Saints Cosmas and Damian, the miracle collection of Saints Cyrus and John, and the healings of Saint Artemius. I shall argue that these collections together constitute a well-defined group, one that differs in kind from other contemporary Byzantine hagiographical records. This focus on the narrative aspects of these sources is justified because as early Christian incubation emerged it adopted not only elements of the pagan ritual, but also ancient narrative records of temple sleep. The transformation of dream cures and their textual and literary expression developed in parallel, and both were rooted in the preceding pagan practice. Consequently, and rather oddly, these Christian collections of dream healing bear a closer resemblance to the incubation records of Antiquity than to contemporary Christian hagiographical genres (in the form of the narrative, not, of course, in their theology).

The Byzantine miracle collections that record incubation proper (those dedicated more or less exclusively to temple sleep) form a small but homogeneous corpus. They were closely modelled not only on the Greek incubation records but also on each other. Their spatial and chronological distribution attests to the popularity of the incubation cult sites and confirms, beyond any doubt, that incubation was a firm and deeply rooted practice with its own unique aspects both in regard to cultic ritual and in the way this ritual was recorded. These incubation miracle collections form a significant proportion of Byzantine hagiography; hence our sources are far from being solitary examples. The uniqueness of these miracle collections and how they developed is the subject of this study.

The first step will be to broadly introduce the cult practice of ancient incubation (Chapter 1) and its literary background (Chapter 2): ancient pagan and Christian aretalogies (the narratives of miracles), ancient incubation records, the Gospel miracles, and the early Christian miracle narratives, the latter most often connected to the saints' *Lives*. Scholars in the past few decades have radically reinterpreted the umbrella term 'aretalogy'. Mark van Uytfanghe spoke of the *chimera of aretalogy* when he redrew the generic-thematic-theological definitions and literary traditions of subject.[5] His hypothesis did not aim to define a single genre, but sought to bring a better understanding of the literary atmosphere of pagan and Christian Late Antiquity to the study. He therefore discarded the categories of genre-definition, introducing instead the concept of *hagiographic discourse*. Such discourse was limited neither to Christianity nor to literature, but was emblematic of a mode of expression for Greek, Christian, and Jewish thought of the time. In my work, a brief description of how genre categories (such as aretalogy or even hagiography) became superseded will be followed by an outline of the tradition of Greek incubation miracle collections (with special attention paid to the recent hypotheses of G. Guidorizzi and Marco Dorati),[6] and by an enquiry into the literary characteristics and requirements of the dream-cure records. The impact of Jesus's miraculous healing on the rhetoric of the incubation narratives will be addressed briefly.

Certainly, there was another half-literary, half-cultic Christian precedent to the early Greek Christian incubation narratives, even if it was an indirect one. The term *libelli miraculorum* referred to the custom of keeping a miracle archive in churches, a phenomenon that not only secured the memory and authority of the miracles but inevitably moulded them into a narrative. Through the

---

5 Van Uytfanghe, 'L'hagiografie'.
6 Dorati, 'Funzioni e motivi'; Dorati and Guidorizzi, 'La letteratura incubatoria'.

process of authenticating and conserving the miracles, the local community were kept aware of the presence of such records. The non-incubational miracle catalogues of the early Church will be considered in their capacity as indirect models that served as a background for incubation narratives.

Chapter 3 addresses the emergence of incubation rituals of Christian physician saints and their respective miracle collections: Cosmas and Damian, Cyrus and John, Artemius, and, in a different vein, within the cult of Saint Thecla. Throughout this work, but especially in the first three chapters, I make extensive references to other scholars' views and often give a detailed outline of how these viewpoints evolved or were challenged. I chose to do so, at the risk of slowing the narrative of my own research, for two reasons. First, much of the important secondary literature, with indispensable contributions from scholars writing in Spanish, German, Italian, or Latin over a period of a hundred years, is hard to access, and the contrasting arguments are often difficult to follow. Second, I would like to articulate their research ideas fairly, even if time, new trends, or succeeding generations of scholars have shunted them aside. We owe to these past scholars the texts themselves, as well as their conviction that these texts and cults were unique and important to study. We should accept their invitation to build upon their views.

Hopefully, this enquiry will demonstrate that there was not just one 'cult of the saints', even at the cost of challenging Peter Brown's model, which (as fine as it is) has become the exclusive model for understanding the formation of late antique sainthood. The development of the Christian incubation cult of these saints was clearly different from what is generally recognized in the cult of martyrs, holy bishops, or living ascetics. Moreover, as the cult practice of incubation took shape in the early Church in a particular fashion, so did the incubation records, which, in many ways, are quite unlike other specimens of Byzantine *miracula*.

Once I have described the collections of miraculous dreams found in incubation records, in Part II I turn to the sources and formative processes that moulded these collections, asking how the early Christian incubation miracles were shaped into stories, texts, recorded narratives, and literary works. Based on what the sources themselves say about their background, I map out the layers of transmission that can be identified within the collections themselves. The analysis of the sources of miraculous cure is best begun with the textual and pictorial evidence provided by the most important material evidence of the cult experience, namely votive tablets and images (Chapter 4). Besides examining the images as records and hence sources for the stories, I also show how pictorial representation shaped the narrative of the incubation dream.

The next element in shaping the stories was the oral tradition that emerged around the site of the cult. These narratives were formed and directed by temple/church propaganda and by pilgrim word-of-mouth. Oral transmission was an important factor in narrative formation because it was not only a way of transforming events into a narrative or providing material for such, but also a significant aspect of the cultic experience. Chapter 5 examines the individual miracle collections in detail in order to address the following questions: (1) What are the textual indications that these miracles were transmitted orally? (2) What occasions (cultic or everyday) provided the framework for storytelling gatherings? (3) Who were the carriers of this oral tradition? Were they the tellers of miracles or the immediate identifiable informants of the hagiographers? (4) What narrative references attest to the spread of these stories? More importantly, how were these miraculous cures narrated and how did this telling of miracles, in turn, become part of the story itself? (5) What is the role of the real presence of orality and its narrative representation in the miracles?

When the miracle collections were recorded, the purpose was not to establish an exclusive canon of texts, in contrast to the gospel tradition. Two intentions were involved in the production of a written text: first, the desire to record past miraculous events to reinforce the believers' hopes that such miracles would happen to them as well; second, depending on the personal aspirations of the hagiographer, the intention to compose a literary work. Besides the internal set of variables signalling the formation of the miracle collections, I shall use works on oral traditions from the fields of anthropology, classical philology, and New Testament studies that focus on separate aspects of orality.

I then introduce the person behind the records: in the midst of shaping the narrative and moulding it into a compositional whole, into a proper collection, we find the person of the hagiographer — alongside others. Chapter 6 on the hagiographers will address how they reflected upon their own work of composition and research. Here, I will seek answers to further questions, such as, What is the relationship of the hagiographer to the text? or In what sense can the hagiographer be regarded as author, narrator, performer, and redactor? Are they the recorders of the texts or creative composers? How did these particular Byzantine hagiographers depict their own role, what forms did their self-display or self-characterization take, and what emerges without their conscious effort? The hagiographers' personality and their literary ambitions certainly left their marks on the structural development and compositional features of the collections.

Part III complements the latter survey by focusing on a structural analysis of the texts and on the conscious shaping of the compositions, born out of literary ambitions that often aimed high and were marked by the hagiographers' individual compositional styles. In the impressive literature on Byzantine hagiography, there are surprisingly few articles that treat hagiographical sources from a literary point of view, and even fewer that deal with them in terms of literary theory. Without subscribing to any such theory in particular, my analysis remains focused on the miracle narratives and includes a mapping of their structure, the miracle groups, and the narrative technique. Thus, Chapter 7 looks at the collections' compositional structures, individual characteristics, structural development, and thematic groupings, in addition to analysing the miracle stories in each collection. Before these structural investigations,

I will briefly consider how each hagiographer establishes credibility, creating the literary and concrete reality of the narrative, as well as the reality of the miraculous. After analysing each collection as a whole, narrative techniques are the subject of Chapter 8. These include story patterns, folktale motifs, narrative devices such as wordplay and jokes, the function of dialogues, scenic duality, and the narrative compulsion to return to expected endings. I attempt here to identify the logic of the narratives. In 1960, Festugière raised the question of hagiographical folk motifs, and in the 1970s, other topoi came to the attention of scholars, while contemporary Byzantinists have analysed hagiographical motifs in a more literary-narrative context. In this chapter, I shall concentrate on some of the individually developed nuclei of miraculous stories such as the invitation dream, the finding of curative objects, and the narrative and theological role of repetition.

Chapter 9 has two parts. The first one analyses the impact of medical knowledge on the dream content of incubation patients, illustrating what E. R. Dodds described as the culturally dependent dream pattern. The second part examines the narrative role of doctors in the miracles by highlighting the situations in which the medical craft is presented in dreams. The closing chapter of this part (Chapter 10) looks first at the contemporary social reality represented in the stories, determined in part by the personal credo of the hagiographer, but also by the religious context around the cult place. I shall consider purposeful and accidental testimonies and attitudes towards pagans, heretics, and Jews, and explore the promotion of theological truths and the presence of contrasting orthodoxies. Certainly, the most articulated of these truths and orthodoxies reveals what this sort of hagiography shows about the 'other', in the broadest sense. Within the period of this study, these 'others' may include not simply Greeks (pagans) in their quality as non-Christians, but 'others' marked by their learning (philosophical, rhetorical, or — in the case of physicians — medical), the last guardians of *paideia*, the traditional Greek education. The unbelievers present in the miracle stories posed a challenge to these miracles and the theological message behind them. They were resistant pagans, Greeks, or Jews, heirs to a great cultural tradition. Prominent among them were doctors, who presented a (perhaps more narrative than real) rivalry, or simply fulfilled a necessary role by viewing healing from a different perspective. Less unusual in view of later hagiography is the presence and representation of the many sorts of heretics of the day, hence the definition of an orthodoxy that can be quite varied.[7] In this context theological propaganda is hardly surprising; what deserves particular attention is how the hagiographers chose to apply their anti-heretical measures. It is noteworthy how hagiography, this apparently fixed narrative form, gave resonance to contemporary sentiments and to changes in its immediate social

---

7   For the period in question, see on this Allan, 'The Definition and Enforcement of Orthodoxy', and Booth, *Crisis of Empire*.

surrounding. Here the position taken towards Jews and the surprisingly rapid accommodation of anti-Judaic rhetoric will be a key example. One of the aims of the collections was theological propaganda. This was accomplished by contrasting the faith of the saints to that of their patients, where both parties were ready to express a neat dogmatic credo. The uniqueness arises when the patients, the saints, and the cult itself could change their theological position; thus, two versions of miracle stories emerged, naturally with two differently interpreted orthodoxies.

The final part of the last chapter addresses the aim of the recording of these miracles, such as entertainment, local cult propaganda, or the dissemination of theological truths. Here I highlight the surrounding circumstances of telling and listening to the dream-miracle narratives. This communal aspect of the cult experience is all the more important because pilgrims not only underwent the rites together, but concurrently told and listened to miracle stories that instructed, oriented, encouraged (or discouraged), and entertained them. The instances of stories that direct our attention to their own mise-en-scène help us form an idea about how 'informal' this sort of performance was and incite us to ask how telling miracles was integrated into the customary practices of the cult place (or even into the liturgy). The mode of expressing the expected unexpected, that is, the logic of the miraculous events, brings us back to those characteristics of the narrative which arose simply by its being told. The worshipper was psychically prepared through the entertainment function of the narrative, through 'becoming an audience'.

The conclusion sums up the broader hagiographical aims of the incubation narratives, and their cultic and narrative singularity. I shall summarize in what respects the Byzantine incubation collections differ from contemporary Byzantine miracle corpora, in what respects they conform to the hagiographical models of the time, and in what respects they reach back and draw on the ancient paradigms of incubation practice and literature. In several aspects, the records of incubation healers were closer to the (pagan) Greek narrative and cultic models than to the other Byzantine miracle collections or New Testament paradigms of miraculous cures. The Christian incubation miracles reflect the survival of a pagan practice with its own narrative tradition. This practice and its narrative left noteworthy traces in the Christian miracle stories, with elements foreign to mainstream Byzantine hagiography. However, the most fascinating development (and one not at all predictable with the arrival of Christianity) was this interconnectedness itself: that the existence of a ritual and its way of expression went on hand in hand.

Part I

Cults and Records

CHAPTER 1

Greek Incubation

The divine physician was expected to make prescriptions that were the paradoxical reverse of normal human therapy, and he did not disdain the use of magical drugs. But he was not required to suggest a different, essentially religious aetiology of diseases. His was secular medicine, with an injection of supernatural power.[1]

The ancient practice of temple sleep is closely connected to the concept that, during the dream, the soul is freed (to some extent) from its physical bounds and contacts the world of the gods more freely.[2] This spiritual aspect of dreams gained an important place in Greek religion.[3] The dream-concept in literature, first formulated by Homer, was but one of the manifold dream-mythologies.[4] Dream, at times also closely related to death, soon found its expression in the thought world of philosophy.[5] The ritual application of dreams had two main purposes: oracular and curative. These quite different needs, physical and spiritual, found their common medium in temple sleep.[6] The essence of the incubation practice was that the sick or those who wished to receive an oracle went to the sacred place of the divinity with the explicit goal of sleeping there and experiencing, in a dream, an epiphany of the god.[7]

---

1 Parker, *Miasma*, p. 249.
2 From the numerous publications, an overall outline is given by Hanson, 'Dreams and Visions'; van Lieshout, *Greeks on Dreams*, and more recently Harris, *Dreams and Experience*; for a psychological context of incubation, see Meier, *Healing Dream and Ritual*.
3 Brelich, 'The Place of Dreams' and the curious book of the ethnopsychologist Devereux, *Dreams in Greek Tragedy* and more recently Walde, *Die Traumdarstellungen in der griechisch-römischen Dichtung*.
4 Amory, 'The Gates of Horn and Ivory'; Messer, *The Dream in Homer and Greek Tragedy*; Lévy, 'Le rêve homérique'.
5 The dream concepts of Heracleitos, Democritos, Plato, and Aristotle and their interpretations have been summerized by van Lieshout, 'Philosophers on Dreams', in his *Greeks on Dreams*, pp. 64–164.
6 The sources of oracular dreams are collected in *Graecorum de re onirocritica reliquiae*, ed. by Del Corno; compare with Del Corno's two other works: 'I sogni e la loro interpretazione nell'età dell'Impero' and 'Ricerche sull' oniricritica greca'.
7 On the terminology of incubation: Deubner, *De incubatione*, p. 6; Fernandez Marcos, *Los Thaumata*, pp. 27–28; Lopez Salva, 'El sueño incubatorio'; Renberg, *Where Dreams May Come*, pp. 8–9. Recently Ehrenheim argued that there was no need for a special terminology for incubation; any word for sleeping could have referred to incubation if used in connection with any Asclepieion: Ehrenheim, 'Identifying Incubation Areas', pp. 238–39, and I agree with Ehrenheim. This statement is even more valid with regard to the Western Christian sources (not addressed here), where we often read that the pilgrims accidentally fell asleep, right in the church or at the tomb. In my eyes, such de-emphasizing of incubation was the

Many of the famous incubation places have been excavated and well documented, and our knowledge about the sites are complemented by several types of archaeological finds, such as votive offerings and inscriptions. In addition, a great number of ancient written testimonies and references have survived from both Greek literature and historiography. Taken together, these sources form a solid base of information about the incubation ritual and its local variants around the Mediterranean from the fifth to fourth centuries BC onwards. This overview will set the stage for our analysis of the Christian incubation material.[8]

Within the cults of Greek incubation deities and heroes, there was no clear-cut division between the healing and the oracular aspects, yet in accordance with the spheres of their divine competence, healing incubation was primarily the task of Asclepius and later of Isis and Serapis. In addition, there are a significant number of other local healing deities, whose cults included incubation heroes, and locally worshipped healing cults, some of whom claimed widespread fame, such as Amphiaraus in Oropos and Trophonius in Lebadea.[9]

Asclepius: His Myth, his Cult

Asclepius had a unique place among the deities of Greek religion. The ambiguous nature of his human and divine being, the various stories and theories of his origin, and the healing practices at his places of cult all endowed him with special attributes. Greek religion had several other healing deities, other places of incubation and divination, flourishing local cults of heroes, and mortal physicians who obtained divine features. All of this diversified further under the impact of Egyptian and Eastern healing gods.[10] Nevertheless, because of his divine healing function, Asclepius was the most popular hero-god. Due to this popularity, his wondrous interventions, and owing to a somewhat radically non-Olympian nature, he was seen by the spreading religion of Christianity as its greatest enemy and a true rival of Christ. His mixed nature was present already in his ambiguous mythical origin: Did a mortal physician endowed with extraordinary knowledge become a god in his own right, or did a deity amalgamate the elements of a heroic cult?[11]

---

hagiographers' intention to obfuscate the pagan associations of voluntarily going to sleep at a sacred site.

8 Neatly assessed by Ehrenheim, *Greek Incubation Rituals*, pp. 23–109, and Renberg, *Where Dreams May Come*, pp. 115–308.
9 For more on the oracular and healing aspects and examples, see the valuable insights of Rohde, *Psiche*, ch. 4 on heroes, esp. its section 10.
10 An overall picture is given about ancient healing deities in the excellent monograph of Jayne, *The Healing Gods of Ancient Civilizations*.
11 The two parallel versions are presented by Farnell, *Greek Hero Cults*, esp. ch. 10, 'The Cult

Asclepius was originally a pre-Olympian deity with a strong chthonic character (that is, related to the underworld and the earth), the traces of which can be observed in the incubation ritual attached to him.[12] In modern interpretations of his myth, his figure is represented either as a chthonic hero, or as a pre-Olympian chthonic deity whose sphere of power increasingly diminished after the establishment of the Olympian pantheon and, as a result, became specialized in healing. Asclepius also had something of a solar aspect that first manifested itself in his mother (see below for the etymologies of her names) and later manifested in his association with Apollo, as expressed in his saving and healing activity.

Thessalia is the mythical birthplace of Asclepius: the legendary country of medicine (Cheiron, Mount Pelion) and magic (witches). His mother Coronis ('raven'), the daughter of Phlegyas, was also worshipped under the names of Aigle ('bright one') and Boibe (or Phoibe, but in other places her name is Arsinoe). According to Hesiod,[13] Coronis was bathing in Lake Boibe when Apollo saw her; Asclepius was the fruit of their love. Phlegyas, unaware of the divine child in his daughter's womb, gave Coronis to Ischys (the 'Mighty'). Pindar speaks of the unfaithfulness of Coronis, punished by the deadly arrows of Artemis, and he remarks that Apollo saved his little son from the flames that followed the murder, entrusting him to Cheiron the Centaur to be taught the art of healing.[14] According to a later version, Coronis arrived with her father in Epidaurus and abandoned the child on a hillside, where a she-goat suckled him and a dog guarded him until a shepherd found the boy. This myth was reported by Pausanias, together with the two other versions, and he concluded: 'Another proof that the god was born in Epidaurus is the Epidaurian origin of the most famous Asclepieia […]. I find evidence of a belief in Asclepius as a god from the beginning; it was not just a reputation built up in the course of time.'[15]

Asclepius is also distinguished from the Olympian gods by his connection with death and the deceased: he was able to raise the dead (by the tradition:

---

of Asklepios', pp. 234–79; the contrasting interpretations are best formulated by Kerényi, *Asklepios*; and by Ludwig Edelstein in *Asclepius*, ed. and trans. by Edelstein and Edelstein, II, pp. 1–138.
12 Cf. Rohde, *Psiche*, ch. 5.1 on the cult of chthonic deities.
13 Hesiodus, Fr. 122 and 123 (= T21–22).
14 Pindar, *Pythiae*, III, lines 1–58 (= T1); the Cave of Cheiron and the valley near Lake Boibe were famous for their abundance of medical herbs. Kerényi, *Asklepios*, p. 100: 'Pindar saw Chiron as a dead god; and that he was in a twofold sense: first as a chthonic deity and *hieros iatros* who died and did not die; secondly, in the sense that Greek religion increasingly excluded such contradictory products of the older, more primordial mythology from its pantheon, regarding them merely as characters of heroic legend. Yet the strange contradiction which, for the healers of Thessaly and probably for the Greek physicians of a later day, found its expression in Chiron has remained perhaps a contradiction inherent in the medical profession itself.'
15 Pausanias, *Guide to Greece*, II. 26. 7; all the quotations of Pausanias are translated by Peter Levi.

Capaneus, Tyndareus, Hippolytos, Glaukos).[16] More importantly, Asclepius was a god who died: his tomb in Epidaurus was visited by the same worshippers who might have experienced the miracles of a god that is active in his temple through epiphanies in dreams or in the form of animals. He himself fell victim to the lightning bolt of Zeus. This paradoxical double trait of death and its conquest is attested in the cult by the fact that, in both Tricca and Epidaurus, a grave of Asclepius was shown to visitors, a practice that fit quite nicely with the living, divine presence in the sanctuary. In the Third Pythian Ode, Pindar recalled the legend that the hero Asclepius met the wrath of Zeus for resuscitating a dead man and, together with the latter, was punished by death.[17] Pindar's remark (we must seek *from the gods*) indicates that Asclepius's punishment was not due to his greed or violation of the order of life and death, but his violation of this (new, i.e. Olympian) hierarchy. With the takeover of the Olympians, myth made Apollo the father of Asclepius. An angry Apollo killed his mother Coronis, now shown as a mortal, before she gave birth, and the baby Asclepius was snatched from her womb on the funeral pyre.

Except Kerényi, most historians of religion interpret the early testimonia on Asclepius as proof that, unlike Pausanias, their authors (Homer, Hesiod, and even Pindar) saw Asclepius as a hero.[18] Accordingly, he was worshipped as such in his birthplace, Tricca, until the southern divine cults swept over the north. Prior to this, towards the late seventh to early sixth century BC, Asclepius immigrated to Epidaurus, that is, the worship of Asclepius had spread southward from its Thessalian origins,[19] with his personality gaining new elements at each step along the way. When he reached Delphoi and Phocis, he found himself confronted with Apollo. The myth represents a compromise between the followers of these two healing gods: Apollo is integrated into the myth as Asclepius's father, and having received the title of *Apollo Maleatas* that was only used in the context of his ties to Asclepius, he began to foster a further

---

16 It is enough to recall Artemis in Euripides, *Hippolytus*, lines 1437–38: 'Farewell, I must not look upon the dead. My eye must not be polluted by the last gaspings for breath'; and compare it to the *Alcestis*, lines 122–29 (T67): 'were life's light in the eyes of Phoebus' son [...] for he was wont to raise the dead, until there smote him the fiery thunder hurled by Zeus'. I wrote in detail on the connection between death and the healing activity of healing gods and healing saints in Csepregi, 'Disease, Death, Destiny'.
17 'Gold shining in his hand turned even that man, for a handsome price, to bring back from death a man who was already caught. And so the son of Cronus hurled his shaft with his hands through both of them, and swiftly tore the breath out of their chests; the burning thunderbolt brought death crashing down on them. We must seek from the gods what is appropriate for mortal minds, knowing what lies before our feet, and what kind of destiny we have.' Pindar, *Pythiae*, II, lines 55–61 (trans. by Gildersleeve).
18 For the summary of the different opinions, see *Asclepius*, ed. and trans. by Edelstein and Edelstein, II, pp. 1–138.
19 From Tricca to Ithome, across the borders of Aitolia to Oichalia, to Minyean Northern Boiotia, rested for a time at Orchomenos, near the Lebedeian shrine of Trophonius, then to Hyettos, Thespiai, and Thisbe; his arrival at Phocis 'resulted in a clash of interests': Jayne, *The Healing Gods of Ancient Civilizations*, p. 244.

spread of his son's cult. In exchange for this, Asclepius did not establish cults of healing and prophecy at Delphoi (Apollo integrated the figure of Paian, the first Greek healing deity, into his mythology in a similar way). Kerényi saw the figure of Asclepius as god of the liminal, grey zone between death and healing, which captures the two sides of Asclepius's divine nature: the bright and sun-like, and the darker death-aspect.

The forms of invocation or epithets of Greek deities always emphasize the nature of the god. Asclepius/Asklepios (whose name in Greek might contain the word *epios*, gentle) was called Σωτήρ, the Saviour, φιλάνθρωπος or φιλόλαος, the lover of people, at Epidaurus Συγγνώμων, the Considerate. Among the epithets of the god we also find that of Asclepius Παῖς, Asclepius 'the Child' in Hellenistic times,[20] both for his attention to children in his healing and as an expression of the tenderness of devotees towards his figure.

Incubation Cures on the Stelai of Epidaurus

If a worshipper of Asclepius visited Epidaurus after the fourth century BC, he or she could see remarkable inscriptions carved on stone slabs, stelai. The cures performed by the god had been recorded initially on these small plaques, which provided the basis for the formation of the *Iamata*, 'Healings', the edited version of the miracle cures that were redacted by the temple personnel. These are the stelai Pausanias described: 'In my day there are six left of the stone tablets standing in the enclosure, though there were more in antiquity. The names of men and women healed by Asclepius are engraved on them, with the diseases and how they were healed.'[21] In 1881, during the excavations led by P. Kavvadias, four stelai came to light. Two of them, Stelai A and B, were entirely readable, while C and D contain miracles in a fragmentary condition. Altogether, seventy miraculous cures can be identified and about fifty of them can be read.[22] Lynn LiDonnici has carried out a masterly analysis of the formation of the *Iamata*, using the votive material and the oral traditions concerning the sanctuary as source material.[23] When the *ex voto* tablets covered the entirety of the temple's walls, they were collected and inscribed on stone slabs. With

---

20 Farnell, *Greek Hero Cults*, pp. 276–77. The collection of the god's names are in T266–76.
21 Pausanias, *Guide to Greece*, II. 27. 3.
22 LiDonnici, 'Tale and Dream' and her *The Epidaurian Miracle Inscriptions*; LiDonnici follows the transcription of Hiller as it was published in *Inscriptiones Graecae*; Emma Edelstein follows the transcription of Herzog, *Die Wunderheilungen von Epidauros*. I follow the generally accepted continuous numbering; for the miracles of Stelai A and B (1–43) I provide the translation of Edelstein (T423); for the miracles on Stelai C and D (44–70) I use LiDonnici's translation.
23 LiDonnici, 'Tale and Dream', pp. 20–82 ('Compositional Background') especially the part 'Source Material for Tales', pp. 40–49; and Herzog, *Die Wunderheilungen von Epidauros*, pp. 56–57.

the subsequent developments of the cult and the enlargements of the temple complex, these inscriptions were written and rewritten. Although it was the most famous Asclepieion in classical Greece, Epidaurus was by no means the only one with such popularity. Recently, both Jürgen Riethmüller and Milena Melfi undertook the task of collecting and systematically describing the hundreds of Greek Asclepieia,[24] a giant work to be paired with Emma Edelstein's collection of the written testimonies.[25]

The inscriptions recording the cures in the sanctuaries of Asclepius provide a colourful picture of what may have happened before and during incubation. An even more detailed description is in Aristophanes' *Ploutos* (lines 659–738), from 408 BC, which is our earliest literary narrative of incubation. Another important written source, telling at length what happened before, after, and during incubation, is the account of Aelius Aristides from the second century AD.[26] The sick (often coming from afar) first underwent (ritual or bodily) purification rites specific to the cult site.[27] For the preparatory rites, the *Iamata* uses general terms ('when he had performed the preliminary sacrifices and fulfilled the usual rites ...'), but it often underlines the importance of providing sacrifices before the cure and offerings afterwards.[28] A short period of abstinence was generally required: for example, a few days abstinence from wine, certain types of meat, fish, and bean, the latter being an old Pythagorean taboo. These observances operated partly on a psychosomatic level, partly on a magical one. To all of this, there was added a sacrifice and a vow that specified the tribute that the patient would pay if they were healed.[29] The required internal preparation was summed up in the inscription at the entrance of the Asclepieion at Epidaurus: 'Pure must be he who enters the fragrant temple; purity means to think nothing but holy thoughts.'[30]

---

24 Riethmüller, *Asklepios*; Melfi, *I santuari di Asclepio in Grecia*.
25 T23–24; for a new assessment of the epigraphic evidence, see Girone, *Iamata*.
26 Behr, *Aelius Aristeides and the Sacred Tales*, II, 30–31.
27 The rites accompanying incubation are well described in Deubner, *De incubatione*, esp. ch. 2, 'De incubationis ritibus symbolisque'; Caton, *The Temples and Ritual of Asklepios*; and Taffin, 'Comment on rêvait'.
28 A very detailed description, both about the documented and the only supposed preliminary rites, can be found in Ehrenheim, *Greek Incubation Rituals*, ch. 1, 'Rites and Rules'.
29 T423.5. The most popular animal-sacrifice was the cock, as one might remember the last words of Socrates. Besides its spiritual-symbolic interpretation, the cock had a down-to-earth meaning: it was the cheapest animal sacrifice. To get an idea about a visit to Asclepius, see the amusing description of Herondas (*c.* 250 BC): *Mimiambi*, IV. 1–95 (= T482); for the meaning of Asclepieian piglet sacrifice in connection with the Eleusin mysteries, see Burkert, *Greek Religion*, p. 268.
30 The inscription survived in several texts, the earliest of which is Theophrastos, *On Piety*, from *c.* 340 BC and quoted by Porphyrius's *De abstinentia* II. 19 (= T318); a new dating, however, has recently emerged, in Bremmer, 'How Old Is the Ideal of Holiness?', whose hypothesis is that the inscription cannot be from Theophrastos and locates it around the year 0.

Rituals accompanying incubation varied: at some sites outside of Epidaurus, patients slept on the skin of the animal that they sacrificed. This is noteworthy because, in a normal sacrifice, the skin would be given to the officiating priest. Aelius Aristides mentions that the incubants at Pergamon wore white linen clothes. Another source from Pergamon that dates from the imperial period speaks of ten days of abstinence and bathing. Another set of preliminary rules mentions the white chiton as well as brimstone and laurel, the prohibition on wearing belts, rings, or shoes when approaching the deity, and refers to 'pure white sacrificial victims garlanded with olive shoots'.[31]

There is one characteristic that declined in later Christian practice: the incubants were required to stretch themselves out on the ground to obtain direct contact with the earth itself.[32] In the ancient concept of healing (especially in the case of a chthonic deity), this contact with the earth was essential. The Asclepieian symbols, the rod and the serpent, represent this intermediary connection between the earth and the god.[33] As Euripides attests, not only healing, but also dream itself comes from the earth: 'O holy Earth, mother of dark-winged dreams!'[34]

The indispensable presence of water inside or next to the sacred area (not necessarily medicinal or thermal water) not only had a symbolic value but contributed to the ritual cleaning of the patients and often served as part of the cure. The presence of water was highly significant in the cult of Asclepius. The spring or bath often lay within the precincts of the sacred temple-complex and was part of the scenery or a means of the miraculous cure. Its importance was so great that A. Duprez attributed the absence of the Asclepius cult in inland Syria to the lack of water there.[35]

The actual place of incubation in Epidaurus was the *abaton*, a long sacred colonnade near the temple whose name ('forbidden', 'inaccessible') indicates its taboo character. We know that those patients or their companions who did not practise incubation slept in what archaeologists call Building E or in the nearby theatre.[36] Aelius Aristides speaks of special lodgings for the nights when one was not an incubant in Pergamon; Pausanias tells us that the future emperor Antoninus Pius built in Epidaurus — besides other buildings —

---

31 T513 Inscriptio Pergamena.
32 In the case of Saint Symeon Stylite the Younger, we see the phenomenon working in the opposite direction: the soil of the hill was considered blessed because of its contact with the saint via the column raising towards the sky; in his healing practice, this blessed earth served as eulogy, a condensation of the saintly power; see Vikan, 'Art, Medicine and Magic', p. 68.
33 See Schouten, *The Rod and the Serpent of Asklepios*, p. 55; cf. the incubatory practice in the cave of Trophonius where the believer had to descend into a subterranean place of cult.
34 Euripides, *Hecuba*, line 70.
35 Duprez, *Jésus et les dieux guérisseurs*, p. 71; on the close associations of occidental pre-Christian healing cults (incl. incubation) with water and on the ritual worship of water, see Rousselle, *Croire et guérir*.
36 For the excavation reports, see Kavvadias, *Fouilles d'Épidaure*.

houses for the dying and for women who were to give birth, whose presence was prohibited inside the sacred precinct.[37]

In the archaeological analysis of the Epidaurian temple complex, we find degrees of sacredness or levels of sanctity within the sanctuary area. Bearing in mind the Christian concept of sacrality, thaumaturgic value of relics, and the power of proximity to certain places (the altar, the tomb of the saints, etc.), the Greek view of this aspect becomes still more important.[38] The 'ultrasacred' character of the rotunda in Epidaurus, the *tholos/thymelé* (whose original function is still a mystery, due to what is believed to be a deliberate silence in the ancient texts),[39] and the obstacle it posed to the enlargement of the temple precinct indicate that there were places where the deity was believed to be especially present.

The Epidaurian stelai show how the direct and intimate conduct of Asclepius is strikingly un-Olympian. The approachability of the god and the familiarity between the healer and the worshipper were completely foreign to the ancient deities of the old religion. These attitudes are those of a personal religion characterized by human helplessness in the face of illness and a healer's attentive care.[40] An expression of this directness may also be found in the Asclepieian epiphany itself. For an ancient Greek, a face-to-face encounter with a deity was rarely an auspicious event.[41] In the language of myths, catching sight of the real figure of a god or goddess most often meant death or blindness, while in contrast seeing Asclepius was a healing experience. Within the framework of incubation, the god's appearance to his worshipper meant healing; indeed, the recognition of the healer by the dreamer was an essential element of dream-healing because the sufferer made the journey to the sanctuary in order to meet the god. In contrast with the Christian physician-saints, Asclepius rarely appeared in disguise; his shape-shifting merely reflected the different ways in which his divinity could appear. Patients at Epidaurus frequently encountered the Asclepius of the temple statue — a bearded, sweetly smiling man leaning on a stick — but he could also appear as a young boy, a snake, or a dog. Outside of epiphanies, these sacred animals could also appear in the company of the god as fellow healers.

---

37 Pausanias, *Guide to Greece*, II. 26. For the difficulties in identifying incubation dormitories and for examples in some prominent Greek Asclepieia, see Ehrenheim, 'Identifying Incubation Areas'; in some cases, as in Pergamon, there were more incubation halls, used by a different clientele.

38 For how the notion of sacred place changed while reusing Greek temples as Christian churches, see Hahn, Emmel, and Gotter, eds, *From Temple to Church*; the problem in the Christian context is well presented in Boesch Gajano and Scaraffia, eds, *Luoghi sacri e spazi della santità*.

39 Deubner calls attention to the *tholos* in KDM14. See Deubner, *De incubatione*, p. 70.

40 For its presentation with regard to the ancient (primarily) healing deities, see Festugière, *Personal Religion among the Greeks* and Nock, *Conversion*, p. 56.

41 On epiphany, see Versnel, 'What Did Ancient Man See When He Saw a God?'.

The familiarity of Asclepius with his patients is evident in his treatment of patients. He is kind and gentle. He is also jocular, posing oracular riddles and enigmatic dream prescriptions. This intimate attitude and similar enigmatic prescriptions are evident in Christian dream-healers as well.

The Cures of Asclepius

And those who came to him afflicted with congenital sores, or with their limbs wounded by grey bronze or by a far-hurled stone, or with their bodies wasting away from summer's fire or winter's cold, he released and delivered all of them from their different pains, tending some of them with gentle incantations, others with soothing potions, or by wrapping remedies all around their limbs, and others he set right with surgery.

Pindar, *Pythian*, III, lines 47–54

In the earliest temple records of Asclepius's incubation healings, the cure of the sick is immediate: most often the dreamer experienced an immediate miraculous intervention, initiated by a word or a touch of the god or as the result of a quick surgery. The sick person would awake from the dream and leave the sanctuary healed.

A few centuries later, the methods of divine cures that were experienced in dream, along with the duration and circumstances of the miracle, underwent a significant change. Although the ritual of incubation fundamentally remained the same, immediate cures were replaced by dream prescriptions. Asclepius's treatments became complex, and his advice concerning concoctions, poultices, baths, gymnastics, and diets only led to cures over time, although they were considered no less miraculous. Typical in this respect is the inscription of Iulius Apellas,[42] or the extensive dream prescriptions of Aelius Aristides,[43] as well as the Tiber Island inscriptions, all from the second century AD.

---

42 'When I arrived at the temple, he [Asclepius] told me for two days to keep my head covered [...] to eat cheese and bread, celery with lettuce, to wash myself without help, to practice running, to take lemonpeels, to soak them in water, [...] in the bath to press against the wall, to take a walk in the upper portico, to take some passive exercise, to sprinkle myself with sand, to walk around barefoot, in the bathroom, before plunging into the hot water, to pour wine over myself [...] to take milk with honey [...] he said I should use dill along with olive oil against my headaches [...] to gargle with a cold gargle for the uvula [...] and the same also for the tonsils. He bade me to inscribe this. Full of gratitude I departed well.' T432 (= IG² 1, 126), c. AD 160.

43 He recorded his experience with Asclepius, giving extensive details of his own sufferings, cures, dream-prescriptions in the work *Hieroi Logoi* (Sacred Tales): *Aelius Aristides: The Complete Works*, ed. and trans. by Behr; cf. Harris and Holmes, eds, *Aelius Aristides between Greece, Rome and the Gods* and most recently Petsalis-Diomidis, *'Truly Beyond Wonders'* and also Behr, *Aelius Aristeides and the Sacred Tales*.

Analysts of the miraculous healing narratives identified two phases in Asclepieian incubation methods,[44] summarized pithily by Ludwig Edelstein: 'the god learned medicine'.[45] I lean towards another explanation, namely that the two healing methods are not two distinct phenomena. Rather, there was only one method, of which the later, more elaborated dream prescription 'was merely an extension and development of the primitive treatment'.[46] The contemporary practice of medicine had been changing. After the initial spread of the Asclepieia, which coincided with the formative period of Hippocratic medicine, the second peak in the popularity of incubation healing was the second century AD with Pergamon being its centre. The second century AD was the time, and Pergamon the place, of Galen.[47] By this time, the patients who turned to the temples had a different experience of cures and doctors. They were dreaming about (both metaphorically and actually) new medical methods that involved diets and long-term treatments. The cultural experiences and the medical knowledge of the dreamer were broadened and became more refined, together with the methods of medical science itself; hence, Edelstein's idea can be reversed: the patients learned medicine.

Judging from the early miraculous cures, the medical expertise of Asclepius is nevertheless striking; he performs complicated surgical operations, pours a medicinal liquid into the eye of a patient, releases pus, sets bones, and expels bile stones. Since its mythical beginnings of Asclepius learning the use of medical plants from Cheiron (and later in Cos and Epidaurus),[48] Asclepieian healing already had a close connection with scientific medicine and Hippocrates. As Helen King writes:

> Rather than Hippocratic medicine breaking 'free' from temple medicine, there is evidence that temple medicine copied Hippocratic and subsequent secular medicine; for example in the late fourth century BCE surgery was in vogue, and the Asklepios seen in dreams duly practiced surgery. But, being a god, he kept ahead of the real world, performing operations superior to any on offer there. When compound drugs were fashionable, Asklepios used them too, but his were invariably more effective. One could argue

---

44 Lecos and Pentogalos, 'Early and Late Asclepieia'.
45 *Asclepius*, ed. and trans. by Edelstein and Edelstein, II, ch. 3, 'Temple Medicine' (pp. 139–80); for the contemporary evaluation of his interpretations, see the Introduction written for the second edition by Ferngren: *Asclepius*, ed. and trans. by Edelstein and Edelstein, I, pp. xiii–xxii; Herzog saw the impact of the medically trained temple personnel behind the success of therapies (*Die Wunderheilungen von Epidauros*, pp. 59–61, 65–71), while Ludwig Edelstein emphasized the natural process of healing (*Asclepius*, ed. and trans. by Edelstein and Edelstein, II, pp. 168–73).
46 Thrämer, 'Health and Gods of Healing (Greek)'; cf. Hamilton, *Incubation*, p. 42.
47 For an overview on Hippocratic and Galenic medicine, see Nutton, *Ancient Medicine* as well as King, ed., *Health in Antiquity*; with an outlook on Byzantine medicine: Temkin, *Hippocrates in the World of Pagans and Christians*.
48 On this 'kinship' between Cheiron and Apollo and Asclepius, cf. Kerényi, *Asklepios*, pp. 97–100.

that the success of Hippocratic medicine actually led to an increase in the Asklepios cult, with patient expectations rising and cures for a wider range of symptoms being sought.[49]

Meanwhile, it is important to emphasize that Hippocratic medicine also maintained and cherished this interconnection — and in its own way exploited it. Not only was Hippocrates a priest of Asclepius, but all Greek physicians at that time were the 'sons', cult-representatives, and disciples of the god; people in the Christian seventh century still referred to them as Asclepiadai rather than doctors.

To understand how temple healing and professional medicine intermingled, or more precisely, how they coexisted in parallel and mutual correlation, it is enough to recall the legend that Hippocrates copied the temple votive inscriptions and applied their methods in medical practice,[50] in the medical contests in honour of Asclepius,[51] and later in the traditions surrounding Galen.[52] Galen, in addition to testimony of his personal experience of Asclepius's healing methods and his respect for temple healing, left an acute observation about the functioning of such divine instruction:

> Thus at any rate even among ourselves in Pergamum we see those who are being treated by the god obey him when on many occasions he bids them not to drink at all for fifteen days, while they obey none of the physicians who give this prescription. For it has great influence on the patient's doing all which is prescribed if he has been firmly persuaded that a remarkable benefit to himself will ensue.[53]

---

49 On the symbiosis of medicinal and ritual healing in Antiquity, see King, 'Comparative Perspectives on Medicine and Religion', p. 281; in a broader cultural context: Kleinman, 'Concepts and a Model for the Comparison of Medical Systems as Cultural Systems' and his *Patients and Healers in the Context of Culture*.
50 Pliny the Elder, *Historia Naturalis*, 29. 1. 4, called attention to this anecdote as a testimony to the fact that, besides the interconnection of the two healing traditions, it was important that the prerequisites of temple cures were consciously and systematically archived. Thus, documentation of the religious experience was meant to serve posterity and not only the short-term situation. Although not sparing his criticism, Artemidorus also records (*Oneirocritica* IV. 22) that in his time dream-cure records were stored at Pergamon, Alexandria, and other places. Many have tried to attribute the origin of medicine to such votives. His praiseworthily sober argumentation saw, in these tablets, the dreamer's actual medical knowledge — or if the record was too complicated, the intentions of the recorders.
51 *Asclepius*, ed. and trans. by Edelstein and Edelstein, II, p. 212.
52 I have in mind, for example, his own recovery at the hands of Asclepius himself, on the basis of which Galen decided to become a physician: 'the ancestral god Asclepius of whom I declared myself to be a servant since he saved me when I had the deadly condition of an abscess'. Galenus, *De Libris Propriis*, 2 = T458. The most recent treatment and the critique of the positivist approach, citing the newest archaeological and theoretical results, is Horstmanshoff, 'Asclepius and Temple Medicine in Aelius Aristides' *Sacred Tales*'.
53 Galenus, *Commentarius in Hippocratis Epidemias* VI. iv; Sectio IV, 8 = T401.

This psychological factor and the respect for the divine doctor explain perfectly how Asclepieian healing worked. When we detect changes in the curing methods, it is more fruitful to see them as shifts of emphasis, just as Eric Dodds labelled 'dream patterns as culture patterns'.[54] In other words, these medical cures represented a culturally dependent reshaping of dream experiences and the expression of a renewal of the community's cultural and current medical knowledge.[55]

Asclepius and Christ

> And again when they [sc. the gentiles] learned about the prophecies to the effect that He [sc. Christ] would heal every disease and would raise the dead, they brought forward Asclepius.
>
> Justinus, *Apologia* 54.10[56]

Asclepius's efficacy as a divine physician, his mythology (being born to a god and a mortal woman, being killed and resurrected as a god), and his immense popularity were attested by hundreds of sanctuaries well beyond the frontiers of the Greek-speaking world, and above all by his facet as Soter/Saviour.[57] His complex figure as Healer-Deliverer rendered him to be a powerful rival of Christ.[58] The lines from the famous paian of Isyllus, from around 300 BC, praise him as 'the reliever of illness, the granter of health, great boon to mankind. Hail Paean, Asclepius, increase your maternal city of Epidaurus, send bright health to our hearts and bodies, hail, Paean, hail, Paean'.[59]

An Attic inscription of the second century AD preserves a prayer to Asclepius:

> These are the words of thy loving servant, o Asklepios, child of Leto's son: how shall I come into thy golden house, O blessed one, O God of my longing, unless thy heart is favourable to me and thou art willing to heal me and establish me again in thy shrine, that I may behold my God

---

54 Dodds, *The Greeks and the Irrational*, ch. 4 ('Dream Pattern and Culture Pattern'); for the Christian context, see Le Goff, 'Les rêves dans la culture et la psychologie collective'.
55 I wrote about it in detail: Csepregi, 'Changes in Dream Patterns'.
56 T332.
57 On what it meant, see Nock, 'Soter and Euergetes'.
58 First Harnack, 'Medicinischen aus der altesten Kirchen geschichte', p. 89, and more recently Krug, *Heilkunst und Heilkult*, pp. 120–87; Rüttimann, 'Asclepius and Jesus'; some important ancient testimonies: Justinus, *Apologia*, 22.6 (T94), 21.1–2 (T335), 54.10 (T332); Justinus, *Dialogus*, 69.3 (T95); *Acta Pilati*, A. I. 216 (T334); Lactantius, *Divinae Institutiones*, IV. 27. 12 (T333); Clement of Alexandria, *Stromateis* V. 1. 13 (T336); Arnobius, *Adversus Nationes*, I. 49 (T584); Eusebius of Caesarea, *De Vita Constantini*, III. 56 (T818); Eusebius Hieronymus, *Vita Hilarionis*, 2 (T818a).
59 T594 (= IG 1. 128) *c.* 300 BC.

who is brighter than the earth in spring-time, Thou alone, O divine and blessed one, art mighty; thee that lovest compassion, the Supreme Gods have granted as a mighty boon to mortals, as a refuge from their sorrows.[60]

The wording evokes the language of the Psalms, while Asclepius's late antique representations as a child relate him to the figure of Jesus.[61] From the second to third century AD, we have records of a statue by a certain Boethos representing Asclepius as a newborn infant.[62]

Even to Christian apologists, the reality of the Asclepieian miraculous cures and the importance of the role they played in everyday life were a social reality. The strongest parallel was with Jesus the healer, a performer of miraculous cures, to whom the Greeks instinctively opposed their own wonder-worker. For the Greeks, it was no novelty that the blind should see and the lame should walk. It was in this context of rivalry that the background of Asclepius was reshaped (e.g. the fatherhood of Zeus and his 'ascension', his becoming a star) to complete the comparison as attested by Justinus:

> And when we say also that the Word, who is the first-birth of God, Jesus Christ, our teacher, was produced without sexual union, and that He was crucified and died, and rose again, and ascended into heaven, we propound nothing new and different from what you believe regarding those whom you esteem the sons of Jupiter [...]. Asclepius, who, though he was a great healer, was struck by a thunderbolt, and ascended to heaven.[63]

In the eyes of early Christians, Asclepius's lively, extremely widespread, and active cult, in contrast to the rather anaemic devotion to the Olympian deities, made him their bitterest enemy. Additionally, he had alarmingly Christ-like characteristics. The early Christian testimonies do not seem to challenge the reality of Asclepieian miracles but instead labour to characterize the miracles as deeds of the Evil One, or, as Lactantius calls Asclepius, the 'archdemon'.[64] It is not surprising that the Greeks regarded Christ either as one who healed

---

60 In Farnell, *Greek Hero Cults*, p. 277 (taken from the *Corpus Inscriptionum Atticarum* 3. 171a).
61 For the artistic borrowings for Christ's figure from Asclepius, cf. Dinkler, *Christus und Asklepios*; Hauck, 'Gott als Arzt'; Nutton, 'From Galen to Alexander', p. 7: At Caesarea Philippi, a statue that was traditionally supposed to represent Jesus and the woman with the issue of blood has been plausibly argued to have been either a statue of an emperor with the epithet *Soter*, Saviour, or one representing Asclepius. For the significance of the statues of Asclepius to Christians, Nutton also directs to Eusebius, *Historia Ecclesiastica*, VIII. 18 and to the *Passio IV SS Coronatorum* in *AASS* November 3; the interconnectedness of the representation of Asclepius and Christ is well illustrated also by Mathews, *The Clash of Gods*, pp. 69–72, with images of Jesus healing in figures: pp. 35–45.
62 T599 (= IG XIV 967a) mentions 'the divine child, [...] who has just been borne by his mother'; cf. T600.
63 Justinus, *Apologia*, 21.1–2 (= T335).
64 Lactantius, *Divinae Institutiones*, II. 16. 11: 'nam illuc daimoniarches ipse in figura sua sine ulla dissimulatione perlatus est' (= T849b).

in the name of Asclepius or as a false Asclepius. To this, the *Acta Pilati* also bears witness:

> They say to him [Pilate]: he is a sorcerer and he casts out the devils in the name of the Devil who rules the devils, and everything is obedient to him. Pilate says to them: it is not possible to cast out devils in the name of an impure spirit but rather in the name of the god Asclepius.[65]

There were words, however, which definitely impressed the Christians: the inscription on the Epidaurian temple, 'Pure must be he who enters the fragrant temple; purity means to think nothing but holy thoughts.' Clement of Alexandria considered this inscription as a forerunner of Christ's sayings and linked it to another temple, 'for there is the sanctuary of God, set up over the three foundation stones, Faith, Hope, Charity'.[66]

Cult Continuity?

When confronted with these deeply rooted beliefs, the early Church had to face the challenge they posed and adapt to them, integrating genuinely pagan dream practices into its own system of beliefs. Christians already had their own traditions for religious dreams (the Old Testament dreams) and for miraculous healing (the deeds of Christ).[67] I am interested in this confrontation between Christian and pagan traditions, and how the Church succeeded in modifying ancient dream healing by turning its cultic use to its own advantage and incorporating it into the cult of the saints.

When the increasingly authoritative Church confronted the practice of temple sleep, it had to define its attitude towards fields that were essential parts of the incubation ritual: miracles, dreams, medicine, and magic. The early Church took a strong line against divination by dreams, even banning professional dream interpreters from taking the Eucharist.[68] It also subordinated dream interpretation to the Church hierarchy, restricting theological significance to the dreams of bishops or other higher Church authorities. The Church was quite wary about Christian incubation due to the uncontrollable origin of the dream medium (viz. God-sent or demon-sent) and the pagan reminiscences of the practice.[69] Official regulations for incubation, either pro

---

65 *Acta Pilati*, A. I. 216 (= T334).
66 *Stromateis*, v. 1. 13 (= T336).
67 On the theme in general, see Le Goff, 'Le christianisme et les rêves'; Smith, *Jesus the Magician*.
68 Stroumsa, 'Dreams and Visions in Early Christian Discourse', pp. 193–94; a broad overview: Kelsey, *God, Dreams, and Revelation*; Cox Miller, *Dreams in Late Antiquity*; also Kruger, *Dreaming in the Middle Ages*.
69 A recent overview on Christian incubation that emphasizes the context of dreams and divination as issues highly problematic for Christian theology is in Graf, *Roman Festivals in the Greek East*, pp. 241–67; the exact opposite is presented by Wiśniewski, 'Looking for

or contra, are missing, and the only administrative record we have is Canon 38 of the Council of Carthage in 251, which, on the insistence of Augustine, forbade the incubation practised in martyr shrines. The prohibition was not necessarily issued due to the practice of incubation for healing, but more because of dreams that claimed to locate new relics of saints.[70]

On the field of dreams and healing, Christianity came up against two other traditions. One was the dream culture of Jews, a positive, Old Testament way of communicating with Yahweh, which provided another background for the Christian attitude to dreams during its formation in the second to fifth centuries AD.[71] (There are traces of a possible incubation practice in the Old Testament.)[72] Dreams were also connected to a radically different way of healing, the Greek medical tradition. Greek doctors observed the dream experience in order to help diagnose the mental and physical state of the patient.[73] The Hippocratic author of the *Epidemics* includes dreams ('of what kind and when') among the features to be observed (1. 23); Book IV of the *Regimen* is dedicated entirely to dreams, describing the method of interpreting dreams for diagnosis, establishing correspondences between certain dream phenomena and malfunctions of the body, and providing an outline of preventive therapy based on the dream-diagnosis. Christianity also had its psychosomatic dream interpreters: in the fourth century, Gregory of Nyssa maintained that dreams reflect the sickness of the soul, and Euagrius Ponticus similarly used dreams to identify the state of the soul and the emergence of illnesses.[74]

Christianity became a healing religion primarily as a response to Asclepieian (Isean, Serapieian, etc.) healing cults. It was a way to meet a social demand for healing hitherto addressed by the healing cults of pagan deities that had immense popularity and importance. That is to say, bodily healing was not an inherent part of Christianity from its start. Rather, miraculous cures should

---

Dreams and Talking with Martyrs', who argues that incubation was 'the only Christian divinatory practice which was proudly described in literary texts' and links the success of the ritual to Christian concepts about dreams and their religious application. For a complete picture on the oracular practices, see Wiśniewski, *Christian Divination in Late Antiquity*.

70 Cf. Stroumsa, 'Dreams and Visions in Early Christian Discourse', p. 194; Dagron, 'Rêver de Dieu et parler de soi', p. 40; about relics indicated by dreams: Maraval, 'Songes et visions comme mode d'invention des reliques'.

71 Husser, *Dreams and Dream Narratives* and his *Le songe et la parole*.

72 On possible incubation dreams in the Old Testament (for example, 1 Kings 3. 4–15 or Isaiah 65. 4) cf. Husser, *Le songe et la parole*, 'Première partie: Le songe royal et l'incubation', pp. 27–125, and his *Dreams and Dream Narratives*, pp. 172–76; Ehrlich, *Der Traum im Alten Testament*; Oppenheim, 'The Interpretation of Dreams in the Ancient Near East', p. 188.

73 Cf. for an overview Oberhelman, 'Dreams in Graeco-Roman Medicine'; for particular authors, cf. van der Eijk, 'Divination, Prognosis and Prophylaxis' and his 'Aristotle on "Distinguished Physicians" and the Medical Significance of Dreams'; Holowchak, 'Interpreting Dreams for Corrective Regimen'.

74 Gregory of Nyssa, *On the Making of Man*, XIII. 'A Rationale of Sleep, of Yawning, and of Dreams', pp. 546–50; Euagrius Ponticus, *Capita practica ad Anatolium*, II. 54–56, in PG 40, cols 1245–48.

be interpreted primarily as miracles and the miracles as signs, based on the message of the New Testament. The theological explanation of the healing miracles of Jesus interprets his miracles as signs of his being the true Messiah. From here, there was a long process in which the new cultural experience in the field of miraculous healing influenced the Church to undertake the role of healing, a task soon to be made part and parcel of its self-definition. By the fourth century AD, the process was reflected in the figure of *Christus Medicus* (who was known earlier but became more popular at that time). The cults of physician saints also arose in the same period, as ancient medical traditions became Christianized.

On Christian Incubation: The Survival of Cult Practices and Cult Sites

Theodosius II (AD 408–450) issued an edict in 435 that aimed to determine the fate of pagan sanctuaries, including those where incubation had been practised. The edict ordered the destruction of those pagan temples and cult buildings that were still intact or partly standing. Although the efficacy of this order is dubious, the edict included a significant phrase when delegating the fate of the edifices to the discretion of the executing magistrates:

> all shrines, temples, and sanctuaries of them, if they are still standing intact even now, we order to be destroyed, according to the command of the magistrates (*praecepto magistratum*), and expiated by setting up the symbols of the venerable Christian religion.[75]

Other considerations were probably added to this condition, depending on the locations of the buildings, their material value, or their state of preservation as well as factors such as the way the cult site was used or the presence of cult statues. Thus, the fate of the cult buildings could be varied: on the rarest occasions, the buildings, left in their original state, were used as Christian places of worship.[76] The complete and systematic destruction of temples was similarly exceptional (such as with the Asclepieion in Corinth and Pergamon, or the infamous plundering of the Alexandrian Serapeion).[77]

---

75 *Codex Theodosianus*, XVI. 10. 25: 'cunctaque eorum fana templa delubra, si qua etiam nunc restant integra, praecepto magistratuum destrui conlocationeque venerandae Christianae religionis signi expiari praecipimus.' In my analysis I follow Alison Frantz's article, 'From Paganism to Christianity'; she sees the phrase *praecepto magistratuum* 'as a loophole to allow the magistrates to exercise their discretion', who, 'as good Athenians, [...] would have had no great enthusiasm for performing their duties' (p. 200).
76 For examples from Greece for all the variants, see Spieser, 'La christianisation des sanctuaires païens en Grèce'.
77 Spieser suggests that Christians were particularly hostile to *soter* deities like Asclepius, Serapis, and Isis exactly because of the characteristics and importance of the cult; see also

More often, temples that had long ceased to function as cult places and were deteriorating into ruin were transformed into Christian cult sites. Even in such cases, the Christian buildings were mostly erected near the former cult places and not directly above them, often using the building material of the previous sanctuary.

Two exceptions to this use and reuse of cult places are worth mentioning, since in all likelihood they attest to the continuity of healing cults and perhaps, in both cases, the continuity of healing incubation. The first example is that of the Athenian Asclepieion on the Acropolis, which had always held an exceptional status among the cult places at Athens. Christian architects seem to have deliberately avoided the city centre and especially the sites of previous temples. With the Christian takeover of the city, a Byzantine church likely dedicated to Saint Andrew was erected on the site of the Asclepieion in the fifth century AD. The Christian construction incorporated the entire temple precinct, including the former incubation hall, the sacred spring, and the *katagogeion*, a large square building with courtyard. Andrew was regarded by the late antique Greek Christians as a patron of healing.[78] Although the opinions concerning the fate of the Asclepieion differ, scholars agree that the Christian practice replaced the ancient cult, more or less, over a single generation. T. Gregory has suggested that both the healing aspect as well as the incubation practice survived without interruption.[79] Between the sixth and seventh centuries, a large basilica of the *Hagioi Anargyroi* (i.e. Saints Cosmas and Damian) was erected over the place of the former Asclepieion, replacing the smaller church. Another church dedicated to Cosmas and Damian was likewise erected over the Asclepieion in Piraeus.

---

the remark of Frantz, 'From Paganism to Christianity', p. 195, n. 50: 'the idea of the Christians savagely attacking all sanctuaries of Asklepios because of their addiction to magic arts is unconvincing'.

78   Gregory, 'The Survival of Paganism in Christian Greece'; Gregory claims that Christians destroyed the temple, while Frantz saw a gradual process in the fate of the Asclepieion: 'More probably, the Temple of Asklepios, under pressure of the imperial edicts, was deconsecrated, but not yet destroyed, shortly before Proclus' death in 485, and its destruction, whether at the hands of the Christians, by earthquake [yet this is refuted by Frantz herself], or from natural decay, occurred toward the end of the fifth century or the beginning of the sixth, to be followed after the closing of the schools in 529 by the construction of the church in the midst of the temple's ruins' (Frantz, 'From Paganism to Christianity', p. 195); more on this theme with further examples: Chandrasekaran and Kouremenos, eds, *Continuity and Destruction in Alexander's East*; the most recent treatment of the question, focusing on sanctuary space of big cities: Busine, ed., *Religious Practices and Christianization*.

79   And although his argument concerning incubation seems rather weak, his conclusion is convincing: 'Chronological considerations allow us to be certain that the pagan associations of the place were still alive when the church was built and the architectural and epigraphic evidence suggests that healing was still carried out in the same place.' Gregory, 'The Survival of Paganism in Christian Greece', p. 239.

An additional example reveals another important aspect. The Christian basilica of Dor, located on the coast thirty kilometres south of Haifa, was established in the mid-fourth century after the town had lost its commercial significance.[80] Its excavator identified an incubation hall in the western part of the church related to a cult of two 'unnamed' saints. The excavation also revealed that the church had been deliberately erected over a Greek temple, which fell victim to a fire (and, in the excavator's opinion, to the devastation of the angered Christians). The foundation of the pagan temple may reach back to the seventh to sixth centuries BC; at the turn of the fifth to fourth centuries BC, it had been transformed into a cult place of Apollo, which may have come under the jurisdiction of Asclepius over time.[81] Even if continuous incubation practice cannot be demonstrated, the Christian reuse of the site as a diocesan see and as a pilgrimage 'stop over' on the way to holy places began soon after the preceding cult ended.[82]

By no means do I wish to insist on the concept of cultic continuity and the direct takeover of cult sites. Regarding Christian incubation saints, I shall examine each cult site individually. I am aware that, when looking at the history of a cult site, one can easily be mistaken in assuming cultic continuity if the function of the place shows the same characteristics over centuries. One example of such typical mistakes was the opinion of many archaeologists about the healing cults at the Tiber Island in Rome.[83] The island had once been one of the first and foremost healing sites of Asclepius. Centuries later, it hosted the healing cult of Saint Bartholomew, which established the hospital that still operates today. The history of ritual healing that is long attached to the site has recently been re-examined, and on the basis of archaeological evidence and textual history, its continuity was refuted by Hugo Brandenburg.[84] I underline two salient points from his argument that we should keep in mind regarding the Christian takeover of cult sites. First, one cannot ignore a gap of centuries; the lack of evidence for the use of any cult place does not provide evidence of cultic continuity. At best, it must remain a hypothesis. Second, the religious history of a place is just one of its characteristics. Its religious history may not provide the only reason for the continuity or cessation of cult activity. The case of Tiber Island shows how an island is a perfect location to put sick people, pagans and Christians alike, just as it explains why it functioned as a prison in the intervening centuries.

---

80 There is an ongoing excavation by the Hebrew University of Jerusalem. Until the final publication, the project website presents the available excavation reports and a thorough bibliography, <http://dor.huji.ac.il/>.
81 Dauphin, 'From Apollo and Asclepius to Christ'; yet how she identifies the Asclepieian takeover remains unclear. Her view is also challenged by Renberg, *Where Dreams May Come*, pp. 540–41.
82 On the fate of healing divinities in Christianity, see Saintyves, *Les saints successeurs des dieux*.
83 Besnier, *L'Île Tibérine dans l'Antiquité*.
84 Brandenburg, 'Esculapio e S. Bartolomeo nell'Isola Tiberina'.

The cult of Asclepius and the features of his cult, with dream-healing among them, did not always make contact with Christianity directly. In some places, the practice had been absorbed by the figure of another intermediary deity. This was the case where Hellenistic healing deities fused with ancient Semitic deities. The cult of Asclepius especially proliferated in Syria and Phoenicia by assimilation with the cult of the Phoenician healing god, Esmun. Under Esmun's aegis were the thermal baths of Gadara, where incubation was also practised (though it is uncertain if it occurred under Asclepian influence).[85] It is also supposed that incubation became part of the cult of Serapis, the god of prophesy, as a result of the Greek influence. The two deities were so closely related that, in the Serapeion of Memphis, daily libation was performed for the honour of Asclepius, while in the Serapeion of Alexandria, an Asclepius cult-statue was installed.[86]

The impact of the Asclepius cult on Judaism is reflected in Jerome's reproach against the aping of pagan customs and in his repudiation of incubation:

> Nothing of a sacrilegious nature did the people of Israel refrain from, not only performing sacrifices in gardens and lighting incense on stones but also sitting or dwelling in sepulchres and sleeping in shrines of idols, where they were wont to lie on the outspread skins of sacrificial victims, for the purpose of learning the future through dreams. The heathens, in their delusion, celebrate this in the shrine of Asclepius up to the present day, and [in the shrines] of many others which are nothing but tombs of dead men.[87]

In the vicinity of Jerusalem, near Lake Bethesda, there was a temple dedicated to a healing deity in the second century AD. On coins and *ex votos*, the cult was identified as dedicated to Asclepius-Serapis. During the reign of Herod, the presence of a nearby Roman military fort facilitated the functioning of the

---

85 Duprez, *Jésus et les dieux guérisseurs*, pp. 68–69.
86 Duprez, *Jésus et les dieux guérisseurs*, pp. 82–83; here Duprez also quotes the ancient testimonies and modern interpretations concerning this entanglement: Pausanias, *Guide to Greece*, VII. 26–27; Tacitus, *Hist.* IV. lxxxiv: 'Deum ipsum Serapim multi Aesculapium quod medeatur aegris corporibus coniectant'; 'le nom d'Esculape semble mis ici [in the Serapeion of Memphis] pour celui de Sérapis. Ces deux divinités dans le temple desquelles les malades venaient chercher remède à l'aide d'incubation et de songes se confondent souvent dans l'esprit des Grecs', quoted from Brunet de Presle, 'Mémoire sur le Sérapeum de Memphis', p. 562. Serapis amalgamated in the same way other healing and non-healing deities as well: Zeus, Hades, Osiris, Dionysos, and Helios Asclepius; more on his relation to incubation: Renberg, *Where Dreams May Come*, pp. 329–93.
87 Jerome, *In Isaiam Commentaria* XVIII. 65 (PL 24, col. 632C). 'Nihil fuit sarcilegii quod Israel populus praetermitteret, non solum in hortis immolans et super lateres thura succendens sed sedens quoque vel habitans in sepulcris et in delubris idolorum dormiens, ubi stratis pellibus hostiarum incubare soliti erant ut somnis futura cognoscerent. Quod in fano Aesulapii usque hodie celebrat error ethnicorum multorumque aliorum, quae non sint aliud, nisi tumuli mortuorum.' T294.

healing cult. In all likelihood, this ancient healing cult site functioned in the time of Jesus as well, on the margin of official Judaism. The healing of the sick at Lake Bethesda in John 5 encourages a new interpretation of the superiority of Jesus the True Healer over the previous healing cult.[88] There were attempts to interpret some Old Testament descriptions of dreaming as incubation, and the most plausible examples are Samuel's sleeping in the church and Psalms 17, 63, 91.[89] An odd source of information on Judaic incubation practices may be found in Strabo reporting Moses' approval of incubation: 'He [Moses] taught that those who made fortunate dreams were to be permitted to sleep in the temple, where they might dream both for themselves and for others.'[90]

Peter Brown outlined the emergence of the saints' cult, especially the birth of the martyrs' cult, in the Western Mediterranean.[91] However apt and influential his model has been, it cannot be applied to the cults of incubation saints. Healing saints, *thaumaturgoi*, are already a somewhat distinct category, and we can feel the unease of the Church when accounting for the miracle-working capacities of such figures.[92] Returning to the proper incubation saints in the Greek-speaking Mediterranean, the whole practice of incubation was very much linked to the preceding pagan cult practices because the place was essentially more important to the cult than was the figure of the healer. In the case of Greek incubation healers (among them heroes like Amphiaraus and Trophonius), 'tomb and altar were joined', something that Peter Brown saw as typical only for the Christian cult of the martyrs.[93] In Epidaurus, Asclepius's tomb was near his sanctuary, while Amphiaraus and Trophonius died being swallowed by an opening of the earth (just like Thecla) and their cult practice evolved around the place of their 'tomb'.

The incubation cult places that were Christianized were related to urban centres. Even at the beginning of their cult, they were not on a cultic or geographical periphery, as were many of Brown's examples. Furthermore, not one of the Christian incubation saints was a proper martyr, although with time passing, they became known and venerated as such. Although Thecla, the legendary companion of Saint Paul, was tried in front of ferocious animals, she was saved and died a peaceful death. According to the earliest

---

88 Duprez, *Jésus et les dieux guérisseurs*, pp. 94, 127, 178; on the continuity of cult and on their attachment to the cult space, especially in the cases of healing cults: p. 95.
89 A good bibliography on the biblical studies of dreams and supposed incubation practices: Caquot, *Les Songes et leur Interprétation*; see also McCasland, 'The Asclepios Cult in Palestine', pp. 227–30, and more recently Bar, 'Incubation and Traces of Incubation in the Biblical Narrative'.
90 Strabo, *Geographica*, XVI. 2. 35 (trans. by Jones).
91 Brown, *The Cult of the Saints*.
92 This unease is articulated by Kazhdan, 'Holy and Unholy Miracle Workers'.
93 Brown, *The Cult of the Saints*, p. 9; in contrast to that, 'the forms of cult for heroes and for the immortal gods tended to be kept apart' (*The Cult of the Saints*, p. 5); see Farnell, *Greek Hero Cults*, esp. p. 238 on the great resemblance between rituals at a hero's tomb and of earth-deities.

layer of their legend, Cosmas and Damian also died a peaceful death, and it was a sort of hagiographic necessity that they were shaped into martyrs; they had to be forced into one of the larger categories of saints. Their historical character is dubious, and their legendary traits offer a valuable insight into the making of saints (both in the cult as well in hagiography). Saint Artemius, undoubtedly a historical figure, was executed as a criminal, but because it was Emperor Julian who ordered his death-sentence, he also became a martyr. Cyrus and John were imaginary beings, invented for the sake of their cult, and no martyrdom tale developed around their figures. Rather, the close link of these saints with healing connected them to their pre-Christian cultic predecessors. In the following chapter, I show how they were further linked to the cult places themselves. Except for the latecomer Artemius, all of these incubation healers replaced a previous pagan healing figure.

CHAPTER 2

The Literary Background of the Collections

One of the most significant features of the ancient practice of temple sleep is that the basic characteristics of both the cult practice and the way of recording the sacred cures remained essentially similar, even in the context of the theologically different Christian ritual.

When we have a building — a Greek temple, for example — we can quite safely reconstruct its subsequent Christian history if we have evidence for it. For instance, Christians could reuse the physical material. They could place there another cult figure, a martyrion, or erect a church to a saint in order to deter the attraction of the pagan site. Sometimes, cultic memories were so strongly attached to a site that a very similar cult function continued (as in Aegae). Sometimes, however, we see an apparent continuity, which then turns out to be a reinvention, as with the use of Tiber Island to receive sick people. My examples come from the realm of incubation, but it is obviously an ever-present phenomenon during the first centuries of Christianity. With regards to the composition of miraculous cures, the similarities with the ancient Greek votive texts are clear enough, but the real work is to analyse the maze of miracle stories when they are already set firmly into the context and genres of Christian literary traditions.

When I state that the Christian incubation practice and the way of recording it conformed to the pagan models, it must not be forgotten that the Christian recorders had centuries of literary forms and modes of expressions at their disposal — both as a choice and as a constraint. The Greek *Iamata* literature and the saints' miracles had never been placed next to each other by the Christian authors (as I am now doing) to highlight the differences and similarities. I hope to prove that, instead of insisting on literary continuity, we need to be aware that we are confronting a situation in which the ritual practice itself demanded to be expressed in a very similar form. Reginald Grégoire made some very subtle distinctions when identifying pagan rituals in Christian legends. These legends were either a prolongation of a pagan religious act, when the Christian appearance conceals its pagan meaning, or a reinterpretation of a pagan ritual in a new, Christian frame, where the Christian discourse eliminates the pagan meaning.[1] I think that the literary background of the legends helps us observe the difference between the Christian incubation stories and their pagan predecessors; that is, how Christian they were. Yet the literary analysis will reveal another of their important characteristics: how much these miracle texts differed from their contemporary Christian hagiographic texts, or more pointedly, how very un-Christian they were, if read with a previous knowledge of Greek incubation cures.

---

1 Grégoire, *Manuale di agiologia*, p. 193.

The Miracle Record as Literary Artefact

Immortalizing the miracles in literary artefacts may be what the beneficiary of the miracle offered as his votive gift, just as a craftsman offered a piece of his work in exchange for the cure. The tragedy-writer Aristarchos, a contemporary of Euripides, wrote a tragedy titled *Asclepius* as a *charistérion*, or thanks-offering, for the god (T455). If one looks back now on the vast mass of divine poetry and prose that is preserved or referred to in the testimonies, one can safely state that there was a rich literature dedicated to Asclepius and other healing divinities. Asclepius, from the beginning of his healing activity, had many poets, rhetors, and philosophers in his devotees who repaid his healing with works of art. Aelian delights in pointing out that Asclepius was wont to take care of the educated (T456), and the testimonies give the impression that the god was the special protector of this class of people. He was reputed to have inspired or requested literary pieces; he was credited with giving the literati the ability to accomplish their task (T610) of writing poetry and prose.[2] The writing (or redacting) of the miracle collection out of gratitude for the cure played a similarly important role in the textual-literary formation of the Christian healing miracles discussed here: the hagiographers of Thecla and of Cosmas and Damian, and Sophronius explained this as the motivation of their enterprise. I find it important to emphasize this personal aspect that was involved in motivating the redaction of many incubation miracle collections because it is a detail that has often been overlooked in scholarly debates.

The twentieth century saw the emergence of extensive research in Byzantine hagiography,[3] which resulted in such monumental works as Stephanos Efthymiadis's collective research companions, his miracle catalogue, or the state-of-the-art hagiography database at Dumbarton Oaks,[4] in addition to the individual works of numerous scholars. Many of the attempts to interpret the literary records of miracles focused on the question of genre. An incomplete list of these genres would include aretalogy,[5] *miracula*, hagiography, biography

---

2   *Asclepius*, ed. and trans. by Edelstein and Edelstein, II, p. 206. Ludwig Edelstein also pointed out that, on the one hand, singing surely had an important role in the cult, and on the other that this sort of patron position holds true for Serapis as well. He listed some famous literary figures who worked under the guidance of Asclepius, among them Apollonius, Theopompus, Sophocles, Aischines, Plutarchos, Domninus, and Hermocrates, Polemon, and Proclus (*Asclepius*, ed. and trans. by Edelstein and Edelstein, II, pp. 206–08) — and the list cannot be complete without Aelius Aristides.

3   For its use in social history, which was in many respects pioneered by Evelyne Patlagean, whose œuvre started with her 'Ancienne hagiographie byzantine et histoire sociale'.

4   Efthymiadis, ed., *Ashgate Research Companion to Byzantine Hagiography* and his 'Greek Byzantine Collections of Miracles'; <http://www.doaks.org/research/byzantine/resources/hagiography-database>.

5   From Reinach, 'Les Arétalogues dans l'Antiquité', to Longo, *Aretalogie nel mondo Greco* and Smith, 'Prolegomena to a Discussion of Aretalogies'.

(and its pagan-Christian genre connections),[6] the late antique novel, the literature of dream interpretation, parables, 'pagan hagiography', the Gospels,[7] *paideusis*, and *psychagogia*.[8]

These genre categories seem to have lost their appeal today, together with the concept of genre itself. Michel de Certeau and Mark van Uytfanghe demonstrated how illusory it is to deal with the concept of aretalogy and hagiography in terms of genre.[9] They did away with the concept, and in their footsteps, it seems wiser to use the term 'hagiographic discourse', both in the ancient (pagan) and the Christian context alike. From the kindred areas of literature, ancient biography, and martyr acts, van Uytfanghe transferred two essential elements that are valid for the formation of ancient and Christian miracle narratives: one is the suggestion of Charles H. Talbert, who argues that rather than seeking to characterize biographies by their formal elements, one should enquire what role these texts fulfilled in their original social, intellectual, and spiritual environment.[10] This is analogous to the 'two milieus' theory of Herbert Musurillo, namely that the same stimuli in similar circumstances call for analogous answers.[11] Taking this line of thinking further, van Uytfanghe saw this theory as applicable for imperial–late antique hagiographic discourse. He emphasized that the analogies, borrowings, mutual influences were all shared, yet he warned against seeing a direct origin when comparing literary materials, that is, a straightforward genealogy behind every similarity.[12] Van Uytfanghe's definition of the hagiographic discourse was challenged by Felice Lifshitz,[13] who objected that van Uytfanghe's theory continued to concentrate on the textuality of hagiography, and that by making the literary context almost the exclusive one, he forgot about the historiographic and political framework of these sources. However, Lifshitz did not aim at formulating a more precise definition of hagiography: her goal was the negation of this category, or more accurately stated, the demonstration of its inapplicability for the period preceding the nineteenth century. She argued that the nineteenth century, and in a certain respect, also the twentieth century, considered the

---

6   Connecting aretalogy with biography: Cox, *Biography in Late Antiquity*.
7   Kee, 'Aretalogy and Gospel'.
8   Cataudella, *Critica e estetica*.
9   De Certeau, 'A Variant: Hagio-Grafical Edification'. On defining how hagiography functioned as an 'open genre', cf. Rydén, 'New Forms of Hagiography', p. 550, and also 'Hagiography is not a genre' wrote Rapp, in her 'For Next to God, You Are my Salvation', p. 63.
10 Van Uytfanghe, 'L'hagiografie', p. 148; Talbert, 'Biographies of Philosophers'; cf. also Rapp, 'The Origins of Hagiography' and Rydén, 'Ueberlegungen'.
11 Musurillo, 'The Pagan Acts of the Martyrs'.
12 'Dans cet optique, on pourrait dire de manière quelque peu triviale que, généralement parlant, dans le milieu hellénistique, le milieu juif et le milieu chrétien, ce discours était alors "dans l'air". Des récits et motifs particuliers pouvaient être empruntés, mais ils pouvaient tout aussi bien "circuler" parallèlement en des endroits différents et dans des traditions différentes' — van Uytfanghe, 'L'hagiografie', p. 170.
13 Lifshitz, 'Beyond Positivism and Genre'.

division of the historical from the legendary to be important; this problem did not exist for the authors/redactors of previous centuries. As Lifshitz argues,

> The entire historiographical transformation of the late nineteenth and early twentieth century involved the redefinition of the category of that which is true, against which falsity could be measured. [...] The concept of 'hagiography' is a historiographical construction and, *ipso facto*, an ideological tool. It is a tool that had no function in the ninth, tenth, and eleventh centuries, and thus as a conceptual category did not exist.[14]

In connection with Byzantine hagiography and autobiography, a similar claim was repeated by Martin Hinterberger, who gave a more specific history of these words and concepts.[15]

Since Lifshitz's arguments concern Western hagiography, it is worth citing a Western example. Although calling the saints' *Lives* and miracle catalogues of medieval Christianity to account for a clear division between the legendary-literary and the historical is indeed futile, the question, nevertheless, was raised even before the twelfth century. At the beginning of the sixth century, a decree attributed to Pope Gelasius (492–496) strongly questioned the status of hagiographic texts, and it deleted the *Passiones* from the official liturgy. Although the ban was lifted under Pope Hadrian I (772–795), the argument itself is worthy of attention. It stated that such texts (i.e. hagiography) are on the one hand not historical enough, since their authors are unknown; yet on the other hand, they are too historical, in that they extol individual, personal merits instead of the universal divine grace.[16]

---

14 Lifshitz, 'Beyond Positivism and Genre', p. 113.
15 'The seventeenth century French neologism "hagiographie" originated from the Latin *hagiographa*, which, as its Greek equivalent ἁγιόγραφα, since the Middle Ages has been defined as the final portion of the Hebrew scriptures (Psalms, Proverbs, Lamentations); in modern Greek the equivalent of "hagiography" is ἁγιολογία, whereas ἁγιογραφία and its derivatives ἁγιογράφος, etc. mean "painting of holy icons", "painter of holy icons", etc. Only during the twentieth century did the word "hagiography" obtain its current meaning.' Hinterberger, 'Autobiography and Hagiography', pp. 139–40, n. 1.
16 'Item gesta sanctorum martyrum, quae multiplicibus tormentorum cruciatibus et mirabilibus confessionum triumphis inradiant. Quis catholicorum dubitet maiora eos in agonibus fuisse perpessos nec suis viribus, sed gratia Dei et adiutorio universa tolerasse? Sed ideo secundum antiquam consuetudinem singulari cautela in sancta Romana ecclesia non leguntur quia et eorum qui conscripsere nomina penitus ignorantur et ab infidelibus et idiotis superflua aut minus apta quam ordo fuerit esse putantur; sicut cuiusdam Cyrici et Iulittae, sicut Gregorii aliorumque eiusmodi passiones quae ab ereticis perhibentur compositae. Propter quod, ut dictum est, ne vel levis subsannandi oriretur occasio in sancta Romana ecclesia non leguntur. Nos tamen cum praedicta ecclesia omnes martyres et eorum gloriosos agones qui Deo magis quam hominibus noti sunt devotione veneramur.' Pseudo-Gelasius, *Decretum de libris recipiendis et non recipiendis* IV. 4; in English (my translation): 'likewise [can be read] the deeds of the holy martyrs, which are shining from the multiple sufferings due to the tortures, and from the triumphs worthy of admiration that arise from their confessions of faith. Who of the Catholics would doubt that they

The suspicion of the decree about the historicity of the texts harkens back to their literary status. Yet Lifshitz's warning that hagiographic texts are inseparable from other manifestations of the cult still holds. The juxtaposition of the literary and historical character of hagiographic texts was likewise formulated by Paul Magdalino. He emphasized that it is precisely the medium of the hagiographic text that establishes the saints' historicity — just as we have seen in the case of Cyrus and John.[17]

Scott Johnson, in his recent search for literary models for the miracles of Thecla, made Herodotus and paradoxography their main (or in his view, their only) literary precedent and argued that the miracles of Thecla consciously imitated Herodotus in a paradoxographical model. Hence, he denied a place for Thecla's collection among the *miracula* literature and fundamentally questioned her status as an incubation healer. Johnson defined Thecla's miracles as part and parcel of paradoxography.[18] Yet he ignored the problem that the main feature of paradoxography is that such stories are neither religious nor personal. They are bookish wonders, not personal experiences of the divine; they have no relation either to cult or to the beneficiary of the miracles. Unlike the highly intimate stories of Thecla's manifestations, paradoxographic tales are rhetorical, literary units. However, what particularly seems to undermine Johnson's hypothesis is that he considered Thecla's miracle collection alone, isolating it from all other early Christian dream-miracle collections. Some of his claims to support his argument are simply not true. For example, he seems to place unjustified importance on the hagiographer's reference to Herodotus, who belongs as much to the self-display of the hagiographer as do the other classical authors he paraphrased (Homer, Plato, Thucydides, or Euripides and Xenophon) among the group of representatives of Greek learning. But Johnson's solution seems unsatisfactory, even if we were to keep the category of genres. Maria Girone has already pointed out that Herodotus could have

---

    managed to endure the greater parts of their sufferings not because of their own strength, but tolerated everything with God's grace and help? But according to old custom, with the greatest caution, they are not read in the Holy Roman Church, because the names of those who wrote [these texts] are not properly known and because the unbelievers and ignorants think that they are useless and less proper than it should be; for instance, the [accounts of] a certain Cyricus and Julitta, or the Passions of George and others are regarded to have been written by heretics. For this reason, as I said before, they are not read in the Holy Roman Church, so that no pretext for casual mockery could arise. Nevertheless, we devotedly venerate, together with the aforesaid Church, all the martyrs and their glorious sufferings, which are better known to God than to men.'

17 'The hagiographic text', writes Magdalino, 'allows us to study the dynamism of the model projected by the text, even where the model behind the text eludes recovery or turns out to be fabricated; in other words, it gives historical meaning and function to those holy men who never existed in the flesh.' Magdalino, 'What We Heard in the Lives of the Saints', p. 85.
18 Johnson, *The 'Life and Miracles of Thekla'*; beyond doubt, this is the most 'literary' approach to early Christian miracles published for some time. The part on paradoxography is ch. 4, 'Greek Wonders', pp. 172–220. Cf. Honey, Review of Johnson's *'Life and Miracles of Thekla'*.

served as a literary model for the fourth-century Isyllus paean from Epidaurus, comparing the Asclepius epiphany of the paean and Herodotus VI 105, the epiphany of Pan.[19] Paradoxography, as Johnson also noted, was a bric-à-brac genre, characterized by the lack of structure and overall composition. On the other hand, Thecla's miracles have strong cohesive elements: the miracles concern a single figure, they are performed at one site, are conveyed mostly through dreams, take place within one generation, and we should not forget to mention the structuralization of the text, such as the thematic grouping (see below). But the merit of Johnson's analysis, regardless of genre attribution, lies in placing the emphasis on a literary approach to the corpus. Yet, when criticizing the previous scholarship's social-historical interest in the miracles, he forgets the literary milieu Dagron outlined: the literary activity, the rhetorical contests, and the presence of famous rhetors among Thecla's clientele. This renders invalid his opinion that the composition of the *Life* and the *Miracula* was a personal pastime and not intended for the public. We know from the diary-keeping pilgrim Egeria's travel memoires that the earlier version of Thecla's *Life* was read to Egeria in the church, so it is likely that others could have also participated at the public readings around the sanctuary, especially when the cult site became even more famous and a representative miracle collection was made.[20]

Greek Incubation Records: Votives and Temple Redactions Become Literary Narratives

Greek miracle narratives of incubation and other types of miraculous healing were often recorded and kept in sanctuaries. About the Serapis temple at Canopus, Strabo states that 'there are some who write down the cures, while others record the miracles of the oracles of this place'.[21] It is important to recall that the textual recording of miracles, healings, and dream-visions at places could be a ritual requirement: 'Everyone who goes down to Trophonios is obliged to dedicate the story of whatever he has seen or heard, written out on a wooden tablet.'[22] The ritual order of recording the miracle could have been conveyed by the cult personnel, but the divinity may have also called for it directly. This is attested, for example, by the verb στηλογραφεῖν, often used on second-century AD confession stelai from Asia Minor. The god might tailor his order to the dreamer, requiring the inscription of the miracle story or the compilation of a whole collection; as Iulius Appelas (*c.* AD 160) informs us at the end of his long votive inscription, Asclepius repeatedly 'ordered' him what to do: 'He bade me also to inscribe this. Full of gratitude I departed

---

19   Girone, *Iamata*, pp. 50–51.
20   *Travels*, 22.2–23.6, in Wilkinson, *Egeria's Travels*.
21   Strabo, *Geographica*, XVII. 1. 17.
22   Pausanias, *Guide to Greece*, IX. 39. 4.

well.'[23] At the same time and at the explicit order of Asclepius, Aelius Aristides also recorded his dream-relationship with the god. His stay in the temple and his literary enterprise lasted for several years, and his motivation to immortalize the god's fame and his special connection to him was identical to the devotion of Sophocles, which prompted him to write his Asclepius-Paean, still famous in the imperial period.[24] There is an interesting Christian source about Greek temple records: the *Passio Sanctorum Quattuor Coronatorum*, which claims that the recording of the Asclepieian miraculous cures could have been requested by the emperor himself. The source attributes to Diocletian that he immediately ordered to build a temple of Asclepius in the Baths of Traian in Rome, and also to make a cult statue from marble. When it was ready, he gave order that all the cures that happened in that temple should be written down with inscriptions on metal tablets of the praecons (that is, tablets that the praecons put out for public viewing)[25] Diocletian was a persistent antagonist of the martyr acts (the emperor who actually promoted the Asclepius cult was Antoninus Pius). Yet the value of this note is not at all insignificant: it bears testimony to some sort of systematic work collecting and archiving the Asclepieian *Iamata*. Critically, the results of this systematization were aimed for public disposal.

Marco Dorati noticed a differentiation in these cultic records. He identified the earlier votive objects as manifestations of individual piety. When the individual dedications underwent a selection and were written on a stele, they were shaped into a narrative, to be read within the temple; this was a successive level of miracle recording. He emphasized that these inscriptions did not originate from the healed individuals but from the temple itself.[26] This was, however, not the final stage. Dorati suggested that the fate of incubation miracle stories might have been similar to the formation of oneirocritic literature.[27] By the Hellenistic era, a large corpus of literary records had developed which could obtain popularity outside the range of cultic healing. It consisted of books whose subject was miraculous healings and divine dream epiphanies.[28] Oracular type incubation and dream interpretation produced a rich literary material,[29] which also included numerous dream-healing miracles, and it enables us to question how vast literary collections, similarly

---

23 T432.
24 T587, 588, 589, 590.
25 'et statim iussit in termas Traianas templum Asclepii aedificari et simulacrum fieri ex lapide proconisso. Quod cum factum fuisset, praecepit omnes curas in eodem templo in praeconias [i.e. "tabulas publice a praecone praepositas"] aeneas cum caracteribus infigi.' Deubner, *De incubatione*, p. 75, n. 1.
26 Dorati, 'Funzioni e motivi', pp. 92–93.
27 Dorati, 'Funzioni e motivi', p. 94.
28 Cf. Dorati and Guidorizzi, 'La letteratura incubatoria', p. 346; cf. also Halliday, 'Some Notes on the Treatment of Disease in Antiquity', p. 286.
29 Cf. *Graecorum de re onirocritica reliquiae*, ed. by Del Corno.

to the oneirocritic literature, could be composed from the raw material of incubation dream cures.[30] A precious source, Artemidorus, attests that Geminus of Tyre collected the dream prescriptions and healings of Serapis into three books, Demetrius of Phaleron into five books, and Artemidorus of Miletus in twenty-two books.[31] This body of material probably formed part of a literature of a particular kind that grew up around Serapis: the lists of dream prescriptions and dream interpretations.[32] In the case of the Serapeion of Canopus mentioned by Strabo,[33] it is uncertain whether we are dealing with proper miracle-lists and booklets, or he simply had in mind the written testimonies of the votives that were a familiar sight from other cult places. In his Serapis hymn, Aelius Aristides wrote about the 'ἱεραι θηκαὶ βίβλων ἱερῶν' (sacred boxes with sacred books),[34] which quite likely refers to miracle narratives archived in the sanctuary. To sum up, there existed in the imperial period at least two channels through which divine miraculous events associated with dreams and ritual healing became fairly widely known: the material around the cult place, from which the primary votive form received a narrative elaboration, and what was archived in the temple but probably travelled far in accordance with the fame of the sanctuary. On the other hand, there existed the (non-cultic) dream literature, out of which emerged works that belonged to the world of popular entertainment, to the 'letteratura del consumo', as Dorati and Guidorizzi put it.[35]

In the introduction to his collections, Thecla's hagiographer mentions that, at the great incubation and oracle cult places of Greece (in Dodona, Delphoi, at the spring of Castalia, and at Pergamon, Epidaurus, and Aegae), the supplicants received a written answer. It is more likely that the hagiographer's remark meant that these answers (i.e. the most famous of them), just like other miraculous deeds of the deities, spread in written form. On the basis of the hagiographer's critique of them, it seems that not only their content but their style and literary topoi were well known to him, most probably from his reading. As for the direct literary precedents of Christian incubation narratives, both Thecla's hagiographer and Sophronius make mention of the written recorded material at the cult place, the miraculous cures of Sarpedonius and Isis, which were known to them.

---

30 Dorati and Guidorizzi, 'La letteratura incubatoria'; in the epigraphic material of the great Greek curative sanctuaries, it is a question whether we can see a clearly outlined incubation literature, as the authors suggest.
31 Artemidorus, *Oneirocritica*, 2. 44 and 4. 22. Cf. *Graecorum de re onirocritica reliquiae*, ed. by Del Corno, pp. 111, 138–39.
32 Longo, *Aretalogie nel mondo Greco*, p. 28; Dorati and Guidorizzi, 'La letteratura incubatoria', pp. 346–47; and Del Corno's Introduction in his Artemidoro, *Il libro dei sogni*, p. xxvii.
33 Strabo, *Geographica*, XVII. 1. 17.
34 Cf. Versnel, 'Religious Mentality in Ancient Prayer', p. 62, n. 258; A. Duprez also spoke of *aretalogoi* in the cult of Serapis: *Jésus et les dieux guérisseurs*, p. 73.
35 Dorati and Guidorizzi, 'La letteratura incubatoria', p. 346.

The recording of these miracles and the shaping of them into a literary mould is of the utmost importance. Its effect was analogous to what would later happen around Christian cult places; from the moment that the miracles were recorded in the sanctuary, on stelai around it, or in books, the dissemination and reading of the stories and their cultic significance were all enlarged. Both in Antiquity and in the forming of saint cults, miracle stories concerning the miracle-worker were organically linked to the cult place itself. Hippolyte Delehaye traced the history of these miracle catalogues back to the testimony of Augustine's *De civitate Dei* XXII, where he suggested that the beneficiaries of the miracles would compose short, written records of the events, which in turn were presented to and approved by the local bishop.[36] Afterwards, these *libelli* were to be stored in the church. Delehaye argued that, at the time, the practice of the *libellus* seemed natural and the idea of recording had to arise nearly everywhere where such memorable miraculous events occurred.[37] He also connected the phenomena to the record-keeping in the sanctuaries of Asclepius and pointed out the essential similarities between the features of the *Iamata* and Christian miraculous cures. Recording and keeping these miracles had a double purpose: episcopal approval established a sort of control through the documentation of miracles and the standardization of testimonies. The practice might have taken root at other places as well,[38] but it is difficult to assert that there was such a practice of systematic archiving in booklet form in Byzantium.

The spread of the stories beyond the boundaries of the cult place had variegated effects. First, the local cult that was advertised by the miracle stories attracted pilgrims to their place and away from other, similar cult figures. Just as the Epidaurian stelai were concerned not with the fame of Asclepius but of the Asclepieion of Epidaurus, and the miracle stories incorporated their rivalry with the defeat of the Asclepieion of nearby Troizen, the collection of Thecla is likewise focused on the importance of the Seleucian shrine. Secondly, a famous sanctuary became a magnet in attracting the most representative stories of the cult figure. This must have happened with some of the miracles of Cosmas and Damian, which were amalgamated into a single corpus celebrating the Cosmidion in Constantinople. A third aspect is that far-spreading miracle narratives (which, as they became more and more distanced, were often stripped of their local features) advertise what is general in the cult, enlarging the universal character of the miracle worker

---

36 Delehaye, 'Les premiers "Libelli Miraculorum"'.
37 Delehaye, 'Les premiers "Libelli Miraculorum"', p. 433.
38 Cf. also Augustine's *Sermones* 320–24, and van Uytfanghe, 'La controverse biblique', p. 211, also with regard to the change in Augustine's attitude towards contemporary miracles; cf. Brazzale, *La dottrina del miracolo in S. Agostino* and de Vooght, 'La notion philosophique du miracle chez saint Augustin'; Hardon, 'The Concept of Miracle'; see also Boesch Gajano, 'Verità e pubblicità'; recently a valuable contribution to the position of miracles, esp. related to relics: Wiśniewski, *The Beginnings of the Cult of Relics*, esp. ch. 2, 'The First Miracles'.

and the circle of 'witnesses'. This circle grew from a group around the healed person in the sanctuary into *all who read and believed* the miracle stories. Of the incubation miracles of Isis, Diodorus Siculus wrote: 'In proof of this, as they say, they advance, not legends, as the Greeks do, but manifest facts; *for practically the entire inhabited world is their witness, in that it eagerly contributes to the honours of Isis because she manifests herself in healings*. For standing above the sick in their sleep she gives them aid for their diseases and works remarkable cures upon such as submit themselves to her.'[39]

When the narratives of cultic events were no longer limited to the area of the sanctuary, the miracle worker and their miraculous stories could become separated. This could happen either when the stories started to retain (or acquire) a local colouring, or by expanding towards the universal patterns of miracle literature.

An important aspect of this separation (in part its cause, in part its result) is that the miraculous motifs, the narrative elements, and the most varied units of the narration have a life of their own: the same story can be connected to several heroes, like the miracle of the mute woman or the paralytic man, which figures among the miracles of Cosmas and Damian and Saint Menas, but was apparently performed by Cyrus and John as well. However, Sophronius purposefully did not want to record those miracles of Cyrus and John which were worked by other saints. Instead, Sophronius gave priority to those deeds that were attributed to his subject-saints alone: 'This present miracle I wrote down, because it is not written in the collection of those others.'[40] His note on this subject of multiple attribution and the travelling of miracles also attests to the fact that he knew these stories in a written form. In addition, the spread of the Sophronian miracle corpus is well illustrated by the fact that some of his miracle narratives would be translated in tenth-century Naples by the hagiographer of Saint Agnellus — who was also an incubation healer.[41] A. B. Lord wrote about the functioning of living, oral compositions:

> The fact that the same song occurs attached to different heroes would seem to indicate that the story is more important than the historical hero to which it is attached. There is a close relationship between hero and tale, but with some tales at least the *type* of hero is more significant than the *specific* hero. It is convenient to group songs according to their story content, or thematic configurations, because songs seem to continue in spite of the particular historical hero; they are not connected irrevocably to any single hero.[42]

---

39 Diodorus Siculus, *The Library of History* I. 25. 4–5 (trans. by Oldfather; emphasis mine).
40 In the epilogue of MCJ30.
41 Mallardo, 'L'incubatione nella cristianità'; cf. Dorati, 'Funzioni e motivi', p. 114, n. 87.
42 Lord, *The Singer of Tales*, p. 120.

Lord's statement holds equally true for the stories of pagan and Christian *thaumaturgoi*, with the emphasis that the main character's historical or a-historical mythical-fictitious being did not influence the migration of these motifs. Moreover, what may seem more significant in the case of our healers is that the type of the hero is more important than the religious and ideological texture surrounding his figure and cult. The typology, the turning points, and the form-world of the stories around the cult-figures of incubation healing were permanent, independently of the pagan-Christian context.[43]

The Relationship of Incubation Narratives to Biblical Miracles and Early Christian *Miracula* Literature

In direct relation to Christian healing miracles were the preceding healing miracles of Jesus and the narrative shape that these stories acquired in the New Testament. Their impact was not only literary and theological,[44] but they provided a new paradigm of miraculous healing from a medical point of view. They accomplished this by turning back to the model of the immediate cure instead of the longer curative process that characterized the later healings of Asclepius. If we examine the incubation miracles closely, it is striking that the saints are perceived to act as medicine men rather than *thaumaturgoi*. They do not use the means that Jesus used to heal: words or a touch. They give individual councils, and they have more than one remedy. Even the habitual wax is not uniformly applied, as it is mostly recommended to treat the already miraculously operated scars, to be taken orally as pill or liquid for internal problems, or to be smeared on the patient's exterior. Gestures like the laying-on of hands or the sign of the cross are also not instrumental but additional to the miraculous remedy,[45] and they only come from the Christian repertoire when the miracle story motif would not interrupt the pattern of the incubation tale's narrative.

The same holds for the healing acts of Jesus. The incubation saints' imitation of Jesus is more rhetorical and supplementary to the narrative,

---

43 Giulio Guidorizzi applied the Proppian model for the *Life of Saint Elias the Younger*, and he underlined that in the narrative of the *Vita*, just as in the tales, the characters did not matter, but their functions did: 'Motivi fiabesche nella agiografia bizantina'.
44 Achteimer, 'Jesus and the Disciples as Miracle Workers'; Bonner, 'Traces of Thaumaturgic Techniques in the Miracles'; Funk, 'The Form of the New Testament Healing Miracle Story'; Hardon, 'The Miracle Narratives in the Acts'; Kee, *Medicine, Miracles and Magic*; Kee, *Miracle in the Early Christian World*; Kelber, *The Oral and Written Gospel*; van der Loos, *The Miracles of Jesus*; Neyrey, 'Miracles, in Other Words'; Pilch, 'Insights and Models'; Pilch, 'Understanding Biblical Healing'; Pilch, 'Understanding Healing in the Social World'; Remus, *Jesus as Healer*; Remus, *Pagan–Christian Conflict over Miracle*; Rüttimann, 'Asclepius and Jesus'; Smith, *Jesus the Magician*; Theissen, *The Miracle Stories*; Tinker, 'Medicine and Miracle'.
45 For example, KDM4, 9, 21 or KDM27.

rather than constitutive of it. The Christian stories often end by establishing a parallel between the healers and Christ, especially if the patient can be compared to some beneficiary of healing in the Gospel: being lame, blind, or having faith as great as the paralytic who was shepherded down from the roof. It is particularly true for the miracles of Cosmas and Damian: the obligatory closure of the narrative ends with thanksgiving to Christ, the saints' healings often emphasized as a reflection of the example set by Jesus and the thaumaturgic charisma that he endowed on his disciples. Despite the Christian references inserted into the story, the half-sentence analogies, and the quotations, the biblical relationship of the miracle stories is only secondary and easy to detach from the narrative. (I emphasize that I am not discussing the theological aspects of Christian miraculous healings, but the formation of the narrative.) The biblical rhetoric inserted into the stories (mostly at their beginning or end) remains rhetoric. To illustrate how the imitation of Christ's gestures by the saints can be forced and out of place, I would like to recall one of the miracles of Cyrus and John. In MCJ46, the saints, through the medium of dreams, follow Jesus's example in John 9. 7–11 and send their patient to the Lake of Siloam (they also advised the sick man to bathe, as was the case in so many other incubation counsels). However, the sick man in the Egyptian Menouthis protested that the blind man of the Gospels was near the pool of Siloam, and he would need to undertake a costly journey to go to Jerusalem. Instead of healing the man themselves, the saints provided the patient with money for the journey! The way that Sophronius told this miracle shows that the mismatch of the biblical imagery in this story must have greatly amused him (if he was not the one who invented it).

In the theological message of the miracles, the *salus* (healing and salvation) given by Christ is naturally emphasized alongside the repeatedly stressed possibility of obtaining physical and spiritual healing. Notably, these healings are expressed in the framework of the story. The dream miracles follow an independent paradigm: the narrative is more determined by the microcosms that called these stories directly to life, the cult practice tradition of dream healing.[46] Previously, I have talked about the travelling of certain motifs and of stories that became attributed to various saints. As far as our collections allow us to observe, this interlacing of narrative units primarily exists within the realm of the incubation miracle collections.

---

46 This loose relationship between the theological-religious background and the narrative was articulated by Dagron in connection with Thecla's corpus: 'Les Écritures ne sont dont pas ici une référence sacrée, et une réalité indépassable, mais un modèle religieux et littéraire adaptable et transportable, à partir duquel on composera une sorte de christianisme de clocher. Ces déformations ne sont pas imputables à l'hagiographie en général, mais à la culture de notre hagiographe, chez qui les mots, les images, les croyances du christianisme s'accrochent infailliblement sur les schémas conceptuels du paganisme des cités.' *Vie et miracles*, ed. and trans. by Dagron, p. 156.

Marie-France Auzépy examined Byzantine miracle-literature from the point of view of the social background of the genre.[47] She distinguishes three phases in the development of miracles in the Eastern Church and characterized them in the following way: The communal consensus required for the functioning of miracles comes into being in the second half of the fourth century AD, in close connection with the cult of relics and the development of hagiography as a genre.[48] She interprets the seventh century as the greatest point of change: an atmosphere of general crisis (the loss of Jerusalem and the Eastern provinces, the Arab threat), which might have lent credence to faith in miracles. In the Greek-speaking areas, the *vitae* became rarer over the course of the seventh century, and *miraculum*-literature spread. With the exception of Thecla from the fifth century, all the incubation miracle collections that I am addressing here are from the seventh century. The collection of such minor incubation saints such as Saint Demetrius by John of Thessalonica dates from AD 610 and that of Saint Therapon by Andrew of Crete is from the eighth century. During the eighth century (the period of Iconoclasm), the *miracula*-stories, as a genre, are temporarily pushed into the background.[49] In the ninth century, miracles again become an article of faith, but at the same time, the genre undergoes important changes. Miracles involving the painted image of the saints Cosmas and Damian became an argument for the use of icons at the Second Council of Nicaea, held in 787.[50] The council convened to support icon worship, and the episode reflects the process by which image and relic attain an equal status. Orthodoxy, being forced to integrate the belief in miracles, attained a degree of control over them, made them a part of the liturgy, and incorporated them into the hagiographic tradition.

With the spread of miracles in liturgical use, especially at the places of cult which were connected to the services performed by the healer saints, the miracle narratives received a new function in addition to their existing function as a mere record of the events that happened. They received a pedagogic dimension with the intention of deepening the faith of the believer.[51] As a result, the actual event of the miracle and its written record accord with certain criteria. For example, there was a demand for witnesses and the need for proof of illnesses and their cures. Additionally, special attention was paid to sacral objects, acts, and the piety and truthfulness of the patient (a process more traceable in Western hagiography). Auzépy, discussing the

---

47 Auzépy, 'L'évolution de l'attitude face au miracle'.
48 According to Auzépy, the spread of the cult of relics 'bastardised' the miracle.
49 On the connection between the rise of icons and the popularity of miracle accounts in the same period, cf. Cameron, *Christianity and the Rhetoric of Empire*, pp. 212–14.
50 KDM13 and 15.
51 See Maraval, 'Fonction pédagogique', and also Déroche, 'Pourquoi écrivait-on des recueils de miracles?'.

treatment of miracles, speaks of 'localised' and 'codified' miracles,[52] and Sigal of 'controlled' miracles.[53]

Natalio Fernandez Marcos, who approached this issue from a different perspective, rightly noted that the narrative of incubation miracles and their religious-theological background are clearly separated. While I explain the fidelity to the ancient form in the Christian corpora by indicating that the narrative pattern inherited from ancient incubation was so strong that it subordinated the formation of the Christian practice to its own rules, Fernandez Marcos attributed the distantiation of the form and content to the fact that the narrative structure of incubation was a mere tool for Sophronius's own ends (the propagation of the truths of Chalcedonian orthodoxy), and he spoke about the 'limitless credulity of the author'.[54] For my part, I see this 'credulity' as the adherence of Sophronius (as of the hagiographer of Thecla and the other saints) to the genre requirements of the miracle narrative. Sophronius emphasized that he wanted this work to be a masterpiece in its genre; an unavoidable condition of which was the most refined display of the most wondrous miracles.

---

52 Auzépy, 'L'évolution de l'attitude face au miracle', p. 46: 'Le miracle est devenu patrie intégrante de la foi orthodoxe, mais il a été contrôlé, à la manière byzantine, en agissant sur le cérémonial et non sur les institutions: il a été liturgisé […], il est devenu l'objet de récits codifiés répétés aux offices et il a été localisé dans les églises auprès des reliques et des icônes.'

53 Sigal, *L'homme et le miracle*, pp. 149–55.

54 'En los Thaumata se conserva el mismo esquema de la incubatio, las mismas fórmulas para las epifanías, un comportamiento de los santos muy parecido al de Asclepio. Pero junto a esta, tenemos la impresión de que la incubatio se emplea como un recurso retorico más con el fin de transmitir una serie de ejemplos y doctrinas. Todas las narraciones de milagros son tendenciosas desde el momento que están escritas con un parti pris dogmático y con una finalidad cerigmática o propagandística. Pero en los Thaumata, la exaltación cerigmática de los santos invade todas las narraciones y hace de ellas un himno de alabanza en el que todos los datos van acordes con el entusiasmo desatado y la credulidad sin límites del autor.' Fernandez Marcos, *Los Thaumata*, p. 167.

CHAPTER 3

The Christian Incubation Saints

Their Cult Sites and their Miracle Records

The Cult of Saint Thecla

Saint Thecla was probably the most celebrated female saint of early Christianity.[1] According to her legend, she was a noble virgin of Iconium (today's Konya, in Turkey) in the first century, and having heard Paul preaching, she left her family and became Paul's follower. She was known as the female apostle and the protomartyr among women. Twice she was miraculously saved from being burned and being eaten by wild beasts. She travelled with Paul and met a peaceful death. Note that in the original version of her legend she did not die a martyr death. Her companionship with Paul, the stories of her wanderings where she forsook marriage for an ascetic and missionary life, her trials, and her miraculous escapes were all given literary form in the *Acta Pauli et Theclae*, composed in the second century AD, in the style of a Hellenistic novel.[2] The figure of Thecla is exceptional for many reasons. Being a woman, she was qualified for particularly feminine tasks, both in her lifetime as well as in her posthumous miracles, and she is often a starting point today for medieval women's studies.[3] The veneration of her cult is first attested in Asia Minor, in places where she allegedly stayed during her life and which figure in the *Acta*: her hometown Iconium, Antioch which she visited with Paul, Myra, and Seleucia, her resting place before her cult spread to Byzantium, Egypt, and the West.[4] Equally significant was her connection to Paul and her role in ascetic literature as a female hagiographical model for women opting for saintly life.[5] This distinction between male and female resulted (as Stephen Davis argues) in Thecla being paired as a thaumaturgic saint to the male thaumaturgic saint of the greatest distinction, Saint Menas.

---

1 For her cult, her life, and her miracles, including a description of the surrounding social milieu, see *Vie et miracles*, ed. and trans. by Dagron, and Davis, *The Cult of Saint Thecla*.
2 *Acta Pauli et Theclae*, BHG 1710–16; critical edition: *Acta Apostolorum Apochrypha*, ed. by Lipsius and Bonnet; English translation: James, *The Apocryphal New Testament*.
3 From the numerous examples: Burrus, *Chastity as Autonomy* and Misset-van de Weg, 'Magic, Miracle and Miracle Workers'.
4 Cf. Davis, 'Pilgrimage and the Cult of Saint Thecla'.
5 Athanasius (fourth century AD), *On Virginity*. On the significance of this gender balance, Stephen J. Davis wrote: 'In the minds of ancient male authors, a woman could imitate a male exemplar only in a partial and generic sense because she would always be encumbered by the differentiation of a female body and the assumed weakness of the female will. In this context, writers would present women as the most suitable ideals for other women, while rarely (and reluctantly) citing them as examples for men.' 'Pilgrimage and the Cult of Saint Thecla', p. 312.

Thecla is also extraordinary with respect to her miracle-working capacities. She often seems to act independently, and we do not find an emphasis on the saint being the servant or intermediary of God in miraculous events, which is ubiquitous in other saints' hagiographical records. The same independence characterizes the cult practices surrounding Thecla: she is neither a clear-cut incubation healer, nor exclusively a healer. She rather embraced all aspects that a healer would (just like Asclepius) and acts as helper in a range of matters.[6] Nevertheless, it is beyond question that her post-mortem modus operandi at her earliest cult sites was incubation. This is made clear in the first lines of her miracle collection. When justifying Thecla's practice of adopting a formerly pagan ritual and sending incubation dreams, the hagiographer drew a conscious distinction between Thecla's dream-advice and that given by the ancient divinities: 'Such are, to quote but a few examples from the many, the oracles of demons: misguiding, malevolent, of bad faith, mere apparitions, tricks, full of obscurity and lies. In contrast to this, what are the remedies and predictions of the saints? They are clear, they tell the truth, they are simple, holy, perfect; indeed worthy of God who grants them.'[7]

In Seleucia and in nearby Aegae, she took over the ritual practice of temple sleep from the preceding pre-Christian cults. If incubation was adopted together with the cult site at these locations, it explains why Thecla never became completely associated with incubation elsewhere in general, as it happened with Cosmas and Damian, a saintly pair whose cult brought dream healing to their various places of worship. Besides her other places of worship (in Aegae, Alexandria, Mareotis, and Egypt), Thecla had three churches dedicated to her in Constantinople.[8] One was in the Sykae district, which certainly existed in the second half of the fifth century (and where the Monophysite Fravitas served before becoming patriarch of Constantinople (489–490), having been nominated by Emperor Zeno).[9] Procopius attests that Justinian had constructed another church before becoming emperor (527) near the Julian Port, probably on the top of the steep hill that descends towards the Sea of Marmora.[10] Thecla's third church was in the Blachernai quarter. At least by the mid-tenth century, there was already an oratory dedicated to her in the Blachernai Palace. This was probably the building that Emperor Isaac Comnenus I enlarged into a proper church in 1059.

However, the most important place for Thecla's cult was Seleucia (Silifke / Meriamlik in today's Turkey), the capital of Isauria in Asia Minor. It was described in the *Acta Theclae* as the place where the saint died peacefully and

---

6 I elaborate on this phenomenon in Csepregi, 'Disease, Death, Destiny'.
7 In the Prologue to the miracles, *Vie et miracles*, ed. and trans. by Dagron, pp. 288–89.
8 Janin, *La Géographie Ecclésiastique*, pp. 148–50.
9 The church figures in Malalas's description of the naval battle in 515 between Marinus the Syrian and the Thracian Vitalian. It was where the spectacular Greek fire was used for the first time. Malalas, *Chronicle*, XVI. 16 (trans. by Jeffreys, Jeffreys, and Scott).
10 Procopius, *On Buildings*, I. 4 (trans. by Dewing).

was buried. Besides this detail in the *Acta*, we have archaeological evidence at our disposal,[11] as well as other textual sources about Thecla's cult place. Egeria visited the site in AD 384, and in her *Travels* she recorded her favourable impressions of the church on a hill. She wrote of the presence of 'innumerable monastic cells for men and women' and the beauty of the shrine located there, encircled by a wall.[12]

From the fourth century AD, the cult site witnessed a huge development. Because of its favourable geographical position, Seleucia was a significant stop on the eastern trade route, and it owed its prosperity to the splendid festivals, grandiose buildings, and a blooming intellectual life. The numerous miraculous cures effected by Thecla are in part the cause and in part the result of the thaumaturgic fame of the place, perhaps also connected to the thermal baths surrounding the site. After Egeria's visit, the church precinct was enlarged and a small basilica was constructed over a cave, a place of great importance for both Thecla and her pilgrims. In the miracle collection, this cave is described as a favourite dwelling place of the saint (probably before the time that the church was built) and a centre of devotion within the cult site from the fourth century onwards. Fortunately, the earliest parts of the miracle collection originate from this period.

The growing popularity and significance of the cult site affected the reworking of Thecla's legend. The *Acta Theclae* became independent from the *Acta Pauli*, with which it was previously paired, and it received a new ending in response to the new circumstances. In this ending, instead of dying peacefully, Thecla disappeared into the ground over the cave. That the rock opened and swallowed the saint naturally explained the absence of her relics; at the same time, it provided an odd blend of a saint dead and not quite dead. This cave church was further enlarged in the fifth century AD (probably shortly after 476) at imperial expense. This financial support was due to both Thecla's general popularity as well as her 'promise' to the dethroned Emperor Zeno that he would recover his imperial power from the usurper Basiliscus. Shortly afterwards, the prophecy was fulfilled in AD 476, and the emperor had a large church erected in honour of Thecla, replacing the small basilica.[13] The expansion and embellishment of the cult buildings continued in the sixth century (with two other churches and a public bath and cisterns) in order

---

11 Herzfeld and Guyer, *Meramlik und Korykos*, pp. 38–46; cf. Davis, *The Cult of Saint Thecla*, pp. 36–39. For an archaeological analysis of the takeover of the site, see Bayliss, *Provincial Cilicia*, pp. 89–90. For geographical references of the cult site, for the plans of the cult buildings, and for a detailed description of the sacred precinct, with a summary of the results of the excavators Herzfeld and Gruyer: *Vie et miracles*, ed. and trans. by Dagron, pp. 55–73, with abundant bibliography and drawings.

12 Egeria, *Travels*, 23. 2–4.

13 A three-naved church, longer than eighty meters; for the plans, cf. Davis, *The Cult of Saint Thecla*, pp. 211–12.

to meet the growing demands of the numerous pilgrims.[14] The splendour of the cult site not only lay in the architectural beauty so admired by Egeria, but also in a concept foreign to Western hagiography; the saint, in fact, inhabited the cult place and moved about in it like in a house.[15]

The soon-to-be-written collection of her miracles would empower Thecla with the characteristics of the divinities formerly associated with the site. Her 'being swallowed by the earth' may well have been related to the chthonic nature of her cultic predecessor, a local hero named Sarpedon or Sarpedonius.[16] Erwin Rohde, in his *Psiche*, dedicated special attention to the cave deities and to the god-hero-tomb triad associated with Apollo and Asclepius. He wrote that, under the figure of several Greek heroes, there was hidden the cult of a minor local deity, whose dwelling in the surrounding land, inside the earth, was considered his or her tomb. Rohde emphasized that after their divine natures were lowered into those of mortal heroes, these figures were truly considered to inhabit the space of their cult. Following this line of thought, he made important observations about the chthonic character of incubation figures and healing heroes; he particularly mentions Sarpedonius, linking him with similar healer-heroes as Mopsus, Amphilochus, Teiresia, Protesilaus, Menesteus, Autolico, and even a female incubation figure, Hemithea, who was giving both oracles and cures. Rohde also dwells on the problem of how the Homeric Sarpedon might have ended in Cilicia and, quite remarkably, presents another figure called Sarpedon, completely different from the Homeric one. This is the dream-oracle-giving figure described at Thecla's site too, with the suppliants visiting his tomb; allegedly, he is the Cretan Sarpedon, the son of Europa, the brother of Minos.[17]

Thecla's miracles clearly indicate that Sarpedonius was also credited with performing cures through incubation. Even after the establishment of Thecla's cult, some pagan supplicants coming to the site held him to be the author of miraculous cures. These events took place in Thecla's only other shrine

---

14 Cf. Euagrius Scholasticus, *Historia Ecclesiastica*, III. 8; ed. and trans. by Bidez and Parmentier, pp. 107–08 — the German edition and translation with the Greek text of 1898. The emperor was also on good terms with Saint Daniel the Stylite, who foretold him in person the calamities awaiting him and his successful overthrow of the usurper; a detailed description of the events is found in in the *Vita Danielis* 68. c. ff, in English in *Three Byzantine Saints*, ed. and trans. by Dawes and Baynes.

15 'On ne peut souligner plus énergiquement cette conception populaire qui fait habiter le saint, invisible à l'ordinaire, dans sa basilique, comme dans un palais. A Séleucie, le peuple avait le vif sentiment de la présence de Thècle. On savait que elle aimait à se tenir dans une sorte de vestibule un peu écarté [...] ou dans la grotte voisine de la fontaine. Car elle aime le calme et la solitude', wrote Delehaye, 'Les recueils antiques', p. 54; on the concept of Eastern saints inhabiting the church: Bozóky, 'Le miracle et la maison du saint'.

16 On the figure of Sarpedonius and the variants of his name, see *Vie et miracles*, ed. and trans. by Dagron, pp. 85–88, and Johnson, *The 'Life and Miracles of Thekla'*, pp. 123–26.

17 Rohde, *Psiche*, p. 159.

where incubation was practised: near the town of Aegae, long famed for the incubation sanctuary of Asclepius.[18]

Thecla's other cult predecessor, who also exercised her function as *soter* — not so much as a deliverer of individuals but rather of the community and town under her protectorate — was Athena.[19] Athena clearly had connections with healing, as her name Athena Hygieia attests;[20] 'Athene of Health' was represented as a running figure with a serpent on her shield.[21] One sculpture of Athena Hygieia is known from fifth-century BC Athens, and three Roman replicas are preserved in the Museum of Naples (the Athena Farnese), in the Hope Collection in England, and in Cividate Camuto (Museo Archeologico della Valle Camonica). The importance of Athena to the town of Seleucia in the fourth century is shown also on the evidence of coins.[22]

It was Athena's features that could be seen in a Thecla who took up arms and fought for Seleucia when it was in peril, together with her patronage of literature and the typically feminine tasks of a virgin-warrior. Hence, the complexity of Thecla's incubation cult, arising from that fact that she was not only a healer-saint but a *soter* in a wider sense of the word. Although she took on many other saving roles from the cultic environment, her name and her cultic function were associated with healing: 'Thecla, the physician' as a grave-inscription from Seleucia attests.[23]

The attributes of Athena that were attached to Thecla by the hagiographer had a personal aspect as well; it was not simply a matter of cultic replacement. The hagiographer, apparently to show off his literary ambitions, emphasized an image of Thecla as patron and a bit of a Muse: she is called *philologos kai philomousos*. For the hagiographer, both he and the bishop were similar to Diomedes, being under the guidance and the protection of Athena.

The Miracle Collection of Thecla

The collection of Thecla's forty-six miracles was written in several phases, probably around the year AD 468 and surely completed before 476. Additions by the same hagiographer can be clearly traced. The miracle collection is a pair with the saint's *Vita* written somewhat earlier by the same hagiographer.[24]

---

18 There are two miracles in the collection connected to Thecla's cult place at Aegae, MT9 and MT39. On incubation cults in Aegae, see later in this chapter.
19 For Dagron (*Vie et miracles*, pp. 84–85) Athena was a literary topos, the real rival being Sarpedonius, while E. Lucius regarded Thecla rather as heir to Athena; cf. Lucius, *Die Anfänge des Heiligenkults*, p. 206.
20 Cf. Suda s.v. *Athena Hygieia* and Pausanias, *Guide to Greece*, I. 23. 5.
21 Peter Levi in Pausanias, *Guide to Greece*, I, p. 65, n. 134.
22 Lucius, *Die Anfänge des Heiligenkults*, p. 206.
23 CIG IV, 9209 (*Corpus Inscriptionum Graecarum*, ed. by Böckh and Niebhur); Linda Honey called attention to this testimony in her review of Johnson's '*Life and Miracles of Thekla*'.
24 The *Vita* and the *Miracula* are compared in *Vie et miracles*, ed. and trans. by Dagron, pp. 19–23; the *Vita* is analysed extensively in Johnson, *The 'Life and Miracles of Thekla'*, pp. 15–66.

Both Thecla's *Vita* and the *Miracula* survived among the works of Basil of Seleucia, but the real hagiographer was an opponent of Basil's, an anonymous rhetor from Seleucia and a man of traditional Greek learning, who, as a layman or perhaps a priest, came into close contact with Thecla and her sanctuary.[25] After that and on several occasions, he became a beneficiary of Thecla's thaumaturgic miracles and experienced the saint's protection over various affairs in his life; at the urging of a friend, he recorded, collected, and redacted the miracles as a gift of thanksgiving.

In his thematic arrangement of the miracles, the hagiographer produced a true artistic composition. At one point, the collection had come to an abrupt end (with MT 44), yet the hagiographer took up the task once again and continued the collection. Although he calls Thecla his sole source of inspiration, he informs us that in collecting these miracles he carried out systematic research, including fieldwork in neighbouring places, interrogation of eyewitnesses and relatives of the healed persons, and exploitation of textual material kept in the church. The core of the narrated miraculous events was formed by those miracles that (at most) took place over a century, or what the hagiographer estimates as memory stretching back roughly three generations. The literary cultic records available at the cult place, like the oral tradition surrounding it, related the way Thecla's cult functioned up until the time of the collection, and also recollected the activity of her predecessors at the site, Athena and Sarpedonius. Compared to the other incubation collections in my survey, the geographical range of the saint's activity seems to have been more limited. The majority of the beneficiaries of the miracles came from Seleucia or from the province of Isauria. One patient came from Constantinople, another from Antioch, and another from Tarsus. Two patients came from Cyprus. It appears that the saint did not specialize in long-distance miraculous interventions.[26]

A notable feature of the corpus is that it often made contemporary ecclesiastical events the core of the miracle story. These include personal conflicts, contrasting theological positions, and the individual character of the bishops of Seleucia. The hagiographer also took a position on issues of heresy and orthodoxy and, at the same time, portrayed himself as a spectator of the town's society and its festive and everyday faces. Thus, he could describe that Thecla's intervention was made manifest in the case of a stolen wedding ornament or in a cattle epidemic, and also when the enemy threatened the town. The hagiographer mentions the pagan written material that he knew about; hence his references to Greek cultic healing and oracular records are far from being simply some literary topoi. Moreover, Johnson totally disregards the attested existence and (vivid) memory of the previous incubation healer

---

25 On the person of the hagiographer and his work, see Dagron, 'L'auteur des Actes et des Miracles de Sainte Thècle'; and in the introduction to his edition of the collection: 'I. Une œuvre et son auteur', *Vie et miracles*, ed. and trans. by Dagron, pp. 13–30.

26 All of these aspects are described in detail in *Vie et miracles*, ed. and trans. by Dagron, p. 24.

of the site. What seems to particularly undermine his hypothesis is that he considered Thecla's miracle collection alone, isolating it from all the other early Christian dream-miracle collections.[27]

The attribution of Thecla's miracle collection to Basil of Seleucia determined its fate; it was transmitted together with the *Acta Pauli et Theclae* until the tenth century. Afterwards, the *Vita* and the *Miracula* were treated independently in the manuscript tradition.[28] The *editio princeps*, together with the *Vita* of Thecla by Simeon Metaphrastes, was published by Pierre Pantin in 1608 in Antwerp and dedicated to Philip III, king of Spain; this text (with a lacuna of ten miracles) was to be adopted into the *Patrologia Graeca*.[29] Its classification, among the works associated with the king's name, meant that the miracle corpus with its forty-six miracles was transmitted in more or less unadulterated form.

The tone of Thecla's miracles is strikingly intimate. This arises from the personal character of the work, the hagiographer's knowledge of ancient literature, philosophy, and religion, his references to details of his own private life, and his personal piety towards the saint. These characteristics reveal him to be perhaps the most congenial of Byzantine hagiographers. By frequent use of references to classical authors, he seems to have tried to establish a Greek Christian *paideia* while writing his hagiography and tried to secure a place for Thecla's miracle collection within it.

Cult Practice and Cult Place: The Case Study of Aegae

Isocasius, the learned rhetor and pagan court official under Leo I (457–474), turned to Thecla and benefitted from a miracle she performed; all that the saint did was scold him for remaining a pagan after the miracle.[30] Isocasius appears in a group of miracles that have great rhetors as protagonists, including the hagiographer himself, who, it seems, wished to place himself next to such a personality. Besides presenting Thecla's magnanimity towards someone who does not acknowledge her superiority over Sarpedonius and showing the saint as a patroness of literature, the story has another important aspect. The miracle did not take place in Seleucia but in Thecla's church at Aegae. Isocasius had a special connection to this place: his career as a grammatician and sophist started here; from this town he conquered Antioch and Constantinople.

---

27 With similar conclusions Honey, Review of Johnson's '*Life and Miracles of Thekla*'.
28 For details, see 'La Tradition manuscrite et les principes de l'édition', *Vie et miracles*, ed. and trans. by Dagron, pp. 140–51.
29 The seventeenth-century Vaticanus codex that, by virtue of its antiquity and good quality, had been the most frequently copied version had a large lacuna: ten miracles were missing from its beginning, from MT1.18 to MT18.18 (cf. *Vie et miracles*, ed. and trans. by Dagron, pp. 142–43). The edition of Pantin, the text of the *Patrologia Graeca*, and Festugière's translation were prepared from this incomplete manuscript.
30 MT39; in 467 Isocasius was arrested and accused of being a pagan, but in the end he was acquitted; cf. *Vie et miracles*, ed. and trans. by Dagron, pp. 91–92.

Thecla has another miracle related to Aegae (MT9), and the hagiographer has an interesting comment about the place: he praises Aegae as a town famous for its piety. Did he mean the worship of Asclepius? Or was he discussing some new, Christian associations?

Aegae (Cilicia, Turkey) was a noted pilgrim site, and the fame of its temple of Asclepius rivalled that of Pergamon in the Greek Near East, where, we know for certain, the miraculous dream cures of the god were recorded and stored on temple inscriptions.[31] The temple of Asclepius at Aegae entered into the story of Apollonius of Tyana, the wonder-worker of the first century: Philostratus (c. 170 – c. 245/47), who wrote the *Life of Apollonius*, said that Apollonius chose the temple of Asclepius at Aegae as the place of his apprenticeship and that Asclepius expressed how he was pleased by Apollonius's presence.[32]

Philostratus was in the company of the emperor Caracalla and Julia Domna in 215 when, after Pergamon, they visited Aegae and made a sacrifice to Asclepius. In the third century, Aegae appears to be a bustling pilgrim centre where both tourist business and cultural activity were booming. The emerging Christian Church had to face the challenge that this site presented. In his *Ecclesiastical History*, the Christian Sozomenus attributed the destruction of the temple to Constantine in the year AD 331, noting that this temple (together with Aphrodite's temple in Aphaca) 'had been most distinguished and venerable to the ancients. As to the Aegeatae, they boasted that those with them who were sick in body were freed of their disease because the demon appeared at night and healed them.'[33] Eusebius wrote the following words about Asclepius and this temple: 'with thousands excited over him [sc. Asclepius] as if over a saviour and physician, who now revealed himself to those sleeping [in the temple at Aegae], and again healed the diseases of those ailing in body'.[34] Here he emphasizes (perhaps involuntarily) the popularity of the incubation practice, of 'the demon worshiped in Cilicia, whom thousands regarded with reverence as a possessor of saving and healing power, who sometimes appeared to those who passed the night in his temple, sometimes restored the diseased to health'. The same passage also describes, in great detail, the destruction of the Asclepieion.[35]

---

31   On the Asclepius cult in Aegae in general, see Ziegler, 'Aigeai, der Asklepioskult'; for the analysis of some particular inscriptions, see Robert, 'De Cilicie à Messine et à Plymouth'.
32   *Vita Apollonii*, I. 8 (Philostratus, *The Life of Apollonius of Tyana*, trans. by Conybeare); a more far-reaching parallel is between Apollonius and Christ, cf. Bernard, *Apollonius de Tyane et Jésus*.
33   Sozomenus, *Historia Ecclesiastica*, II. 5 = T819.
34   *De Vita Constantini*, III. 56 = T818.
35   *De Vita Constantini*, III. 56 = T818. 'For since a widespread error of these pretenders to wisdom concerned the demon worshipped in Cilicia, whom thousands regarded with reverence as the possessor of saving and healing power, who sometimes appeared to those who passed the night in his temple, sometimes restored the diseased to health, though on the contrary he was a destroyer of souls, who drew his easily deluded worshippers from the true Saviour to involve them in impious error, the emperor, consistently with his practice

It is doubtful, however, whether it was destroyed this way or whether it was destroyed at all. Some scholars think that if Constantine actually destroyed the temple, he did it for political reasons because Aegae took the side of Licinius, his opponent.³⁶ I would like to emphasize that, whether or not the Asclepieion was indeed destroyed, the description of its destruction, as a narrative tool, was used in a very powerful way to attest Christianity's victory. The latest surviving inscription about the cult of Asclepius comes from Epidaurus in the year AD 355: the dedication of Mnaseas, priest at the Asclepieion of Aegae of Cilicia.³⁷ This shows that, regardless of the condition of the building by the 350s, healing activity continued within it, albeit in reduced circumstances.

Rather unexpectedly, Aegae soon witnessed a second intellectual and cultic revival during the reign of Emperor Julian, who opposed Asclepius to Christ:

> Asclepius, having made his visitation to earth from the sky, appeared at Epidaurus alone, in the shape of a man; but afterwards he multiplied himself, and by his visitations stretched out over the whole earth his saving right hand. He came to Pergamon, to Ionia, to Tarentum afterwards; and later he came to Rome. And he travelled to Cos and thence to Aegae. Next he is present everywhere on land and sea. He visits no one of us separately, and yet he raises up souls that are sinful and bodies that are sick.³⁸

This praise of Asclepius as a healer is even more significant if we recall that Julian's personal physician was Oribasius, the most important medical scholar of that time. We know that he was involved in producing state-of-the-art medical knowledge because he wrote his major works at the request of the emperor. It was Oribasius who went to consult the Delphic oracle on behalf of the emperor in 362 and received one of the last answers of the Pythia, declining the help Julian offered in the restoration of the site:

> Tell the king, the splendid hall fell to the ground.
> Phoebus no longer has his house, nor the prophesying laurel,
> nor the speaking well. The speaking water has dried out.³⁹

---

and desire to advance the worship of him who is at once a jealous God and the true Saviour, gave directions that this temple also should be razed to the ground. In prompt obedience to this command, a band of soldiers laid this building, the admiration of noble philosophers, prostrate in the dust, together with its unseen inmate, neither demon nor god, but rather a deceiver of souls, who had seduced mankind for so long a time through various ages. And thus he who had promised to others deliverance from misfortune and distress, could find no means for his own security, any more than when, as is told in myth, he was scorched by the lightning's stroke. (2) Our emperor's pious deeds, however, had in them nothing fabulous or feigned; but by virtue of the manifested power of his Saviour, this temple as well as others was so utterly overthrown, that not a vestige of the former follies was left behind.'

36 See Steger, *Asklepiosmedizin*, p. 100 and n. 168.
37 IG, IV² 438: Ἀσκληπιῶι Αἰγεώτηι ὁ ἱεροφάντης καὶ ἱερεὺς τοῦ σωτῆρος Μνασέας Ἑρμιονεὺς κατ' ὄναρ τὸν σλβ'.
38 Julian, *Against the Galileans*, 200B, in *The Works of the Emperor Julian*, trans. by Wright.
39 *Passio Artemii*, 96.1284.45–47, Cedrenus 1.532.8–10; cf. Thompson, 'The Last Delphic Oracle'.

Julian's devotion went alongside his plan to restore important cult buildings. During the spring of the year 362, Count Julian, the emperor's uncle, wrote a letter to the emperor and outlined a plan for the restoration of the temples in the East. Julian agreed to all of the details; however, he requested that the sanctuary of Apollo at Daphne take precedence.[40] Count Julian proceeded with zeal to repossess temple property and reconstruct Asclepius's temple in Aegae. This temple must have been in a condition to properly resume its function quite quickly, since there are records of patients practising incubation from that time. Among them we find Libanius, one of the most eminent intellectuals of the fourth century (*c.* 314–394), who was a friend of the emperor Julian and a teacher of John Chrysostom and Theodore of Mopsuestia. Libanius, in his work *For the Temples*, on the one hand mourns the 'injury done to the place', while on the other hand praises that 'now the people, whom their illnesses require the hand of Asclepius, attract to Cilicia',[41] and from his letters, we learn more about his attachment to Asclepius and the pagan intelligentsia that flourished around the place. This pagan revival also inspired Libanius's sophist friends, Demetrius and Acacius, in Tarsus: Demetrius composed two orations on Asclepius, and Acacius composed one. Libanius paid attention to these activities at Aegae, partly because of his close connections with the extended clan of Demetrius and Acacius, but more importantly because of his intimacy with the god of healing due to his chronic migraines. Before he was able to visit the sanctuary himself, Libanius requested that Demetrius seek a dream oracle on his behalf and sent him copies of the two orations on the god.[42] We learn from his Letters 707–08 that his brother also travelled to Aegae in late winter or early spring 362 in the hope of receiving an oracle from Asclepius, that is, medical advice normally resulting from incubation. During his illness in 367, Libanius visited the temple himself,[43] and one of his letters bears testimony to its restoration under Julian.[44] For this restoration, we also have a Christian account with a rather different emphasis: transforming its restoration into a miracle. The heavy columns of the Asclepius temple could only be moved at great costs and major difficulties by the 'Hellenes', and they managed to only lift one of them; even that one they were only able to move to the threshold where they were eventually unable to bring it out. The returning Christian bishop after Julian's death 'easily righted it again and returned it to its spot'. The *History* of Zonaras tells the events of 362, making the fate of the temple's columns emblematic of Julian's whole reign.[45]

---

40 Julian, *Letter*, 29.
41 Libanius, *Oration*, 30. 39: in *Selected Works*, trans. by Norman.
42 Libanius, *Letters*, B 146, 147, and 148 also speak of the Asclepieion of Aegae.
43 Libanius, *Oration*, 1. 143.
44 Libanius, *Letter*, 695.
45 *The History of Zonaras*, 13. 1–19, ed. and trans. by Banchich and Lane, p. 174. 'He (Julian) set his army in motion against the Persians and arrived at Tarsus, a famous city of Cilicia. When he had arrived there, Artemius, the priest of Asclepius, approached him — for in Aegae

In all of these accounts, pagan or Christian, the writers never forget to underline that Aegae had a famous Asclepieion. It is quite natural then, that in the case of Aegae we are dealing with a quite smooth transmission of cult memory, as Thecla's hagiographer in the mid-fifth century still seemed to know the records of the temple of Asclepius that Libanius mentioned in his letters.[46] The hagiographer did not treat this pagan past as an inconvenient rival; nor did he dismiss it as godless nonsense. With the inclusion of Aegae and other cultic sites preceding Thecla's, he managed to turn the pagan background into a positive hinterland, a source of legitimacy and credibility for Thecla's miraculous powers. In this way, the saint could nicely fit her cult activity into the piety of the town of Aegae, which piety had a strong Christian tradition as well.

In Christian hagiography, Aegae was not famous for Thecla. It acquired a symbolic significance because of its connection to Asclepius and ritual healing in a less spontaneous way. In Christian hagiography, Aegae became most emblematically attached to Saints Cosmas and Damian, the doctor-saints and incubation healers par excellence.

The Cult of Saints Cosmas and Damian

The trajectory of the cult of this pair of physician-saints is perplexing. Their figures and the way they could have been worshipped proved extremely flexible. Additionally, as their cult spread quickly over the entire Mediterranean, subsequent features complemented their legend in each of the major emerging cult places.[47]

The earliest layer of their legend locates them in Syria, calling the town of Cyrrhus their hometown, which also became the place of their peaceful death and burial. At this phase of the legend, they were healers and miracle workers but not yet martyrs. The hagiographical demand soon emerged to make them martyrs, and this was the time when Aegae entered the story. Aegae became the scene of their martyrdom during the reign of Diocletian, under the

---

(this, too, a city of Cilicia) there was a renowned temple of Asclepius — and requested that he restore again to the temple of Asclepius the columns which the archpriest of the people of the Christians had removed and upon which he had built his church. The transgressor straightway commanded that this be done at the bishop's expense. Then the Hellenes, when they, with much labor and with the greatest cost, had barely taken down one of the columns and moved it with machines as far as the threshold of the door of the church, even after a great length of time were unable to get it outside. They abandoned it and departed. And after Julian had died, the bishop easily righted it again and returned it to its spot.'

46 Libanius, *Letter*, 695. 2.
47 *AASS* September 27, 428–99; *St Kosmas und Damian*, ed. by Deubner; *Sainte Thècle, Saints Côme et Damien*, ed. and trans. by Festugière; Luongo, 'Il *dossier* agiografico'; *Cosmae et Damiani*, ed. by Rupprecht; and Wittmann, *Kosmas und Damian*.

prefect Lysias.⁴⁸ Cosmas and Damian also had their important parallels: the brother and sister saints Zenobius and Zenobia, who were also martyred at Aegae by Lysias, were also regarded as incubation healers.⁴⁹ These two figures seem to have had a great impact on the formation of the legend of Cosmas and Damian.⁵⁰ Asclepius's celebrated cult in Aegae doubtlessly influenced both narratives.⁵¹ And it would be from Aegae that the cults of the two saints started to spread and soon covered the whole eastern Mediterranean and Rome. Interestingly, there is another holy doctor who came to be linked to Aegae: Saint Thalelaius, allegedly a physician from Lebanon who, during his lifetime, cured the sick with his medical skills and miraculous powers.⁵² When he was captured in Cilicia, he was brought to the governor Theodore at Aegae and beheaded in 284. He became numbered among the holy *anargyroi*, saints who took no payment, along with Cosmas and Damian and Cyrus and John.

With regards to Saints Cosmas and Damian, one of the most unusual things is that, because of their popularity, they multiplied. Hence there are three pairs of Saints Cosmas and Damian, the so-called Asian (that is, from Asia Minor), Roman, and Arab pairs, with three different *Passiones*, and three *Vitae*. Each pair has a different place of birth and their own feast day.⁵³ We can begin to answer the question of how and why this pair of saints became tripled by consulting Deubner's monograph:⁵⁴ The Asian pair of saintly physicians met

---

48 They were among other saints who were reported to have suffered martyrdom at Aegae, by the order of Lysias: Saints Claudius, Asterius, Neon, Domnina, and Theonilla; cf. *AASS August 23*.
49 *AASS* October 13, 259–73.
50 Ludwig Deubner and Ernst Lucius long debated which *Vita* had had been the model for the other, i.e. the legend of which pair of saints came into being first. Both scholars, however, were in agreement about the impact of Asclepius. *St Kosmas und Damian*, ed. by Deubner, p. 64; Lucius, *Die Anfänge des Heiligenkults*, p. 260.
51 Ernst Lucius also identified the beginnings of the saints' cult in Aegae and saw in Asclepius the catalyst of incubation healing (Lucius, *Die Anfänge des Heiligenkults*, pp. 259–61).
52 On his cult, see Brocker, 'Der heilige Thalelaius, Texte und Untersuchungen'.
53 According to the first, the so-called *Asian Vita*, the mother of the saint-pair was a certain Theodote. (On the motif of the missing father in the saints' *Lives*, see Guidorizzi, 'Motivi fiabesche nella agiografia bizantina', p. 467); these 'Asian' saints decided to heal both men and beast for free. They were buried at a place called Pheremma. They are not described as martyrs. Their feast day is November 1. The saints in the second pair, from the *Passio Romana*, were Christian doctors in Rome who healed and converted Emperor Carinus but suffered martyrdom because of the jealousy of the court physicians. Their feast day is July 1. This *Vita* was not accompanied by miracles. The saints of the third pair, from the *Passio Araba*, by way of their Arabic origin, were wandering doctors who praised Christ through their medical practice; during the reign of Diocletian and Maximian they arrived in Aegae in Cilicia, and there they were led to the prefect Lysias, where they suffered martyrdom together with their three brothers. To the versions of this last *Vita* altogether seven miracles belong. A detailed list of the different versions with their manuscripts, including the oriental ones, is provided in van Esbroeck, 'La diffusion orientale de la légende des saints Cosme et Damien', pp. 69–70.
54 *St Kosmas und Damian*, ed. by Deubner, p. 60.

a peaceful death, and this motif formed the basis for the various versions of the legends. The absence of a martyrdom indicates it is likely that Christianity was already the state religion at the time of the formation of the legend. They were moulded into martyrs by hagiographic necessity. As Deubner remarks, there was a need to place the thaumaturgic saints into a larger category, and since they fit neither among the ascetics nor among the confessors, they were claimed as martyrs.[55]

Scholars have explained the tripling of the saintly pairs by the fact that their cult sprang up in different locations, or that we are dealing with parallelly emerging cults,[56] while Ehrhard saw the origin for this multiplicity chiefly in their various feast days.[57] According to Ernst Lucius, the reason for the diversity arose from the efforts of three different localities claiming the tomb of the saints for themselves.[58] As Deubner demonstrated, the three pairs can be immediately reduced to two because the Arabian martyrs had no real cult in the Eastern Church, and only the Roman and the Asian pairs had their feast days on 1 July and 1 November, respectively. In contrast, only the Arab pair of saints had a cult in Rome and in the Western Church.[59]

Cult Places, Cult Predecessors, and Texts: Cyrrhus, Pheremma, Rome, Constantinople

The cult of Cosmas and Damian spread rapidly, as is attested by the churches erected in honour of the 'Asian' pair.[60] A church was dedicated to them around the year AD 400 in Aleppo, and two others in the fifth century AD in Edessa and in Cyrrhus (the latter together with 'their bones'). We know of a Cosmas and Damian church dated to the sixth century AD near Jerusalem, while John Moschus preserved the memory of a church and monastery (where incubation was probably practised) within the city of Jerusalem itself.[61] A knightly order was established in their honour in Palestine, Procopius Carthophylax made mention of a church in the ninth century in Pamphilia, Saint Sabas built a church to them in Cappadocia,

---

55 And, using a somewhat circular argument, the Asians must have been the first of these saint-pairs, since it is less likely that martyrs would have been replaced with non-martyrs in the miracle collections.
56 *St Kosmas und Damian*, ed. by Deubner, p. 40, who refers to Mezzadri, *De actis ss. Martyrum Cosmae et Damiani*, p. 14, who formulated this hypothesis already back in 1750.
57 Ehrhardt, 'Forschungen zur Hagiographie der griechischen Kirche', p. 109.1.
58 Lucius, *Die Anfänge des Heiligenkults*, p. 256.
59 *St Kosmas und Damian*, ed. by Deubner, p. 71.
60 *St Kosmas und Damian*, ed. by Deubner, pp. 81–82.
61 The *Pratum Spirituale*, 127 (PG 87.3, col. 2990) speaks about a hesychiast nun, Damiana, who before entering the convent was attached to the church of Cosmas and Damian in Jerusalem, and spent Friday nights in the church. Cf. Luongo, 'Il *dossier* agiografico', p. 38 (the text does not seem to me to necessarily attest to incubation since these visits may just as well have been related to a vigil).

there are traces of their cult from the seventh century onwards in Galatia and in Mysia, and important Byzantine ruins were found on the island of Dascalio as well as in Phocis and in Dyrrachium, all dating to before AD 518. A church dedicated to Cosmas and Damian with a spectacular mosaic floor was excavated in the Jordanian town of Gerasa (today Jarash), dating to AD 530–533. Based on the Greek dedication inscription, the church was built from donations by five individuals under the patronage of Paul, bishop of Gerasa.[62] In fourth-century Alexandria, Patriarch Timothy converted a temple of Serapis into a church dedicated to Honorius, the son of Theodosius I, which also became known as the church of Cosmas and Damian. We do not know when this happened, but it definitely happened by the end of the seventh century when John of Nikiu wrote about it. This may or may not be the same church of Cosmas and Damian that we read about in Sophronius's *Thaumata*, written at the beginning of the seventh century.[63]

Among the unique characteristics of the *Vita Asiatica*, one in particular may have a background in reality, a place named Pheremma.[64] The town was probably the same as the Cilician Pheremma, near the town of Cyrrhus, twenty-one kilometres north-west from Aleppo. Cyrrhus was both the supposed birthplace of the saints and the place where their remains were placed (either after their martyrdom in Aegae, or after they died from natural causes).

The town of Cyrrhus took pride rather early in the possession of these relics, as shown both in the name of the town, 'Hagioupolis', as well as in the basilica erected in honour of the saints to which Theodoret (bishop of Cyrrhus from AD 423) bore witness in AD 457.[65] The cult of the saints may have flourished there from the sixth century, as reported by Procopius:

---

62 Hamarneh, 'Cosma and Damian in the Near East'.
63 'And in those days the holy patriarch Timothy [died in 385] built a church of marvellous workmanship in the city of Alexandria [...] that he named after the emperor Theodosius I (379–95). [...] And there was a temple of Serapis in the city, and he converted it into a church and named it after the name of his (Theodosius') younger son Honorius. But this church was also named after the martyrs Cosmas and Damian. It faced the church of St Peter the patriarch and last of the martyrs.' *The Chronicle of John, Bishop of Nikiu*, 83.37–38; translated from Zotenberger's Ethiopic text by Charles, p. 88.
64 On the evidence of KDM12 where we learn of a sick woman who ever since her childhood had been under the protection of these saints, for 'ἐκ γὰρ τῆς τῶν Κυρρεστικῶν μερῶν τῆς ἀνατολῆς ἐτύγχανεν ὁρμᾶσθαι, ἔνθα τὰ τίμια λείψανα τῶν θαυμαστῶν τουτῶν ἁγίων καὶ θεραπόντων Χριστοῦ Κοσμᾶ καὶ Δαμιανοῦ ἀπόκεινται' (For she came from the parts of Cyrrhus, in the east, where the sacred relics of these wonderful saints and healers of Christ Cosmas and Damian belong). For criticism of Deubner's identification of the place (with Pelusion) and for the overall topography of the miracle collection, see Crum, 'Place-Names in Deubner's Kosmas und Damian'; P. J. Stilting was the first to understand that Pheremma must be near the town Cyrrhus, on the basis of a letter by Theodoret, without knowing the London Codex, which confirmed it. On all this, see Maas, 'Review of Ludwig Deubner's Kosmas und Damian'.
65 Festugière (*Sainte Thècle, Saints Côme et Damien*, p. 121, n. 43) introduced the KDM34, which

> There was a certain utterly neglected fortress in Syria, Cyrus by name, which the Jews built in early times, when they had been carried off as captives from Palestine into Assyria by the army of the Medes and were released much later by King Cyrus; and for this reason they named the place Cyrus, paying this tribute of gratitude to their benefactor. And as time went on this place came to be neglected in general and remained altogether without walls. But the Emperor Justinian, both out of his forethought for the safety of the state, and at the same time as showing especial honour to the Saints Cosmas and Damian, whose bodies lie close by even to my day, made Cyrus a flourishing city and one of great note.[66]

Lucius correctly observed that the scarce evidence that can be deciphered from the account of their miracles does not provide a basis for locating the origin of the cult in Constantinople. This observation will be confirmed by the evidence of the other miracle collection, the *Codex Londoniensis*, which I will introduce below. The same is corroborated by the contents of KDM12, which explicitly attest that the remains of the saints lay in the Syrian town of Cyrrhus.[67]

If their attributes have been correctly identified, the British Museum stucco painting from a sixth-century Egyptian monastic complex (in Wadi Sarga) seems to portray characteristics of the Arab pair: It represents the Old Testament martyrdom scene of Ananias, Azarias, and Misael in the burning furnace, painted between the figures of Cosmas and Damian. The three brothers of the saints appear below this scene.[68] The oldest known iconographic representation of Cosmas and Damian, however, was painted much earlier, namely the mosaic in the church of Saint George in Thessalonica, dated by Artelt to AD 379–395.[69]

---

refers to the relics being in Constantinople. Hence, he claimed, together with Lucius, that the growing number of places where the relics were guarded led to the multiplication of saints.

66 Procopius, *On Buildings*, II. xi. 2–5 (trans. by Dewing).
67 Deubner dismissed it as an inorganic element, similar to the mention of the five saints in certain manuscripts (which would lead to the conclusion that it is the Arabian saint-pair that was erroneously related to the miracles. On the evidence of the Suda (s.v. 'Christodoros Thebaios'), where it was noted that this Christodorus from Thebes put together a collection of the miracles of Cosmas and Damian, Lucius reached the conclusion that the saints must have exercised their thaumaturgic powers outside of Constantinople as well. Deubner however, also considered this story an elaborated version of the Constantinople corpus. (I did not find the Suda mentioning that Christodorus wrote on Cosmas and Damian.)
68 The saints here are not represented as twins. Dalton, 'A Coptic Wall Painting from Wadi Sarga'.
69 Luongo, 'Il *dossier* agiografico', p. 40; a photograph is in Skrobucha, *Kosmas und Damian*; English translation as *The Patrons of Doctors*; for more on their (mostly Western) iconography, see Artelt, *Lexicon der christlichen Ikonographie*, vol. 7 (1974), cols 344–51, s.v. 'Kosmas und Damian'; and his *Kosmas und Damian*; David-Danel, *Iconographie des Saints Côme et Damien*; Julien, Ledermann, and Touwaide, *Cosma e Damiano*; its modern veneration is assessed by Duffin, *Medical Saints*.

Cosmas and Damian in Rome

It was the Arab pair that entered Rome. Moreover, Ludwig Deubner concluded that the Arab version was fabricated for the use of the Roman cult sometime in the fifth century. Hence, these Byzantine saints appeared as noteworthy exceptions in Rome before the conquest of Justinian.[70] Recently, Beat Brenk investigated the motives for the saints' entry to Rome and for the location of Cosmas and Damian's church, built in 527 by Pope Felix IV (526–530), in the middle of the Forum Romanum — I briefly follow his observations.[71] After rightly questioning the historical reality of the saints, Brenk focuses on the iconography of the mosaic in the Roman church, which represents them in the company of Saints Peter and Paul together with Saint Theodore, and argues that it was King Theodoric (AD 452–526) who granted the church to Pope Felix IV. Saint Theodore is represented together with Cosmas and Damian in a fifth-century mosaic found in Apamea, Syria, and the three saints (Theodore, Cosmas, and Damian) can also be associated in their churches in Gerasa, Jordan. The Byzantine emperor Anastasius (491–518) showed a particular veneration for Saint Theodore. If we consider that it was Anastasius who recognized Theodoric as king of Rome, the selection of the church-site for the famous doctor-saints, together with Saint Theodore in one of the most prominent places of Rome, might have been a gesture to Byzantium that was supported by Theodoric's political heirs as well. Another, more legendary account tells that Amalasuntha, daughter of King Theodoric, gave the pope a rectangular building which, speculation goes, was the library of the Temple of Peace, and an adjoining circular building which was thought to be a temple dedicated by Emperor Maxentius to his son Romulus. In any case, it was to the Arab pair that Pope Felix IV dedicated the still beautiful basilica. At the time, there were already five churches dedicated to Cosmas and Damian, among them the oratory built by Pope Symmachus (AD 498–514). The basilica was built in an area of Rome that was considered the medical quarter, replacing a structure that was part of Vespasian's Forum of Peace.[72] Interestingly enough, the church of Cosmas and Damian came to stand for the medical quarter; in the fifteenth century, Pope Martin V assigned the church S. Lorenzo in Miranda to the pharmacists' guild, probably influenced by the fact that, near S. Lorenzo, there stood the church of Cosmas and Damian, the patron

---

70 Deubner speaks about shorter and longer Greek versions, the former extant in two manuscripts, from the eleventh to twelfth centuries, and the latter in another manuscript from the fourteenth to fifteenth centuries. This latter manuscript, interestingly, is full of Latinisms; cf. *St Kosmas und Damian*, ed. by Deubner, p. 80, n. 1.

71 Brenk, 'Da Galeno a Cosma a Damiano'.

72 Over time, the basilica went through numerous changes, with deterioration followed by restoration, with additions and reconstructions. In 1503, the basilica was consigned to the Third Order Regular of St Francis for maintenance (formally transferred in 1512), and this religious order manages the basilica to this day.

saints of doctors and barbers.⁷³ During the plague of AD 590, a procession of supplicants seeking a cure started off from this church.⁷⁴

Incubation was connected to their cult place in Rome as well, in the Chapel of the Physicians in the Santa Maria Antiqua, built and frequented by Greeks living in Rome. Thus, incubation was part and parcel of a Byzantine environment and was practised probably first by the Greek Christians living in Rome. Recently, it has been pointed out that there is a niche carved into the wall at floor level (unlike the other niches in the church that are consistently at eye level) that may indicate incubation in the Chapel of the Physicians.⁷⁵ According to another hypothesis, the medical character of the S. Maria Antiqua might have been the result of the associations with the Lacus Iuturnae, with its water that was thought to have healing capacity, as well as with the temple of the Dioscuri, Castor and Pollux, in the immediate neighbourhood.⁷⁶

In the end, Rome made her own pair of saints. In the *Passio Romana*, Cosmas and Damian are depicted as living in Rome as Christian physicians who were denounced by Emperor Carinus (AD 283–285). After the locals hid them in a cave, they were arrested and interrogated by the emperor. They threatened Carinus that he would become as distorted as his thoughts, and indeed this is what is said to have occurred — his head turned backwards. The miraculous healing of the emperor was followed by the latter's confession of faith, and the saints could leave in peace. However, a final martyrdom was needed. The emperor's jealous physicians lured them into a trap and stoned them. What brought this version of the legend into being? In the competition of the Eastern Church with the Western Church, did demand arise for a martyr-pair of Saints Cosmas and Damian, resulting in a new 'Roman' pair?

All this variation reveals the enormous flexibility of their cult; meanwhile it renders irrelevant the question of which 'original' pair of saints superseded which 'single' ancient healer. A similar elasticity can be observed in the exceptionally convoluted hagiography of the saints. Their legend is multilayered and tangled because of the numerous sources. This tangling occurred because it adopted

---

73   Some interesting details about the fate of this church can be read in Giuseppe Vasi's 1761 *Roman Itinerary*.
74   The sanctuary had previously been dedicated to either Urbs Roma or Romulus (the son of Emperor Maxentius); for bibliography, see Luongo, 'Il *dossier* agiografico', pp. 41–42; for interpretations agreed with and those rejected by Deubner regarding the church, see *St Kosmas und Damian*, ed. by Deubner, pp. 73–74.
75   Knipp, 'The Chapel of Physicians', p. 12. About the establishment of the cult of Cosmas and Damian he wrote that 'the installation of a cult of Eastern medical saints at S. Maria Antiqua was probably not merely due to the ancient connotation of the site, but also had its cause in a predominantly Byzantine environment: the administration on the Palatine, the emergence of a Byzantine quarter, the wave of immigrants from Egypt in the seventh century, and the specific dedication of the nearby diaconiae' (p. 8).
76   Tea, *La basilica di Santa Maria Antiqua*; Osborn, 'The Atrium of S. Maria Antiqua', p. 207; also Aronen, 'La sopprainvenza dei culti pagani'.

so willingly the hagiographic characteristics and necessities of the moment, be these about the number of the saints, their persons, their lives or deaths, or the places and times where they were active. The more recent inclusion of the oriental texts into the scope of research has modified interpretations on some important issues that were based on the surviving Greek and Latin texts.[77] The research history on Cosmas and Damian is splendidly described by M. van Esbroeck, with the inclusion of Syriac, Arabic, Coptic, and Georgian manuscripts.[78] However, even if we had the 'earliest' *Vita*, it would be futile to search for the *real* or *original* legend; these legends, by their very nature in the early formation of Christian places of worship, were created to answer to the demands of the surrounding community.

Cosmas and Damian in Constantinople

When writing about the pre-Christian history of Constantinople, a Byzantine historian from the sixth century AD named Hesychius of Miletos referred to a legend that Byzas, the mythical founder of the city who erected a temple next to water for Castor and Pollux, healed his people.[79] Deubner connected this reference to the incubation cult of the Dioscuri, citing in support of his argument a miracle from their collection (KDM9) where a pagan visited the saints, addressing them as Castor and Polydeices.

This miracle led him to believe that (1) the cult predecessors of Cosmas and Damian were the Dioscuri,[80] and (2) the cult originated in Constantinople. Though it was not the original place of the cult, there is a sort of consensus about the primary importance of Constantinople in the incubation cult of Cosmas and Damian. Nevertheless, it is far from easy to

---

77 On a Syriac *Vita* surviving in a fifth- to sixth-century manuscript: Bedjan (v. Bedian), *BHO* 210; with translation and commentary: Weyh, *Die syrische Kosmas – und Damian-Legende*; W. E. Crum vindicated the attention being paid to the Coptic–Arabic version of the legend, published by Sulaimân: *Tuḥfat az-zamān fi sīrat-al-farīsain Quzmān wa Damyān*; Crum pointed out that the version in the Cairo manuscript survived not only in Arabic but in a Coptic version as well; the narration of the *Vita* is followed by seven miracles, of which three were not found either in the Deubner corpus or in Rupprecht. The seven miracles are also present in the Arabic Cairo manuscript and in the Coptic codex (Pierpont-Morgan, MS 856). Van Esbroeck emphasized that at the beginning of the collection the Coptic introduction placed the story of the saints in Petra, evidence that Petra had been christian before it became Islamized (see the next note).
78 Van Esbroeck, 'La diffusion orientale de la légende des saints Cosme et Damien'.
79 Hesychius, *Origines Constantinopolitanae*, ch. 15, ed. by Preger, p. 7; quoted in Deubner, *De incubatione*, p. 79.
80 Deubner, *De incubatione*, p. 77; Harris, *The Cult of the Heavenly Twins*, esp. pp. 96–104 on the connection between Castor and Pollux and Cosmas and Damian. A rejection of Deubner's fundamental thesis on the basis of the Syriac legend is contained in Maas, 'Review of Ludwig Deubner's Kosmas und Damian'; another rejection of the Christian identification of the Dioscuri from a standpoint different from Maas may be found in Delehaye, 'Castor et Pollux dans les légendes hagiographiques'; see also Franchi de' Cavalieri, 'I SS. Gervasio e Protasio'.

locate where the miracles took place. We know of six Cosmas and Damian churches in the capital:[81]

1–2. Κοσμᾶς καὶ Δαμιανὸς ἐν τοῖς Βασιλίσκου was built by Justin II (AD 565–578) together with his wife, Sophia, as an offering of thanks. This is according to an epigram from the Anthologia Palatina I. 11 'for the victory over illnesses and the barbarians' (ἐπὶ νίκαις κατὰ νόσων καὶ βαρβάρων); Janin claims that it was identical with the church of the saints in the town quarter of Dareios (Κοσμᾶς καὶ Δαμιανὸς ἐν τοῖς Δαρείου), which is known to have been built by Justin II in AD 569, north-west of Port Sophia.[82]

3. The church in the Zeugma town quarter, the Κοσμᾶς καὶ Δαμιανὸς ἐν τῷ Ζεύγματι, was founded by Saint Proclus, bishop of Constantinople (AD 434–446), according to the patriographers. Although it was never mentioned in the synaxaries, it stood until the end of the twelfth century near the Forum of Constantine.

4. The church of the monastery of the patriarch Euthymos (Κοσμᾶς καὶ Δαμιανὸς ἐν Ψαμαθέῳ) was erected around AD 890.

5. The fifth one was a monastery of Cosmas and Damian, also called the Monastery of the *Anargyroi*. On the basis of meagre documentation, it can be safely said that it was founded by a *logothetes* (secretary of the state) and fell into ruin at the time when the Latins overran Constantinople. It was later rebuilt and made independent by Theodora, the widow of Emperor Michael Paleologos VIII. We know nothing about its location, although we can be sure that it is not identical with the monastery of the Cosmidion.

6. The Cosmidion, a church and a monastery-complex erected on the shores of the Golden Horn, was one of the most beautiful and most frequented churches in Constantinople. Janin identified the titular saints as the Roman martyr-pair because their feast day was on 1 July. According to tradition, it was founded by Paulinus, *magister officiorum* and a schoolmate of Emperor Theodosius II (AD 408–450). Paulinus was accused of a liaison with Empress Eudocia, and for this reason, the emperor tried to have him killed. According to the legend, the killers only succeeded in cutting off his ears. This was interpreted as an intervention by the saints, who would have naturally been displeased if the construction of the church in their honour had remained incomplete. On the basis of a story told in various sources, the construction of the church may have taken place around AD 439. Although the role of Paulinus in connection to the church cannot be ascertained, it is sure that the Cosmidion stood in the Paulinus

---

[81] Janin, *La Géographie Ecclésiastique*, pp. 284–89.
[82] Janin, *La Géographie Ecclésiastique*, p. 284, while Ebersolt speaks of two different churches, *Sanctuaires de Byzance*, pp. 98–99.

quarter of the city, that is, on the property of a man called Paulinus. About the monastery adjacent to the church, we do not know exactly when it was built; the first known mention of it comes from AD 518. Procopius describes the church in the following way:

> At the far end of the bay, on the ground which rises steeply in a sharp slope, stands a sanctuary dedicated from ancient times to Saints Cosmas and Damian. When the Emperor himself once lay seriously ill, giving the appearance of being actually dead (in fact he had been given up by the physicians as being already numbered among the dead), these Saints came to him here in a vision, and saved him unexpectedly and contrary to all human reason and raised him up. In gratitude he gave them such requital as a mortal may, by changing entirely and remodelling the earlier building which was unsightly and ignoble and not worthy to be dedicated to such powerful Saints, and he beautified and enlarged the church and flooded it with brilliant light and added many other things it had not before. So when any persons find themselves assailed by illnesses which are beyond control of the physicians, in despair of human assistance they take refuge in the one hope left to them, and getting on flat-boats they are carried up the bay to this very church. And as they enter its mouth they straightforward see the shrine as on an acropolis, priding itself in the gratitude of the Emperor and permitting them to enjoy the hope which the shrine affords.[83]

About a hundred years later, on 5 June 626 AD, the Avars plundered the church during their siege of the city, and three years later the church was set on fire. Yet, thanks to the popularity of the saints, the church did not lie in ruins for long. At the end of the tenth century Agapius, patriarch of Antioch, became responsible for the Cosmidion monastery. Later, Michael IV (1034–1041) fortified and enlarged the building complex, and it is at this time that the exterior sacred precinct, gardens, marble mosaics, and a bath were constructed. The privileged status of the church remained as late as 1453, the year of its (supposed) destruction. The exact place of its sanctuary cannot be identified. The building was often named and renamed after the surrounding area — either after the Paulinus quarter or after the Brachys or Lympidarius quarters. The London Codex repeatedly refers to this church as the church of Cosmas and Damian in the Blachernai (CL7, 17, 18, 20, 37 and KDM18). It must refer to the famous church of Mary of the Blachernai, and the testimonies of Russian pilgrims confirm the proximity of that church.[84] The detailed description of the miracles could make it possible to reconstruct some important parts of the interior of this church.

---

83 *On Buildings*, I. vi. 5–8 (trans. by Dewing).
84 Ebersolt, *Sanctuaires de Byzance*, p. 98, and Janin, *La Géographie Ecclésiastique*, p. 299.

The Miracle Collections of Cosmas and Damian

Kosmae et Damiani Miracula (Deubner)

The larger and better-known collection, called here KDM on the basis of the critical edition (*Kosmae et Damiani Miracula*), is a compilation and redaction based on thirty-six manuscripts, presenting forty-eight miracles from various periods and places. It chiefly contains the cures obtained through incubation in the church of the Cosmidion in Constantinople, probably covering a period from the fifth/sixth to the thirteenth centuries. The earliest layer may date to the sixth/seventh century, the collection being continuously enlarged until the thirteenth century. Ludwig Deubner organized the miracles in chronological order and distinguished six series of miracles:

I   (with a prologue) Mir. 1–10

II (without a prologue) Mir. 11–19

   Mir. 20 is an addition, being originally in the fifth series.
   These first two collections were written by two different authors, but it is likely that the author of section II united the two collections and wrote the prologue at the head of the first series.

III (with a prologue) Mir. 21–26, written by a sick man cured in the church, at the request of a person named Florentius.

IV (without a prologue) Mir. 27–32; this series is thought to be an extract from a longer collection, probably written by the author of section III.

V   (with a prologue) Mir. 33–38; the author is different from the previous ones; the miracles are shaped into individual stories, often having separate prologues and endings. This series survived in a tenth-century manuscript.

VI (with a prologue) Mir. 39–47; written by the deacon Maximus (thirteenth century) in an elaborate style with references to contemporary history.[85]

   Mir. 48 was performed in the saints' lifetimes and does not belong to any of the six series. This 'miracle of the black leg' was, however, probably the best known of the saints' cures, especially in the West, and numerous paintings attest its fame.[86]

---

85 On the textual history of this part only, see the article of Talbot, 'Metaphrasis in the Early Palaiologan Period'.

86 For example, Fra Angelico (1438–1440), Museo di San Marco, Florence; the painting in Ditzingen near Stuttgart (1490); or Master of Los Balbases (*c*. 1495), *The Miracle of Cosmas and Damian*, in the cathedral of Burgos, Spain; cf. Zimmermann, *One Leg in the Grave*.

Sophronius, in the miracles of Cyrus and John,[87] mentioned two miracles of Cosmas and Damian, KDM1 and 24, which suggests that the content of the first three series (perhaps with the miracles ordered differently) was circulating together by the beginning of the seventh century. Of the parallel miracles of the London Codex and the KDM, the last in Deubner's chronological line that is present in the London Codex is KDM33. This means that the account of the miracles in the first five series were surely known and copied in ninth-century Egypt.

The London Codex (Rupprecht)

In 1907, an Arab shepherd who was pasturing his flock in the neighbourhood of a ruined monastery near Edfu found a number of codices. The excavations following the discovery unearthed a (supposed) library from a (supposed) Coptic monastery. News about the finds spread fast, and the English collector Robert de Rustafjaell bought the manuscripts.[88] In addition to the largely Coptic material (among them a Nubian vellum with the miracles of Saint Menas from the tenth to eleventh centuries), there was also a Greek manuscript. The ninth- to tenth-century codex is now in the British Library and is referred to as the *Codex Londoniensis* or London Codex.[89] In 1935, a disciple of Deubner's, Ernst Rupprecht, edited the Greek text.[90]

The codex contains an alternative version of Cosmas and Damian's miracles, written in simple Greek, in a manner similar to an inventory. During his time, Rustafjaell argued that the London Codex pointed to an earlier phase of

---

87   MCJ30.
88   Rustafjaell, *The Light of Egypt*. Rustafjaell writes as follows: 'Here [in Edfu] I met the supposed finder himself, who agreed, for a small remuneration, to take me to the spot where he said he had dug them out. On the last page of two of the manuscript references are made to a monastery to which they were dedicated, named "St Mercurius on the mount at Edfu", and I was greatly surprised when the Arab piloted me to a place about five miles west of Edfu on the fringe of the desert plateau, where, he said, was a Coptic monastery. This monastery proved to be a white building of the Oriental type, standing within its own enclosure, and further partly surrounded by the dark brick ruins of what must have once been a very large building' (pp. 4–5). It is uncertain if these manuscripts were indeed found where it was claimed, or if they really belonged to this monastery. Besides the questionable tale of the Arab, it was not uncommon for monasteries to buy up the libraries of other churches. Books could also be transferred to larger places for safety or as gifts between various communities. Rustafjaell continues: 'The most important of the Coptic manuscripts is the Apocryphal Narrative of Christ's descent into Hell by the Apostle Bartholomew; this, the Greek manuscript relating to Saint Cosmas and Saint Damian and the small, insignificant-looking Nubian volume of the tenth century [with the miracles of Saint Menas] were left, because, from their appearance, they seemed to have no particular value compared with the larger and better preserved books selected from the find, before I obtained possession of the remainder' (p. 5).
89   Cod. Lond. Add. 37534; fully digitalized: <https://www.bl.uk/manuscripts/FullDisplay.aspx?ref=Add_MS_37534>.
90   *Cosmae et Damiani*, ed. by Rupprecht.

the cult, noting the unpretentious style and the straightforward narration.[91] Rupprecht called it 'the oldest Greek version we know' ('antiquissimum quod novimus exemplum graecum').[92] The question of its precedence, however, cannot be decided only on the simplicity of its style; one must not forget that a lowering of style could also occur in popular hagiographical works.[93] The London Codex *Vita*, at its beginning of the miracles, follows the *Vita Asiatica* and does not speak about the pair of saints as martyrs. In addition to this, the text unmistakeably identifies twice the origin of the saints' cult by their hometown and burial place, Pheremma near Cyrrhus. Besides the fourteen miracles that figure in this collection alone but not in the KDM, the uniqueness of the London Codex lies in its Egyptian colouring and in its Monophysite position.[94]

The hagiographer divided the corpus into forty-seven sections with each miracle story receiving a unique number and a title. There is a huge lacuna in the codex, with miracles 12–20 missing. The hand is easily readable, and there are painted floral decorations in colour. An encomium to Archangel Michael is found at the end of the codex written by another hand.[95] This edition naturally calls for comparison with the later, Deubnerian version of the miracles, which has not only survived in a great number of manuscripts but also differs at various points from the London Codex. For the moment, I will point out two of its special characteristics, one regarding its form, the other its content: firstly, unlike in the Deubner texts, the miracles here do not start with short introductions or epilogues, and they end with short doxologies; secondly, although the Deubner versions are longer, these shorter miracles contain more precise descriptions of the illnesses.

The Cult of Saints Cyrus and John

The Greek Church recognizes seventeen saints as *anargyroi*. Cyrus and John were probably the first of the saints to be called in this way. More often, the name was later applied to Cosmas and Damian and came to generally denote saints of an unselfish, succouring type.[96] Healing without accepting money

---

91 Rustafjaell, *The Light of Egypt*, p. 90: 'The text of the manuscript [...] in all probability refers back to an original of greater antiquity than those of any of the current texts.'
92 *Cosmae et Damiani*, ed. by Rupprecht, p. vii.
93 Claudia Rapp in her 'Byzantine Hagiographers as Antiquarians', p. 36, complemented the picture of the lowering of the style, the simplifying, and the abbreviating given by Ševčenko, 'Levels of Style in Byzantine Prose', p. 301; a thorough outline of past research, including all other textual genres beside hagiography, is given by Patlagean, 'Discours écrit, discours parlé'.
94 I wrote about this in detail: Csepregi, 'The Theological Other'.
95 The codicological description of the text: *Catalogue of Additions to the Manuscripts in the British Museum in the years MDCCCCVI–MDCCCCX*, 1912, p. 73; Halkin, 'Publications récentes', pp. 374–81; including some photographs, Rustafjaell, *The Light of Egypt*, pp. 89–98.
96 The term *anargyroi* only came to be used after the issuing of the Theodosian edict, when

was not a unique characteristic of this pair of saints.[97] It can already be found among the precepts of Hippocrates in regard to the poor and foreigners.[98]

As in the case of the cult place of Thecla, the thaumaturgic site lay at the core of the cult of Saints Cyrus and John in the Egyptian Menouthis, which owed its significance to Isis, the previous healer there. In their case, we possess a precious piece of evidence about the conscious replacement of the ancient healer with a Christian cult, as engineered by Cyril of Alexandria in order to challenge the tenacious fame of the miraculous cures of Isis.[99]

The site, Menouthis (now Abukyr) near Alexandria, was significant in Late Antiquity for two main reasons. Firstly, it fell within the sphere of influence of the pagan intellectuals of Alexandria; secondly, it was significant because the Serapeia of Alexandria and Canopus influenced the development of the characteristics of the place. Incubation was practised at the Serapeion of Canopus, just as it was in the Iseion of Menouthis.[100] With the advent of Christian pilgrimages, the importance of Menouthis was geographic, as it not only lay on the pilgrim route leading to the Holy Land, but it was also close to one of the most renowned healing sanctuaries of Egypt, Saint Menas in Abu Mina.[101] The individual figures of the saints established here seem rather

---

the Asclepius temples were closed around the beginning of the fifth century AD: Miller, *The Birth of the Hospital*, p. 224. n. 26. In Delphoi there stood a Hagios Anargyros shrine; see David-Danel, *Iconographie des Saints Côme et Damien*, p. 17; about the sanctuary: Foucart, *Mémoire sur les ruines et l'histoire de Delphes*, II, p. 6.

97 And this free healing should be more nuanced, as done by Déroche, 'Vraiment anargyres?'.

98 'I urge you not to be too unkind, but to consider carefully your patient's superabundance or means. Sometimes give your services for nothing, calling to mind a previous benefaction or present satisfaction. And if there be an opportunity of serving one who is a stranger in financial straits, give full assistance to all such. For where there is love of man, there is also love of the art.' Hippocrates, *Precepts*, 6 (trans. by Jones).

99 Herzog, 'Der Kampf um der Kult von Menuthis'; Sansterre, 'Apparitions et miracles à Menouthis'; Takács, 'The Magic of Isis Replaced'; Montserrat, 'Pilgrimage to the Shrine of SS Cyrus and John'; and most recently Gascou, 'Les origines du culte des saints Cyr et Jean'.

100 Diodorus Siculus, *Bibliotheke*, I. 25, 2–5: 'As for Isis, the Egyptians say that she was the discoverer of many health-giving drugs and was greatly versed in the science of healing; consequently, now that she has attained immortality, she finds her greatest delight in the healing of mankind and gives aid in their sleep to those who call upon her, plainly manifesting both her very presence and her beneficence towards men who ask her help. In proof of this, as they say, they advance not legends, as the Greeks do, but manifest facts; for practically the entire inhabited world is their witness, in that it eagerly contributes to the honours of Isis because she manifests herself in healings. For standing above the sick in their sleep, she gives them aid for their diseases and works remarkable cures upon such as submit themselves to her; and many who have been despaired of by their physicians because of the difficult nature of their malady are restored to health by her, while numbers who have altogether lost the use of their eyes or of some other part of their body, whenever they turn for help to this goddess, are restored to their previous condition.' Diodorus Siculus, *The Library of History*, trans. by Oldfather.

101 Menouthis (Abukyr) near Canopus, some twenty kilometres from Alexandria to the east. On the name of the place, cf. Deubner, *De incubatione*, p. 90, and Montserrat, 'Pilgrimage to the Shrine of SS Cyrus and John', p. 260.

insignificant. They acquired their entire role (including their name and healing function) as the new, Christian occupants of the cult site. Two deities should be mentioned with regard to the cultic predecessor: Isis, whose incubation cult was adopted by Cyrus and John, and Serapis, who was closely related to Isis and similarly provided miraculous healings through incubation.[102]

The role fulfilled by the shrines of Asclepius created a cohesive force among the pagan Greek intelligentsia in the face of advancing Christianity. Similarly, the cult places of Isis and Serapis were of great importance for the teachers and students at the Alexandrian university, who together formed a sort of Neoplatonic 'order' in the fourth century AD. In AD 391, the patriarch of Alexandria, Theophilus, and his monks, the 'tall brothers',[103] destroyed the Serapeion and publicly defiled its sacred cult objects. Following this desecration, the Serapeion was pulled down. Theophilus had a church built over its site, named after Emperor Arcadius. A similar fate befell the Serapeion in Canopus and the Iseion in Menouthis; the latter was transferred to the monks by Theophilus in order to be transformed into a church of the Evangelists.[104] Nevertheless, the cult of Isis retained its influence, not only among pagans but in the surrounding Christian communities as well, due to her powers of miraculous healing.[105] After 412, Theophilus's successor and nephew, Cyril of Alexandria (AD 412–444), tried to gain control of the situation by establishing a Christian healing cult in the immediate vicinity of the Iseion. This new cult was centred on the relics of those two saints whose resting place Cyril learned in a dream.[106] Who were these saints? Cyril initially sought for the relics of a Saint Cyrus, but when the bones were unearthed,

---

102 The primary sources on the two deities: Vidman, *Syllogae inscriptionum religionis Isiacae et Sarapicae*; their interpretation: Vidman, *Isis und Sarapis*.
103 The monks were used as a sort of private army of Cyril for his wide-ranging interventions in ecclesiastical matters and in the civic life of Alexandrian Jews, intellectuals, pagans; see Dzielska, *Hypatia of Alexandria*; for a more general context, cf. Wipszycka, 'La Christianisation de Égypte'.
104 On the basis of an inscription in the A. Bernand-collection, the church of the Evangelists was a new construction, built in the vicinity of the Iseion which remained intact (Bernand, *Le Delta égyptien d'après les textes grecs*); cf. Sansterre, 'Apparitions et miracles à Menouthis', p. 71, and McKenzie, *Architecture of Alexandria*, p. 247.
105 The different context of the worship of Isis and Serapis is outlined by S. Takács: Isis, as opposed to Serapis, was one of the most ancient Egyptian deities, the wife of Osiris and the mother of Horus. The worship of Serapis had a serious political connotation, relating to the emperor-cult. Hence, the position taken against it by Christian authorities should be interpreted in this context as well. 'As long as she (Isis) did not or could not be thought to interfere with Christianity, as long as she was solely identified with healing, and as long as there was no equally powerful "local" Christian alternative, there was no other entity which served her function and thus her position remained secure.' Takács, 'The Magic of Isis Replaced', p. 503.
106 Cf. the already mentioned work of Maraval, 'Songes et visions comme mode d'invention des reliques', with Sansterre's objection, viz. that this event was not part of the typology of Maraval (Sansterre, 'Apparitions et miracles à Menouthis', p. 80, n. 17).

the remains of two bodies were found; thus, a Saint John was added to Saint Cyrus. This is the first mention of these saints, who were unknown before.[107] That Cyrus was the most important of the pair is reflected in two aspects. His name Cyrus (Kyros = Lord) contrasted with the epithet of Isis: Kyra = Lady. Additionally, it was Saint Cyrus who gave a new name to the town that later became Abukyr, deriving from Abba (father) Cyrus. These connections, along with the supposed identity of the saints (in their lifetimes, one was allegedly a soldier and the other a monk) were articulated by Cyril in the homilies that he wrote for their translation.[108]

Deubner suggested that Cyril himself devised the characteristics of the two saints, based on the model of the saint-pair Cosmas and Damian who were of great renown at that time. Following their popularity, the saints were transformed into 'martyrs' and even 'brothers'; Occasionally, it was attributed to Cyrus that he practised the profession of medicine in his lifetime.

The three Cyrilian homilies were read aloud in Canopus and Menouthis during the translation of the relics. They represent the first written records of the Christian cult of Cyrus and John. From these homilies, we can deduce that Cyril introduced these saints not only to eradicate a pagan cult of Isis,[109] but in order to replace incubation practice as well.[110] However, the mere presence of the saints did not prove sufficient for the establishment of an efficient Christian cult, while Isis continued to attract pilgrims. Some sixty to seventy years after the translation, Isis still exercised immense power over her supplicants, and written sources speak of the scandal of her secret worship (in the account of *Vita Severi* by Zacharias Scholasticus),[111] and there is no firm evidence of a functioning Christian cult of Saints Cyrus and John. Hence, several hypotheses arose. E. Wipszycka rehabilitated the thesis of L. Duchesne, who suggested that it might have been not Cyril, but rather Peter Mongus, the patriarch of Alexandria between AD 482 and 489, who introduced the cult of these saints.[112] However, Peter Mongus was a Monophysite, and thus his name

---

107 On the versions and evaluation of their *Vitae*, see Nissen, 'De SS. Cyri et Johannis Vitae formis'.
108 Sansterre, 'Apparitions et miracles à Menouthis', p. 71, with reference to Cyril's homily: XVIII, III in PG 77, col. 1105A.
109 Takács, 'The Magic of Isis Replaced'.
110 Sansterre, 'Apparitions et miracles à Menouthis', p. 72. Sansterre here also calls attention to an apology by Cyril in which, rejecting the *Contra Galileos* of Julian, Cyril confirmed his aversion towards incubation with a commentary on Isaiah 65. 4, using his interpretation of Isaiah to show that Jews practiced incubation only when they turned to false deities; he rejects the practice in Christianity along with dream interpretations (Jerome, in his commentary on the locus, recalled the *pagan* custom of incubation); cf. Cyril, *Contra Julianum*, PG 76, cols 1024–25, esp. col. 1024CD.
111 Zacharias Scholasticus, *Vita Severi*, 16–18, and 20–22; cf. Herzog, 'Der Kampf um der Kult von Menuthis'; as a result, Petros Mongos demolished the privately owned house where her worship, together with the saved cult objects, had been practised in secret.
112 The question was addressed most recently by Grossmann, 'Zur Gründung des Heilungszentrums'.

could have been replaced with Cyril's name after an orthodox revision.[113] Other scholars generally agree about Cyril being behind the initiative but maintain that the establishment of the two saints' cult had shown no direct results by that time.[114] As the pagan shrine of Menouthis was strongly connected to a circle of prestigious Greeks, the Christian cult site may have been linked to the patriarchal family whose local representatives were Theophilus and Cyril;[115] its eventual decline might have been the wish of Cyril's successor who was his adversary.[116] Recently, Jean-Marie Sansterre proposed that the figures of Cyrus and John were introduced by Cyril and in accordance with his goals, without the incubation rite. In his third homily, Cyril affirmed: 'Come then, all, who have been erring for long, at our place nobody patches up dreams [...]. Despising then the old wives' tales and the dirty jokes of the fortune-tellers, come to the really true physicians.'[117] Sansterre's key phrase was 'οὐδεὶς γὰρ ἡμῖν ὀνείρατα πλάττεται' (nobody patches up dreams), and he quoted it in support of his argument that the ritual of temple sleep with dream consultations was not taken over. In the *Patrologia Graeca* Angelo Mai, however, was of a different opinion; he thought that Cyril intended to juxtapose bad, pagan dreams to pious, Christian dream. To the words 'nobody patches up dreams' he added the following comment:

> Cyril here talks about and reproaches the superstitious and treacherous dreams, which ritual was frequently talked about not only in connection with the cult in Menouthis, but also attached to the Asclepius sanctuary and healing place in Alexandria. On the other hand, there are good dreams, sent by good angels, which is a pious thing to believe, and even more, those dreams sent by the holy martyrs Cyrus and John; and Sophronius told a great number of such dreams in his book written about the miracles of the abovementioned martyrs.[118]

---

113 Duchesne, 'Le sanctuaire d'Aboukir' and refers to a similar event where the name of Cyril replaced that of Bishop Theodore in Mopsuestia.
114 Thus, Delehaye in his 'Les Saints d'Aboukir'; Cozzolino, *Origine del culto ai santi martiri Ciro e Giovanni*, p. 95; and also Montserrat, 'Pilgrimage to the Shrine of SS Cyrus and John'.
115 Various scholars (M. Dzielska, G. G. Stroumsa) have recently emphasized how Cyril coordinated his spheres of influence, acting in parallel on ecclesiastical, political, and social concerns.
116 Montserrat, 'Pilgrimage to the Shrine of SS Cyrus and John', p. 263.
117 The third homily, read on the occasion of the translatio, PG 77, col. 1106.
118 'Superstitiosa ac fallacia somnia intellegit, reprehenditque Cyrilus, cujusmodi non in Menoutheos tantum cultu, verum etiam in Aesculapii Alexandrino fano nosocomioque saepe dictitabantur. Caeteroqui bona somnia, et a bonis angelis, ut credere pium est, atque a sanctis martyribus Cyro et Joanne immissa, in volumine suo de praedictorum martyrum miraculis Sophronius permulta narravit.' Compare it with the distinction Thecla's hagiographer made between the Sarpedonian false dreams and the true ones of Thecla, *Vie et miracles*, ed. and trans. by Dagron, p. 289.

However, the cult failed to attract the previous clientele of Isis in this way. The sacred character of the place was too closely related to incubation.[119] In order not to be defeated, the saints were forced to combat Isis using her own methods; one of Menouthis's names was 'True', after her truthful advice offered in dreams.[120] Hence, incubation and dream miracles were added to the saints' healing repertoire, and by the sixth century, the practice of ritual sleep had received the acknowledgment it merited in the Christian cult.

It is a coincidence that the same Emperor Zeno, whose recovery of his throne resulted in the enlargement of Thecla's cult place, also played a role in the cult of Menouthis. He indirectly provided powerful state help for retaliation against the cult of Isis. The scandal of the uncovering of a conspiracy by Illus and Pantrepius against the emperor in AD 484, was followed by a large-scale persecution of Greeks. Many Alexandrian scholars who remained faithful to the cult of Isis fell victim to it, and after a denunciation, the cult place also fell victim.[121] The closeness of Alexandria and the adherence of teachers, students, and sophists (I also include physicians here) to the ancient religion presented a great challenge to the rival Christian cult. The numerous pagans and learned physicians featuring in the miracle collection who had developed a strong aversion to the saints had not merely a hagiographical or narrative role but also reveal principles of the Greek philosophical and scholarly tradition. Their personages and what they represent serve as the best indicators for what the hagiographer, in contrast to Thecla's hagiographer, intended to include in his Christian *paideia* and what he would exclude from it. In the stories that involve these pagan scholars, and where they are put to shame or defeated in argument, the hagiographer's point was often not to comment on their attitude towards the saints, but rather to stage a showdown with this scholarly worldview.

During his career, Cyril participated at the translation of relics indicated by a dream: in 415, a certain presbyter named Lucian, of the village called Caphargamala (= 'Gamaliel's house', near Jerusalem), had a dream (repeated three times) while he had been sleeping in the baptistery (!). The rabbi Gamaliel appeared to him and described how he had buried Saint Stephen in

---

119 Sansterre, 'Apparitions et miracles à Menouthis', p. 74.
120 Oxyrinchus Papyri XI, 1380. 63; cf. Montserrat, 'Pilgrimage to the Shrine of SS Cyrus and John', p. 258, who drew direct comparisons between two other Isiac inscriptions from Menouthis in Vidman, *Sylloge inscriptionum religionis Isiacae et Sarapicae*, nos 403, 556a.
121 Herzog, 'Der Kampf um der Kult von Menouthis', p. 122; the ancient source for these events is the *Vita Severi* by Zacharias Scholasticus, which he wrote in order to defend Severus (the bishop of Antioch) from accusations of Hellenism (i.e. paganism) (Zacharias Scholasticus, *Vita Severi*; other references by Herzog to other sources pertaining to the cult of Menouthis (besides the homilies of Cyril and the *Thaumata*): Socrates, *Historia Ecclesiastica*, v. 16 and works of Sozomenus, Rufinus, Eunapius, Damascius — Herzog, 'Der Kampf um der Kult von Menouthis', p. 117, nn. 2, 3, 4. Sansterre's no less adventurous account of the events directed the reader to the collection of Bernand, *Le Delta égyptien d'après les textes grecs*.

his house.[122] In 439 (or 438), a basilica was erected at the supposed place of his martyrdom in the vicinity of Jerusalem and was dedicated to Saint Stephen the Protomartyr. It was commissioned by Empress Eudocia and Juvenal, and they asked Cyril of Alexandria to inaugurate it.[123]

The church of Cyrus and John at Menouthis is apparently depicted on a mosaic church floor at Jerash, in the church of Saint John the Baptist, from around AD 531.[124] At the time of the literary redaction of the miracle collection of Cyrus and John (i.e. the beginning of the seventh century AD), the sanctuary flourished as a miraculous healing centre. On the basis of the descriptions in the miracles, a vivid picture can be drawn of the richness of the building-complex and about the social standing of some of its visitors. Deubner diligently collected mentions of the temple personnel in the stories; meanwhile, the hagiographer organized the miracles into separate groups based on the provenance of the beneficiaries and underlined the range of action exercised by the fame of the cult place. In all likelihood, the church complex weathered the hardships of the Persian attacks in 618. Later, it continued to function under Muslim authority. After the ninth century, we have no evidence that the cult still functioned; with the passing of time, the worship of the saints shifted to Rome and Constantinople. In Constantinople, they had a church in the Arcadianae district and another in the Sphorakion, that is, on the plateau to the east of the Nurosmaniye mosque, near the Hagia Sophia.[125] In Rome, they became popular during the period of Byzantine rule in the seventh and eighth centuries. Cyrus was treated as the more prominent saint, and the first chapel dedicated to him coincides with the seventh-century flow of Greek immigrants from Egypt after the Arab conquest of Alexandria (including their hagiographer, Sophronius).[126] In Rome, there were four or five churches dedicated to them (or to Cyrus alone), and in the Santa Maria Antiqua, the church that hosts the Chapel of the Physicians, Saint Cyrus is the most prominent figure, appearing four times on the frescoes.[127]

---

122 The text is in Vanderlinden, 'Revelatio Sancti Stephani'; cf. Maraval, 'Songes et visions comme mode d'invention des reliques', and Berardino, 'Guarigioni nel contesto della traslazione delle reliquie di S. Stefano'.
123 *BHO* 955 and PG 85, col. 469.
124 McKenzie, *Architecture of Alexandria*, p. 247, with a photo.
125 Cf. Janin, *La Géographie Ecclésiastique*, p. 304 and his supplementary map; also Deubner, *De incubatione*, pp. 108–09, and Cozzolino, *Origine del culto ai santi martiri Ciro e Giovanni*, p. 166, with quotation of the pilgrim sources.
126 Cozzolino, *Origine del culto ai santi martiri Ciro e Giovanni*, pp. 189–92: 'Storia del culto per i SS. Ciro e Giovanni nella città di Roma'.
127 Knipp, 'The Chapel of Physicians', p. 19.

The Miracle Collection of Cyrus and John: The *Thaumata*

Seventy miraculous cures by the saints were collected and reworked in a high literary style by Sophronius, himself a beneficiary of a dream cure, between AD 610 and 614. It is possible to date this collection so precisely because, although the collection abounds in references to religious intolerance, there is no mention of the fall of Jerusalem in AD 614.

The hagiographer Sophronius was probably born around the year AD 550, near or in Damascus, and his praise of the city opens the description of his own cure in the seventieth miracle, the last in the corpus. After studying rhetoric, Sophronius became a monk in the monastery of Saint Theodosius near Bethlehem. He later travelled to Egypt where he formed a life-long friendship with John Moschus. Together they travelled through Palestine and Phoenicia, and upon their arrival in Alexandria, they became friends first with the patriarch Eulogius and from AD 607, with his successor, John the Almsgiver. After the fall of Jerusalem in 614 to the Persians, they went to Rome, where Moschus wrote his *Pratum Spirituale* and dedicated it to Sophronius. After the death of John Moschus around 630, Sophronius returned with the remains of his friend to the monastery of Saint Theodosius, where he again became involved in the theological and political debates of his time. After a short stay in Constantinople, in AD 634 he reappeared in Jerusalem where he was elected patriarch and four years later witnessed the entry of Caliph Omar into the city.[128]

In the *Laudes* (written at the head of the collection) and in the last miracle of the corpus describing his own cure, Sophronius recalled that he turned to the saints because he was afflicted with an eye ailment. He dedicated his work as a gift of thanksgiving for his recovery.

The full *Thaumata* only survives in a single copy from the tenth century (*Vaticanus Graecus* 1607) and an *editio princeps* by Angelo Mai, adopted by the *Patrologia Graeca*. For his critical edition, Natalio Fernandez Marcos also took another version into consideration, the *Codex Berolinensis Graecus* 220, which only contains a random selection of fifteen miracles. Fernandez Marcos dated this codex to the tenth to eleventh centuries, adding an important remark that the selection of the Berlin Codex on various occasions filled the lacunae in the Vatican manuscript.[129] After considering further manuscript versions, Jean Gascou recently published a new French translation with a detailed guide in the textual matters regarding the collection.[130] Fernandez Marcos

---

128 Cf. Fernandez Marcos, *Los Thaumata*, pp. 1–11; for more details on Sophronius, see Vailhé, 'Sophrone le sophiste et Sophrone le patriarche', and Schönborn, 'Sophrone de Jérusalem (Saint)'.
129 The two codices are described in Fernandez Marcos, *Los Thaumata*, pp. 231–37.
130 *Sophrone de Jerusalem: Miracles des Saints Cyr et Jean*, ed. and trans. by Gascou.

explained the notable absence of variants and copies by arguing that these miracle narratives were so closely connected to the cult place of Menouthis that they never reached a wider Christian reading public.[131]

I agree with Fernandez Marcos's argument, yet there is another reason for the limited distribution of these miracles. These miraculous stories emphatically propagated Sophronius's theological position in the context of Christological and heretical debates. When these tensions moved into the background, this propaganda (especially outside of the Egyptian context) hardly generated any wider interest. What marks out the corpus of Cyrus and John as unique from the other incubation miracle collections treated here is that heretics are emphatically present as agents in the narrative, mirroring earlier and contemporary Christological debates in a striking fashion. Again, the presence of heretics in the collection can be attributed to the characteristics of the cult place, namely its location in Egypt. After the Synod of Chalcedon (AD 451), a greater part of Egypt remained faithful to the Monophysite credo, and it is possible that the church in Menouthis was Monophysite for a while. However, the redactor of the saints' miracles, Sophronius, was a Chalcedonian, and either out of personal conviction or in order to exonerate the saints from the accusation of Monophysitism, Chalcedonian theology was introduced into the account of their activities.

We do not know whether Sophronius took the *Thaumata* with him to Rome. It is quite likely that he made some propaganda for the miraculous healing of the saints. The first partial Latin translation of the miracles was made by Boniface, *consiliarius* to Popes Benedict II (684–685) and Sergius I (687–701). Boniface translated the *Laudes* and the first twelve miracles. His efforts were supplemented by Anastasius Bibliothecarius during the papacy of John VIII (872–882).[132]

The Cult of Saint Artemius

While the *Thaumata* is a perfect example of the hagiographer's dogmatical opinions, Saint Artemius provides the most illustrative example of the way a cult could become orthodox. By the seventh century, Artemius had become one of the most renowned incubation healer-saints in Constantinople.

What is known of Artemius from the historical sources?[133] In AD 356, Emperor Constantine commissioned him to bring the relics of the apostle Timothy to Constantinople, and a year later, those of Andrew and Luke. From AD 360, Artemius was a *doux* of Egypt. In this capacity and as a zealous Christian, he took part in the profanation of the Serapeion of Alexandria and

---

131 Fernandez Marcos, *Los Thaumata*, p. 227.
132 PL 129, col. 706.
133 Cf. Dummer, 'Fl. Artemius dux Aegypt' (I owe this reference to Vincent Déroche).

the destruction of its cult objects and votive offerings. Hearing the numerous denunciations of his behaviour, Julian sentenced him to death,[134] but nothing indicates that he died as a martyr. A note by Ammianus Marcellinus from the fourth century AD refers to accusations of criminal activities against him.[135] The *Church History* of Theodoret from the mid-fifth century (*c.* AD 444–450) mentions his destruction of pagan sculptures, while only vaguely outlining the (Arian) story of the martyrdom, which was to be elaborated in the fifth century.[136] For a long time, it was only supposed that Artemius was an Arian, mostly based on a remark in Photius's *Bibliotheke*, and on Philostrogius's lost Chronicle, which mentioned Artemius with profuse praise. A more serious piece of evidence comes from the *Life of Saint Pachomios*, which demonstrates with certainty that Artemius was an Arian and explains how he came into contact with incubation during his lifetime and how he could become an incubation healer after his death:

> And it happened after this, as the holy bishop Athanasius was being sought by the Emperor Constantius at the instigation of the enemies of Christ, the Arians, that a certain general by the name of Artemius received authority and was searching everywhere for him. And as a rumour spread, 'Is he not hiding among the monks of Tabannesi, for he loves them?' the duke [!] sailed up for this purpose. As he was sailing up, it happened by chance that Theodore himself was sailing down to visit the monasteries of the brothers near Hermapolis. As he drew near the upper monastery called Kaior, he saw the duke sailing up; the Lord made him understand what was going to happen and he revealed it to the brothers. The brothers wanted to turn back and arrive before him lest he should trouble the brothers at Phbow, but Abba Theodore told them, 'He for whose sake we have come so long a way to visit

---

134   According to the (now lost) ecclesiastical history of the Arian Philostrogius, Julian's charge was far more serious, namely that Artemios, by the order of Emperor Constantine, actively participated in the execution of Gallus. Cf. Grosdidier de Matons, 'Les *Miracula Sancti Artemii*', p. 263; on the various versions of his *Passio* (also translated into Armenian, Georgian, and Old Church Slavonic), see Lieu, 'From Villain to Saint and Martyr', who argued that the *Passio* was written in Constantinople by John the Monk, whose identification with John of Damascus by John of Rhodes still lacks secure foundation.

135   Ammianus Marcellinus, *Res Gestae*, XXII, 11: 'Artemius ex duce Aegypti Alexandrinis urgentibus atrocium criminum mole supplicio capitali multatus est', 'Introduction', in *The Miracles of St Artemius*, ed. and trans. by Crisafulli and Nesbitt, p. 1.

136   On the variants of the Artemius-martyria, esp. on the role of Apollo and Asclepius, see 'Introduction', in *The Miracles of St Artemius*, ed. and trans. by Crisafulli and Nesbitt, pp. 2–6; on p. 28, n. 3: 'Theodoret states that Artemius "smashed most of the idols" and for this reason Julian "not only stripped him of his property" but had him beheaded.' This statement is similar to the description of Artemius's fate as it is found in the year AD 363 in the *Chronicon Paschale*: 'And Artemius, who was the *dux* of the diocese Egypt, since in the period of his office under Constantius the Augustus of blessed memory he had displayed great zeal on the behalf of the churches, had his property confiscated and his head cut off in the city of Alexandria, since Julian had a grudge against him.'

His servants is able to take care of this affair without there being any grief.' Having said this, he went on to the monasteries. 138. When Artemius came to the monastery he ordered the army to keep watch around the monastery by night, armed as during war. He himself sat with his lieutenants within the monastery, outside the synaxis, having archers standing by him on both sides. Seeing this the brothers were afraid. But a holy man called Pecoš, whom we have mentioned above, exhorted the brothers to keep courage in the Lord. The duke asked through an interpreter, 'Where is your father?' Abba Pecoš answered, 'He has gone to the monasteries.' And he said, 'The one who comes after him, where is he?' They showed him Abba Psahref, the Great Steward. And [Artemius] told him privately, 'I have an imperial order against Athanasius the bishop, and he is said to be with you.' Abba Psahref replied, 'He is indeed our father, but I have never yet seen his face. Still, here is the monastery.' After he had searched and not found him, he said to those in the synaxis, 'Come, pray for me.' They said, 'We cannot, because we have a commandment from our father not to pray with anyone who follows the Arians' — for they saw with the duke one of the Arians who was acting as bishop — and they left. So he prayed alone. And as he fell asleep in the synaxis by day, he woke up with a bleeding nose and was troubled — we do not know for sure what happened to him — and full of fear, he said, 'When that happened to me in the vision, I hardly escaped death with God's mercy.' Thus he withdrew. When Abba Theodore returned and heard these things, he gave praise to God.[137]

Vielleux, the editor of the *Life of Pachomios* added:

> Egypt was ruled by a governor (*hegemon*), that is a civilian authority, and by a military general, called duke, *dux*, who resided in Alexandria. We know from the Index to the Festal Letters that Artemius searched for the fugitive Athanasius in 360. The Greek *Vita* adds that it happened during the persecution of the Emperor Constantius (353–61) against Athanasius. Artemius was sentenced to death by Emperor Julian in 362, probably as a criminal and not because he was Christian. Nevertheless, and despite his Arian past, later he was venerated as a martyr. This may explain why he does not appear as a persecutor in the present story told in the *Life of Pachomius*.[138]

It seems that the cult of Artemius first gained ground among the Arians in Antioch, and probably thanks to his successful miraculous healings, his fame spread far and wide. By the fifth century, he was ascribed the honours

---

137 The First *Vita Graeca*, 137–38: *Pachomian Koinonia*, trans. by Vielleux, I, pp. 395–97. I owe this reference to David Movrin.
138 *Pachomian Koinonia*, trans. by Vielleux, I, pp. 291–92, n. 185.2.; without mentioning the vision, the story was also told in the *Bochairic Life of Pachomius* 185a in *Pachomian Koinonia*, trans. by Vielleux, I, p. 182.

due to doctor-saints and his relics were translated to Constantinople. Supposedly, a deaconess named Ariane sent the relics to the capital, perhaps with the intention of erecting a church in their honour. The relics ended up in the church of Saint John the Baptist, which was in all likelihood built by Emperor Anastasius I (AD 491–518); hence, the *translatio* would have taken place in the last years of the fifth century at the earliest.[139] In this version of his story, it seems his Arian past had become forgotten to such an extent that, in the seventh century, in the collection of his miraculous cures Arians were fiercely attacked along with other heretics and non-Christians.

The relics of Artemius were placed in the church of Saint John the Baptist, in the quarter of the capital called Oxeia. We do not exactly know why there, but this place was to become the scene of the incubation miracles that were collected and organized into a miracle-corpus during the seventh century. In the field of ritual healing, Artemius specialized in curing male hernias,[140] while the female patients were treated by his less prominent colleague, Saint Febronia.[141] Specialization was not unheard of among either the ancient Greeks or Christian cultic healers. For example, Cosmas and Damian were known at the beginning of their careers as experts in curing barren women. Saint Euphrosyne specialized in cures against infertility, Saint Anastasia dealt with mental patients, while Saint Modestus healed animals. Cosmas and Damian directed the woman seeking a cure for her oxen to Modestus: 'O woman, we are not allowed by God to work cures for animals, for this grace has been granted to Modestos, the great high priest from Jerusalem, if you will go to him he will cure your oxen'.[142] The Byzantine miracle collections attest that even if there was no absolute specialization, as in the case of Artemius, certain sanctuaries, saints, and cult places were more concerned in some illnesses than others.

---

139 Cf. Rydén, 'Kyrkan som sjukhus', p. 3.
140 A contemporary of the collector of the miracles, Paul of Aigina, a famous Alexandrian physician, professor, and surgeon, in the sixth book, chapters 61–66, of his medical encyclopaedia gave full details of the various forms of hernias and a hernia operation; cf. Rydén, 'Kyrkan som sjukhus', p. 5.
141 Saint Febronia was from Nisibis and suffered martyrdom during the reign of Diocletian. On her *Passio*, see Simon, 'Note sur l'original de la Passion de Sainte Fébronie' and Halkin, 'La Passion grecque des Saintes Libyè, Eutropie et Léonis', p. 295; the English translation of her *Vita* with commentary appears in *Holy Women of the Syrian Orient*, ed. by Brock and Ashbrook Harvey; more on her *Vita* in Chiesa, *Le versioni latine della Passio Sanctae Febroniae*, pp. 368–95.
142 For Saint Euphrosyne, see *AASS* November 3, 861–77; for Saint Anastasia, cf. Kaplan, 'Le miracle est-il nécessaire au saint byzantin?', p. 174; for Modestus the quote is from the *Passio et Miracula Modesti* in Magoulias, 'The Lives of the Saints as Sources of Data for the History of Magic', p. 252.

THE CHRISTIAN INCUBATION SAINTS   91

The church of Saint John the Baptist in the Oxeia lay close to what is today the Grand Bazaar of Istanbul.¹⁴³ In Nesbitt's description: 'The name of the quarter derives from the hill's steep declivity toward the Golden Horn […]. The church was situated opposite the Bath of Dagistheos, a complex that began to arise during the reign of Anastasius, but was not opened until 528. […] The Bath was not very far from St John's and very likely situated along the Mese, the broad avenue leading to the Hippodrome, to the east of Constantine's Forum.'¹⁴⁴ The collection itself supplies evidence that there was a hospital or hospice near the church that had physicians and assistants who were offering hospital care and which must have been of some importance.¹⁴⁵

Nesbitt, based on some indications in the miracles, suggested that the church, having seen better days, had become dilapidated and ill funded by the second half of the seventh century when the collection was written. In the period after the miracle collection was put together, Lennart Rydén has observed a conspicuous lack of continuation of the Artemius cult. He sought an answer for the apparent disappearance of incubation practice in that, 'Artemius did not belong to the great and well-known saints, that his cult lacked social standing, that his healing activity was valid almost exclusively for a single illness, about which one was unwilling to speak.'¹⁴⁶ The last known mention of the church comes from the end of the eleventh century, but the healing cult of the saint underwent a change sometime earlier. Cyril Mango writes: 'It may be worth pointing out that there is no mention of the martyrion of St Artemius as a centre of healing after the period of the Iconoclasm and that in Byzantine iconography the Saint is normally portrayed as a warrior having, for some obscure reason, the features of Christ, not as a physician.'¹⁴⁷ Artemius, however, was always depicted as a warrior, as he was an imperial officer (there existed an interesting interplay between the representations of healer/helper types and warriors).¹⁴⁸ Warrior attributes can also be observed

---

143   On the church, see Maas, 'Artemioskult in Konstantinopel'; Janin, *La Géographie Ecclésiastique*, p. 58, pp. 433–34; Mango, 'On the History of the *Templon*'; Sodini, 'Les cryptes d'autel paléochrétiennes'; 'Introduction', in *The Miracles of St Artemius*, ed. and trans. by Crisafulli and Nesbitt, pp. 8–19; the architectural plan of the church: Mango, 'On the History of the *Templon*', p. 42; *The Miracles of St Artemius*, ed. and trans. by Crisafulli and Nesbitt, p. 319.
144   'Introduction', in *The Miracles of St Artemius*, ed. and trans. by Crisafulli and Nesbitt, p. 8.
145   The Cristodotes hospital.
146   Rydén, 'Kyrkan som sjukhus'; Rydén's further arguments concerning the possible causes included economic instability and the fact that Artemius was primarily the patron of merchants and artisans in the capital, not of aristocrats. His other speculation sounds less convincing, namely that with time the Byzantines came to feel shame in matters concerning hernias. Cf. Rydén, 'Kyrkan som sjukhus', pp. 13–14.
147   Mango, 'On the History of the *Templon*', p. 41. The reproduction and interpretation of a tenth-century image of Artemius appears in Lehmann, 'Ein Reliefbild des Heiligen Artemios'; Artemius is depicted in a group of saints, together with Saints Cosmas and Damian, Saint George, and Saint John the Baptist among others, in Bees, 'Weiteres zum Kult des heiligen Artemios'.
148   Cf. Belting-Ihm, 'Mediomagische Praktiken und die Reaktion der Kirche', pp. 199–226, in

in the dream apparitions recorded in the miracles. It was in the likeness of a Byzantine official that Artemius found his way to Rome: in the Santa Maria Antiqua, at the Chapel of Theodotus, there is a votive icon from around the mid-eighth century with a male and female saint-pair and an inscription with the name 'Scs Armentise', probably referring to Artemius.[149]

What is known about the incubation practised in Constantinople in the church of the Forerunner? Artemius did not inherit an incubation cult site. Nothing was known about the Antiochian beginnings of his miraculous healings, nor even what the medium of healing was. At the time his cult came to Constantinople, temple sleep was a widely popular practice at the cult places of the capital.[150] The worshippers of Artemius were allowed to sleep in the left nave, which was locked off during the night with bars. Rydén plausibly argued that the right nave was designed for the use of women, in what might have been the Chapel of Saint Febronia.[151] Peter Grossmann has confirmed that such parallel distributions (not just that in the left nave and right nave washing rooms and latrines on both sides were for men and women, respectively) were common in churches where incubation was practised.[152]

One of the characteristics of Saint Artemius's cult practice was to light an oil lamp in honour of the saint in the church, perhaps next to the relics (but also in the patient's home as well). Such lamps were also offered as a votive gift after a successful incubation, but more importantly, they often played a role in the miraculous cures. Incubation was practised, surely but not exclusively, on the night between Saturday and Sunday, following the Saturday evening vigil. The Saturday night vigil was one of the most important 'institutions' at the cult place. There was an organized lay sodality around it, and Saturday night was also the time that the thaumaturgic wax (holy lamp oil) was distributed. In all likelihood, this was the occasion when miracle stories were told and listened to.

---

which she traces back the knightly figure on horseback to the Heros Equitans Epiphanens, around 400 BC, who returns from the dead in desperate situations. Gods succouring sick people often come on horseback, almost always with a weapon in their hand. Hundreds of such figures were found in Greece but also in Egypt, Syria, and Palestine, dating to the second to third centuries AD. King Solomon was also represented as a horseman who defeats the sickness-causing demon, often a female figure. The horseman continues its popularity in a Christianized form, e.g. the Saint George type figures on sixth-century amulet finger-rings.

149 David, 'L'église Sainte-Marie-Antique', p. 486, and Knipp, 'The Chapel of Physicians', p. 20.
150 Grosdidier de Matons was also of the opinion that the incubation cult of Artemius was based on the model of the practice in the Cosmidion.
151 Cf. Rydén, 'Kyrkan som sjukhus', pp. 7–8; also Lieu, 'From Villain to Saint and Martyr', p. 56.
152 Grossmann, 'Late Antique Christian Incubation Centres in Egypt', p. 127.

The Miracle Collection of Artemius

The corpus of Artemius is relatively easy to date and interpret within the context of the saint's healing cult.[153] The text as we have it now was written around AD 658–668 (probably with a larger insertion around AD 692), in Constantinople. The Greek text was edited by Papadopoulos-Kerameus; several scholars have formulated theories about possible divisions of the miracles and the phases of redaction, recently analysed by Vincent Déroche.[154]

The scene of the forty-five miracles of Artemius was his cult place in the capital, the church of the Forerunner. In Artemius's case, there was no rival cultic predecessor; we hear only in passing about competition between the saintly healers of the city. The focus of the text moves between strictly set chronological boundaries. The hagiographer was probably officially associated with the saint and the cult place. He might have been a member of the saint's lay confraternity, formed around the all-night vigil, and even one of the protagonists of the miracles.[155] He describes the physical characteristics of illnesses and their cures using professional terminology, showing himself to be familiar with the medical practices of Constantinople. The fervent invectives against doctors, as well as non-orthodox Christians, heretics, and Jews, are a distinguishing feature of the collection. These short outbursts are probably later insertions, as their form and content differ from the content of the miracles. While the anti-heretical invectives could be derived from the hagiographer's authentic opinion (later interpolations or not), their attack on the medical profession should be interpreted more carefully. John Haldon likely attributed slightly too much weight to these anti-medical invectives, whereas we can see them partly as narrative features, partly as a naturally emerging polemic in the case of a healer saint (a rival to doctors) and whose miraculous cures were a counterpart of contemporary medical science (in a separate chapter, I closely examine the role of doctors, both narrative and real, in the realm of the miracles together with the opinion of the Church on medicine). Denigrating heretics and attacking physicians were well-known features of hagiographical propaganda, to some extent present in all of these collections.

---

153   First published by Papadopoulos-Kerameus, *Varia graeca sacra*; the second edition is *The Miracles of St Artemius*, ed. and trans. by Crisafulli and Nesbitt; the third edition and French translation is under preparation by Vincent Déroche, who has kindly sent me his manuscript. For a thorough analysis of the text as a whole, see *Les Miracles d'Artémios*, ed. by Déroche.
154   Delehaye, 'Les recueils antiques', p. 33; Haldon, 'Supplementary Essay', pp. 33–35; *Les Miracles d'Artémios*, ed. by Déroche, 'La rédaction: Ses dates, ses procédés et ses sources,' p. 204.
155   A hypothesis by Efthymiadis, 'A Day and Ten Months in the Life of a Lonely Bachelor', p. 3, and earlier by Rydén, 'Kyrkan som sjukhus', p. 15, n. 5. I shall address his person in detail in the chapter on the incubation hagiographers.

Another characteristic of Artemius's collection is that the hagiographer knew the city intimately and depicted a vivid picture of everyday existence and customs in Constantinople. He certainly did not limit himself to matters concerning the church or those pertaining to the religious sphere. He acquaints the reader with the labyrinth of the streets and merchants of Constantinople, the network of circumstances surrounding the patients' family life, their economic situation, and the particulars of their professions. Attention was also given to the traditions characteristic of the church, in addition to its interior. The patients of Artemius were typically from Constantinople (often craftsmen and traders) who were sometimes already connected to the church in some manner (for example, as a member of the all-night vigil fraternity); patients coming from afar were usually merchants, sailors, or ship-owners.

Incubation Practice Attached to Other Saints

The practice of sleeping in the church to obtain a cure or experience a vision could easily be attached to different types of saints, just as it was a common ritual in classical and late antique Greek religion. A glimpse at other figures who in some way were connected to incubation will lead us to rethink the notion of 'incubation saints'. Insisting on such a group as a separate saint-type or looking for the definition of such a category can lead to faulty conclusions. Incubation was closely connected to the saints that I introduced previously; as their miracle collections attest, in a certain period, incubation was often their emblematic activity, even if they were occasionally associated with other actions. Peter Grossmann showed how incubation could be a secondary function of an ordinary church: just as a side nave could be suitable for the ritual, a saint's cult could also have such side activities that varied with time and place. What is fascinating is the existence of the ritual itself, with all its variations, and the fact that these 'incubation-saints' warn us that the 'holy man' type of saint or the martyr-saint were by no means the only saint types. To illustrate how differently temple sleep could be linked to figures so different to each other, I will give an overview of saints in whose cults incubation played a minor role — or for whom we simply do not have enough sources.

Saint Therapon

The only document that has come down to us concerning Saint Therapon, whose very name means 'Healer', is a collection of fifteen miracles, compiled around AD 695–710, often attributed to Andrew of Crete.[156] Although little can be learned about the saint himself from this text, in all likelihood Therapon

---

156 The edition of the Greek text: *Laudatio Therapontis*, in Deubner, *De incubatione*, pp. 113–34; its analysis: Haldon, 'Tortured by my Conscience'; Haldon discusses here the questions of attribution and dating as well.

was a bishop in Cyprus in the third century AD who suffered martyrdom. What is certain is that the patients of Therapon practised incubation, and holy wax and lamp oil often figured among his prescriptions.¹⁵⁷ The location of his incubation cult is more uncertain: his remains were rescued from the barbarians attacking Cyprus in the 650s and were brought to one of the churches of the Holy Virgin in Constantinople. I believe that this church was the famous church of Mary in the Blachernai, as Deubner has already suggested.¹⁵⁸ The first miracle tells the story of a demon-possessed man who wanted to hurl himself down from the wall of the Blachernai. In a vision, he is sent to the church of Mary, called Elaia. The Elaia quarter was at the other side of the Golden Horn bay, in today's Galata, where Janin and Haldon located Therapon's cult.¹⁵⁹

In addition to the unlikely suggestion made to the demon-possessed man to cross the city for the saint's help, I think that there are two circumstances that confirm the hypothesis that Therapon carried out his incubation ritual in the church of Mary in the Blachernai quarter, similar to the manner that Saint Artemius settled with his relics and incubation practice within the church of the Forerunner. The first is that both Cosmas and Damian's church and Thecla's church were located close to the church of Mary in the Blachernai quarter, where incubation, it seems, was in vogue in the sixth to seventh centuries. The second confirmation is that we know that incubation was practised in the church of Mary in the Blachernai: it is attested in the *Vita* of Irene of Chrysobalantion.¹⁶⁰

Therapon, like Artemius, was likely to have been Egyptian in origin, or was closely connected to Egypt in some way because there was an Egyptian martyr who specialized in curing rabies that went by the name of Tarabô.¹⁶¹

The text of his miracles was first published by Angelo Mai in the *Acta Sanctorum*, based on an eleventh-century manuscript. Deubner discovered a later, twelfth-century manuscript and attached his critical edition as an appendix to his *Incubatio* book and wrote an introduction to it.¹⁶² The text mentions the city being attacked by barbarians, which Deubner related to the attack on Constantinople in 626 by the Slavs and Avars, while Delehaye was more sceptical about this reference. John Haldon dates the collection to the end of the seventh / beginning of the eighth century, where the reference

---

157 Delehaye, 'Les recueils antiques', pp. 38–39.
158 Deubner, *De incubatione*, p. 125 and pp. 106–07; Lopez Salva, 'El sueño incubatorio', pp. 154–55.
159 Janin, *La Géographie Ecclésiastique*, p. 183; according to John Haldon, Therapon's incubation cult was located in the Zotikos foundation in the Pera region across the Golden Horn: Haldon, 'Supplementary Essay', p. 34. On the church building itself: Janin, *La Géographie Ecclésiastique*, pp. 255–56.
160 *Life of Irene, Abbess of Chrysobalantion*, ed. and trans. by Rosenqvist, pp. 57–59. Cf. Kaplan, 'Le miracle est-il nécessaire au saint byzantin?', p. 174.
161 Auzépy, 'La carrière d'André de Créte'.
162 Deubner, *De incubatione*, pp. 113–19.

could be to the city's siege in 717–718. The *Laudatio Therapontis* describes the miracles as taking place in Constantinople, and the laudatory passages and the fact that its hagiographer often addresses the audience suggest that it was meant to be read to the congregation of the church, and it was certainly read in Constantinople in the early ninth century.[163]

Isaiah the Prophet

In Constantinople, in the church of Saint Lawrence, the prophet Isaiah also acted as a minor incubation healer. His relics from Jerusalem were transferred to this church at an uncertain date. According to some Byzantine chronicles, perhaps his relics were transferred around the years 433–434 or in the mid-sixth century. The only confusing detail is that there were at least two churches of Saint Lawrence in Constantinople: one in the Blachernai, the other constructed by Pulcheria in the Plateia quarter. The Greek collection of Isaiah's miracles was published by Delehaye.[164] This miracle collection clearly indicates that the Saint Lawrence church in the Blachernai quarter was the location of the miracles.[165] On the other hand, the church of Saint Isaiah stood next to the church of Saint Lawrence in the Plateia quarter. Janin suggested that, by the time of the arrival of the relics, the church in which Emperor Marcian and Empress Pulcheria had decided to house them was not yet ready; this is why the relics became deposited temporarily in the church of Saint Lawrence nearby. Although we are unable to decide which of the two Saint Lawrence churches was the home of Isaiah, I would like to add a further reference: one of the protagonists in Cosmas and Damian's miracles was affiliated with the church of Saint Lawrence but nevertheless went to the Cosmidion (which was situated in the Blachernai). Whichever of the churches housed the relics, we have no mention of the church's functioning after the twelfth century. This is also the time from which the surviving manuscript of Isaiah's miracles dates, although it clearly records earlier phases of the incubation cult. The text, written in literary Attic Greek, cannot be older than the seventh century because it mentions the *protospatarios* (3.7), an office that was created in the seventh century. In this manuscript, the hagiographer affirmed that he was recording contemporary miracles to which he was an eyewitness. The nineteen miracle-narratives are quite Epidaurian in their character and conform to the narrative pattern of incubation miracles. Each of them has the name of the patient, and some give their profession too. Three miracles state the cause of the illness as well. The miracle collection has a prologue and an epilogue.

---

163 For which, see Auzépy, 'La carrière d'André de Créte', p. 10, n. 66.
164 Delehaye, 'Synaxarium et miracula S. Isaiae prophetae'; cf. also Delehaye, 'Les recueils antiques', pp. 39–40.
165 Delehaye, 'Synaxarium et miracula S. Isaiae prophetae', p. 257; references to the church are in Janin, *La Géographie Ecclésiastique*, p. 146 and pp. 312–13.

Saint Michael the Archangel

In Near Eastern Christianity, Saint Michael was regarded as a miraculous healer, closely associated with cult places around water sources.[166] We can discover traces of incubation in the Byzantine cult of Archangel Michael that was similar to his early worship in South Italy, where an earlier incubation cult was functioning in the neighbourhood. On Monte Gargano in Apulia, we know about the cult of Podaleiros, Asclepius's son, where we can even find the memory of sleeping on the skin of the sacrificed ram.[167] The most famous part of the cult site, the cave where Michael is believed to have appeared in the fifth century, is the same site where the incubation cult of Calchas the seer flourished earlier.[168] Michael was also honoured as a healer in Egypt and in the Phrygian towns of Colosse and Hierapolis, where Asclepius and Hygeia had previously been worshipped.[169] Remarkably, in the Arabic version of Cosmas and Damian's Syriac legend, Saint Michael saved Cosmas and Damian together with their three brothers.[170] As I noted earlier, at the end of the miracles of Cosmas and Damian in the London Codex, there is a hymn to the archangel Michael, written by another hand.

Michael had a church in Anaplous, on the left side of the Euxine, which was allegedly built by Constantine and restored by Justinian in the sixth century. We find a description of its colourful marbles, golden decorations, and rotunda in Procopius (*De Aed.*, I. 8. 2–19). Sozomenus refers to the church in Anaplous as being in the Hestiae. There was another church dedicated to Saint Michael, also restored by Justinian; this was the famous Saint Michael in the Sosthenion quarter.[171] Malalas attributed this as well to Constantine, telling the story of how the emperor, passing by the Sosthenion quarter, saw an angel dressed as a monk inside a pagan temple that was allegedly founded by the Argonauts. At night, the angel returns to the emperor in a dream and reveals himself to be the archangel Michael.[172] The legend was a popular one with later writers. Janin gave a very plausible suggestion for its popularity: it was a rival church to the Michaelion in Anaplous that claimed a (more credible) Constantinian foundation. Thus, its location on a pagan site and its appearance in the emperor's dream was a boon for this church. Janin adds

---

166 Saxer, 'Jalons pour servir à l'histoire du culte de l'archange Saint Michel'; for the most recent overview, see Arnold, *The Footprints of Michael the Archangel*.
167 Rohde, *Psiche*, p. 133.
168 For the most spectacular example in Western Christianity for the establishment of the cult of Saint Michael, see Otranto and Carletti, *Il Santuario di S. Michele Arcangelo sul Gargano*.
169 Deubner, *De incubatione*, p. 65.
170 The Arabic legend was published by Sulaimân, *Tufhat az-zamān fī sīrat-al-farīsain Quzmān wa Damyān*; summary in Crum, 'Place-Names in Deubner's Kosmas und Damian', and van Esbroeck, 'La diffusion orientale de la légende des saints Cosme et Damien', pp. 65–66.
171 Maury, 'Du temple appelé Sosthenium'.
172 Malalas, *Chronicle*, IV. 13 and XVI. 16.

that the earliest references to the Sosthenion from the first years of the sixth century speak about it as a church that is already famous.[173]

There are several pieces of evidence that an incubation cult of Michael existed in the Sosthenium (= 'being saved'). The ecclesiastical histories of Sozomenus from around AD 440 and those of Nicephoros preserve some of Archangel Michael's incubation miracles.[174] The name Sosthenium refers to the *soter* aspect of the occupant of the cult place, and L. Deubner has already suggested that Michael had not been the first incubation healer in the church, and in the hooded figure he saw Thelesphoros, Asclepius's helper.[175] Besides these references in Greek, some ten healing miracles of Michael came down to us in Coptic, translated by E. Amelineau.[176] Miracles 6–10 record miraculous healing through incubation with the patients sleeping in Michael's church.

Regarding S. Michael in Athens on the place of the former Asclepieion, there are scholars who discern a transition of the cult into an incubation cult.[177]

Saint Dometius

The hagiographical dossier of Saint Dometius is extremely complex. Dometius was a fourth-century minor incubation healer who became connected with the city of Cyrrhus and with Cosmas and Damian. His legend is complex mainly because of the variety of heresies associated with his cult.[178] Paul Peeters distinguished two Dometiuses: the healer of Mount Cyrrhus was Saint Dometius the Physician, while there was another Saint Dometius, called the Martyr or the Persian.[179] Yet their two legends complement each other; in Peeters's view, the hagiographer of the less well-known Dometius the Physician consciously referred to the town of Cyrrhus in order to have the reader recall the figures and the efficacy of the famous *anargyroi*, Cosmas and Damian. The hagiographer of Dometius the Persian, on the other hand, dated the activity of his Dometius earlier, urged on by the (by that time,

---

173 Janin, *La Géographie Ecclésiastique*, p. 359; and also Janin, 'Les sanctuaires byzantins de saint Michel'.
174 Sozomenus, *Historia Ecclesiastica*, II. 3. 10–12 (PG 67, cols 940ff), Nicephoros Callistus, *Historia Ecclesiastica*, VII. 50 (PG 145, cols 1329ff); cf. Deubner, *De incubatione*, p. 65, and Sansterre, 'Apparitions et miracles à Menouthis', p. 72.
175 Deubner, *De incubatione*, p. 66, Thelesphoros, 'who brings the end', was the hooded companion of Asclepius. (About representations of Thelesphoros and on his relationship with Asclepius, see Kerényi, *Asklepios*, pp. 88–90, and also Kerényi, 'Telesphoros'.) Deubner's other suggestions for possible healer-predecessors include the Argonauts, Apollon Iasonius, Serapis, or a local healer called Sosthenes.
176 Amelineau, *Contes e romans de l'Égypte chrétienne*, s.v. Michael.
177 See Deubner, *De incubatione*, pp. 65–67; Hamilton, *Incubation*, pp. 139–43. For the history of the Asclepieion Acropolis at Athens: Frantz, 'From Paganism to Christianity'; Gregory, 'The Survival of Paganism in Christian Greece', and Gregory, 'The Christian Asclepieion at Athens'.
178 Parmentier, 'Incubatie in de antike hagiografie'.
179 Peeters, 'S. Dometios le martyr et S. Dometios le médecin'.

significant) popularity of Dometius the Physician, as well as by a sense of rivalry. How did he become associated with incubation? According to his Syriac *Vita*, the saint was once miraculously cured near a hill called Cyrrhus, and from that time onwards, he also practised this thaumaturgic gift. Based on the testimony of the Greek *Vita*, Dometius once went to the martyrion of Saints Cosmas and Damian in the town of Cyrrhus, where he encountered a patient who had practised incubation for a long time to no avail. Dometius suggested to him that, instead of incubation, he should take the Eucharist. When he did, a cure was finally achieved for him.

Parmentier explained the dichotomy between the two Cyrrhuses by saying that Dometius may have had a Nestorian healing cult on Cyrrhus hill, in juxtaposition to the Monophysite healing cult of Cosmas and Damian in the city of Cyrrhus. We learn from an AD 514 sermon of Severus of Antioch that, in his time, there was a Monophysite church of Saint Dometius in Antioch where incubation was practised. Severus wrote that Dometius was from Cyrrhus and contrasted him to the 'Nestorian' Theodoret, bishop of Cyrrhus (AD 423–457). Out of this hagiographical chaos, the most likely conclusion might be that a Nestorian incubation cult was first formed around Dometius in order to counterbalance the nearby Monophysite dream-healing cult of Cosmas and Damian. With the passing of time, the figure of Dometius was 'reprogrammed' by the Monophysites. Thus, he became a converted former Nestorian that they could use in their fights with Theodoret. Incubation played an important role in both cases, either the negative approach of the Greek *Vita* or the positive one of the Syriac *Vita*. His fame and his incubation cult reached the West: Gregory of Tours tells a miracle story about a Jew who went to the Basilica of Saint Dometius in Syria to undergo incubation but considered himself unworthy of sleeping inside the church.[180]

Saint Demetrius

Saint Demetrius should also be mentioned along with other incubation healers; the early martyr lists connected him to Sirmium. Yet, from the sixth century, his figure became entwined in the texts with the town of Thessalonica.[181] This connection with Thessalonica was to become the backdrop to the (partial) incubation miracles surrounding his relics. Three different pictures emerge about the circumstances of Demetrius's life and death in his three surviving *Vitae*. One version tells that, in his rage, Emperor Maximian had him executed in Thessalonica. Demetrius was described as either being of humble origin or a noble senator or general. His miracles are recorded in three books; the first two of them are edited by Paul Lemerle.[182]

---

180 Gregory of Tours, *In Gloria Martyrum*, 99.
181 About how his cult changed places, see Delehaye, *Les légendes grecques des saints militaries*, pp. 103–08.
182 *Les plus anciens recueils*, ed. and trans. by Lemerle; all three versions are in PG 116,

Collection I is a collection of fifteen miracles by Bishop John of Thessalonica. These stories are, for the most part, incubation miracles from the first part of the seventh century. Miracles 1–4 are cures through incubation; Miracles 7 and 11 are punishment miracles, although they provide rich details about the incubation practice in his church in Thessalonica. In Miracles 8–9, Demetrius saves the city during a famine; in Miracle 10, he cures Emperor Maurice from a disease of the intestines. Miracle 12 speaks of extinguishing a fire in the granary with particulars about the saint's feast day, while Miracles 13–15 speak of the attacks of the Avars. The historical facts in the stories help to date the collection, from which we know that Eusebius was the archbishop and Maurice was the emperor. In addition, one of the manuscripts (1517, Mazarineus, Bibl. Nat. Paris: fol. 135) names the hagiographer as John, archbishop of Thessalonica, who was indeed contemporary with the events described. Thus, the collection can be dated to the years 610–630.[183]

The second collection (six long miracles) comes from a different hagiographer and does not speak about incubation or healing miracles in general, but includes the attacks on Thessalonica by the Avars and Slavs (partly during the time of John, partly after his death). This book dates to the second half of the seventh century.

Book III (five miracles) addresses incubation in Miracles 1, 2, and 4. This book is a later redaction, written after the year 904 when the city was plundered. It differs greatly from the two earlier books because it is less rhetorical. The incubation miracles follow the customary dream-healing narrative pattern. The hagiographer remains anonymous.

Thessalonica, especially the calamities that befell the town and its inhabitants, was at the centre of this collection. Besides information on illnesses and the catastrophes of wars, the third collection provides rich historical details concerning the Slav attacks. By the tenth century, Demetrius had chiefly become a warrior saint. In his attributes, he resembled Saint George and was often represented next to him. A fascinating characteristic of these miracles is that, although they speak the language of Byzantine hagiography more familiar from elsewhere, they rely on the well-known narrative schemes when it comes to the incubation miracles.

Saint Menas

Saint Menas, a third-century martyr, was one of the most important saints in Egypt, not the least because of his capacity as a healer. His cult started in the fifth century when, on the then forgotten spot of his burial some thirty-five kilometres west from Alexandria, miraculous cures started to

---

cols 1081–1426; a good overview of the collections and on the saint's figure is given by Delehaye, 'Les recueils antiques', pp. 57–64; cf. Frendo, 'The Miracles of St Demetrius'.
183   Laurent, 'Sur la date des églises Saint Démétrius et Sainte-Sophie à Thessalonique', p. 425.

happen. Among these miracles, the daughter of Emperor Zeno was healed. She was taken to the spot in Mareotis and, in a dream, Menas appeared to her and told her who he was. When she woke up, she was cured and the emperor ordered a cathedral to be built there. This church of Abu Mina was one of the most popular destinations of pilgrims, especially for sick people. Menas's miraculous cures are attested by the great number of Menas ampullae, little clay flasks in which pilgrims carried home oil or water received at the holy site. In the church of Abu Mina, there is archaeological evidence that can be interpreted as traces of incubation (I shall return to this shortly).[184]

The textual evidence of Saint Menas's miracles is similar to the archaeological evidence; clearly, he was not exclusively an incubation healer, but temple sleep was part of his cult and several references confirm this. The thirteen miracles that were first published from a manuscript in Moscow include the same story (Miracle 5) that we also know from Cosmas and Damian: the incubation healing of a paralytic man and mute woman; Miracle 7 also records incubation. Many of the other miracles (1, 3, 5, 6, 9, 10, 12) make clear references not only to patients seeking a cure but also to the saint's epiphany in a dream (6, 9, 10, 13). Miracles 4–8 apparently follow the narrative of *ex voto* tablets.[185] Yet this is only what is preserved in the Greek material, whereas several miracle stories of Menas survive in Arabic, Coptic, Ethiopian, and even some in Armenian and Nubian.[186] The oldest Coptic manuscript from 892 occasionally reveals details relating to incubation that the Greek text does not mention.

Some Other Saints Associated with Incubation

We have testimonies for a Saint Ptolemy: there are no Greek texts that survive, but a seventh-century miracle collection in Arabic (perhaps originally from Coptic?) informs us that Saint Ptolemaius was also cured by incubation in his church at Ishnin near Oxyrinchus.[187]

Without going into a detailed analysis, it is worth calling attention to another, Egyptian account of incubation miracles almost contemporary to the *Thaumata* of Menouthis from the second half of the seventh century. Agathon, an Alexandrian Monophysite and the successor of the patriarch Benjamin (AD 626–665), wrote a book that recorded the incubation healings that took place in the church of Saint Macarius (Abû Maqâr). The Greek original was

---

184 Grossmann, 'The Pilgrimage Center of Abû Mînâ' and Grossmann, *Abû Mînâ: A Guide to the Ancient Pilgrimage Center*.
185 Miracles of Saint Menas: BHG 1256–69.
186 Some of the published material: Budge, *Texts Relating to Saint Mêna of Egypt*; Devos, 'Le Juif et le Chrétien, un miracle de Saint Ménas'; and Devos, 'Les miracles de St Ménas en éthiopien'; Devos, 'Un récit des Miracles de S. Ménas en Copte et en éthiopien'; *Apa Mena*, ed. and trans. by Drescher; Jaritz, *Die Arabischen Quellen zum Heiligen Menas*.
187 Cf. 'Les miracles de Saint Ptolémée', ed. and trans. by Leroy.

translated into Arabic, with the misleading title given by the translator: *Book of the Consecration of the Church of Benjamin*. Several dream cures took place in this church on the day after its consecration by Benjamin. A boy with leprosy told a certain Agathon that Macarius had appeared to him in his dream and healed him so that his illness and all the spots and the wounds on his body became attached to his garment.[188]

To some extent, Saint Luke of Steiris in Boeotia should also be numbered among the ancient practitioners of incubation. His *Vita*, written by an anonymous monk sometime in the 960s, contains some cases of incubation among his posthumous miracles. Temple sleep was a rather ubiquitous ritual, not one confined exclusively to certain cults. His miracles provide variants of the modes of ritual sleep. Miracle 13 informs us that, according to the cult practice of the place, it was necessary for the patient not only to sleep near the tomb of the saint but also to be the only one to sleep there. Another miracle (10) reveals an alternative mode of incubation, not alien to the previously mentioned collections,[189] where the patient practised incubation in his dream, although they were actually situated far from the church (while visiting the saint's tomb in their imagination, the patient prayed that they might be able to visit the tomb after they were healed).[190] Marco Dorati also discussed some other saints who had a subsidiary incubation function: he speaks of Saint Nikolaos, who was also a healer, and incubation was practised in his church in Constantinople.[191] It is worth mentioning Saint Stephen, whose twenty miracles are candidates for being considered the earliest Christian incubation miracles, dating from the beginning of the fifth century AD.[192]

By way of concluding, I would like to point out a question of basic importance. Are there saints we can call incubation saints? I think, yes. There are saints whose modus operandi at a given place and time was primarily temple sleep. However, I do not want to press this category further than it could actually be applied. As we can see, there are saints' cults where incubation was only part of their repertoire, or when it was practised with great variation. The examples also showed that there are saints who only took up incubation in very particular circumstances, like the ones in Constantinople or in Aegae or when associated with other strong incubation cults or healers, and there are saints who carry this ritual with themselves. The colourful picture of the miracle collections confirms the same impression that we can receive from the

---

188 Coquin, *Livre de la consécration du Sanctuaire de Benjamin*, pp. 177–85; here the healer appearing in dream was a tall man, in a monk's habit, with a beard covering his chest.
189 Thecla's hagiographer recorded a dream in which he was practicing incubation, MT12.
190 Connor, *Art and Miracles in Medieval Byzantium*, p. 98.
191 Dorati, 'Funzioni e motivi', p. 94, n. 17: on the basis of the *in vita* miracles, referring to Anrich, *Hagios Nikolaos, der Heilige Nikolaos in der griechischen Kirche*, I, pp. 3–6.
192 PL 41, cols 833–54; cf. Dorati, 'Funzioni e motivi', pp. 96–97, n. 21, for incubation saints in the West.

archaeological evidence, as Peter Grossman recently discussed in connection with the church of Saint Menas:

> direct traces showing that incubation rites were once practiced here do not survive. But it can be inferred that the semi-circular shaped southern hemicycle [...] divided into several differently shaped rooms, was designed by its original builders to locate each of these rooms at an equal distance from the martyr-crypt below the church. These differently shaped rooms can be interpreted as the *enkoimétéria* for the sick. In the corner of one of these rooms there are even the remains of a *kliné*.[193]

Grossman lists further evidence of incubation practice: the presence of the nearby washing rooms and another room for the other latrines — that is, separately for men and women. He continues by describing a small sixth-century Christian sanctuary near Abu Mina in a village now called Sidi Mahmud. It has all that is necessary for incubation practice: instead of the usual sitting benches, there is a continuous row of *klinés* with headrests along the inner northern wall; on the southern side, there are high sitting benches, larger than usual, and a row of beds along the outer side of the northern wall. In the western contra-apse, there was another set of incubation beds and seats, with a burial chamber beneath the ground and even a slot to introduce textiles in order to make contact relics. Grossmann calls attention to another church with remains of *klinés* along the inner sidewalls, the south church of Abdalla Nirqi in Nubia (twelfth century or later), and still another church with interior beds in Hirbat al-Bayudat in Palestine, as well as the church of Saints Cosmas and Damian in South Sinai Firan (ancient Pharan). These features confirm that sleeping in the church was often one of the possible ways of approaching the healer, which was a form of practical contact with the saints. Many cult sites could have had sleeping chambers without becoming a famous incubation centre or even making incubation its main profile. If we take into account the numerous churches where incubation was ancillary to standard practices, this also means that the practice of temple sleep in Byzantine Christianity was much more widespread than we had thought before, and it was not limited to only the few famous cults of incubation saints.

---

193 Grossmann, 'Late Antique Christian Incubation Centres in Egypt', pp. 126–27.

Part II

Sources

CHAPTER 4

Material Sources

The *Ex Votos*

> In the church of the Madonna di Rimedio near Oristano, Sardinia, [...] on a votive photograph glued onto a piece of cardboard a soldier is portrayed in his Sunday best, standing before a back-drop which shows Saint Peter in Rome. A life-size wooden model of an ear is fastened with a ribbon to the corner of the photograph. When a man, either ancient or modern, thanks his god for a cure by offering an accurate replica of the part which had been afflicted, he may be overcome by an acute awareness of the vulnerability of his mortal body, perhaps even heightened at the sight of numerous similar dedications in the sanctuary.[1]

In Antiquity, the closeness of the supplicants to their local deities is reflected in their humble votive offerings, placed with care in the local shrines, which convey the intimacy and devotion incorporated within these simple objects. Though the written and archaeological testimonies tend to be more concerned with the great and famous temples of Antiquity, the faithful paid no less tribute to their local protecting divinities, and even the humble shrines of the nymphs and heroes were full of simple objects of thanksgiving.[2]

Among the situations of life that provided occasion for thanksgiving, recovery from an illness was of overwhelming importance. The temples of the healing gods and heroes were thus the chief destinations for votive tablets recording both modest and lavish gifts. For the Greeks from the fifth to fourth centuries BC, one of the centres of the Asclepieian miraculous healing was Epidaurus. Strabo summarized the essence of this site in the following words:

> Epidaurus, too, is an important city, and particularly because of the fame of Asclepius, who is believed to cure diseases of every kind and always has his temple full of the sick, and also of the votive tablets on which the treatments are recorded, just as at Cos and Tricce.[3]

The *Iamata* and the research on its compositional history supply the study of Christian incubation records with rich parallels, for two reasons. First, the

---

1   Van Straten, 'Gifts for the Gods', p. 112.
2   'Indeed, because of the closeness and familiarity of the local deities, he could have felt more at his ease with them. He could submit all his daily worries to them and, out of gratitude for their help and protection, their shrines were too crowded with gifts which may have been of less value, but were presented with no less piety than the ones in the larger sanctuaries.' Van Straten, 'Gifts for the Gods', p. 79.
3   Strabo, *Geographica*, VIII. 6. 15.

ancient practice of incubation was transformed into the early Christian cult of the saints, and second, the process of the formation of the miracle tales into a textual corpus was similarly influenced by the pagan descriptions of temple sleep. It is not always a continuity, but it is always a dialogue. This lies at the core of the transformation of the incubation ritual and its records, and attention to these changes is very important in order to understand these very particular Byzantine miracle narratives. Hence, an understanding of the role that ancient *ex votos* played, both as sources and in shaping the narrative, will provide a good point of departure and standard of comparison into research on analogous Christian records.

The Varieties of Ancient Greek and Early Christian Votive Offerings

Any object could be used as a votive gift, and an enormous variety of examples has been found in Greek and Christian sanctuaries. Rouse, in his *Greek Votive Offerings*, classified these offerings into four groups:

1. The image of the deliverer: the statues and statuettes in the image of the god were not dedicated for healing by private individuals at an early date, but rather by cities; in the case of Asclepius, snake offerings (as an epiphany of the god) also enter this category.

2. An image of the person delivered from illness (this applies to statues only appearing after the late fourth century BC).

3. A representation of the act or process of healing.

4. Miscellaneous objects including a wide and exotic variety of not only objects but sometimes persons as well. The likeness of a healed child or a child born to a previously infertile couple could be given as an offering, among both Greeks and early Christians. Neither was the practical aspect lacking, with plenty of useful objects offered, including medical tools, restoration work, and carpentry in the temple, food to feed the sick, or money to cover the expenses of a ceremony.[4]

The material used in these votives may also be grouped into categories: wood, clay, or precious metals were all used, and what is more, their usage points to local preferences at the different sanctuaries.[5] In Corinth, for instance, terracotta anatomical votives were preferred; clay and wooden tablets (*pinakes*, or *sanides*) were frequently dedicated, for example, in Samothrake and Lebena. From Athens, Pireus, or Oropos, numerous elaborately carved stone reliefs have survived. The same typology has been found in early Christian votive

---

4 Rouse, *Greek Votive Offerings*, pp. 208–09. More recently, see Petsalis-Diomidis, 'Between the Body and the Divine'; and also Draycott and Graham, eds, *Bodies of Evidence*.
5 For their modern interpretation and examples of the ancient (inscriptional and literary) references to them, see Dorati, 'Funzioni e motivi', p. 92, esp. n. 12 and p. 99.

objects. In Corinth, the Greek model limbs from terracotta dedicated to Asclepius give way to silver anatomical votives, dedicated to Saints Cosmas and Damian, as late as the twentieth century, in their Corinthian church.[6] The material could be secondary to what it represented; anatomical *ex votos* were in use in all over the Mediterranean, and still are, for example, the spectacular wax limbs of San Andrés de Teixido in today's Galicia. These anatomical votives may represent the sick limb or the healed body part.[7] Mary Hamilton saw in all (both Greek and Christian) anatomical votives a representation of the limbs before the cure: 'an image of the member to be healed was set up in the neighbourhood of the god's statue as a sort of guide for the deity'.[8] Votive plaques could also serve as memorial objects, veritable guides for the deity, as Callimachus's teasing poem attests: 'Know that you have received the debt, Asklepios, which Akeson owed you because of his prayer for his wife Demodike; were you to forget and claim it a second time, the votive tablet will serve as evidence.'[9] The frequency of dedicated model limbs can highlight the diseases that occurred locally and/or what special competence the particular temple had.[10] Specialization on a certain disease was certainly not unheard of: the hero Theogenes on Thasos, for example, was especially consulted for healing fevers. The Epidaurian practice probably included placing a clay tablet on the wall, with a figurative drawing of the limb and with a short text on the tablet, comprising the patient's name, hometown, and the individual features of his illness and cure.[11]

The temple personnel regularly removed these objects covering the walls of the sanctuary in order to make room for newer ones. On such occasions, the *ex votos* were recorded, as can be seen from this official (priestly) dedication from the Athenian Asclepieion: 'Nikomachus, a priest and physician dedicates a censer made out of old offerings melted down.'[12] In Athens, there was a board of yearly elected temple personnel whose task was to inspect and catalogue the votives,[13] and the office was of such significant authority that the name of

---

6 Cf. Lang, *Cure and Cult in Ancient Corinth*, p. 31; this little book contains a variety of photographic material on terracotta anatomical *ex votos*.
7 Such as the silver ears and the silver milt, dedications to Asclepius on Tiber Island, from the first (or second) century AD: Girone, *Iamata*, pp. 154–56, also for further reading on anatomical votives.
8 Hamilton, *Incubation*, p. 86.
9 Callimachus, *Anthologia Palatina* VI, 147, in van Straten, 'Gifts for the Gods', p. 71.
10 In Lebena on Crete, for example, it is conspicuous that a great number of those who were healed had suffered from eye diseases, while from Corinth (contrary to the numerous feet, for instance) hardly any eye images have come down to us.
11 For a short stylistic introduction to the basic elements, see Dorati, 'Funzioni e motivi', p. 93, n. 13; for a typology on the basis of the inscriptions from Tiber Island, cf. Rüttimann, 'Asclepius and Jesus', p. 59.
12 Rouse, *Greek Votive Offerings*, p. 206 (= CIA II. 836). For an elaborate survey on such material, see Aleshire, *The Athenian Asclepieion*.
13 Rouse, *Greek Votive Offerings*, p. 198.

its bearer (like the archons) often was recorded on the inscriptions in order to date them. The latest stele found in the Athenian Asclepieia from the fourth century AD includes the name of the priest of the time and is an example of a son dedicating the votive on behalf of his father:

> Hegemachos, son of Krataimenes of Lamptra to Asclepius. Having suffered many terrible ills and seen many visions, [and] having been saved, Eurumedon, son of Hegemachos, dedicated [this] to Asclepius and Hygeia, under the priest Theophilus.[14]

In the early third century AD, the Roman author Aelian wrote about the votive catalogues himself, pointing out the accuracy of the practice, mentioning that 'the catalogues indicated the missing votive offerings and so did the empty spaces where the votive offerings had been set up'.[15]

Another typology of votive offerings focuses on their function. The purpose of such dedications was always to honour the deity, either thanking them for help already given or in order to implore future protection. As Theophrastos noted, the twofold aim of the practice was similar to the motivations for offering sacrifices.[16] So-called acknowledgement votives are a group of cult objects that expressed the help received or the miracle experienced by those who dedicated them, while offerings made before the manifest divine intervention occurred are known as invocational votives. Although acknowledgement votives were more common in Antiquity, invocational votives are also found in Asclepieian practice. A curious instance is a votive from the Athenian sanctuary of Asclepius: the first part of the inscription contained the invocation; the second part contained the acknowledgement.[17]

Many of the above-mentioned votive practices were continued by early Christians.[18] At first, the principal destinations for Christian pilgrims were the lands of the Bible. Occasionally, the journey itself also meant the fulfilment of a vow; besides these places, many pilgrims who were seeking cures hastened to far-famed ascetics and miracle-working saints. They left behind gifts that hardly differed in their colourfulness from ancient *ex votos*: 'ornaments in vast numbers, which hung from iron rods: armlets, bracelets, rings, tiaras, plaited girdles, belts, emperors' crowns of gold and precious stones, and the insignia of an empress', wrote the Piacenza pilgrim in 570 about the votive objects placed at the Holy Grave.[19]

---

14 Girone, *Iamata*, pp. 36–38; English translation Johnson, *The 'Life and Miracles of Thekla'*, p. 205.
15 Aelian, *De Natura Animalium* VII. 13 = T489.
16 *Peri eusebeias*, Fr. 12. Cf. van Straten, 'Gifts for the Gods', p. 66; distinguishing between sacrifice and offering, he defines the first as edible, the latter as non-edible.
17 The dedication of the temple servant Diofantos is in Girone, *Iamata*, pp. 31–34.
18 On Christian votive gifts, cf. Kötting, *Peregrinatio religiosa*, pp. 398–410; Vikan, *Byzantine Pilgrimage Art* and Vikan, 'Art, Medicine and Magic'.
19 The Piacenza Pilgrim, *Travels*, 18 (around AD 570), in Wilkinson, *Jerusalem Pilgrims before the Crusades*, pp. 129–51.

There was a group of Christian anatomical votives on small silver plaques from northern Syria from the sixth century AD.[20] They had large eyes moulded on them, some of which belonged to the invocational type, with the inscription, 'Lord, help, Amen'. Others of the acknowledgement type bear the words 'In fulfilment of a vow'. In early Byzantine art, the testimonies of pilgrimage and personal devotional art are far more commonly in the form of objects beseeching help or tokens or *eulogiai* endowed with miraculous power. Anatomical votives can also be found among the multiplicity of votives rendering thanks for healing. Theodoret of Cyrrhus confirmed that the practice was not at all unusual in Byzantium:

> Christians came to the martyrs to implore them to be their intercessors. That they obtained what they so earnestly prayed for is clearly proven by their votive gifts, which proclaim the healing. Some bring images of eyes, others feet, others hands, which sometimes are made of gold, sometimes of wood.[21]

An incised bronze cross that was connected to Saint Thecla from sixth- or seventh-century AD Syria represents an example of the invocational votive. The cross, which is now at Dumbarton Oaks, may have been set into a wall or column, probably in a shrine or chapel dedicated to Thecla. In the upper centre, there is a bust-portrait of Thecla as intercessor, in the *orans* position, while an invocation on behalf of four dedicators was written across its surface: 'St Thekla, help Symionis and Synesios and Mary and Thekla.'[22] There is also pilgrim-graffiti, inscriptions beseeching help that, even without the votive objects, often bear important witness to the circumstances under which the saints were implored.[23] For example, the invocation of a sick woman in a graffito from Abydos attests that Saint Cyrus was invoked together with Cosmas and Damian and Saint Kollonthos.[24]

The ubiquitous presence of the votives, the way they covered the temple walls, their colours, their varieties of form, and not the least the cures that they advertised exercised a great impact on those who arrived at the sanctuary — not only aesthetically but in the psychological sense as well.[25] Nevertheless, the practice must have remained the same in Christian times.

---

20 Baltimore, Walters Art Gallery, 57. 1865. 560; fig. 38 in Vikan, *Byzantine Pilgrimage Art*, p. 45, and Vikan, 'Art, Medicine and Magic', p. 66, fig. 1.
21 Theorodet, *Graecorum Affectionum Curatio*, 8, 64; translation from Vikan, *Byzantine Pilgrimage Art*, pp. 45–46.
22 Vikan, *Byzantine Pilgrimage Art*, p. 44.
23 On these pilgrim graffiti, cf. Vikan, *Byzantine Pilgrimage Art*, p. 44.
24 Papaconstantinou, *Le culte des saints en Égypte des Byzantins aux Abbasides*, p. 238.
25 A literary description of such a visit in Herondas (*c.* 250 BC) *Mimiambi*, IV, the women's amazement in the Asclepieion of Cos: '–La! Cynno dear, what beautiful statues! What craftsman was it who worked this stone, and who dedicated it? –The sons of Praxiteles – only look at the letters on the base, and Euthies, son of Prexon, dedicated it. [...] –Only look, dear Cynno, what works are those there! See these, you would say, were chiselled by Athene

Archaeological findings are surprisingly scarce, and written sources referring to votives dedicated after healing are also rare.[26] The Christian incubation miracles offer again a very useful insight into material about which other types of hagiographic records usually remain silent. In what follows, I shall investigate the way votives appear in the miracle texts. I discuss votives first as sources, as firsthand material for textual recording; afterwards, I shall analyse them as agents in shaping the miracle narratives themselves.

The Votive Objects as Sources

Votive gifts did not simply bear witness to the miracles by their presence. They were closely connected with the direct representation of the cures, to their oral dissemination, and their pictorial and textual recording.[27] LiDonnici has demonstrated how it was possible to find traces in the *Iamata* tales of the *ex votos* that served as a starting point of these miraculous tales which themselves went through repeated priestly redactions and which were, with the passing of the years, recopied and reorganized, receiving a new order as well as different emphases. In this case, the rewriting of the stories from the votives illustrates the development of an increasingly compact, shorter form. Despite the ad hoc nature of the survival of the finds from Epidaurus, we occasionally have both the original votive and the *Iamata* inscription composed based on it. A large block of stone near to the sanctuary was found, bearing the following inscription:

> Hermodicus of Lampsacus
>
> As an example of your power, Asclepius, I have put up this rock which I had lifted up, manifest for all to see, an evidence of your art. For before coming under your hands and those of your children I was stricken by a wretched illness, having an abscess in my chest and being paralysed in my hands. But you, Paean, by ordering me to lift up this rock made me live free from disease.[28]

---

herself – all hail, Lady! Look, this naked boy, he will bleed, will he not, if I scratch him, Cynno; for the flesh seems to pulse warmly as it lies on him in the picture' (T 482).

26 Vikan, *Byzantine Pilgrimage Art*, p. 45.
27 Two pictorial examples: on a Boiotian vase-painting next to a serpent there are suspended anatomical votives, which suggest that the image shows Asclepius and Hygeia (photo in Lang, *Cure and Cult in Ancient Corinth*, p. 18, fig. 16); the other is the well-known relief of Archinos for the Amphiareion at Oropos (Athens, National Museum 3369) showing the double aspect of divine healing, the miraculous dream (in which the A. cures the patient's shoulder) and parallel to this the view from the outside: Archinos lying on a bed and, while he is asleep, a serpent licking his shoulder. That all this happens in the temple precinct is indicated by a votive tablet behind the bed. More on the relief and also about the representation of votive tablets on reliefs in van Straten, 'Daikrates' Dream', p. 4, esp. n. 41.
28 IG IV 1, 125 (third century BC) = T 431.

This is a rare instance in which one can compare the inscriptional evidence with that of the priestly redaction and contrast the elements that were retained or dropped:

> Hermodicus of Lampsacus was paralysed in body. This one, when he slept in the Temple, the god healed and he ordered him upon coming out to bring to the Temple as large a stone he could. The man brought the stone which now lies before the Abaton.[29]

Due to the literary form of the *Iamata*, which aimed at a condensed, concise rendering of carefully selected miracles, the ordinary is excised from the story. The irrelevant abscess must go, and the patient is not only paralysed in his hand but in his whole body; the 'children of Asclepius' disappear from the scene, giving way to the single figure of the god, while the healing performed by the god's hand is transformed into an explicit reference to incubation. Moreover, the means of the miraculous cure is referred to with its exact location.[30]

Another characteristic of votive objects is what LiDonnici has called 'stock-influence': the cured patients could select from the votive goods of craftsmen plying their wares around the cult place and choose the votive object they thought the closest to their own case. The range of goods that was offered was probably more or less stable, only allowing for some limited, occasional additions to the ready-made tablets. The form-repertoire of these votives and their inevitable uniformity represented an important source for the compilers of the miracle catalogues. Their presence in and around the temple was no less significant for the sick supplicants still awaiting the cure because they could find encouragement in them. More importantly, the patients could consult their 'cases', in order to interpret the cure that was suggested in a dream.

There is a group of Greek votive reliefs that are of special importance for incubation studies: they were set up in accordance with a dream, and at the same time, usually represent the dream experience, or the dreaming person. Van Straten called them *kat'onar* (= 'according to a dream') offerings, that is, objects dedicated as a consequence of a dream.[31] His examples range from the fifth century BC to the second/third centuries AD and include well-known carved marble reliefs to Asclepius and Amphiaraus, more modest pieces dedicated to the Nymphs and the Charites, to Hermes, Nemesis, various figures like Zeus and Apollo, to Angdistis and Attis, Men and Meter. There were examples from the Lydian and Phrygian confession stelai as well.[32] The simultaneous representations of cures and dreams on reliefs that were dedicated

---

29 T423.15.
30 A detailed rendering of the text and the various interpretations concerning it are in Girone, *Iamata*, pp. 53–55.
31 Van Straten, 'Daikrates' Dream', p. 3.
32 Elaborate lists of the divine addressees and dedicators of dream *ex votos* (with his terminology, provenance, and dating) is in van Straten, 'Daikrates' Dream', pp. 21–27, and photos

to Asclepius and Amphiaraus are well known and have been amply discussed by other scholars as well.[33] The wider existence of such dedications, including those outside the context of the better-known incubation cults, revealed the popularity of the dream votive type as such.[34]

Ex Votos *in the Christian Incubation Narratives*

It is now time to turn to the Byzantine incubation collections. In what context did votive gifts appear in the miracles? What were these gifts? What did the characters in the miracle narrative and contemporary readers make of them? Most importantly for the formation of the stories in the Christian context, what did the hagiographers do with them? That is, how did votive tablets serve as sources for their stories?

In Saint Thecla's miracles, we find that the hagiographer simply mentions riches and gold as votive gifts (MT12). In his church in Constantinople, Saint Therapon cures a man through incubation; this man dedicated a votive tablet made of wax to his healer; this tablet recorded the miracle and was probably placed somewhere on the church wall: 'τοῦ τε πάθους καὶ τῆς ἐλευθερίας τὸν θρίαμβον ἐγκήροις ἐστηλίτευσε πίναξιν'.[35] Interestingly, the votive objects themselves could also be distributed, in accordance of the vow. The first miracle of Saint Demetrius tells how the saint healed the wealthy Marianos. Afterwards, the man left the church, collected a large number of valuable objects made of gold and silver as well as a large sum of silver coins, and brought them back to the church, whereupon he distributed them to the poor and the sick who gathered from all over the city. The hagiographer says that the scene was recorded on a mosaic on the external wall of the church.[36]

Yet there were far more intriguing votive gifts. We can compare the same miraculous story that survived in the two different versions of the miracle corpora of Cosmas and Damian (CL6, KDM3). In a dream, the saints cryptically announce the remedy for the sick patient: to burn and drink the pubic hair of Cosmas. As he wonders what to do, in the (presumably later) KDM collection, we see him consult the votive tablets that are described as hanging on the walls of the church. This act conveys an idea of the expansion of the cult of Cosmas and Damian and, more importantly from the compositional point of view, identifies one of the sources of the hagiographic record. Moreover, the text

---

of them on pp. 29–38; cf. also the first part of Chapter 10, below, on sin and illness and the references to the confession stelai.

33   Hausmann, *Kunst und Heiligtum*.
34   For other examples besides van Straten's article, see Dorati, 'Funzioni e motivi', p. 93, n. 13, and Girone, *Iamata*, pp. 133–35; the latter analyses a dedication of two dream figures, two statues of Oneiroi, in gratitude for regained eyesight through incubation from Lebena, third century AD (IC I. XVII. 24).
35   *Laudatio Therapontis*, 12. 22–23, in Deubner, *De incubatione*, p. 127.
36   *Miracula Demetrii*, 1, 23–24, *Les plus anciens recueils*, ed. and trans. by Lemerle, I, p. 56 and p. 67.

says that it took the patient several days to go through all the votives! It was no less significant that men relied on such records in seeking to interpret their dreams (in the Christian collections, we hear nothing about church personnel helping to interpret the saints' message). Regarding the solution to the bizarre prescription, we are informed that there was a sheep named Cosmas who was brought in (according to the KDM) as an offering to the church. In an attempt to condense the story and suppress one detail as spurious, the miracle story omits the information contained in the London Codex miracle, that is, the sheep was named after its donator, himself also Cosmas.

In the miracle of Cyrus and John (MCJ49), we find a pig as a votive gift. In the church of Saint Menas in Mareotis (MM13), there were also pigs. In the atrium of Thecla's church, there was a garden with birds, the function of which has been variously interpreted. Peter Grossmann considered it a poultry farm and claimed that these animals were donated primarily to feed the poor,[37] as were probably the pigs mentioned above. Who knows what function the lamb and the deer served, described in the miracles as wandering freely among the patients? Elsewhere Thecla's garden has been called a veritable zoo; birds were donated because of their exotic character, both to please and entertain those present at the church precincts as well as to attest the wealth and uniqueness of the shrine far and wide.[38] These votive birds made their presence more conspicuous in those miracle stories where, just as with the sheep above, donated animals are the agents or means of the cure. In MT24, a child with a disease in one of his eyes was taken to Thecla by his nurse. In the atrium of the church, writes the hagiographer, there were a great number and variety of birds, doves, cranes, and geese, as well as swans and pheasants, that were brought to the church for entertainment or as votive gifts, and all these birds were dedicated to Thecla. One of the cranes pierced the diseased eye of the child, but when the frightened spectators examined the wound, this act turned out to produce the remedy, since the eye, 'as if it were pierced by the physician's lancet and incised with medical skill', was emptied of the liquid that obscured sight and the child became well. Several Asclepieian cures also come to mind, not only those involving the deity's epiphany, where the god healed with the help of a dog or a serpent or the deity took an animal form, but also one cure quite akin to Thecla's bird that cured miraculously: 'of Chios with gout. While awake he was walking towards a goose who bit his feet and by making him bleed made him well'.[39]

As children playing with the votive animals offered a pleasant sight to Thecla's suppliants, a deer dedicated to Cosmas and Damian must have also been a source of entertainment as it walked among the patients who lay in their church. The man with the withered arm in CL8 laughed as he tried to

---

37 Grossmann, 'The Pilgrimage Center of Abû Mînâ'.
38 Vikan, *Byzantine Pilgrimage Art*, p. 44; cf. Kötting, *Peregrinatio religiosa*, p. 156.
39 T423.43 on Stele B.

chase away the deer after it chewed the sleeves of his cloak. As the amused spectators did not help him, he began to try desperately to move his arm, and the thus the deer was recognized as the means of the healers' grace.

There are examples where the due offering is precisely prescribed by the healers themselves. In one instance, Saints Cyrus and John meticulously bid their healed patient to return to his hometown, plant a grapevine in their names, tend it, and harvest and press the grapes. In due time, the wine produced from the grapevine had to be divided. The patient was free to sell one half as he liked; the other half of the wine was to be carried yearly to the church and distributed there among the needy.[40] In the second part of the same miracle, we read about a type of votive gift already familiar from the Asclepieian corpora: the dedication of the object itself that caused the illness.[41] In this miraculous story, a woman was gripped by intestinal pains. She delivered a stone as big as an egg, which she ordered to be hung above the tomb of the saints. There the stone remained 'for many years, as a memorial to the miracle' and may well have served as a starting point of the tale for Sophronius or his informant.[42]

In the collection of Artemius, there is no explicit mention of tablets that record the cure on them, but more is said about votive gifts, most frequently a lamp that is lit in honour of the saint or simply the cost of the lamp oil. This sort of lamp, however, whether lit in the church or in the patient's house in the name of Artemius, was often also the vehicle for the cure. The routine act of lighting it was an act of devotion as well as the catalyst for Artemius's intervention (as in miracle MA11). The holy lamp-oil, however, was mostly applied as an ointment or swallowed by the patients. We witness this curative technique in Saints Cosmas and Damian as well: one of their miracles describes how disgusting this mixture of oil and wax actually was — drinking it was considered a test of faith itself (KDM16). The saint could order or suggest that a votive lamp be dedicated, but the patient might take the initiative. In Artemius's cult, a votive gift might comprise the organization of a banquet, a common meal for the fellow incubants, as well as regular attendance at the all-night vigil, the *pannychis*. These two votive acts will be addressed in detail later when communal occasions for telling and listening to miracle stories are discussed. Meanwhile, Artemius was also surrounded by the usual votive offerings. The hagiographer duly informs us, if not about the character of the objects, then about their location. The cured left their objects not on the walls of the chapel but on and around the lead coffin of Artemius, 'the saint's holy coffin of lead, where his living relics are stored, where the gift of cures

---

40 MCJ48.
41 Cf. T423.12, 13, 14, 30, 32, 40, where the objects causing the illness (head of an arrow, stone, etc.) might have been depicted on the votive tablet or left as a votive gift, but surely described in the text itself.
42 MCJ48; cf. also Fernandez Marcos, *Los Thaumata*, p. 170.

bubbles up, where patients' thank-offerings for cures effected by the saintly megalomartyr are stored' (MA33).

Similar to Hermodicus's dedication (which survives in both its original and edited forms), in the Christian context, votive tablets recording the miracle in a few words can sometimes be compared with the longer story of the hagiographer. A unique healing votive embedded within the miracle narrative can be found in the *Thaumata* (MCJ69), and its existence offers an invaluable clue to the mechanism of Sophronius's creative fantasy:[43]

> I, John, coming from the town of Rome, having been blind for eight years, after having been waiting here patiently, through the miraculous power of Saints Cyrus and John, have regained my eyesight.[44]

Sophronius the Sophist knew his craft well and was able to weave a flowery story around these words, starting with a panegyric on Rome (so broad was the saints' sphere of action!), and afterwards, telling in detail how the miserable patient spent all his money on doctors and when they failed, finally turned to the holy healers. There are two especially noteworthy features in this narrative. Sophronius made the precise location of the inscription the basis of his story, interpreting the word *here* quite literally. In his version, the patient took up his abode at the entrance of the sanctuary, having made a vow not to enter the church until he received his cure — and *there* he stayed, suffering *for eight years*, exposed to the unpleasantness of the weather. In a further twist, what figures in the votive text as eight years of blindness, Sophronius transformed into eight years spent in front of the church.[45] Nevertheless, the most inventive part of the tale follows: when the saints at last had mercy on the man and healed him by placing their finger upon his eyes, Johannes awoke in the middle of the night and immediately inscribed on the wall, near to where he had been lying, his testimony to the miracle. Thus, the actual location of the votive inscription contributed to the formation of the story. This formative factor, already mentioned briefly by LiDonnici in connection with the *Iamata* tales,[46] was dramatically exploited in this instance. This precious reference helps us see how Sophronius could build his story from scratch, and at the same time, it attests to the way votives could be used as direct source-materials to the written record.

This inscription on the wall as a memento of the miracle bears close resemblance to those inscriptions, the *proskynemata*, that are not properly votive tablets, yet they were important records of the pilgrim's experience and are also familiar in the context of incubation. These remembrances were

---

43 On most points I follow Delehaye's analysis of how 'Sophrone enfile ses perles', Delehaye, *L'ancienne hagiographie byzantine*, pp. 62–63.
44 'Ἐγὼ Ἰωάννης πόλεως τῆς Ῥώμης ὁρμώμενος, τυφλὸς ὀκτὼ χρόνους γενόμενος ἐνθάδε διὰ τῆς τῶν ἁγίων Κύρου καὶ Ἰωάννου δυνάμενος προσκαρτερήσας ἀνέβλεψα'.
45 Connecting the *okto khronos* not to the *tuphlos genomenos*, but to *proskarterésas*.
46 LiDonnici, *The Epidaurian Miracle Inscriptions*, p. 52.

commonly written on the walls of sanctuaries in Egypt. Dorati remarks, 'What renders these texts of interest is the fact that these, being directly executed by the beneficiary of the miracle, escape, at least in theory, certain demands of serial production that mark the commissioned objects.'[47]

Although the texts on the original votive tablets did not find their way into any of the other miracles retold by Sophronius, he includes stories for which such concise votive narratives almost certainly served as the point of departure. In these narratives, the layers of the texts can be neatly peeled off from the core of the story, reducing it to two or three words; this can be observed in MCJ6 and 7: Geddaius with a fistula; Menas from Alexandria, with a paralysed leg and whose story might have implied competition with the Saint Menas shrine, not far away from Menouthis. In the word-spinning of the hagiographer, this skeleton narrative was fleshed out with elements that were well known from other early Byzantine miracle collections (the miracles of Cosmas and Damian were known to Sophronius). Likewise, in the futile medical treatment that preceded the miracle or the herbal dream-recipes of the saints, Sophronius's creative imagination provided the stories with detours that can be only loosely connected to the plot. In this way, in MCJ7, he lingers on the theme of how the lame Menas had previously been swift-legged as a goat in the meadow, a quality he shared with Asael in the Bible. In a similar fashion, Sophronius continues with descriptions that were not at all essential to the stories (how the paralytic lay on his litter and was transported by others to the church, and the like).

These stories, which can be stripped down to the scheme of 'name-town-illness', are to such an extent rhetorical (with their literary and everyday commonplaces, biblical analogies, and Sophronius's moral diversions or his praises of the patient's town) that besides the incubation miracle itself, they often lack organic narrative schemes including such elements as the patient falling asleep, the dream appearance of the saints, the dialogue between the patient and the healer, conflicts between faith and doubt, as well as the circumstances under which recovery was experienced.

In the first miracle of the corpus (MCJ1), the text describes how Sophronius's sources are layered on top of each other, and the existence of a votive inscription as a source can be reasonably supposed. The basic details are these: Ammonius, *octaviarius* (collector of the eighth part tax) from Alexandria, with scrofula on his throat; this is data that can safely come from the votive inscription. Yet the remedy, the poultice prepared from bread mixed with holy wax, and the way the patient obtained his cure must have been difficult to squeeze

---

47 Dorati, 'Funzioni e motivi', p. 92, n. 13. Cf. also Festugière, 'Les Proscynemes de Philiae' — the word literally means 'act of worship', but here the testimony, the memorial to the act of worship; Dorati further mentions that it is possible to connect to these *proskynemata*, even if just in passing, those temple and magical papyri 'which render the formulae and the procedure that are to be used within the practices related to incubation'. For incubation examples of these memorial wall-inscriptions, see Dorati's same note.

into the terse few words of an inscription. Sophronius also records that the patient had sixty-seven scrofulae, as counted not only by the witnesses to the miracle, but also as they were collected after they had fallen down from the sick man's throat and the church servants suspended them in the church for a few days in honour of the saints. Sophronius thus probably had at his disposal a considerable body of oral material as well, either from the priests or the church personnel themselves, or from their successors. From them, he could have obtained information that this Ammonius was an arrogant individual (a detail we would hardly be likely to read in the patient's own version), that Ammonius had to obtain spiritual purification through repentance, and that becoming humble was a condition of his recovery. However, his haughtiness broke through afresh and so he relapsed into his illness, for which the saints gave him a new prescription of humbleness: namely, that he was to carry water for the other patients. This sort of service, affecting all the church community, probably remained as a vivid memory in the sanctuary. This last example raises questions that remain valid for the overall issue of votives, such as their social implications, their relation to literacy, or on the more practical side, how they were stored, and whether we can speak of some kind of archives in the church.

Objects with the Healing Saints' Names and Images

Before turning to the miracle stories with images, where images were used to enhance the saints' miraculous healing power, we may first think about the art objects, amulets, or medical tools bearing the name or image of doctor-saints, which served to establish a link between the function of the object and the thaumaturgic capacities of the healers.[48] An example connected with Cosmas and Damian is a seventh-century gold and niello box housed in the British Museum that bears an inscription of these saints' names. Gary Vikan called it an 'amuletic pill box' and described it in the following way:

> octagonal in outline, and bears on its obverse two scenes from the Palestinian christological cycle: the Nativity and the Adoration of the Magi. The back side shows a cross-on-steps whose arms terminate in what are probably the letters of a magical number, name, or phrase; around its circumference are the words: 'Secure deliverance and aversion [from] all evil', while into the edge of its octagon is inscribed: 'of Sts. Cosmas and Damian'. That these famous holy doctors are named leaves little doubt that this was a medical amulet — i.e. that the 'evil' from which its wearer should be delivered was first and foremost that of ill health.[49]

---

48 Cf. with many images Schlumberger, 'Amulettes byzantines anciens à combattre les maléfices et maladies'.
49 Vikan, 'Art, Medicine and Magic', p. 84.

Vikan also sustained that 'the power for deliverance came from the locket's very shape, from its imagery and from its words, but more than any of these, it must have come from that sanctified bit of material, "of Sts. Cosmas and Damian" that this capsule once contained'.[50] He assumed that the locket held some of the saints' customary all-purpose healing wax, which in this way became a *eulogia*. I would rather suggest that *any* material (ritual, magical, or actually medicinal) was rendered more effective by the saints' names inscribed on the container of the material, regardless of its content. An antique example for a similar context is a *cylix* bearing a dedication to Asclepius, found during excavations at Scornavacche in Sicily. Its words suggest that it contained the balm used in the cure and was left as a thanksgiving offering to the god.[51]

Another piece of art connected to our doctor-saints reveals how help was intended to be secured by way of a double invocation, one of a general nature, and the other more direct, with its addressees specifying the focus of the request, namely bodily help. A bronze cross from the eastern Mediterranean, held in the Metropolitan Museum and probably dating to the sixth/seventh century AD, has the images of Mary with the child Christ, Peter and Paul, and Cosmas and Damian, from top to bottom on its four arms, with St Stephen in the centre holding a censer and an incense box. It has an inscription on the horizontal cross arm, 'Christ, help [me]'; on the lower arm, as if in a concentrically narrowing circle, the invocation reads: 'Saint Cosmas and Damian, grant [me] your blessing'.[52] Medical tools were often decorated with the name or images of Cosmas and Damian.

Closer to what Vikan called 'invocational votives' was an important group of holy objects in the field of ritual healing that were associated primarily but not exclusively with living saints such as the Stylites, although they can also be found in our rather a-historic incubation-miracle records as well. These vary from elaborate tokens with images on them to the earth or clay surrounding the saint's dwelling. Lamp oil or candle wax, burnt by the saint's relics or in the saint's name, often had a similar function. These pieces, in Vikan's words 'of portable, palpable sanctity', were often situated at the intersection of the magical and religious; they were used as *prophylacteria*, empowered by the saints' name or by his image on it. At the turn of the fourth to fifth centuries AD, iconical representations could be endowed with and transmit magical-miraculous powers, for example, in connection with a thaumaturgical plant growing near an image of Christ.[53] The coins and ampullae bearing the images of saints, such as the ones that are well known from the cult places

---

50 Vikan, 'Art, Medicine and Magic', p. 84; Vikan's further examples, which I shall refer to, may corroborate this thesis, but as we do not know the real content, it is pointless to divide sharply between the possibilities.
51 Girone, *Iamata*, p. 37.
52 Vikan, 'Art, Medicine and Magic', pp. 84–85, and fig. 28.
53 Eusebius, *Historia Ecclesiastica*, VII. 18. 2; cf. also Kitzinger, 'The Cult of Images in the Age before the Iconoclasm', p. 94.

of Saint Symeon or Saint Menas, played an enormous role in affirming the miracle-working aspect of images, and the overlap between the depicted figure and the saint's power. Such healing icons, endowed with miraculous power by their contact with or representation of the saint, were far too important to be regarded as mere pilgrim-souvenirs.[54]

Images and Art Objects in the Miracle Stories: Their Role in Healing and in the Narrative

In all its forms, miraculous healing offers a rich body of material for the study of the role that images played in the thaumaturgic process or in the recognition of the miracle.[55] My intention cannot be further from entering into the debates (both Byzantine and contemporary) on the veneration of icons, iconoclasm, and the cultural and religious significance of the public use of icons.[56] Instead, I focus on the role that images played during the process of miraculous healing, both in the ritual itself and within the miracles stories that recorded the events. In some cases, we are dealing with actual icons that were put on display inside the church. In other cases, real or imaginary icons appear in the patients' dreams, while on other occasions we encounter images that depict the miracle and became a testimony together and within the story, while elsewhere the inclusion of an image into the miracle account can also be fictional and thus function as a narrative tool.

The role of images primarily manifested itself in connection with three central issues:

1. Images can be used to ensure the healers' miraculous presence: A true representation of the healer (i.e. his presence) not only heightened the miracle but also widened the range of the healer's thaumaturgic activity.

---

54 For more on the cult image and votive image, see Belting, *Likeness and Presence*, pp. 82–87.
55 The literature, both ancient and modern, on the topic is vast; I focus on examples concerning images and healing miracles. As a starting point, see Kitzinger, 'The Cult of Images in the Age before the Iconoclasm'; Maguire, 'Magic and Christian Image'; Speck, 'Wunderheilige und Bilder'; on the connection between iconoclasm and miracles, cf. Kaplan, 'Le miracle est-il nécessaire au saint byzantin?', pp. 170–71; with Coptic examples, see also the rich study of Heijer, 'Miraculous Icons and their Historical Background'; a more specific research direction is using hagiographic texts as sources on art objects: Kazhdan and Maguire, 'Byzantine Hagiographical Texts as Sources on Art'.
56 A condensed overview of the chief issues and bibliography can be found in Belting, *Likeness and Presence*, ch. 8; some important works from the overwhelming literature: Grabar, *L'iconoclasm byzantine*; Bryer and Herrin, eds, *Iconoclasm*; Barber, *Figure and Likeness*; Cormack, *Writing in Gold*; sources: Mango, *The Art of the Byzantine Empire*, pp. 149ff; on theological aspects, see Beck, *Kirche und theologische Literatur im byzantinischen Reich*, pp. 296–320; Barnard, *The Graeco-Roman and Oriental Background of the Iconoclastic Controversy*; Cameron, 'Images of Authority'; and Cameron, 'The Theotokos in Sixth-Century Constantinople'.

As the following examples demonstrate, images in healing could act in several ways, not only as figurative representations of the healer, but through the image-bearing material it could sometimes even become the means of the cure.

2. Images could play an important role in the narrative of healing, either within the miraculous event (e.g. the healer coming down from a picture), or as a possible record of the miracle (painting made as an *ex voto*) and, in some cases, as reference point for the written composition (miracle scenes depicted in the sanctuary, visible in the hagiographer's times).

3. Images could be key to recognition and identification. The further importance of the visual representation of the healer lay in the visual character of the ritual practice itself, that is, the dream-medium. In the incubation ritual, the visual representation of the healer was instrumental because *seeing* his figure was already a miracle in itself. In order to make the figure of the healer recognizable, it seems to have been equally important to see their images either before the miracle as a preparatory tool or after the appearance, as confirmation or identification.[57]

These issues are often present together in our miracles involving images; hence instead of sticking separately to these aspects, I am going to analyse a few miracle narratives that best represent these issues and highlight how they achieve their functions.

From a narrative point of view, icons could play a great variety of roles in the formation of the miracle stories, just as in effecting the cure.[58] Images in healing miracles often serve to widen the range of the saint's action. Images could be used as tools to identify the healer that was seen in the dream, similar to the use of icons as *prophylacteria*. Instances where they are used as the actual means of the cure are also well represented in the incubation miracles. When seen first in a dream or when the saint came deliberately in disguise, a recognition scene had to follow. These recognition scenes usually took three forms.

1. The saints could declare who they really were (e.g. KDM9).

2. The experience of the miracle verified their identity (a very common ending).

3. The patient compared the dream-figure to the depiction of the saints. Saints who appear in this manner allowed the image to perform as a separate narrative unit in the story, inserting a phase between the miracle and the recognition of the miracle-workers. It was quite common, as is evident in

---

57 On the topos of recognition, see Dagron, 'Holy Images and Likeness', pp. 30–31; on images and dreams pp. 32–33.
58 For further examples, outside the healing context, see Hahn, 'Picturing the Text'.

the following example, that the image-bearing object was itself the means of the cure.⁵⁹

Sergius, an elderly guard of a granary, prays to Artemius to cure his hernia, starting with an apology for his immobility and an excuse for his inability to go himself to incubate in the sanctuary:

> 'For you know both that I am an old man and that I cannot leave the granary and wait upon you. For if I leave it, they will employ another and I will be deprived of both my position and my livelihood, unable to do even this job.' These and similar things he would say whenever he went to pray to the saint. While he was sleeping at the granary, the saint appeared to him one night. The old man seemed to see the Administrator of the Granaries. And the saint approached him and said: 'You sleep a great deal and are neglecting the granary. Look, pay attention, lest what is here be stolen.' Giving him a gold coin, he said: 'Take this that you may drink.' In fact it was a salve. After Sergius woke up, he was pleased with the gift of the coin. For while still drowsy with sleep, he believed he actually held the gold coin. But when he opened his palm and fingers and found that he possessed a wax seal bearing an image of the saint, coming to his senses, he recognized the miracle that was worked upon him and that St Artemius was the one who had appeared to him. Immediately softening the seal, he anointed his genitals and as soon as the softened wax of the seal touched him, instantly he became healthy and glorified God and the holy martyr. (MA16)

It is likely that this kind of wax piece with the saint's image had been made in bulk in the cult of Artemius.⁶⁰ To confirm this hypothesis, we can turn to the well-known custom of these image-bearing tokens at the cult sites of the Stylites, or the fifth-century miracles of Saint Theodore,⁶¹ and to confirm the piece of wax, a similar one was given to the dreaming patient in the miracles of Cosmas and Damian (KDM22).

In addition to widening the saints' thaumaturgic sphere, the image could serve as a point of departure for the miraculous event or the meeting with the saints. Likewise, it could also become the means of deliverance, in a different way than my above quote, where it was melted and swallowed or applied directly on the body. In order to examine how the image could become a catalyst for the miracle, as if they were the saints' direct agents, the best example is offered by an often-quoted miracle of Saints Cosmas and Damian.

---

59 A thorough analysis of image-bearing tokens and the textual records of the same healing cult made in connection to Saint Symeon Stylite the Younger is provided by Vikan, 'Art, Medicine and Magic', pp. 73–75.
60 Cf. Déroche, 'Vraiment anargyres?', p. 157, who attributes this initial hypothesis to Lennart Rydén.
61 *AASS*, November 4, 69, where it is mentioned a 'small seal (*sphragis*) made of wax'.

KDM13 tells the story of Constantinos, a soldier who was a devotee of the saints. He served in Laodicea, where he was married. Since Constantinos lived far from Constantinople, he kept a small, painted image of the saints with him. His wife eventually developed an abscess on her jawbone. Constantinos lamented that they lived too distant from the capital and thus could not visit the church of Cosmas and Damian for the healing wax. His devotion to the saints was embraced by his wife who listened eagerly to the stories of speedy miracle cures performed by the saints, and she wished to approach them herself. When she did so, their image and the testimony of her husband's worship was forgotten. The following night, the saints appeared to the woman in dream 'in their likeness as they are represented' and reassured her about their presence and help. Without recognizing the saints, she told the dream to her husband and gave a detailed description of the figures she had seen. Her husband recalled the attributes of the saints, and their icon that he had with him suddenly came to his mind; by bringing it forth, the wife confirmed the saints' identity on the basis of the painting. After healing her, as a special reward for their faith, the saints announced in another dream that she would find a piece of wax under her pillow in order to ensure that she would never become ill again.

The story has some features that are worth considering in the wider context of icon worship as well: it shows an image of the saints transformed in front of our eyes. This reflects a larger body of narratives in which a painted artwork or a memorial of one's devotion to these particular saints visually transforms into an object of veneration. It also highlights the interconnectedness of the icon in the household, in the private sphere, and its relation to the church space, recalling the image of the saints as depicted in the church and bringing the ritual usually practised in the church into the home. The interplay between the private and public place of worship is also articulated by attributing these spheres to a woman and a man and by setting the private devotion in the realm of the family home, linked to a female protagonist.[62] Furthermore, here the icon was the means of cure to such an extent that when the miracle was quoted during the Second Council of Nicaea in 787, the comment upon it was, 'this clearly shows that it was through their icons that they appeared to the woman and healed her'.[63] On the other hand, the painted image was instrumental to the recognition of the saints, confirming a posteriori their identity.[64] However, the worshipper most often sees the image first, and that

---

[62] On the role of private icons and the inclusion of women in the miracle stories with images who epitomize the private sphere, see Cameron, 'The Language of Images', p. 19, also her *Christianity and the Rhetoric of Empire*, pp. 201–03.

[63] Mansi, *Sacrorum Conciliorum Nova et Amplissima Collectio*, XIII, cols 64–65; ref. in Dagron, 'Holy Images and Likeness', p. 31; the original text can be read online: <http://patristica.net/mansi>.

[64] Cf. also the examples of portraits of saints painted after the saint's appearance in dream: Dagron, 'Rêver de Dieu et parler de soi', p. 42, n. 23.

works in his or her own imagination and renders the healer recognizable when they appear in a vision or dream.

In this case, the miracle attested to the cultic usefulness of the image. It served as proof to all the other miracles: those recounted by the husband within the story and those that occurred in the church, and thus to the miracle collection itself. More importantly, the icon physically made the saints present, so that Ernst Kitzinger could write:

> The tale stands out among a host of similar ones by the fact that the beneficiaries not only make no effort, by prayer or action, to secure divine assistance through the icon but are not even aware of the presence of the icon, at least when it first begins to operate on their behalf. The story dramatizes the objective power of the icon, which is shown to be effective regardless of the faithful's consciousness. Its key theme, however, is the actual presence of the saints in the image.[65]

As I interpret it, the first dream-appearance of the saints was initiated by the husband's recollection of them: of their miraculous curative power and their cult place that was so familiar to him through the miraculous stories associated with them. The self-same miracle was recorded in the London Codex as well (CL25), and it is worth pointing out the differences between the two narratives. In the KDM version, the husband wished to be in Constantinople so that he could take his wife to the church of the saints in order to practice incubation there. In the London Codex, however, Constantinople is not even mentioned, and the husband wishes to have with him the image of the saints that, he was convinced, would suffice for the cure. Afterwards, the wife began to invoke the saints:

> Yet the heart of her husband was even more anxious for her. He himself, in accordance to his custom of carrying the image of the saints, forgot about it and addressed his wife in this way: 'What shall I do with you, woman? *If now I had brought with me the image of the saints or the wax from their church, if you beseeched them, and anointed yourself with the wax, you would be healed.*' On hearing these words, the woman started praying to them, saying: 'Servants of Christ, Cosmas and Damian, the doctors of incurable diseases, deem me worthy of finding a cure from you, and deign me soon your holy sanctuary.' (my italics)

Following the first dream appearance,

> awakening from her dream, she told in detail what she had heard from the saint in her dream, and *asked him* [her husband] *to bring her their image.* For meanwhile the husband recalled that the image was with him. He

---

[65] Kitzinger, 'The Cult of Images in the Age before the Iconoclasm', p. 148.

showed the image of the saints then, and the woman cried out of joy that they were indeed those whom she saw in the dream. (my italics)

I would like to compare this miracle to a non-incubation miracle story that involves Saints Cosmas and Damian and their image (which I will later analyse in detail in Chapter 9). It comes from the *Vita* of Theodore of Sykeon and describes the helping presence of the icon of Cosmas and Damian, its equivalence with the saints' power, and its role in calling forth the dream appearance:[66] Theodore was gravely ill and retired to his room. Above his bed, he had long kept an image of Saints Cosmas and Damian, a testimony of his continuous devotion towards them. When Theodore fell asleep, the saints appeared in his dream in the manner that they were depicted on the icon and behaved in a way familiar to their incubation miracles. They acted as visiting doctors, taking Theodore's pulse and discussing between themselves what they needed to do. The mere presence of the icon is of interest here because Theodore neither addressed the saints nor prayed to the image. The picture watched over Theodore and advanced the healers' appearance. My hypothesis is that this miracle from Theodore's *Vita* attests that, in connection with widely known incubation healers such as Cosmas and Damian, the narrative pattern describing their healing was incorporated into non-incubation hagiography. The dynamics of telling the miracle were identical to those found in the narratives of incubation miracles.

This last miracle leads us to the theme of recognition and the healers' visual attributes in dream appearances. The role of the cult-image cannot be overestimated in the practice of incubation. Van Straten wrote of Asclepius's cult statue: 'Sometimes the god would go on even further in assimilating his appearance to the image his devotees knew best, and appear in the shape of the statue.'[67] This is true for Christian dream-healers as well. The healer was not merely recognized by his close resemblance to their appearance in the dream; recognition drew on an essential aspect of ancient dream-interpretation. One of the criteria for differentiating between the true and false dreams was the extent to which the healers' representation in the dream was in accordance with their customary attire. Hence, a figure clearly appearing with his or her own attributes was more believable and fortunate, while 'gods appearing in a wrong costume may easily lie', as C. A. Meier has put it. Meier interpreted this insistence on the real form of things as a reminiscence of a totemistic attitude.[68] What was seen before, during, and after the dream was necessarily a composite representation of the visual experiences of the dreamer. These images built

---

66 *Life of Theodore of Sykeon*, ch. 39, in *Three Byzantine Saints*, ed. and trans. by Dawes and Baynes.
67 Van Straten, 'Daikrates' Dream', p. 15; cf. Asclepius's statue appearing in dream to Aelius Aristides, that of Asclepius to Domninus, or Pindar's vision *Pythicae* III; also Weinreich, *Antike Heilungswunder*, pp. 137–40, and Brillante, 'Metamorfosi di un'immagine'.
68 Meier, 'The Dream in Ancient Greece', p. 311.

upon each other. This is precisely because the medium of the ritual experience, the dream, could only be perceived in a visual way, as an image:

> A vision of the saint was instrumental to the miraculous cure, and [...] this vision might be induced by a man-made representation of the saint. As incubation was instrumental to healing [...] so a dream vision was instrumental to successful incubation. And the fact that the healing saint is said to appear 'in his customary manner' strongly suggests that representations of the saint (whether on tokens, or as icons or murals) were instrumental to the evocation and confirmation of that vision.[69]

This meant no novelty in comparison to the ancient Greek practice. Christian dream-healers also appeared in dreams as they were represented in their sanctuary, just like Asclepius and Isis. The face-to-face encounter with the deity in the cult of Asclepius was quintessential to the cure, often identical with the cure itself. As Asclepius had to be recognized, his familiar statue in the shrine was in the same way a preparation for the incubation experience, just as were the narratives, the miracles inscribed on stelai, and the *ex votos*. Knowing Asclepius's appearance enabled the dreamer to recognize (and of course, to visualize) him in his usual form. In addition, Asclepius hardly ever came in disguise, unless he arrived in one of his well-known substitute forms: a beautiful young boy, a sacred serpent, or a sacred dog.

The appearance of the Christian healers was more complex. They were not healing deities in their own right but transmitted the miraculous power of Christ, so the mere sight of them did not create a cultic experience as with the Greek deities. They often came in disguise, and hence their image and attributes in the stories receive more emphasis.

The very visualization of the healer in the dream could give insight into the illness-related anxieties of the dreamer. When visiting patients who were fearful of their intervention, the saints often disguised themselves as a family member or the patient's doctor in order to earn their patient's trust (Artemius as the patient's father, MA1; a close friend, MA31). In KDM29, we read about a dreaming husband seeing Cosmas and Damian as the doctors of his ill wife. In another source, we see the panic of the sick person requiring an operation who saw Saint Artemius in the likeness of a butcher with butcher's tools (MA25) or read Cosmas and Damian described as performing surgery with a huge sword instead of a scalpel (KDM1). Investigation into the guises of the healer could shed light on social attitudes as well. The saint could be pictured as one of low rank (a monk, a boy bath attendant, a patient suffering on the latrine) or high up on the social hierarchy (Artemius as a palace nobleman[70]), or a somewhat awe-inspiring stranger (Artemius as the Persian doctor, MA23).

---

69   Vikan, 'Art, Medicine and Magic', p. 73, n. 44; see also Delehaye, 'Les recueils antiques', p. 16, and Kötting, *Peregrinatio religiosa*, pp. 217–19.
70   MA11, 29, 37, 39.

Additionally, the healer could also be imagined quite naturally as the dreamer's immediate superior: the Administrator of the Granaries to a granary-guard (MA16) or a sea captain to a sailor (MA27). When appearing in the likeness of a family member or a close friend, the saint's image reflected the attitude of people whom they consulted about their troubles.

In the stories, the presence of the pictorial representation of the saints shares a particular feature of miraculous healing: they reinforce the healers' ability to operate at a distance. It demonstrates the way these saints operated outside their church when the patient was unable to grasp their image there. The presence of an icon in the stories emphatically widened the geography of miraculous operation.

A more direct relationship can be detected with celebrated icons. It was very likely that the represented figures generated miracle stories, and thus it is possible to speak more confidently about pictorial representation as a source for the textual record. An extreme example is the Passion of Saint Eleutherius, which draws heavily on the pictorial representations in the saint's sanctuary; hence, the scene when the saint is preaching to the animals gained an additional dimension: the beasts, unable to express themselves in songs or in prayer, raise their right paws as if to praise God. 'It seems clear that he [the hagiographer] has seen animals walking in line in mosaic', observed H. Delehaye.[71]

The miracle that I examine below illustrates the way that the depicted figures shaped the cultic experience and the dream-content itself. In KDM30, a patient suffering from a fistula turned to the incubation place of Cosmas and Damian, following a dream invitation extended by the saints. While waiting for the dream visit of the saints, he walked around the church one day and discovered a painting showing Christ and Mary, Cosmas and Damian, and a certain Leontinus, probably the donor of the icon — which means that it was in all likelihood a seated Virgin with the child Christ.[72] This seems to be a pictorial *ex voto* incorporated into the narrative text. Festugière called attention to the hagiographer's expression 'μέχρι τοῦ παρόντος', 'till today', referring to the fact or creating the impression that the picture was still in place at the time that the miracle was recorded (or told). The patient fervently prayed to the image and accordingly, the following night, experienced the sought-after visitation. Not only did the saints appear, but the Virgin was also among them (presumably just as in the icon). She ordered Cosmas and Damian to heal the man quickly (as duly happened afterwards). The representation of Mary on the picture naturally called forth her presence in the dream and her active role in the course of events. Rather cautiously (as the exact date of the miracle is not known) I would also risk suggesting that her appearance implied an emphasis on her role as *Theotokos* (note that Christ is not the main character, although he is present) and as a higher authority for

---

71 Cf. Delehaye, *The Legends of the Saints*, p. 63.
72 Cf. *Sainte Thècle, Saints Côme et Damien*, ed. and trans. by Festugière, p. 170.

the occupants of the cult place. The ending of the narrative deserves further attention. In one manuscript version, the miracle itself was commemorated in an *ex voto*, and similar to the case of the intervening icon in the story, the hagiographer here also mentioned the precise location, which more than likely was the source of the narrative itself, as his last remark suggests: 'γέγραπται δὲ ταῦτα ἐν τῷ οἴκῳ τῶν ἁγίων ἐν τῇ ἐξευωνύμῳ στοᾷ ἐπάνωθεν τῆς εἰσόδου τοῦ διακονικοῦ, καὶ ἔστιν ἀκριβέστερον ἐν τῇ γραφῇ κατανοῆσαι' (and these things are written in the house of the saints in the left collonade above the entrance of the deacon, and it is more accurate to understand in a written form).[73] Interestingly enough, this formulaic ending figures at the end of another miracle, in the same alternative codex, concluding the miracle with the lamb (KDM3). By all means, we could not know if there were such actual representations, inscribed or painted onto the church wall in these particular cases, but having such a concluding sentence, almost a formula, shows that for the hagiographer and for his audience it was a well-known practice.

In a similar vein, the image of Christ found its way into the narrative in MCJ36. The consciously artistic hagiographer seemingly wanted to attribute special importance to the miracle, judging by the extraordinary length of the story as well as its position within the miracle collection. MCJ36 was placed in the middle of the corpus, and what is more, it represented an opening to a new section of the collection, one which, after the thirty-five miracles that happened to the Alexandrians, comprised the stories of the Egyptian and Libyan patients.

The story is as follows: The heretic patient, Theodoros, underwent a long and complicated sequence of incubations and various attempts from the saints to convert him. A few days later, Theodoros, still unwilling to convert to Chalcedonian orthodoxy, was incubated again. This time, he dreamed of the Saints Cyrus and John, who bade him to follow them. The patient duly went after them until all three arrived at a beautiful, tall church. Upon entering it, they came before a huge icon: in the centre of the picture there was a colourful Christ who was flanked on his left by Mary (*tén Theotokon kai Aeiparthenon*) and on his right by John the Baptist. These figures were complemented by some of the apostles and the collegium of martyrs.[74] The saints adored the Lord by genuflecting and beseeched him to secure the recovery of their patient. Yet Christ did not give a nod of approval, so the saints sadly gave up

---

73 *Sainte Thècle, Saints Côme et Damien*, ed. and trans. by Festugière, p. 103, n. 12 and p. 172, n. 9; although the text says *graphé* and *gegraptai*, the French translation renders it as a painting: 'Ce miracle a été peint dans l'église des saints, dans la colonnade de gauche, au-dessus de l'entrée du diakonikon. Et il est possible de prendre une vue plus exacte de la chose sur cette peinture.'

74 On this so-called *Déesis* iconography and this picture being one of the earliest of it, see Kantorowicz, *Laudes Regiae*, pp. 48–53, esp. n. 129; Kitzinger, 'The Cult of Images in the Age before the Iconoclasm'; and Velmans, 'L'image de la Déisis dans les églises de Géorgie', esp. p. 52.

their intercession and turned to the patient standing next to the icon: 'Do you see that the Lord does not wish to give you health'; the answer, thus, was expected from the nod of the depicted figure of Christ. After some time had passed, they repeated their prayer in front of the icon, again to no avail. But the third time, Christ spoke to them from the painting:[75] 'Give it to him!' The saints then gladly told him that he could be healed and in the following way: he would go to Alexandria, where, in the church called Tetrapylos, he had to fast and then practise incubation. Moreover, he was instructed to rub himself with oil from the lamp that burned before the image of Christ in that church.

In the miracle narrative, the Christ-icon is introduced as part of a dream, regardless of whether such a picture was actually present in the church or not (see below). The iconographic representation of the image, by giving the visual priority to Mary the God-bearer (*Theotokos*), emphasized the theological dogma for the patient as well (who was a follower of Julian of Halicarnassus). The visual message of the invoked image symbolically represented the condition of the cure: the patient's conversion to orthodoxy. On the other hand, the icon seen in the dream formed a link to a real icon, the Christ-image in the Alexandrian church, which eventually became the means of the cure. In this context, an explanatory hypothesis arises: in the incubation practised by the patient, the sacrality of the ritual sleep was derived from the image rather than the sanctuary.[76]

Are we dealing here with a fictitious icon? Kitzinger maintained that the icon in the story might have been a later interpolation:

> Neither the large composition with Christ and the Saints nor the image of Christ in the Tetrapylon can be assumed with certainty to have figured in the original version of the story, since just before the first of these pictures is introduced the narrative changes abruptly from the third to the first person. There is at least a suspicion that originally the story involved no

---

75 Another Byzantine example for a speaking icon of Christ seen in a dream is in Theodosius, *Chronographia*, ed. by Tafel, pp. 97–98: 'Theodosius of Melitene records an incident in which the Emperor Maurice dreamt that he saw a large group of people standing before the icon of Christ on the Chalke Gate of the Palace. Suddenly a voice was heard from the icon saying: "Bring Maurice to me." When the Emperor appeared before the icon, the Saviour spoke and said: "When, O Maurice, do you desire that I punish you? Here or in the future age?" The Emperor asked to be allowed to expiate his sins in this world, and so Christ ordered that he and his entire family be turned over to the usurper Phocas.' Quoted in Magoulias, 'The Lives of the Saints as Sources of Data for the History of Magic', p. 262.

76 Sansterre, 'Apparitions et miracles à Menouthis', pp. 76–77. G. Dagron considers incubation to have been so common that it could be practised at any sacred place, sanctified by, for example, the presence of a holy image. Incubation was certainly not practised only at the celebrated cult sites of Thecla, Cosmas and Damian, or Cyrus and John, but, as he writes, 'dans toute église ou martyrium toute demeure laïque où une simple icône est gage d'une présence sacrée' (Dagron, 'Rêver de Dieu et parler de soi', p. 41).

images at all. On the other hand, the grammatical inconsistency may be due simply to Sophronius's peculiar methods of composition.[77]

Kitzinger also repeated the remark of the *Patrologia Graeca*; the story was known to John of Damascus and was quoted in his *Third Oration*.[78] The miracle was also told at the Second Nicaean Council of 787; hence, it can date no later than the early years of Iconoclasm. Sophronius explicitly says that the protagonist of the miracle became the subdeacon of the church, and at the time of his stay in the Menouthis (610–614), he was still the subdeacon; in this case, he might have been his own personal source of information.

In this miracle narrative, the (perhaps) fictitious icon seen in the dream directed the viewer to an existing icon, while in the London Codex (CL15), a miracle bore testimony to the animation of an image present in the church, which (in a very strange way) became the vehicle of the cure. The miracle speaks about a woman with dropsy who spent more than four months in the church of Cosmas and Damian waiting for her recovery:

> According to the Roman calendar, on the first day of July, on the feast day of the saints, there arrived at the church of God a priest and he asked a serving woman about where the woman with dropsy was lying. She answered: 'Today I saw in a dream, that one of the two [saints] descended from the icon set up opposite to the entrance and with the images of Cosmas and Damian carved on either side of it, with the Virgin Mother of God between them, and went to the miserable woman. He slipped his hand under the woman's clothes and touched her stomach and belly. And I forgot how he came down from the image and I took him for a monk or a deacon and I thought that he put his hand on the sick woman with some ugly intention and told him: 'You are not acting nicely with such behaviour, touching like this the nakedness of this sick woman.'

But the saint reassured her that, within eleven days, the dropsy would gradually withdraw. By the last day (the feast day of Saint Euphemia), the woman would be healed; and this was the way it happened. What gives the miracle its special quality is not just the overcrowding of visual and narrative layers (it was the church servant who saw the dream, not the incubant). She saw the picture which could be seen by everybody in the church; however, she did not tell her dream to the patients, which is usual in the incubation narratives, but to a third party, a priest (we do not know in what way he became involved in these events). However, it is especially interesting how the picture occupies the entire story. It is not the patient who is in the centre of the narrative, and strangely the saints must share the protagonist role with Mary on the icon. The image upsets the narrative.

---

77 Kitzinger, 'The Cult of Images in the Age before the Iconoclasm', pp. 106–07, n. 86.
78 PG, 94, cols 1413 ff.

The theological aspect of the wonder-working image is extolled by another celebrated miracle of Cosmas and Damian (KDM15), which was also cited in the Iconoclast debate at the 787 council in Nicaea, in which story a woman is cured by the plasters scratched from the wall-painting of the saints. Whereas in the miracle above, we saw how the image could shape the story, here we have a model for how the narrative could shape the pictorial content. The painting in the house of the patient could be nothing else but the representation of the saints. In her final despair, a woman with colic scraped plaster off the picture of the saints painted on her walls, and dissolving it with some water, drank it and recovered in an instant. Analysing this miracle, Kitzinger speaks about the complete identification of picture and prototype.[79] A Byzantine source from the same period of the 787 council attests that Iconoclasts turned not only against the miraculous icons, but in the same vein, it forbade the use of the *hagiasmata*, in this case, holy (healing) water.[80]

In the miracle stories above, two paradigms can be observed in the curative use of images representing the miraculous healer:

1. The icon stands entirely for the healer himself. Even within this category, we need to make a crucial distinction between saints presumed to be long dead (like Saints Cosmas and Damian coming down from their image to Saint Theodore[81]) and saints who were still alive. This distinction is important for the latter category because their portraits made them present at one place, while they could be physically present elsewhere. An example is the case of Symeon Stylite the Younger, where a woman calls for the saint's image instead of himself: 'If only I see your image, I will be saved.'[82] In another occasion, Symeon himself says to a man: 'When you regard the imprint of our image, it is us that you will see.'[83] When the image stands for the saint, the patient could be healed without being at the cult place.

2. In the other paradigm, the key element of the cure was an image inside the church through which the saints acted out their wonder-working (either exclusively via the icon as in CL15, or mediating the further cure by appearing in the patient's dream in the form of an icon as in MCJ36 or

---

79 Kitzinger, 'The Cult of Images in the Age before the Iconoclasm', p. 148, see also p. 101, p. 107.
80 The source is a sermon attributed to Constantinos of Tios, attacking the iconoclast emperor Constantine V: 'Not only did he extend his wickedness against the holy icons, but also […] he set at naught the hagiasmata that flowed on account of God's providence towards men, and he called those who made use of them worshippers of water, thus taking the glory away from the intercession of saints, even renouncing the help and intercession of Mary, the all-holy Mother of God.' The Greek text in Halkin, ed. *Euphémie de Chalcédonié: Légendes byzantines*, p. 96; cf. also Maguire, 'Magic and Christian Image', p. 66, who discusses this KDM miracle as well.
81 *Life of Theodore of Sykeon*, ch. 39.
82 *Life of Symeon the Younger*, ch. 118.
83 *Life of Symeon the Younger*, ch. 231.

KDM30). In contrast to this double model for the healing image (inside and outside the sanctuary), Gary Vikan outlined how the textual and pictorial narratives complemented each other in the cult of living saints (his example being Symeon Stylite the Younger). He observed that 'there is not one miracle in the entire *Vita* of the saint where a medicinal eulogia is described as being used in the shrine itself; rather, they were given out to accomplish their cures' somewhere else.[84] In his analysis, the role of the eulogies (pictorial and non-pictorial) applied in ritual healing was developed in such a way that they (regardless of whether they bore the image of the healer or not) served primarily as instruments for long-distance miracles, cures far away from the sacred place.

Our incubation saints did not necessarily work in such a mutually exclusive way. Eulogies are also 'portable sanctities', applicable even at a far distance from the saint, although they could be used in their church as well, often at the initiative of the saints. The rarity of long-distance healing in incubation hagiography indicates that the cult site itself, the very place, was more important than the person of the healer. A further example would also confirm this aspect of incubation (MA11): The mother of a herniated child could not leave her work in the bath to go incubate for the help of Saint Artemius, so she prepared at her dwelling what was a customary offering in the church of the Forerunner before incubation; she lit a votive lamp in the name of Artemius and thus rendered her own place suitable for the saint's dream appearance. In a dream, Artemius came to her in his unmistakeable form and promised (and undertook as well) the recovery of the child.

Artemius's customary lamp was often offered as a votive gift after the cure. Here it sufficed for inducing the saint's visit in the same way as an invocational image. Nevertheless, images also served as commemorative votives for miracles. In the miracle collections, there are pictures which recorded what happened, and this pictorial representation shaped the miracle on its way to becoming a story, reflexively impacting the hagiographer's narrative as well.

In the *Thaumata*, we encounter such a commemorative picture in the form of a large-scale wall painting: the healed man of MCJ28, the rich Nemesius, had the wall around the saints' tomb decorated with a picture representing Christ, John the Baptist, Cyrus (either the saint or the intermediary of the miracle, a lawyer called Cyrus), and himself. It is not unreasonable to suppose that such a work at such a prominent place was seen by Sophronius, who reveals that this Nemesius, the commissioner of the painting and the beneficiary of the miracle, was his source. Because of this personal closeness of the dedicator, the painting was included at the end of the miracle story, even without its direct involvement in the course of events.

---

84   Vikan, 'Art, Medicine and Magic', p. 72.

In the later part of the Cosmas and Damian collection, the same sort of iconographical testimony to the miracle was explicitly identified as the source by the thirteenth-century narrator. In this case, it was the healed woman's *peplos* (cloak), embroidered with gold and silk and representing the figures of the saints and the woman herself. The hagiographer explicitly refers to the *memorial* role of this cloak, writing that it attests to the miracle even after her death and serves as an exhortation for all those who suffer ills in their body to seek refuge from the saints.[85] This indicates that the cloak was on display (probably in the church) even after the woman's death. This miracle (KDM39) is the first of the sixth series. I believe that the image gave such importance to the narrative that the hagiographer decided to place it at the beginning of his series: 'ἄξιον δὲ τῶν ἄλλων προθεῖναι τὸ ἐν εἰκόσιν ἡμῖν ὁρώμενον', 'This [story] which is in front of me in pictures, deserves to be set as the start for the other miracles.'[86]

This remark of the hagiographer turns our attention back to a question touched upon earlier: To what extent are the images that are described in the narrative simply functioning as narrative tools? The described images could possibly be one of the many literary constructions of the hagiographer to render his story more colourful, even visually more appealing, just as it could serve as a certain proof of the existence of the icon: 'I am telling the miracle involving this and this picture in the church' — which could mean a real icon, and could also be a textual icon, created by the hagiographer. In some of the examples quoted above, when the hagiographer referred to contemporary events, their contemporary surroundings, and even expected the reader to see the picture in the church about which he was writing, there is no reason to doubt that those pictures actually existed. The involvement of icons in miracle narratives seems to be more dubious when their presence explicitly serves to convey a theological-dogmatical message, not necessarily as post facto interpolations, but as a case-in-point that the hagiographer wished to instil in the readers' minds.

To sum up the examples I have discussed above, whether textual or iconographical, it is important to underline that votives appear in the miracle narratives in various ways. Most often, these votives were commemorative objects, testimonies to the devotion of the pilgrim and to the miraculous experience itself. Alternatively, by virtue of their (symbolic or financial) value, they aimed at expressing the patient's gratitude. Occasionally, the miracle stories mention them as objects that were already present in the church. In a few cases, these were objects around which the miracles eventually evolved; thus, themselves commemorating the miracles, they became commemorated

---

85   KDM40.31–32, *St Kosmas und Damian*, ed. by Deubner, p. 199: 'καὶ μετὰ θάνατον τῷ θαύματι μαρτυρεῖ καὶ προτροπὴ τοῖς κακῶς τὸ σῶμα διακειμένοις τῆς ἐπὶ τοὺς ἁγίους καταφυγῆς γίγνεται'.
86   Prologue to the sixth series, 40–41, *St Kosmas und Damian*, ed. by Deubner, p. 198.

within the narrative itself. The miraculous story elevated these objects to the level of real or imaginary testimony. This might occur with images, as my examples have illustrated, but it could also occur with inscriptions originally not related to the miracle. Such non-miraculous ecclesiastical testimonies in the course of the miraculous events not only became the centre point of the miracle but also acquired, through the saint's intervention, a greater theological significance. This was the case, for example, with an inscription on a gilded mosaic on the wall of Thecla's church, 'proclaiming to all people the consubstantiality of the holy and sublime Trinity' (MT10). Symposius, then Arian bishop of Seleucia, had attempted to destroy it. The miracle, the accident that befell the workman who was entrusted with carrying out Symposius's order, was Thecla's protective intervention on behalf of orthodoxy. The hagiographer began with the existing inscription. Some damage caused by the attempted destruction was perhaps still visible when the hagiographer wrote about it. By mentioning the misfortune of the worker whose leg was broken as he fell down, the emphasis is on Thecla's anger at the deed. The story was enlarged into another dimension, as the originator of the act, Symposius, later converted to orthodoxy. It would not have been alien to the miracle pattern that he converted as a result of the punishment miracle. However, it seems that the memory of the events and persons was still alive during the lifetime of the hagiographer; therefore, he had to account for the time gap between the two events. He returned, however, to the inscription as the tangible testimony to his story. In attributing Symposius's later conversion to this event, the hagiographer emphasized that the Arian bishop's return to orthodoxy was expressed by his public confession of the dogma inscribed on this very mosaic.

To complement my conclusion, I should stress that votive tablets and commemorative objects played an important role in the shaping of the narratives in another sense as well. I have already mentioned that these stories served to guide the worshippers in shaping their expectations about the customary process of the incubation rites, the appearance of the healer, and how to obtain a cure.[87] Besides this psychological pre-conditioning, the text of the *ex votos* served two main functions. On the one hand, they provided direction to the pilgrims for moulding their experience into the customary pattern, while on the other hand, they served as a device for continuously teaching pilgrims (even if they were not recipients of any miracle) what miracle narratives to tell others beyond the boundaries of the precinct. This same role is emphasized for the recorded miraculous stories of the Epidaurian stelai: to promote the pilgrims to make the right choice amongst the numerous rival Asclepieia. The Italian scholar Marco Dorati wrote:

87 Cf. also Dillon, 'The Didactic Nature of the Epidaurian Iamata'.

It was not only about convincing the pilgrims already present in the temple that they made the right choice, by coming to that temple and not to any other one. Once they left Epidaurus and were back in their homeland, it also equipped them with the tools necessary to propagate the message. They could take home not only their own personal experience but a more ample 'memory' that was, so to speak, distilled through the exemplary stories which the stelai allowed them to learn.[88]

The concise texts of the votive tablets and stories of the miracle records effectively provided the worshippers with proper narrative units and with the most captivating tales about the wonders of the place.

---

88 Dorati, 'Funzioni e motivi', p. 98.

CHAPTER 5

The Oral Tradition in the Miracles

The Christian incubation collections, besides describing a specific ritual, differ in one essential point from other Christian miracle records, even those contemporary with them or written by the same hagiographer. The incubation miracles were formed around a cult, or more precisely, the cult practice of a given cult place. It is important to emphasize that I do not mean around the cult of a saint, but around the cult of incubation, with the miracles that happened and that were collected, retold, and written about at that particular cult site. The cult site often had its own cultic past, and accordingly, the stories could refer to the past or use the associations linked to this past. Those who shaped the cult (and the cult records) could wish to emphasize and use this cultic past as a contrast or comparison with the Christian present of the cult site, or they could willingly remain silent about it. Because the stories were organized around the cult, they often incorporated the earlier phases of the cult, or the memory of the preceding healer. The significance of the oral sources was derived from the central importance of place and practice. The transmission of the stories that formed, stratum by stratum, around the cult place eventually became the hagiographers' sources.

Telling miraculous stories is a form of *storytelling*. This fact leaves its mark on the storyteller, on the listener, and on the tale itself. What exactly should be understood by the telling of miracles? Its oral character also had a particular effect on the written recording of the story; according to the dynamics of the formation and transmission of the miracles, the story from time to time took shape in written records, and then what had been consigned to these records continued to be retold in an oral form. Thus, recording the story did not mean that the text became fixed. Nor were the elements of the story immutable. Just as someone wrote down the narrated story, the storyteller could draw on ready material from the circulating miracle catalogues, a raw material which they felt free to alter. The hagiographer, when he embarked on the project of recording stories, is reminiscent of Collingwood's historian in that the stories find him:

> The Greek historian cannot, like Gibbon, begin by wishing to write a great historical work and go on to ask himself what he shall write about […]. Instead of the historian choosing the subject, the subject chooses the historian; I mean that history is written only because memorable things have happened which call for a chronicler among the contemporaries of the people who have seen them.[1]

---

1 Collingwood, *The Idea of History*, p. 26, quoted, concerning Herodotus, by Hartog, *Le miroir d'Hérodote*, p. 276.

The miracles that accumulated at the cult site form the narrator's source material, and they were like an overwhelming bulk of stories from which he could choose. Thecla's hagiographer expressed this idea by saying that the miracles had invaded him; they were stories that 'wanted to come to light'.[2] The stories that accumulated around the Christian incubation saints embrace several (narrative, but occasionally also material) layers of the cult, and in some places even the pagan predecessors of the cult as well, and can be easily distinguished from other similar Christian testimonies.

In the first part of this chapter, I will try to introduce briefly the questions, methods, and results of disciplines concerned with the study of orality — approaches which have partly been applied to incubation records, but can also be applied directly or in an analogous way to the analysis of Christian dream-miracle narratives. These studies have mostly aimed at detecting the orality *behind* the written records, as identifiable sources, and at discovering traces revealing oral traditions in the composition of the text. In a further section I will be more concerned with how orality was represented (deliberately or accidentally) within the stories and incorporated into the narrative itself. In the present section, I shall examine the presence of orality within the miracle collections. On the one hand, orality lay behind the moulding of the stories into narratives. Their oral transmission is often highlighted by the explicit references of the hagiographers to the oral circumstances of their story collection. On the other hand, there are certain elements within the stories that can only be assumed to reflect probable oral sources. The same phenomenon, the telling of and listening to miracles, acquires a slightly different role in the collections when it also formed part of the narrated events. Most intriguingly, hagiographers occasionally artificially (and artfully) created the illusion of orality as an indispensable element in the miracle narrative. In this way, the hagiographer was able to bring such narrative situations to life, drawing him (and to some extent, the reader as well) into a personal closeness with the beneficiary of the miracle or with one of his or her descendants. Its purpose was not only to create an aura of authenticity, but also to create a rhythm. The storyteller had to present the miracles in sequence, and such a narrative context greatly eased his task. I would like to illustrate this phenomenon of artificially composed orality by comparing two groups of Cosmas and Damian miracles that record the same stories. In referring to artificially created orality, I do not mean that there was no oral transmission at the cult site. It is a narrative technique when the narrator starts his tale by mentioning that he had learnt of such events from the son of the healed (and so on) when, in fact, he was more likely to be working from an earlier written miracle catalogue. Afterwards, I shall discuss the communal, ritualized events of storytelling, as depicted in the miracle narratives. In the closing section, I investigate what happens to the

---

[2] MT 13.

texts when they receive their written recorded form, how the side-by-side existence of the written and oral traditions worked, and what the sources have to tell us in this regard.

The Role of Orality in the Formation and Transmission of the Incubation Stories: Methodologies

When examining the oral sources of the Epidaurian miracle stories, Lynn LiDonnici greatly relied upon the research of Milman Parry and A. B. Lord and the methods of classical philology as these relate to orality (Finnegan, Havelock, Peabody).[3] If we replace the *oral poet* and the *epic singer* with the hagiographer, and the form *poems* with miracle stories, Parry's questions and his network of connections regarding the emergence and transmission of oral texts can become a valid approach to studying the way early Christian miracle narratives were shaped.[4] The research of Milman Parry and Albert Lord focused on the formation and transmission of the Homeric epics and on their re-creation,[5] primarily through the retelling of stories during the performance itself. They focused particular attention on the phenomenon that a poetic text, rooted and surviving in orality, is not only transmitted during its performance, but at the same time is being created as well. This continuous poetic creation during the telling of the stories depended much on the talent of the singer and his poetic repertoire, but it also depended upon the circumstances of the performance on any given occasion. On the one hand, the text-creating performance feeds on a stock of formulae. On the other hand, the narrator carefully followed a narrative logic as well, maintaining the internal coherence of the order of the stories. Illustrating this natural order of things, Lord writes: 'In the case of the horse, the singer begins with the blanket under the saddle and ends with the bit in the horse's mouth. He is ready to be led forth. The descriptions are vivid because they follow the action.'[6]

---

3 Havelock, *The Muse Learns to Write*; Finnegan, *Oral Poetry*; Peabody, *The Winged Word*.
4 Parry neatly defined the aims of research on oral transmission in the following way: '(a) to what extent an oral poet who composes a new poem is dependent upon the traditional poetry as a whole for his phraseology, his scheme of composition, and the thought of his poem; (b) to what extent a poem, original or traditional, is stable in successive recitations of a given singer; (c) how a poem is changed in a given locality over a number of years; (d) how it is changed in the course of its travels from one region to another; (e) in what ways a given poem travels from one region to another, and the extent to which the poetry travels; (f) the different sources of the material from which a given heroic cycle is created; (g) the factors that determine the creation, growth, and decline of a heroic cycle; (h) the relation of the events of an historical cycle to the actual events; and so on and so on'. Parry, 'Project for a Study of Jugoslavian Popular Oral Poetry' (typewritten reports, quoted in the Introduction to the second edition of Lord, *The Singer of Tales*, p. ix).
5 Lord, *The Singer of Tales*.
6 Lord, *The Singer of Tales*, p. 92.

In the early Christian stories of miraculous cures, one finds the same kind of narrative logic. Invariably, the story of the miraculous cures followed a certain 'obligatory' and natural order, for example, the sickness is described prior to the cure. The dream experience or the encounter with the holy healers also always have a logical sequence. The patient learns about the holy healers, they arrive at the cult place, they encounter fellow pilgrims, undergo the rite or the process of falling asleep and dreaming-awakening, and so on. In addition, the formation of the plot of the miracle narratives contained several other components whose origin and coherence within the text derived from the oral transmission of these stories. Lord demonstrated not only the regularities in the way a text assumes its shape while being told, but (and this is more relevant regarding the miracle collections) how even the circumstances of narrating a story and its logical requirements ultimately shape the narrative itself, just as he called attention to the role of the audience in this process.

In regards to the findings of the research of Parry and Lord and its relevance to miracle narrative studies, LiDonnici also made some significant qualifications. She noted that the oral tradition in classical literature usually refers to oral composition, performance, and so on, and that classical scholars have paid scant attention to the 'loose, informal exchange and preservation of non-literary material, especially that which is in "free language", that is, non-formulaic prose. It is more this type of oral activity, the spread of tales and traditions by word of mouth among the suppliants, which I envision to be lying behind some of the *Iamata* tales.'[7] I would like to emphasize this statement, especially because it emerges from the methodologies not only of Classics, but also of anthropology, New Testament research, and contemporary rumour studies as well. The Epidaurian miracles were shaped into texts through several traditions representing sources of different types and of a rich variety. Among them, LiDonnici distinguished traces of (1) the oral tradition that formed around the cult place; (2) the impact of other votives with their own textual and visual narrative; (3) the 'stock influence', that is, the fixed repertoire of pictorial ready-made materials at the cult place and the possibilities they offered when incorporated into the story; (4) the state-sponsored inscriptions and elements of local propaganda; and (5) the priestly editing given to all these factors. She also gave an example of circumstances, which can allow us to suppose that oral source material has been used, for instance 'where tales occur in groups or pairs which are similar thematically but different linguistically'.[8]

Questions about how stories spread and which stories were remembered during the process of oral formation and transfer have been the focus of both anthropological literature of orality in non-literate societies as well as

---

7   LiDonnici, *The Epidaurian Miracle Inscriptions*, p. 53.
8   LiDonnici, *The Epidaurian Miracle Inscriptions*, p. 52.

in rumour studies.⁹ The spread of anecdotes, gossip, and modern legends provides an important parallel for understanding how stories spread, what elements of the story were omitted, and what elements were added during the transmission of the story.¹⁰ LiDonnici used the results of this research in her study of the Epidaurian incubation corpus, although even earlier in the 1970s, they had been applied in the investigation of early Christian oral traditions.¹¹ At the same time, anthropologists also started to take notice of Christian rituals as these relate to the role of orality and storytelling in the pilgrim experience.¹² The most important concept formulated by anthropological orality studies was a concept that accords with the deductions of Parry and Lord: there are no original versions of orally transmitted stories because the content and contexts were continually being reshaped.

Comparable conclusions emerged from another field of oral tradition research. The scholarly literature of New Testament studies is both a treasure mine and a maze. In many aspects, they were pioneers in applying methods of modern literary theories in order to analyse biblical narratives, with the aim of separating the layers of transmission and outlining the very intricate historical and narrative aspects that influenced the formation and dissemination of these texts. Following the steps of Hermann Gunkel, who established a critique to unearth possible indicators of oral tradition in the Old Testament, the works of scholars such as Rudolf Bultmann, Martin Dibelius, and Werner Kelber proposed a critical analysis of the biblical texts without tearing the texts out from their spiritual context.¹³ These are the reasons, paired with their attention to oral folk traditions as well, why I regard their work, especially that of Kelber, as a suitable model for analysing hagiographical texts. Among the schools of New Testament studies, one of the basic dividing lines was the extent to which scholars focused on the concept of the 'original text' and how they were able to distinguish between the categories of oral and written

---

9   The anthropological literature of orality in non-literate societies provides a different point of view. Jan Vansina in his *Oral Tradition as History* calls attention to the fact that oral traditions document the present, not only because they are told in the present but because they embody a message for the present, not necessarily identical with that message of the past; this message for the present is an essential factor in this process of reshaping and reinterpreting the message according to its temporary context. I shall return to this observation in relation to the repetitive character of the miracle narrative and the reshaping of the past theological message of the miracle story within repeated narrative contexts.
10 See the work of Allport and Postman, *The Psychology of Rumour*.
11 Abel, 'The Psychology of Memory and Rumor Transmission'; Theissen, 'Itinerant Radicalism'.
12 Turner and Turner, *Image and Pilgrimage in Christian Culture*.
13 Bultmann, *Die Geschichte der synoptischen Tradition*; Dibelius, *A Fresh Approach to the New Testament and Early Christian Literature*. Werner Kelber summarized (and in part criticized) Bultmann's approach: 'Anonymity, collectivity, and nonliteracy were thus considered the formal attributes of the synoptic tradition, and together they epitomize the concept of Kleinenliteratur. In sum, Bultmann intended to come to terms not with consciously and artistically reflective literature, but in communally shaped and shared folk traditions.' Kelber, *The Oral and Written Gospel*, p. 3.

tradition. In his *History of the Synoptic Tradition*, Rudolf Bultmann regarded his task to be the reconstruction of the 'original form' of the gospel tradition. In attempting to unravel the collective oral tradition, Bultmann revealed the social markers in its language and concluded that the Gospels represented both a continuously growing and stratified tradition.

The opposite to Bultmann's hypothesis of the folkloric, communal, and loose oral transmission was expounded by Birger Gerhardson,[14] who proposed that the transmission of Jesus's teachings might have been by a process similar to that of the rabbinic tradition, with verbatim memorization and exact reproduction of the text. Whereas the Bultmannian model denied all conscious textual creation and emphasized an oral transmission growing by leaps and bounds, by contrast, Gerhardson's mechanical model excluded creative, communal shaping, the independent life of the text (together with its social, literary, and propagandistic contexts), and the personal impact of the transmitters. Subsequently, a new line in New Testament research developed between these two models, building equally on the two previous concepts and criticizing both. This new school looked beyond the borders of its own discipline, and both exploiting the methods of Anglo-Saxon classical-philology in orality research and simultaneously applying the results of anthropology, rumour studies, and sociology, it created a more nuanced picture of the textual history of the Gospels. One pioneer of this research direction was Erhardt Güttemanns,[15] while more recently Werner Kelber has summarized his point in a way that is extremely useful for analysing hagiography as well: 'In approaching Mark's healing stories we encounter a *plurality* of brief tales that are impressive by their *uniformity* of composition and *variability* of narrative exposition, and we seek an explanation for this triple phenomenon in the oral technique of communication.'[16]

When analysing the compositional history of the *Iamata* inscriptions, LiDonnici's aim was to identify the oral aspect *behind* the incubation tales. Her approach in this respect has been the most fruitful, with results that should open up new directions for similar studies on Christian hagiographic material in general. I have been strongly influenced by LiDonnici's handling of the incubation material, and in my analysis below, I will follow some of her observations on the Christian incubation tales and add a new dimension to the oral background that she examined. In addition to questioning *what oral sources were used* in the formation of the collections, I will focus on the internal evidence of the hagiographic narratives about the way the stories circulated orally, how they reached the recorder, and more importantly,

---

14 Gerdhardson, *Memory and Manuscript*; and also his *Tradition and Transmission in Early Christianity*.
15 Güttemanns, *Candid Questions Concerning Gospel Form Criticism*; whereas Werner Kelber follows in the tracks of Walter J. Ong and Jack Goody.
16 Kelber, *The Oral and Written Gospel*, p. 46.

what the hagiographer wished to depict of these circumstances. Orality had a role in the circulation of stories around the cult place, as a source for the recording and compilation of the miracle collections and in the shaping of individual narratives. However, the material once composed took on a life of its own through the pilgrims and patients returning home. Material moulded in this way was told and retold naturally, not only based on the pilgrims' own experience, but through the stories that pilgrims had seen (depicted on images and votives), read (in the miracle collections), or heard from others in the sanctuary or on the journey. Moreover, it was not just the material of the miraculous that they took home, but more significantly, a type of the pilgrim experience in the form of a narrative code, a way of describing the circumstances of dreaming, together with the obligatory attributes of the epiphany and the miracle cure.

Orality, Oral Sources, and Storytelling within the Christian Incubation Miracle Records

'I, for whom the talk (*logos*) is dearer than my homeland': "Ἡμεῖς δὲ οἷς λόγος ἐστὶν τῶν γηΐνων ὑλῶν τιμαλφέστερος' — thus wrote Sophronius in the *Laudes* by which he began the miracles of Cyrus and John.[17] It is difficult to provide an overall picture of the oral layers within the miracle catalogues. There were different degrees of oral tradition in each collection because of the varying — sometimes very conscious — compositional techniques of the hagiographers. From the literary point of view, the two most polished collections are those of Thecla and of Cyrus and John; these collections represent two extremes in the depiction of how sources were handled. Thecla's hagiographer provided the reader with indications at each step that he was offering the fruits of his own personal research, pieces of information that he had sought out directly, and often incorporating into the narrative frame an account of how he had met the narrator. At other times, he lets the reader know that he had travelled to the town of the beneficiary of the miracle to do a sort of field research. We also learn from him that he was familiar with the (written and oral) miracle stories of Antiquity. These pagan narratives may have served as examples for his development of the narrative model. At the cult place itself, a small archive contained the miracle stories of the previous healer Sarpedonius. The memory of the latter's stories was still alive in the oral traditions of the city as well. On the other hand, the 'Herodotean' perspective of the writer should not be neglected: the hagiographer introduced himself as a collector of circulating information. Thecla's hagiographer drew consciously on Herodotus. His direct reference to the ancient traveller is complemented by the impression that the hagiographer leaves in us: the

---

17   PG 87.3, col. 3388C–D.

figure of the researcher, the collector of stories, and the man travelling around in order become informed.[18]

In order to work in an archive, it is indispensable to regard the *written* as more true, more authentic, and safer than the *oral* — even if writing can also lie. 'Hérodote, homme entre l'écrit et l'oral, écoute des gens qui se servent de livres, mais, lui-même, l'idée d' "aller aux archives" du sanctuaire de Saïs ou de Bouto ne saurait l'effleurer: "Je sais pour avoir entendu".'[19]

What gives credit to the presentation of oral tradition as the primary source in the Thecla collection is the geographical and chronological coherence of the stories. The chronological reference points encompassed contemporary witnesses and two earlier generations; this narrated tradition revolved around the city of Seleucia and its surrounding region. What Dagron called the 'vaste *présent* correspondant à deux ou trois générations' enabled the hagiographer to draw (according to Dagron, exclusively) on a body of orally transmitted narrative material, 'that is not yet a tradition and not yet a legend'.[20]

Sophronius followed the opposite method in introducing the sources of his material. Apart from very general and schematic remarks (e.g. that the healed patient told everyone about the miracle that had happened to him), he never refers to his sources. I would even say that he carefully avoided recording them for the same reason that Thecla's hagiographer was so keen to name them. For Sophronius's compositional model was different. He sought to produce a free-flowing narrative, in which he ordered a chain of stories in accordance with his own editorial principles. He created the impression that his own creativity as a 'writer' should be more emphasized than did Thecla's hagiographer, who subscribed to another image of the narrator-self. The metaphor Sophronius used to describe the impossibility of his task was that of Peter, who foolishly attempted to walk on water. Thecla's hagiographer compared himself to one who sought gold, having to first dig and carry away the soil with much labour in order to reach the treasure hidden beneath.

With the other three collections, it is not possible to speak of the conscious literary art of a single hagiographer. The multifaceted layers and their continuous editing allow different glimpses into the formation of the collections. Besides the two corpora of Cosmas and Damian, which more closely resembled inventory-like miracle catalogues, Artemius's *Miracula*

---

18   Hartog formulated the way Herodotus created his own persona in this way: 'Que l'historiant initial, aventuré dans la narration, ait rencontré en elle la fiction, c'est ne pas un accident fortuit: cela même appartient au procès fondamental. Les "sources" d'Hérodote sont fictives, en dépit de sa volonté historienne d'aller en "s'enformant", parce que la fiction appartient au procès de la narration primitive se faisant.' Hartog, *Le miroir d'Hérodote*, p. 291. Johnson (*The 'Life and Miracles of Thekla'*, ch. 4) also noted this Herodotean aspect; however, he did not attribute it to the hagiographer's personal stamp but saw in it a proof for classifying the miracles as paradoxography.
19   Hartog, *Le miroir d'Hérodote*, p. 291.
20   *Vie et miracles*, ed. and trans. by Dagron, p. 25.

fell halfway between a highly ambitious literary artwork and a miracle catalogue. This midway position also holds true concerning the presence of oral transmission, in the extent to which the hagiographer revealed his oral sources and described occasions of communal storytelling within the church. Artemius seems to have been a writer attentive to details and aware of what the rules of incubation-storytelling required, yet he was far from matching the artistic talent of Sophronius or the hagiographer of Thecla. This is why I call his representation of orality a halfway stage between the obligatory rhetoric and reflection on real experience.

Examining the collections individually, what interested me were the following questions: What were the (ritual and everyday) occasions that provided a framework for retelling miracle stories? Who were the carriers of this oral tradition around or beyond the cult place? Who exactly were the storytellers sometimes named either by the hagiographer or by characters in the miracles? In addition, I noted the direct references in the texts that indicate an oral transmission as source of the miracles. I have also tried to show how oral transmission played a role in the spread of miracle stories, and how storytelling was depicted in the miracles themselves.

Occasions for Storytelling

> The telling of tales by pilgrims and by guides is an important part of the pilgrimage experience, and it plays a great role in inducing mental readiness and expectation, not only in pilgrimage, but in many other types of ritual as well. In the case of incubation, however, mental readiness was certainly an important element.[21]

Sick people — as a result of their of their illness situation, their togetherness in ritual practice, or because of the similarity of their experiences and expectations — shared their dreams, the cures they saw or heard about, and they told again and again the encouraging, famous miracles of the cult place. This is attested in the stories themselves where patients are described discussing the healing among themselves, asking for counsel, expressing scepticism, or sharing their common joy. A more specific situation was represented by the ritual context for the telling of the miracles. These occasions played an organized and organic part in the worship of the saints and in the practice of incubation itself.

In the miracle collections, we find three major occasions for the retelling of the miracles: the communal vigil (the *pannychis*), the communal meal (the *agape*),[22] and the feast day of the saint.[23] The practice of the all-night vigil in

---

[21] LiDonnici, *The Epidaurian Miracle Inscriptions*, p. 52.
[22] On eating together in the church, see Smith, *From Symposium to Eucharist*; for its pre-Christian context: Bookidis, 'Ritual Dining at Corinth'.
[23] For a discussion of the communal reading of saint's *Lives*, see Connor, 'The Setting and Function of a Byzantine Miracle Cult', pp. 69–70.

the sanctuary, the name by which the practice was mentioned, and its cultic function can be found already in ancient Greek rituals. There was a ceremony called *pannychis* attached to the cult of Asclepius at Athens, a night ceremony with torches.²⁴ As a Christian ceremony, it contained three antiphons and five prayers. In our Christian miracle records, this ceremony usually took place on Saturday night, and it was during the *pannychis* that the saints' eulogies were distributed, that is, wax, lamp oil, or other sorts of healing objects. According to the stories in KDM30 and the *Miracula Artemii* (MA33), the distribution of the *kerote* occurred in the sixth hour, that is, around midnight. The dreams seen during this night had particular thaumaturgic significance. The all-night vigil was also one of the key occasions when the miracles of the saints were told, thus combining the entertainment function of the stories with spiritual preparation. Storytelling during the vigil can become an element in the story, expanded into a narrative framework. This is the setting of an entire section of Cosmas and Damian's miracles: the hagiographer in KDM21–26 describes how the recently healed patients told their stories during the *pannychis*, one after the other. He describes himself as a listener and recorder and offers his readers and listeners the chance to feel like they were one of the members present at the vigil.

The all-night vigil is best described in the miracles of Artemius. Several special events took place only during the Saturday night vigil. Only at this occasion was it allowed to sleep next to the saint's coffin; this was also the time when the most efficacious lamp oil was distributed and when the hymns of Romanos the Melodist were sung (this is incidentally the earliest known mention of Romanos, besides his own works).²⁵ We learn that there was a lay confraternity for the vigil, of which the hagiographer was probably a member. There are miracles in the miracle collection of Artemius that either took place during the *pannychis* or emphasize its importance. The first of these, MA15, begins by illustrating the devotion of the character through his participation in the *pannychis*: 'There was a certain man in voluntary service [...] who was devoted to the all-night vigil of the Forerunner every Saturday.' The whole miracle situation evolved from the occasion of a man mocking Artemius's all-night vigil and the cures to a man devotedly attached to the vigil: 'A young man named Narses [...] frequently chided the one devoted to the all-night vigil, mocking both the singing of hymns and those involved in it. [...] He even uttered blasphemous words, saying ironically: "Yes, and perhaps Artemius heals hernia patients?"' A punishment miracle follows, when he duly develops a hernia and ends up in the church awaiting the saint's mercy. One day the saint heals him in a dream, and he tells the story to the churchwarden. 'Since it was then the hour for the communal meal, he [the warden] stood up' and verified the miracle himself.

---

24 See Farnell, *Greek Hero Cults*, p. 239, who refers to IG 2.add. 453b.
25 MA19; cf. Rydén, 'Kyrkan som sjukhus', p. 15, n. 19.

The following *pannychis*-miracle (MA18) begins in a similar manner, but in this case, the events evolve during the vigil itself, which, however, was not an ordinary Saturday but rather the *pannychis* held on the night preceding the saint's feast day (i.e. of Saint John the Forerunner, his sanctuary being the one that hosted the relics of Artemius): 'There was a certain man who from tender age used to attend the all-night vigil of the Forerunner [...] this man was burgled as the birthday of the holy Forerunner was dawning.' Because his clothes had been stolen, he was unable to attend the vigil of the feast day. This moves Artemius to appear in dream to the man in his house and reproach him: 'Why did you not go to meet and escort the holy object in procession with your candle, as is customary for you celebrants of the all-night vigil?' A more detailed picture of the vigil and the cure occurring at that time is given in MA33:

> It was a Saturday, the eve of the Lord's day, and the holy night vigil was being celebrated; after the *troparion* had occurred and the three evening antiphons, Theognios stood up and fell back on the bed with the herniated child and the child's father himself. And then he fell asleep and saw the one who is quick to help — the glorious servant of Christ, Artemius — speaking to him: 'Get up, and take some of the prepared wax-salve and anoint your chest and eat some of it. Also anoint the testicles of the child reclining with you, and both of you will be well.' After the working of the miracle the man recounted: 'I woke up immediately at the saint's words. It was already the hour of completing the midnight rites and the occasion for the holy wax-salve to be dispensed at the adoration of the precious life-giving cross. [...] Afterward, when we were healthy, I related to my companion the thoughts that I had in my mind and the requests I made to the martyr and the vision that befell me.'

The miracle from Artemius's corpus that I have recalled here is connected to the Saturday night vigil with the eve of the saint's feast day; moreover, it is an important source for showing how this ritual took place, with frequent participation in the Saturday *pannychis* itself becoming a kind of votive gift. The protagonist of another story was a widow with her sick child. During their stay in the church, the preparations for the saint's feast day began and the child 'assisted capably both in hanging lamps and dispensing water and other necessities on the occasion of the church assembly, namely the feast of the holy martyr'. In exchange for the cure, Artemius made the following request to the mother: 'If your son recovers, frequent the all-night vigil that is celebrated here' (MA36) — a proof, incidentally, that women could also attend the *pannychis*.

MA15 (quoted above) shows us that the communal meal was an everyday practice in the Forerunner's church and not limited to special occasions. An *agape* meal is described in MA5 as an offering made by the patient after his cure. A more common use of the *agape* is mentioned in MA39 where a sick man, after meeting a stranger (Saint Artemius) who encouraged him to have faith regarding his cure, proposed to hold a fellowship banquet (probably in the church). During the preparations, he realized that he had been cured by the saint, and instead of the meal honouring the stranger, they performed the evening doxology with thanksgiving.

In MA35, we read about two *agape* meals. In the first, a man who had waited for two years in vain for the saint's visit organized a farewell *agape* dinner in the church before his departure. During this communal meal, the priests encouraged the man by telling stories in which the saint cured patients returning home: 'While they were dining the clergy were advising George not to give up; for the saint had been known to visit many at sea and in their homes after they had stayed a while and departed.' In the event, Artemius miraculously cured the man during this meal, and this in turn ended with more telling of miracles: 'The diners waiting for him, hearing the shouting, left the table and ran to him. And when they asked why he was shouting, the healed ship-owner reported everything to them […] and *afterward their banquet was a feast full of miracles*' (my emphasis). The second meal was again a thanksgiving offering: 'So on the morrow, having made an offering to the best of his ability he brought it to the martyr, and after having feasted with the holy clerics he departed […] relating to everyone the marvels.'

The vigil could certainly be held in conjunction with the saint's feast day, and just as in Artemius's case, where such an occasion was more festive than on customary Saturdays, so in Thecla's miracles we read about sumptuous celebrations. MT33 gives a very detailed description of Thecla's festival, which lasted several days and drew 'people living in the village and foreigners, men, women, children, employers and employees, military chiefs and soldiers, demos-members and simple individuals, young and old, sailors and peasants'.[26] The parts of the festival were a long vigil, the taking of the Eucharist, and the sharing of a communal meal when everybody could tell what they admired most in the feast. Here there is already mention of the literary talent of the preachers. What this meant is expanded in MT41. On this occasion, there was a literary contest organized in Thecla's honour, when orators could show their expertise in composing and delivering sermons about Thecla and her miracles. One of the peak events of the festival happened during the all-night vigil (MT26): if one kept the vigil on a little hill nearby and remained awake, observing the sky, it was possible to see Thecla flying on the sky in her chariot of fire. But the vigil during the festival did not exclude dreaming: MT29 describes a punishment miracle, with Thecla appearing in sleep to an intermediary during the vigil to announce the death of the wrong-doing bishop.

In the London Codex, we read of a miraculous cure sandwiched between two feast days (CL15). A dropsical woman went to the church of Cosmas and Damian and spent four months there in pain. On the saints' feast day (1 July), a priest arrived in the church and asked a servant girl about the dropsical woman's

---

26 On Thecla's pilgrims, see *Vie et miracles*, ed. and trans. by Dagron, pp. 73–79.

whereabouts. The servant girl recalled the dream that she saw that night: one of the saints descended from an icon in the church, touched the dropsical woman's belly, and announced to the servant girl (who was reproaching him) that the patient would be healed by the feast day of Saint Euphemia, with the pain diminishing each day. In another of Cosmas and Damian's miracles (KDM41), not only did the miraculous cure take place on the saints' feast day, but also each year on this same day from then on the healed man retold the miraculous cure Cosmas and Damian performed on him.

The persons involved in the transmission of the stories included those lay people who moved into the sanctuary and perhaps spent years or even the rest of their lives there (MT19, 43, 46, MA35, KDM34). Occasionally, the healed patient remained in the church after their recovery, sometimes at the request of the healer, or else out of gratitude, dedicating their personal services in thanksgiving for the miracle. A variant of this practice was when the patient spent a long period (even years) in the sanctuary awaiting a cure. For whatever reason, people chose to stay, and the patients who lingered on for years at the cult place were probably significant sources of information about the miracles that had happened to and around them. In KDM34, we learn that there was a barbershop in the church, which was run by a patient who had been cured by the saints. Such a detail serves to highlight another group of actors as well: visitors like the clients of the barbershop or curious sceptics or the heretic flirting with orthodoxy. In short, these were all those people who did not come to the cult place with a primarily ritual aim. They surely listened to the stories of long-term patients and church personnel and probably retold them in turn. There was another group in the miraculous healing records, and in the KDM in particular, that had a similar function (one already familiar from the Asclepieian stories): the servants and family members accompanying the sick person. Similarly, the monks and nuns from the cloister attached to the church[27] as well as pilgrims also helped in making the stories travel. Among pilgrims who listened to and retold stories, we cannot omit Egeria, who, as I mentioned earlier, on her journey to the Holy Land (around 381–384) paid a visit to the cult site of Saint Thecla as well, and in her travel diary, she recorded that the entire *Vita* of the saint was read aloud to them at Thecla's church.[28] These multifaceted groups of informants and audience facilitated the mouth-to-mouth spread of memorable narratives far beyond the network of cult adherents.

---

27 *Vie et miracles*, ed. and trans. by Dagron, pp. 57–58.
28 Egeria, *Travels*, 22.2–23.6: 'Ibi ergo cum venissem in nomine Dei, facta oratione ad martyrium nec non etiam et lectus omnis actus sanctae Teclae.'

Orality in Thecla's Collection

The transmission of the material in the Thecla corpus differs significantly from that of the miracles of Cosmas and Damian or Cyrus and John, whose hagiographers (so Dagron said) had only the talk of the church servants and the votive objects on which to draw.[29] Unlike these other collections, Dagron argued, Thecla's hagiographer drew upon a not yet recorded, living oral tradition. The written and material evidence, however, is not entirely missing from Thecla's miracles; hence, a close look at these sources may produce a reality that is subtly different from both of his statements. When Dagron outlined a geographical radius of the action of the miracles,[30] the places where there was a still active oral tradition about the saint's recent deeds, the collection was recorded and became visible. A chronological survey of the stories,[31] on the other hand, showed that the narrator-hagiographer's knowledge embraced a more or less century-long tradition. The large number of events precisely dated by the hagiographer is significant and unique in its genre. The hagiographer was also keen to picture himself as a researcher of oral tradition, his literary-historiographic ideal confessedly being Herodotus. Nevertheless, the chronological framing of the stories rendered credible the principles of collecting and editing established by the hagiographer in the prologue:

> In order that we may relate a very few of all these many miracles, let me recount those which we have known hitherto, which are commonly acknowledged by many, and which we all know and experienced, some of us to our own personal benefit, while others have heard tell from those who themselves benefited.[32]

What kind of information does the text contain concerning the circumstances of its composition? A handful of inter-related reasons lay behind the hagiographer's motivation for writing. In the first place, he intended his work to be a gift of thanksgiving. At the same time, he was inspired by Thecla and urged on by a friend.[33] In his writing, he occasionally drops two other background features that become known. The first is that the hagiographer was familiar with the ancient prophetic and incubation material, which was partially preserved in written records. He probably had a more intimate knowledge of these records, not simply regarding their existence as an annoying challenge, as Sophronius did, nor sweeping them aside as godless nonsense.

---

29 *Vie et Miracles*, pp. 24, 1.
30 *Vie et Miracles*, pp. 24–25.
31 *Vie et Miracles*, pp. 25–27.
32 'Καὶ ἵνα ἐκ πάνυ πολλῶν ἄγαν ὀλίγα εἴπωμεν, φέρε εἴπωμεν ἅ τε ἡμεῖς ἴσμεν τέως, ἅ τε συνομολογεῖται τοῖς πολλοῖς, καὶ ὧν πάντες ἴστορες τε καὶ ἐν πείρα καθεστήκαμεν, οἱ μὲν καὶ αὐτῷ τῷ εὖ παθεῖν, οἱ δὲ καὶ παρ' αὐτῶν τῶν εὖ πεπονθότων ἀκηκοότες' (trans. by Talbot and Johnson).
33 A certain Achaios; cf. *Vie et miracles*, ed. and trans. by Dagron, p. 21.

Zeus of Dodona, Apollo of Delphoi, the Castalian oracles, and Asclepius in Pergamon, Epidaurus, and Aegae: 'πολλὰ περὶ πολλῶν ἀναγεγράφασι χρηστήριά τε καὶ παθῶν λυτήρια', which, our hagiographer writes, 'are partly tales (*muthoi*) and fictitious things (*plasmata*), ingenious inventions (*kompseumata*) of their fabricators, who wished to attribute to the daimones some power and strength and knowledge of the future, but on the other hand they are often authentic and for many people useful oracles "full of breathing (*gemonta*) ambiguities".[34] Though Dagron writes that this reference to the great oracle-giving sanctuaries 'est purement littéraire et conventionnelle',[35] all the same, if someone mentioned Epidaurus and Aegae he must have had in mind the stories of miraculous cures that happened at these places, either knowing them in their written form or by hearsay. In addition, by criticizing the content of the texts of these miracles and oracles, the hagiographer seemed to refer to a body of material that was known to his audience as well. Sophronius's references in the *Laudes* were much more formulaic: he listed the local Isis among the demons freed by Christ, and also alludes to Loxias's (= Apollo's) tripod, Dodona and Castalia, the bull of Rhodos and Asclepius — even though centuries had passed since these cults had ceased their activity.

The literary reality of the ancient Greek oracle and dream-healing literature undoubtedly inspired the recording of Thecla's miracles, merely by its existence and fame. At the same time, it also directed the way Thecla's miraculous stories evolved. One of the basic layers in the pagan material known to the hagiographer must have been the miracles of Sarpedonius: 'Nobody is ignorant about that Sarpedonius, and we came to know the indeed very ancient legends around him from stories and books.' This seems a clear indication that the hagiographer had both oral and written information concerning Sarpedonius's activity.[36]

The phrase 'nobody is ignorant' (ἀγνοεῖ μὲν οὐδεις), which occurs elsewhere as well, reflects the fact that numerous miracle stories contain elements of knowledge that were shared by the whole community, just as it is a common rhetorical technique to establish a factual background and the idea (and ideal) of shared knowledge about the miracles in question. It appears that the hagiographer consciously competed with the miracle-tales of the rival cult hero because he repeatedly used a very powerful image: Thecla silenced and dumbfounded Sarpedonius, 'she rendered him voiceless, this one with so many voices and so many words uttering oracles, by making the word of the Lord and King a stronghold against him: Keep silence and withhold yourself! In this way, he was muted, left alone, and he hid himself. I think he even left

---

34 The full English text is in Talbot and Johson, *Miracle Tales from Byzantium*, p. 5.
35 *Vie et miracles*, ed. and trans. by Dagron, p. 287, n. 6.
36 'Τὸν Σαρπηδόνιον τοῦτον ἀγνοεῖ μὲν οὐδείς, καὶ γὰρ παλαιότατον τὸ κατ' αὐτὸν μυθολόγημα ἔγνωμεν ἀπὸ ἱστοριῶν καὶ βιβλίων.' MT1; cf. *Vie et miracles*, ed. and trans. by Dagron, p. 291, n. 2.

his tomb and the place where he stayed.'³⁷ Thus, the imagery of total silence dominates; the words of the deity and words about him were muted alike. With an amazing twist, the hagiographer connects the physical presence of the healer with the stories circulating about him and his miracle-working. No miracle-tales told, no cult.

In the same vein, the hagiographer tried to reduce his own rivals and the local rhetors to silence.³⁸ The high level of the literary repertoire mobilized by the hagiographer was also a response to the level of rhetoric that characterized the greatest works of Antiquity. Just as his narrative technique was based on his classical reading, it is not surprising that the first 'narrative' of the miracle collection comprised a Herodotus-paraphrase on dream interpretation.³⁹ Nevertheless, the inspiration for storytelling and for rendering the *words* of the miracle narratives as *miraculous words* originated from Thecla. The merit was hers, not only in the recording of her miracles, but also when during the annual panegyricus-competition, the words themselves became the *thauma* of eloquence:

> I spoke a few words, but the martyr offered her helping hand and her grace to such an extent that, first, I seemed to be a man of some reputation; second, I spoke passably well; and third, I received substantial admiration (*thauma*) for my words which had no admirable feature.⁴⁰

The oral tradition at the cult place must have been old indeed if the ancient name of the place that preceded even the cult of Athena was still known. The oral tradition must have been very intense as well, since the miracles advertising the triumph of Thecla 'were so magnificent that it was impossible even for those who wanted to doubt, not to confess them, not to agree with them, and not to tell and make others tell them', writes the hagiographer.

Who could have been his oral sources? As soon as the hagiographer passed from telling about the large-scale miracles affecting the whole town to individual cases, an odd remark suggests that the beneficiaries of the miracles or the witnesses would, in fact, have allowed such events to descend into oblivion, 'λήθῃ καὶ σιωπῇ παραδόντες' (MT6). Among the still living carriers of memory, there were those who experienced the miracle (e.g. MT11). Such people would also have included the hagiographer himself (MT12, 31), the relatives of the healed person (MT19, 24), the whole community of believers (in connection with miracles concerning the sanctuary) (MT5, 6, 26, 27), the compatriots of the healed patients (MT28, 34, and in MT15 the entire island

---

37 MT1.16–20.
38 See e.g. MT30.
39 Moreover, a dream interpretation of Croesus's dream that unmasked a false dreamer. On Herodotean dreams, see Hartog, *Le miroir d'Hérodote*, pp. 278–79.
40 'οὕτω δέ μοι τὴν χεῖρα καὶ κάριν συνεπέδωκεν ἡ μάρτυς, ὡς εἶναί τι καὶ δόξαι, καὶ εἰρηκέναι μετρίως, καὶ θαῦμα πλεῖστον ἐπὶ μηδενὶ θαυμαστῷ τῶν ἐμῶν ἀπενέγκασθαι λόγων'. MT41.25–27 (trans. by Talbot and Johnson).

of Cyprus, from where the fame of the miracle reached Seleucia). Testimonies also comprised the descendants of the victim, as in the punishment miracle of MT33 which ended in death, and where the victim's family, even after a long time, were still marked by the infamy that arose from it.

There is a more emphatic expression of how direct information was gathered from the participants in the miracles or from the eyewitnesses at the end of MT34, in a phrase that suggested that the hagiographer had even travelled to the town of the beneficiary of the miracle in order to collect the details of the story:[41] 'Τοῦτο δὲ καὶ παρ᾽ αὐτῶν τῶν ἐκείνοιν πολιτῶν, τάχα δὲ καὶ συγγενῶν ἐπυθόμην.' It is plausible that this trip provided the occasion for the hagiographer to collect the other miracles experienced by the citizens of the same town, Eleucia (MT19, 33, 35). That the hagiographer had in mind a sort of 'research publication' is evidenced by the last sentence of MT35: "Ἄπερ οὖν ἔγνωμεν, πάλιν εἰς μέσον ἀγάγωμεν.'

The range of the spreading fame of a miracle could encompass the whole town of Seleucia, 'μάρτυς τοῦ θαύματος ἡ σύμπασα Σελεύκου πόλις' (MT23) — and even the whole region, as it knew no geographical boundaries (MT28): 'These witnesses are not three or four individuals [...] but entire cities and whole communities; those who live between the east and our city, and again those who extend in turn from our city all the way to [the west], [to the diocese] of Asia.'[42] The same miracle informs us about the difficulties involved in the collection of these stories:

> As it is with seekers of gold, who first cut down the woods and dig up the soil, so it is to collect the miracles on the basis of hearsay; those which were covered, as if by a hillock, by time and oblivion, and thus became obfuscated and weak and tended to exclude memory, order, and the place and circumstances of their origin. However, I must say that what I found I discovered only after searching and investigating with difficulty and in the midst of toils.[43]

Elsewhere (MT44) miracles are described as if floating from all directions towards the hagiographer, and in another passage, we again read that 'even that the miracles themselves wanted to come to light', demanding speedy work on the part of the hagiographer: 'therefore, let us not delay, but since the miracle is impatient to bound swiftly into view, let us grant it speed.'[44]

---

41 Cf. *Vie et miracles*, ed. and trans. by Dagron, p. 385 n. 9.
42 'ὅλαι πόλεις καὶ ὅλοι δῆμοι, καὶ οἱ μέχρι τε ἡμῶν ἀπὸ τῆς Ἑῴας παραγινόμενοι, καὶ αὖ πάλιν οἱ ἀφ᾽ ἡμῶν καὶ μέχρι τῆς Ἀσίας ἐκτεινόμενοι' (trans. by Talbot and Johnson).
43 MT28, my translation.
44 MT13, 'μήτε οὖν ἡμεῖς μελλήσωμεν, καὶ τῷ θᾶττον βουλομένῳ προπηδῆναι θαύματι χαρισώμεθα τάχος' (trans. by Talbot and Johnson).

Traces of Storytelling and Handling of Oral Sources in the Collections of Cosmas and Damian

The variants and the multiple editions of Cosmas and Damian's two miracle catalogues provide a wide variety of opportunities for observing narrative situations and oral storytelling, and for this reason, I have dedicated what may appear to be a disproportionate amount of room to the treatment of these episodes. However, as we shall see below, the representation of orality and the handling of oral sources were typical in several ways for the rest of the collections as well. Instead of recapitulating what would hold equally true for storytelling and oral transmission within the miracles of Thecla, Cyrus and John, and Artemius, I will concentrate on features not mentioned so far in my discussion in connection with the collections of Cosmas and Damian, especially characteristics and narrative solutions, and situations of transmission that are unique to one or the other of these miracle collections.

In the two miracle collections of Cosmas and Damian the references to orality invite the reader to consider some of the essential realities of the cult practice and, more importantly, differences between the various phases in the development of the cult.

In the first and oldest part of the KDM (1–10) it is often described, as a narrative solution for transition between the miracles, that the recipient of the previous miracle 'praised Christ and the merit of the saints, proclaiming the miracle he was affected by' (KDM3). Proclaiming the miracle to all present as a form of thanksgiving probably did reflect everyday practice. It seems the miracles told in this way could reach even the ears of non-Christians. In KDM2, a Jewish woman turns to the saints; in KDM9, we are told explicitly that the pagan protagonist of this tale was moved by the spreading fame of the cult site to seek a cure there, allegedly from Castor and Pollux. Would this phenomenon highlight how miracles revolved around the cult place rather than the actual healers? The same story can also be found in the London Codex (CL23). There we do not read of the spreading fame of the healers, but rather we find a precise description of how the sick pagan found his way to the sanctuary: 'Those who were, just like him, faithful to the godless Hellenic religion, carried him to the church of the wise doctors, Saint Cosmas and Saint Damian, but not as to these saints, but to Castor and Pollux, whom the Greeks since long before worshipped as healing daimones of diseases.' The pagan Greek was forced to recognize and acknowledge as a condition of his cure the identity and power of the saints. As beneficiary of the miracle and in both versions of the story he proclaimed the miracle to his fellow pagans, and many of those who listened to his story and the story of his baptism then confessed to Christ.

The miraculous deeds of the saints spread and became the first piece of information for those who were ignorant of the cult (either because of the distance or because they were not Christians). As some of the miracles attest, many would-be patients learned about the cures by such hearsay. The miracle of the wonder-working icon (KDM13) that I have discussed before presents a good example of how these stories were spread. It shows how the healers, even if known only from hearsay, could actually effect cures through long-distance healing. In the miracle in question, the soldier comforted his sick wife by recalling the effective and miraculously fast cures carried out by Cosmas and Damian. As the result of hearing this account of previous cures by the saints, she was filled by a desire to see them and was eventually healed. A more grotesque example of what someone can deduce from hearsay about the saints' competence is the case of the lamenting teacher (*paidagogos*), who, learning from the stories the wonders the saints can perform, turned to them with his problem: his desire to settle in Constantinople and get a job there (KDM18).

Telling about the saints' miracles could represent far more than a customary motif. In the third part of the KDM (21–26) the all-night vigil (*pannychis*) represented an exclusive source for the first-person narrator, and at the same time it provided a cultic and narrative unity for the stories. In this narrative framework created by the hagiographer, he was one of the healed patients, who, with some encouragement, had ventured on the project of recording some of the miracles. He naturally faced (and confronted his readers with) the problem of the vastness of the material: 'In truth, which ones of the miracles could one narrate? Those of today, those of yesterday, those of each day, those which took place for many people, or those for single individuals, those from here or those from elsewhere?'[45] To facilitate the choice, and at the same time in order to establish the (fictitious) narrative situation, he chose those stories that he had heard himself during the *pannychis*, just as the narrator of the Thousand and One Nights made an effort to tell only the tales of Scheherazade. To justify his method of collecting sources, he had recourse to another argument, namely the desire to make the collecting work easier.

In the first miracle of this unit (KDM21) the narrator-protagonist was a recently recovered patient, of whom we learn at the end of the story (from the hagiographer) that ever since the miracle he had become a regular visitor to the church. In this way the hagiographer established a sort of continuity between the time of the narration and that of the recording, and in this way sought to give credit to the story, with both the subject and source of the miracle and the recorder (the hagiographer) being, as it were, living witnesses to these events.

The beginning of the next miracle (KDM22) remained within the rules of communal storytelling. Following directly on from the previous account, another recently recovered patient took up the word. It is remarkable how the *meta tauta* beginnings of the early miracle catalogue, the *Codex Londoniensis*, transform into the description of a process of events, each with an incipit in which one patient had just left when the other arrived. The same framework

---

45 Prologue to the miracles.

remained, only the conventions of storytelling altered. The narrative situation underwent a change in the next miracle (KDM23), where we learn, but only from the interpolated half-sentences, that the sick person himself is narrating the events. Moreover, in the epilogue added to the end of the miracle it is made clear that as soon as the patient left the sanctuary he continued to spread word of the saints' miraculous deeds that he had personally experienced. In the fictitious framework of the narrative of the next miracle, the storytellers within the sanctuary heap up miracle accounts, actually interrupting each other. Thus, while one is still telling his story, another one begins his own. This miracle (KDM24) is noteworthy for several reasons. It was one of the best-known miracles in the corpus and was known to Sophronius too. It was also paraphrased by the hagiographer of Saint Menas. The narrator was once again a healed patient although not the recipient of the cure described in the miracle; he was rather a witness to the miracle, the third patient lying between the two people healed by the same miracle. This storytelling technique, which I call the *narration of the third*, appears on other occasions in the corpus (e.g. KDM26) and in Thecla's collection (as in MT46) as well. It aimed at giving the plot the credibility of oral tradition, a reality-effect.[46] What rendered this transmission unique is that this third narrator was — allegedly — the oral source used by the hagiographer, although for the character who retold the story the source took the form of a *vision*. However, as shall be seen below, given the nature of the story, this narrator must also have been informed by what the dreamers, the protagonists of the miracle, *told* him.

The story runs that on the right side of our ultimate 'narrator' lay a mute noblewoman and on his left side a paralysed man. The saints appeared in dream to the paralysed man and ordered him to approach the woman; when he finally makes an attempt, the mute woman cried out and the paralysed man ran away. In order that the miracle-element of the story should be made clear, it was essential within the coherence of the narrative that the paralysed man would tell his dream, since this legitimized his action and demonstrated the saints' intervention. The miracle that comes next (KDM25) evolved in a similar way. A third character was placed between the husband who doubted the fidelity of his wife and the wife who was unable to prove her innocence. This third character was a blind man whom the saints had told, as a remedy, to rub his eyes with some milk handed to him by a chaste woman. The blind man told his dream to his neighbours. The story reached the ears of the husband, who passed it on to his wife, until the miracle occurs and the husband's suspicions are dispelled.

---

46 This is quite similar to archaic turns of phrase as in classical Greek writers, *hos legousin*, *phēsin, legetai* (etc.) used to warn the reader and to shift the responsibility for its veracity. It is always a question whether such sources actually existed. Herodotus provides a useful parallel. See Murray, 'Herodotus and Oral History'.

The miracle story KDM26 can be traced back to the *pannychis* where the heretic protagonist of the story had learned from hearsay about the miracle working of the saints (apparently from outside the context of the sanctuary) and was seized with a desire to participate in the Saturday night vigil. He was not ill, but the stories he heard had piqued his curiosity. Despite the fact that he was not a patient, the saints appeared to him in dream and proposed a remedy for the ills of the noblewoman lying next to him. In the story, it is seen as a test of his faith in the saints whether or not he would have the courage to report the dream he received. He held back from telling the wondrous event because of the difference in rank between the woman and himself, and even more by the fear that if he told the story, nobody would have believed it and he would just render himself ridiculous. Thus, the *telling of the miracle* was both the prerequisite for the woman's recovery and a test of the man's faith. The heretic eventually told the miracle when the saints provided a material object which was at the same time both the means of the cure and the proof of the man's story. The hagiographer relates that he had been told that although the man remained a heretic, he *put down in writing the miracles of the saints* when the prophecy which the saints had told him concerning his future was fulfilled. This part of the story concludes with an epilogue in which the hagiographer turns to his commissioner saying: 'Here you are, at your request, I have written down the saints' miracles for you; if you like them, I shall send more later'. As Kelber summarized this phenomenon, 'one may thus find inscribed in the newly mediated story a rationale for its own medium history'.[47]

Before I pass on to the role of orality in miracle-writing in the next section, it is worth casting a glimpse at the alternative miracle collection of Cosmas and Damian in the earlier and quite different London Codex. This codex contains valuable items of information concerning orality and storytelling. As mentioned earlier, the miracle stories of the CL are in part identical to those in the Deubner corpus although the order of the stories is different, with no traces of the units found in the latter corpus. The stories KDM21–23 and 25–26 are analogous to the stories of CL33, 34, 26, 11, and 35.

CL33 starts with the customary first words, *meta tauta*, but the descriptions of the repeated cures of the patient and the time frame of the recovery that extends over years placed the patient into a different relationship with the narrator: there is no hint of personal contact or direct oral transmission. That the source was ultimately the healed patient is only mentioned casually in a short sentence: 'He hurried to the saints' church and told what happened to him by the virtue of the saints' — thus, in quite general terms. Likewise, with the other analogous miracles, all begin with the usual catalogue-like *meta tauta*

---

47 Kelber, *The Oral and Written Gospel*, p. 129. According to Festugière, this second set of stories may have also been identical to the following, fourth section of the corpus (KDM27–32). *Sainte Thècle, Saints Côme et Damien*, ed. and trans. by Festugière, pp. 165, 1.

formula. In none of them is there any trace of the framework of communal or personal storytelling set up by the later hagiographer. Nevertheless, in CL35 the moment of the miracle is specified as the Saturday night vigil. The stories that figure in this earlier, less elaborated and rather inventory-like collection show that the hagiographer of the KDM himself created a context of oral tradition for the miracles, an age-old narrative method and one that was to have a long future:

> Nearly all the Holmes stories, therefore, are stories of people who tell their stories, and every so often the stories these people tell feature people telling stories (about what they heard or saw, for example, on the night in question), and if this sounds like a dubiously metafictional observation then we may have forgotten how fundamental such stories within stories have always been to popular art from Homer to *Green Acres*, and how lightly worn.[48]

The fiction of the communal listening to the miracles and the context of direct storytelling does give credit to the hagiographer's compositional creativity, while on the other hand, it was probably the real medium for the transmission of these miracles. However well it accords with the way the community preserved its miracle traditions, it is important that the hagiographer emphatically builds communal listening into the narrative — to the extent of creating the fiction of a direct, personal experience. (A similar technique for establishing authenticity and the reality-effect of storytelling was achieved by involving elders as sources.[49])

The text, although a written artefact, conveys the sense of 'realism' that in its total impact exceeds that of orality. More to the point, this 'realism' is the logical outcome of the manufactured text. Written language, exempt from concerns for self-preservation, is allowed full play. It can live and create its own interior potential.[50]

Most probably, the editor of the KDM miracle corpus worked from written and perhaps oral sources as well, although he transformed both into written descriptions of personal and oral sources. The written text was presented as the miracle accounts were *read aloud* in the church, the oral ones as stories heard from the patients themselves. Generally the *Codex Londoniensis* did not refer to its sources (as sources for the hagiographer) directly from word-of-mouth, although the hagiographer was familiar with the idea of the genealogy of miracles, a tradition that received new layers generation by generation, as he wrote after the first three miracles in a short prologue:

> While these miracles happened right after the consecration of the church of Saints Cosmas and Damian, in the past, we should not ignore those

---

48 Chabon, 'The Game's Afoot', p. 14.
49 See Weinreich, *Antike Heilungswunder*, p. 92.
50 Kelber on the Gospel of Mark, *The Oral and Written Gospel*, p. 116.

miracles that happened afterwards, at our place, through them. *One generation shall praise thy works to another* [...], says David the prophet for the glory of God, urging even now for praise, showing to us, their descendants, similar miracles performed by Saints Cosmas and Damian.

There is no evidence of embedded storytelling in the miracles of the fourth section (27–32) in the KDM collection. Instead, the hagiographer established directness in a different — although not hitherto unknown — way. The telling of tales from two points of view, of the narrator and of the listener, had hitherto taken their form that the patient was the narrator and the hagiographer the listener (together with the others: 'we'). Now, a new aspect of textual formation comes to the fore. It was emphatically the hagiographer who took on the role of 'I', the narrator, while the reader/listener was the public, 'you'. The means to achieve this immediacy, or even intimacy, was by the hagiographer turning to his audience at the end of the narration: 'Do you see, my beloved friend, how the saints succour those whom they love?' (KDM27).⁵¹ The addressee here may still be the real or fictitious friend created above, Florentinus, but there was also a more general audience before the hagiographer's eyes: 'Do you all see of what great things faith in the saint's grace is capable?' (KDM28).⁵² This narrator's aside was expanded to such an extent that by the time KDM31 was written, the miracle itself occupied only a third of the narration with the better part of the text comprising a universal message, packed with biblical references and, at the same time, personalized with a simile about the emperor's servant, and with the hagiographer's aside to his (imaginary?) reader-friend — *do you see, my beloved friend?* Meanwhile in the preceding miracle, KDM30, the narrative employed the old fiction of the directly heard story. At the end of the miracle, the hagiographer remarked that the healed patient remained in the church — and supposedly then became the oral source of the tale.

A more explicit version of this same narrative situation is present in the much later fifth part (KDM33–38) composed by a different hagiographer. This section was introduced by a bulky prologue where the hagiographer describes the motivations for his work, the sources of the miracles, and his own editing principles. He likened himself and his collection to the poor widow with two mites. The first 'partial narration', *meros exégéseōs*, informed the reader right at the start that this was an addition to the already existing miracles,⁵³ something the hagiographer had composed in fulfilment of his vow — although at the same time the hagiographer was also motivated by his desire to record the already familiar stories of the miracles he himself had just heard at first hand. 'As I was listening to the reading of the miracles here in the church': the first words of the prologue provide a valuable witness that there was a written

---

51 'ὁρᾷς, ἀγαπητέ, πῶς φθάνουσιν τοὺς φιλοῦντας αὐτοὺς οἱ ἅγιοι'.
52 'ὁρᾶτε ὅσα μετὰ τῆς τῶν ἁγίων χάριτος ἡ πίστις δύναται'.
53 *Sainte Thècle, Saints Côme et Damien*, ed. and trans. by Festugière, p. 177.

record of the saints' deeds in the cult place which was regularly read aloud and 'written down in various and multiple ways'. However, the narratives of the more recently healed patients represented a fresh source for the enthusiastic recorder: 'as I have heard them day by day, in every hour, [...] either from the mouth of those who were cured, or from those who were eyewitnesses or the servant of the healed person'. The beginning of KDM34 contains reference to yet another group of sources: 'Now I will attempt to tell what I have obtained from pious men, either orally or in writing.'[54] Moreover, the hagiographer attests that he incorporated the exact words of his informants into his narrative (and his use of *phonai* indicates speech, rather than writing).[55] At the same time, this miracle offers an explanation for the presence of barbers within the church of Cosmas and Damian. The protagonist of the story, a butcher with paralysed hands, was ordered by the saints to shave a fellow patient; after this test-of-faith act, he was healed and advised by the saints to remain in the church and establish a barber shop. Hence, he spent the rest of his life there and shaved many of the noblemen of the city.[56] (The hagiographer, in order to demonstrate the veracity of his story, mentioned the contemporary activity of barbers within the sanctuary, confirming the authenticity by claiming that those present barbers were the disciples of that healed butcher, or if not directly his disciples, then the disciples of his disciples.) Remarkably, the story directs the reader's attention to a concrete group of persons, carriers of the oral tradition at the cult place.

The miracle of KDM35 points to a written record as direct source: the beneficiary of the miracle did not narrate what had happened to him, but instead handed it to the hagiographer in a written form; the latter even admitted to have incorporated the patient's own words into the narrative.[57] It can even be an example of a *libellus miraculi*.

From the viewpoint of textual tradition, the sixth part (KDM39–47) of the collection was in a special position. It was the work of the thirteenth-century deacon Maximus, who ambitiously aimed at expressing already known miracles in a better style. He also desired to enrich the collection with stories from his own lifetime.[58] We learn from Maximus that he composed his miracle-group using the stories that reached his ears, and he did it in view of a certain audience: 'for you, my listeners', 'for you, who all gathered here'. The style of address

---

54 'τὸ δὲ νῦν προκείμενον εἰς ἐξήγησιν θαῦμα παρὰ θεοφιλῶν ἀνδρῶν τοῦτο μὲν ἀγράφως τοῦτο δὲ καὶ ἐγγράφως παρελάβομεν'.
55 'ὡς καὶ αὐτὰς τάς ὁσίας αὐτῶν φωνὰς ἐνθεῖναι τῷ διηγήματι' (just as these holy words of theirs add to the story).
56 *Sainte Thècle, Saints Côme et Damien*, ed. and trans. by Festugière, p. 182, n. 11, about the activity of barbers in the church.
57 'ἀνήρ τις [...] διηγήσατό μοι, μᾶλλον δὲ καὶ ἐγγράφως ἐξέθετο (οὗτινος αὐτὰς τὰς λέξεις τῇ προκειμένῃ ἐνέθηκα πραγματείᾳ)' (the man [...] narrated to me, but rather also set it down in writing (whose words I inserted into the subject)).
58 Cf. *Sainte Thècle, Saints Côme et Damien*, ed. and trans. by Festugière, p. 191, n. 1.

may be rhetorical, but it doubtlessly represented an attempt to reconstruct the oral context of miracle narration. What eyewitnesses recalled was rendered as testimony to the sources (at the end of KDM42). The majority of the stories (KDM43–47) were also connected to the monastery — a community around the church complex that was the most natural transmitter of the miraculous events. The hagiographer at some place in the collection remarked that the beneficiary of the miracle was a member of the community. Elsewhere he simply recurs to formulas such as, 'which happened recently and is well known to all of us'.

Orality and Storytelling in Sophronius's Thaumata

When identifying Sophronius's possible sources, Fernandez Marcos included inscriptions, *ex votos*, and oral tradition in the church,[59] in addition to the other Christian miracle catalogues of which Sophronius must have known. However, he attributed little importance to the material-textual sources and emphasized the significant impact of the hagiographer's conversations with church personnel because references to votive or written sources are extremely scarce and only worded in general terms. It seems certain in cases such as the *ex voto* written on the church wall by the patient (MCJ69), the commemorative image (MCJ28), or the egg-shaped stone that had caused a woman's malady and, upon her being cured, was suspended over the saints' tomb as a votive (MCJ48). All these material remains must have been accompanied by stories; only in this way would it have been possible to shape them into narratives. Nevertheless, I do not share Fernandez Marcos's hypothesis about an exclusively oral tradition behind the shaping of the majority of the miracles. It seems wiser to say that Sophronius was the hagiographer who was best at hiding his sources and creating the raw material for his stories out of his personal compositional skill and ways of obtaining ideas, as if he was creating these stories out of nothing. That he preferred to avoid referring to his sources can be compared to the same technique of classical and classicizing historians (like Thucydides or Procopius), a habit that went hand in hand with his classicizing style. But on the other hand, it could have been the case that he wished to create a picture of himself as the only and supreme storyteller — the ultimate and omniscient source of the miracle stories.

There are essentially two types of miracle narratives in Sophronius's collection. There are short, rather schematic stories and extremely detailed, long tales that are often continued on subsequent pages. In the first type of story, reflecting the big impact of the local oral tradition, there was the always-present *name-provenence-illness* of the patient that, in my opinion, suggests that these data were conserved in some way, either on *ex votos* or in a primitive register. The oral tradition might have provided an impetus that

---

59 Fernandez Marcos, *Los Thaumata*, pp. 169–73.

was more concerned about the miraculous content. In the long and detailed stories, Sophronius himself reported that he had heard the miracle from the *oikonomos* or the deacon of the church. MCJ3 is a good example of the first type. At the end of the story, the hagiographer noted that 'this was the story Kalos narrated, the memory of the miracle that was performed on him' (καὶ τοῦτο μὲν τοῦ Καλοῦ καθεστηκέν τε τὸ διήγημα, καὶ τοῦ γεγονότος ἐπ' αὐτῷ θαύματος τὸ μνημόσυνον). (It is worth comparing it to MCJ23, where Sophronius apologized for the paucity of information; here as well only the barest facts were related.)

The *oikonomos* of the sanctuary was doubtless a precious source of stories. In the miracle concerning the *oikonomos* himself (MCJ8), the hagiographer revealed that the healed patients had been of great help in the inscription of the miracles: 'συνεργώντων τῶν δεδρακότων καὶ δρώντων τὰ θαύματα'. This steward of the church, the *oikonomos*, not only must have played an important role in the construction of earlier stories, but his own miraculous experiences also provided rich material for the hagiographer. At the same time, his experiences also showed his certain privilege. Sophronius followed his dreams meticulously for several days, just as he dedicated an equally long narrative to the *oikonomos*'s wife (MCJ9) and to his daughter (MCJ10). Similarly, a detailed miracle described the story of another deacon's daughter (MCJ11) who may be numbered among the hagiographer's informants. In addition, a firsthand story was depicted in MCJ12. Here, not only was the patient the oral source for the miracle, but he was also the commissioner who wanted the story to survive. The grouping of these firsthand family miracles (MCJ8–12) also attests the thematic compositional aim of Sophronius. The *oikonomos* also appeared as a secondary character, for example in MCJ31. Here a certain Theodoros was named as the source of the miracle; the *oikonomos* may have added some details that concerned his role in the event. Thus, the story would have exemplified the way Sophronius used multiple oral sources.

In MCJ28, it is mentioned that a man called Cyrus is staying in the church. However, nothing indicates that he was sick. He was a god-fearing lawyer, wise, and *philochristos*, who plays the role of a mediator in the miracle. The saints give a dream that concerns two patients waiting for the cure and incubation: a poor man and a rich, haughty man, called Nemesius. According to the dream sent to the poor man, he should turn to the rich one for help, but as he is hesitant to do so, our third man, Cyrus, acts as an intermediary. Natalio Fernandez Marcos saw in him some sort of domestic *thaumatologos*, a local miracle-writer, who stayed for a longer period in the sanctuary and collected the stories, or at least remembered them.

A more interesting feature of the story is that the rich patient spreads the news of both his own and the poor patient's recovery by commissioning a monumental decoration. Nemesius commissioned a painting for the wall of the saints' tomb, which represented Christ, John the Baptist, Cyrus, and himself — not at the moment of the miracle but when he voices it to the others in the church. Our hagiographer Sophronius explicitly identified him as his own informant: 'λέξωμεν δὲ καὶ κατ' αὐτὸν ὡς ἐμάθομεν' and 'Νεμεσίων δ' ὁ ταύτης ἡμῖν τῆς διηγήσεως αἴτιος'. Moreover, he wrote that he would use him again as a source: 'ἐπ' αὐτὸν γὰρ πάλιν τρέψω τὸν κάλαμον' (I shall turn my pen on him again).

The notoriety of the patient in itself may guarantee that the miracle connected to his or her person will survive and circulate. In this way was conserved a punishment miracle of an unbelieving Alexandrian lady (MCJ29), who was, already because of her high status, an object of gossip and whose blasphemy against the saints remained a vivid memory (περὶ ἧς ὁ λόγος γεγένηται).

The same assumption can be made for the subsequent punishment miracle, the case of Gesius, the well-known Alexandrian scholar (MCJ30). Such rumours attached to famous personalities, in all likelihood, were circulating beyond the sanctuary; it was circulating in Alexandria as well, sticking more to their figure, rather than to the church. Just like in the miracles of Asclepius, in Thecla's collection we also find famous persons, like the rhetor Isocasius.

The protagonist of MCJ32 is again a notorious person, not only as a silver dealer, but one who openly sustained his pagan beliefs and was imprisoned for idolatry. He fled from prison, and only his paralysis, sent by the saints, forces him to seek the help of Christian holy healers. Just as in the preceding miracle 31, the *oikonomos* appears here again as intermediary of the miracle. Agapius, a pagan, takes communion in order to evade suspicion of not being Christian, and he dies three days later. Similar people in such punishment stories were hardly keen (or, as in the latter case, capable) to spread the miracle. It seems sensible to conclude that the stories around famous or notorious personalities nurtured oral tradition, complementing the information originating from the church personnel. Accordingly, the *oikonomos* Christodorus also makes his appearance in MCJ37 (where the protagonist of the miracle is John, the subdeacon of the church) as well as in MCJ39, in which he is mentioned as the one who assigns a patient their location for incubation, and finally he is mentioned in MCJ40 and 67.

Other carriers of oral tradition besides the long-term patients and the church workers are the *philoponoi* and those who go to Cyrus and John only to adore the relics.[60] The *philoponoi* were secular youths, usually students in formally organized groups, who undertook religious and charity services. They were called *philoponoi* by the Alexandrians; they were Monophysites and were sometimes considered to be fervent attackers of pagans.[61] The picture of them given in the *Thaumata* is of volunteer lay workers helping the patients around the church. In MCJ35, we are shown the *philoponoi* at work, while

---

60 *Philoponoi* are mentioned, e.g., in MCJ35, and also in CL3; on the *philoponoi* generally, see Fernandez Marcos, *Los Thaumata*, pp. 51–52, and Wipszycka, 'Les confréries dans la via religieuse de l'Égypte chrétienne'.

61 Our primary source on this is Zacharias Scholasticus, *Vita Severi*, p. 12; cf. Beck, *Kirche und theologische Literatur im byzantinischen Reich*, pp. 138–39.

MCJ33 and 34 introduce persons who are initially not sick and who go to pray to the relics as an act of devotion.

In MCJ36, we also find a character, Theodorus, who remained for an extended period in the sanctuary, and by Sophronius's time, he was a subdeacon of the church.[62] He was undoubtedly the oral source of the miracle, which is the longest story and the centre of the collection. We learn that Theodorus entered the service of the saints as thanksgiving for his recovery. A similar figure was John, protagonist of the following miracle (MCJ37) and a subdeacon in the church who left behind his heretical past in exchange for life-long residence in the sanctuary. Besides such residents of the church, long-term patients also heard and retold miracle stories. Probably one such patient was the sick heretic of MCJ38 who stayed four months in the sanctuary, while in MCJ39, Sophronius makes the patient tell his story directly (which, even if it is a narrative device, surely attests to real practice).

There is a miracle, MCJ60, that presents the spread of the wonder-working fame of the cult and the way patients could discover the path to their healers. Sophronius writes a handy introduction to the miracle about how people, from near and afar, come to the saints. In this story, the patient arrives from Constantinople, a place that does not lack holy healers. The saints' fame and miraculous power overcomes distance in a rather personal way; the secondary character of the story and the saints' mouthpiece is John the Deacon, familiar from earlier pieces of the collection. He is also from Constantinople, and he is the one who writes to the sick man, urging him to visit Menouthis. What makes the patient obey the words of John the Deacon is not only the shared homeland, but also the fact that John describes the man's illness in his letter. I find this story to be a fascinating piece, exactly because of the mention of the letter. At the same time, it is a variation to the functor of the spreading of the saints' fame by word of mouth, and presents a sort of 'proof', which adds a little miraculous touch to the story before the actual miraculous cure would start. One can be invited by the saints in an invitation dream, advised by friends, or learn about the healers from hearsay — but receive a letter?[63]

Orality and Storytelling in the Miracles of Artemius

The hagiographer of Artemius introduced himself to his readers as a man walking in a beautiful park, who then proposes to tell of all the wonders that he has seen, 'in our desire to write an account of the many miracles of the holy martyr […] of which we have knowledge of some by sight itself and of others by hearsay'. He limited the range of his collection to the period of his

---

62 Sansterre, 'Apparitions et miracles à Menouthis', p. 76.
63 Just as a curiosity, I would like to mention Asclepius's miraculous cure by letter: Pausanias (*Guide to Greece*, x. 38) tells the story of a blind man who received a letter from Asclepius. When trying to decipher the text, he regained his eyesight; the words he saw were: 'two thousand gold pieces'.

own generation, or rather, the collected miracles were limited in this way. 'It may well be that [in the first part of the collection] the first sixteen stories correspond to the class of miracles that have come to the author's attention through hearsay and the remainder to those he has personal knowledge of', speculated Crisafulli.[64] Though the corpus does not offer such a clear distinction regarding oral sources, I have proceeded following the order of the text. Just as above, my focus has not been limited to the oral sources used by the hagiographer, but on the role of orality in and around the miracles and on the way storytelling was described within the stories themselves.

Among the first miracles in the collection, we find the more or less obligatory remark about the way the patients learned of the cult place from hearsay, and often other additional pieces of information. In MA4, an African (with a remark that attests to the range of the saint's fame: 'who had resided in Africa itself') turned to Artemius with his sick child, because 'in conversation some people suggested to him, as they themselves had experienced the martyr's efficacy'. We even see him jotting down the address: 'Upon hearing this, he inquired diligently about the location and wrote on papyrus taking notes, just as they dictated to him, saying: "*To St John the Baptist in the Oxeia, near the colonnades of Domninos.*"' It is notable how the hagiographer, by emphasizing the written recording of the information he had heard, put himself into the shoes of the patient and involved the reader as well in the reality of the situation. At the same time, by doing so, he stepped out from his familiar narrative frame; in order to create the reality-effect, he did not content himself with recalling this simple 'let me write down the address' situation, but he also incorporated the 'written proof' into his story, which, like a formula, identified the saint's dwelling place.[65]

The beneficiaries of the following miracles (MA5 and MA7) also learn of Artemius from hearsay; in the case of the latter, the hagiographer, as proof of the miracle, drew on a parallel between the stories circulating orally about the illness of the cured man and the recovery of his sight: 'whoever had learned of his misfortune, seeing him restored to health, glorified God'.

For prospective incubants, stories about the saint's miracle working were told by lay members of the all-night vigil fraternity and other men and women staying frequently or long term in the church. Just like family members, private doctors, or servants who accompanied the patients, in MA17 we hear about an actor who was brought to the church in order to entertain his sick master. During his stay, the actor did not hide his scepticism, and at the end, he also became a beneficiary of a miracle. The spreading of such miraculous stories was always more efficacious if their beneficiary not only repeated the story of the miracle but also advertised the miraculous medicine (as in MA20).

---

64 In his 'Translator's Preface', in *The Miracles of St Artemius*, ed. and trans. by Crisafulli and Nesbitt, p. xii.
65 On the geographical location of the church, see 'Introduction', in *The Miracles of St Artemius*, ed. and trans. by Crisafulli and Nesbitt, p. 8.

As the result of the miracle, the beneficiary in this case joined the official members of the cult, just as the patient did in MA30, who, the hagiographer says, 'became the church warden. Up to the present time, he excels in this service'. Most probably, he was the hagiographer's firsthand source, just as were the protagonists of MA15, 29, and 33. The narrator of MA21, Stephen the deacon, and *poiétés* of the Blue Faction, must have been such a born storyteller that the hagiographer gave over the word to him entirely. Uniquely in this collection (and indeed, in the five miracle corpora), this is a first-person narrative from beginning to end (in other cases, the first-person narrative relates to the hagiographer himself.) Does this represent an attempt to vary the narrative? Or was the hagiographer faithfully reproducing an individual written or dictated record? Or was this perhaps an officially recorded/stored *libellus miraculi*? It is also possible that the protagonist was a literary man, and he perhaps insisted that his story would reach the audience in the form he composed it. (We saw a somewhat similar case in KDM35, where the beneficiary of the miracle wrote his own record and handed it to the hagiographer.) How a story was told by the personal voice of the healed patient is shown in a complex version in MA32, where we find two stories conflated. As person 'A' was keen to persuade person 'B' about the efficacy of Artemius, he testified to the miracle in the first person; as a result, 'B' turned to Artemius, and his miracle was described by the hagiographer in a direct quotation. Was it 'B' who recalled the circumstances of the narration of the previous miracle together with its exact text, or was it the hagiographer who incorporated the two stories by creating a fictitious (or real?) narrative context?

In MA34, we find a mother described as the one who interrogated her child about the miraculous dream he saw. In MA36, the mother was most likely the direct source for the hagiographer since, he says, 'she (who still survives) enrolled herself in the night office there'. We meet the son in question again, as a grown-up monk, in another miracle; in MA37, he persuaded the patient-protagonist to turn to Artemius.

The collection of Artemius's miracles invites two remarks. There was one sphere where this corpus differed greatly from the other collections, namely, in regard to the nature of the participants (and possible sources) of the stories. In this regard, a conspicuously large number of priests of all sorts figures in the narratives, and not only those who were attached to the cult place, but also priests from other churches in Constantinople as well. Sometimes they acted as protagonists, and sometimes in secondary roles (e.g. the deacon of Hagia Sophia or the abbot and monk from Pege church, MA36–37). These priests seem to have been (in some kind of way) the official or unofficial memory-holders of the miracles. Naturally, this was the group that would have had the most exposure to miracles and were probably prone to sharing their stories (Artemius's hagiographer was also likely to have been some part of the cult personnel). Fernandez Marcos referred to some such a group as the main oral source for Sophronius and he labelled them *domestical thaumatologos*.⁶⁶ However, the *Thaumata* of Cyrus and John, in fact, reveals very little about such persons; their existence seems to have been more plausible for the Artemius-collection. Their involvement in the narrative has another, hagiographical function: agents in the rivalry between the various cult sites of the capital.

The other notable characteristic of the corpus (though examples may be found in Thecla's miracles as well) is that the same figures appear in several miracles. They may be the protagonists of consecutive stories, like George in MA19–20. Elsewhere they appear in different points in the collection, as individuals who had already been helped by the saint in another earlier matter. These overlaps resulted in a peculiar confusion in the chronology of the miracles and the circumstances of their narration. The robbed man in MA18 is found again in MA22 as 'the very same victim of burglary about whom we have just spoken succumbed to severe diseases'. In one case, it is possible to follow the entire life of a character under the protection of the saint. In MA38, another man called George is introduced as a nine-year-old boy, at this time already an assiduous visitor to the church and an *anagnostes* (reader). He felt a vocation for spiritual service, and he sought escape from the family business of money-changing that awaited him. His parents dragged him home, but Artemius, miraculously curing the child of an illness, saved him. In the next miracle (MA39), George is shown growing up under the spiritual direction of a monk, and he again encountered Artemius at the age of twenty-two. In MA40, the hagiographer recalls an event of George's life when he was only eighteen.

Alternatively, it could happen that the main character of a miracle became a secondary figure in another story, like the cured child of MA36 who became a monk and suggested that the patient of MA37 turn to Artemius, persuading him by the example of his own healing story. These narratives show that the hagiographer had received his information directly in a number of cases and that he chose to organize it around certain given figures.

If we reconsider the collections of the four healers in comparison with each other, it becomes clear that from the perspective of the formation of the material Artemius's collection is unique because it lacks cultic precedents. In the other cases, these antecedents left a strong impact on the emergence of the incubation collections in regards to their content, the raw material of the narrator, and his way of collecting it. This was all set against the background of cultic rivalry with the previous healers. That the cult of Artemius was imported into Constantinople, however, isolated the formation and traditional transmission of the stories, or in other words, it retained them within their own context. In the three other cases, we are dealing with a stratification of oral and material cult-traditions; their accidental and conscious shaping into collections are both a sort of archaeology.

---

66 Fernandez Marcos, *Los Thaumata*, p. 171.

Seen under a different light, the collections or corpora of Thecla and Artemius stand apart. These are the collected material of a single hagiographer over a relatively short period of time, and they are confined to a well-defined place. The miracles of Thecla, exactly because of the above-mentioned cultic continuity and the hence further-reaching narrative tradition, embrace a greater time span than those of Artemius, which is described as contemporary to the hagiographer's own generation. In these two collections, the geography of the sacred and spatial distribution of the patients is also more restricted than in the other miracle accounts. Thecla focuses more on her region and town, Artemius on Constantinople and his quarter, the Oxeia. Both the closed chronology and space determined what the hagiographers had at hand when collecting their narrative material. In contrast, the redactors of Cosmas and Damian as well as Sophronius were free to select from a more timeless, diversified, and multiple tradition and from a material that encompassed a wider cultural spectrum.

When it comes to an orally transmitted tradition, we face a two-sided phenomenon. On the one hand, (any) miracle-narration and transmission in general had a real oral context. This was the same case with ancient Greek incubation and with the survival of the practice that it passed on to the Christian cult. On the other hand, this real orality was modified by the demands of literature:

> features of the new [late antique / Christian] narrative manner […] were taken over from traditional oral storytelling. Stylistic assimilation of oral form had presumably begun in late antiquity, but the traits studied here appear with regularity from the sixth century on. The adoption of the oral style by writers of history, that is to say by men of letters, is encouraged and made possible by the fact that the high culture of the period displays new interests of its own that match those popular narrative — in particular the hardening of public life into patterns of ritual and ceremony, and the development of an elaborate inventory of significant and symbolic objects — tendencies that coincide in large measure with the oral-traditional emphasis on gestures and objects. This convergence of high and popular culture leaves its unmistakeable stamp upon the new style, which turns out to be something far more complex than a naturalized folktale manner.[67]

Thus, we are dealing partly with the conservation of orality, and as such, the oral tradition is a *source*. Then again, this orality in the text is a created literary narrative technique that imitated and recalled oral transmission, in this way giving the framework of storytelling to the narrative prose. What is worthy of attention in the miracle collections is that these two phenomena are not only present side by side but are inseparable from each other; the literary form draws on a living tradition, which in turn assumes the composed form of the miracle narrative.

---

67   Pizarro, *A Rhetoric of the Scene*, p. 15.

The Transition from Oral to Written Records

In what follows, I will focus on the impact that the mixing of oral and written material had on the narrative. First, I will do this by examining the explicitly stated motivations for putting the miracle story in writing. One of the most frequently expressed motives for recording the miraculous event was the expressed wish of the healer. The inscription of Iulius Apellas started and concluded with repeated emphasis on what Asclepius ordered (c. AD 160): 'I, Marcus Iulius Apellas, an Idrian from Mylasa, was sent for by the god [...]. In the course of my journey, in Aegina, the god told me not to be so irritable. When I arrived at the temple, he told me to [...] [here follow detailed prescriptions]. He bade me also to inscribe this.'[68] Maria Girone has called attention to other examples of divine orders for the making of written records,[69] a topos that was widespread from the Old Testament to imperial Rome.[70]

The purposes of recording incubation miracles (pagan or Christian) were of many kinds: (1) to fulfil the ritual obligation ordered or expected by the healer; (2) for the healed patient to record their own personal experience and give it the meaning of a cult experience; (3) to induce similar miracles to happen to those waiting to be cured; (4) to propagate the healer's fame and the efficacy of the cult place far and wide; and (5) in many cases, for the personal aims of the recorder. These hagiographic aims could be well expressed openly, often in the prologue of the miracle collection. The rhetorical colourfulness of such prologues has been recently analysed by Thomas Pratsch, outlining the topoi, the metaphors, and the literary allusions the hagiographers used;[71] I list here the motivations and references the incubation hagiographers made to the act of recording itself.

Thecla's hagiographer called his endeavour a 'searching and collecting' (in MT 31: *thamatón erauna kai syllogé*), and we have every reason to suppose that he took pleasure in discovering new stories, tracing witnesses, and organizing the heard material into a written, structured collection.

Sophronius states in the prologue of the *Thaumata* that the lack of written sources urged him to create his collection. When the fame of the saints attracted him to Menouthis, and he became a beneficiary of a miracle, he discovered with surprise the richness of the circulating narrative material. He cites the

---

68 T432; cf. Girone, *Iamata*, pp. 58–70.
69 Girone, *Iamata*, p. 70: Asclepius to Aelius Aristides in the *Hieroi Logoi*, Or. 48, 2K; on the inscriptions from Lebena, III. 10 (Girone), III. 12 (Girone), III. 13 (Girone), and Pergamon IV. 2 (Girone).
70 See Weinreich, *Antike Heilungswunder*, pp. 6–9; Festugière, *La révélation d'Hermès Trismégiste*, p. 318; Girone lists Old Testament orders of this sort from Habacuc 2. 2; Isaiah 8. 1; Jeremiah 30. 2. For Lebena, first century BC (Girone, III. 12–13), III. 15 Lebena, third century AD; Girone, *Iamata*, p. 153, concerning the inscriptions from Tiber Island, on the importance of written evidence for pilgrims in Roman religion.
71 Pratsch, 'Rhetorik in der byzantinischen Hagiographie'.

two groups of written material that encouraged him to record the miracles as Cyril's *sermones* read at the *translatio* of the saints, and the numerous written miracles of the pagan deities. Sophronius unambiguously remarks that these collections were widely known in written form; therefore, it is legitimate to suppose that they also served for him as literary models or anti-models in the field of miraculous healing. Sophronius himself denied the existence of a miracle-inventory kept in the sanctuary, though I do not think that he was sincere but rather wanted to create the impression that he only shaped the orally circulating miracles into structurally unified narratives. On one occasion, he mentions that he worked from written sources: in MCJ8, the first of the miracles concerning Christodorus, he said that Christodorus himself wrote down the miracles of the saints that involved him and his family.[72]

Concerning the miracles of Cosmas and Damian, it is of great importance that the London Codex reported the injunction of the saints explicitly forbidding the creation of a written record of their miracles. At the background of this demand was the imitation of Christ: the London Codex speaks of Saint Cosmas as 'having performed many other sorts of healing, the writing down of which he forbade, quoting Christ, who forbade that his own miracles should come to light' (CL8.27–9.2).

The point is not only that the saints, both by their miraculous healings as well as by keeping silent about them, follow Christ's example, but that the miracles themselves are carriers of a sort of mimesis, so that their written recording is all the more to be avoided because these miracles are also Christ's miracles: mirrors, transmitters, and appendices to the events of the Gospel.

> Saints Cosmas and Damian, having healed already many sick people through the grace given by God, did not want their deeds to become public. It is the saints' custom to hide their merits, so that they would not become like those who seek the approbation of men. As many people urged them to write down together whatever they did in their lifetime while wandering, they replied angrily: 'The grace of healing belongs to God, who does all, at the time and in the way he wants. What he did earlier, is written in the Gospels. Those miracles show that he is the true God.' (CL5.20–27)

This miracle is doubly mimetic: not only are the deeds of the saints the image of Christ's miracles, but the miracle stories reflect each other as well, revealing the universal from the particular:

> You, my dear audience, when hearing the power of the saints' miracles, do not only rejoice, but whatever great miracle you hear that the saints performed, regard these small ones and few in number. Because we could

---

72 Déroche takes the whole collection for these miracles; see his 'Tensions and contradictions dans les recueils de miracles', p. 147.

select for you only a few from the many, to guide you who hear them to believe also the rest of the miracles. (CL5.6–13)

A few written miracles provide a hinterland for the numerous other heard miracles, behind which there are countless other stories. Nevertheless, this concept of the mimetic oral carriers of tradition failed to take root in the case of Christ — an inadequacy of the oral mimetic medium of the disciples that eventually led to the birth of the Gospels.[73]

The Necessary, the Superfluous, and the Additional

When miracles receive their written form, one of the most interesting aspects of the process is what is omitted and what remains of the elements of the story. What do we know about the personality of the characters — or rather, to what extent is what we know of them inherited from the fixed-form votive (name, place, profession, illness), and how much the result of the narrator's imagination, a rhetorical demand to enrich the narrative? On the fate of names and personal details the two disciplines of New Testament studies and rumour studies contradict each other. Lynn LiDonnici summarized these contrasting views when addressing the same question (what was inserted and what was dropped) in the *Iamata*:

> Bultmann held that as the oral tradition developed, names and details would be inserted, reflecting the 'novelistic' concern with the 'characters' in the tradition. [...] However, studies on the transmission of rumour suggest that it is just this type of detail which drops out, rumours becoming vaguer though keeping their basic shapes. [...] This is another example of the mismatch between rumour studies and tradition studies, whether oral or written. Rumour is free, but when even an informal tradition is making the effort to persuade and preserve, it seems very natural for the tradition to *gain* material rather than the reverse.[74]

In his prologue, Thecla's hagiographer brings up the question of personal details and historical authenticity, writing that he sought out and recorded contemporary or somewhat earlier miracles because the content of these could be verified, and on the basis of such 'facts', the rest of the much older miracles, known only by hearsay and lacking these personal details, would also gain credit. This is why he carefully described all names, places, and persons, so that the audience should not have the slightest doubt about the historical truth of the events.[75]

---

73 Cf. Kelber, *The Oral and Written Gospel*, p. 97.
74 LiDonnici, *The Epidaurian Miracle Inscriptions*, p. 55, esp. n. 20.
75 *Vie et miracles*, ed. and trans. by Dagron, pp. 284–85.

Details unmistakeably inserted by the narrator to enhance the exactitude of the miracles are frequent in Artemius, like the one below concerning the space of the sanctuary:

> This person [Artemius appearing in a dream] was coming from the direction of the narthex, preceded by a spotless white dove. Upon entering the nave and then making a turn, he entered the left colonnade through the upper railings proceeding as if in the direction of the sacristy. (MA15)

I doubt if such a detailed account, with the exact topographical description of the interior, could have come to the hagiographer from the dreamer, rather than from a previously written account or based on his own intimate knowledge of the church.

Transmission from oral to written record, with the ever-present details of the given sanctuary, had great importance from the aspect of the rivalry between cult places. The written documents made public at the place, as well as in circulation together with other hagiographical writings, strengthened not so much the fame of the healers but that of the particular healing sanctuary. In this competition, it is rather probable that freely circulating miracle stories became connected in their written form to a specific sanctuary, with the insertion of the place name into the narrative or, as we may suppose in the case of Cosmas and Damian, by relocating the miracle from its previous place to a more famous church.

At the end of this investigation into the presence of stories both as background material and as final products, we arrive at the formation of what Averil Cameron called the Christian discourse, in her *Christianity and the Rhetoric of Empire*. She outlines how holy places attracted their own collection of stories and how stories were formed and attached themselves around particular cult places: 'It was not enough simply to possess relics; the relics had to be given their own discourse.'[76] It is remarkable that the majority of her examples come from incubation places (including, interestingly, Thecla's miracles):

> With earlier exceptions, such as the miracles attached to the shrine of Thecla at Seleucia, collections of miracle stories focused on specific shrines seem characteristically to develop in the East in the sixth and seventh centuries. In the majority of cases the miracles consist of cures associated with the shrine itself, as in the cases of SS. Cosmas and Damian, and St John the Baptist at Oxeia (site of the relics of Artemius) in Constantinople, SS. Cyrus and John at Menouthis in Egypt, and others where incubation was practiced.[77]

---

76 Cameron, *Christianity and the Rhetoric of Empire*, p. 209.
77 Cameron, *Christianity and the Rhetoric of Empire*, p. 211. Thecla's inevitable inclusion in this list, as an integral part of it and not as an exception, speaks to her belonging to Christian incubation healers (this is not the only reason, of course, and her cult and miracle collection obviously have their individual characteristics).

These observations invite a further thought on how a 'discourse' attached to a place can function: if we step outside the Christian framework, we may notice that it is often the case — as most markedly in the case of Seleucia and Menouthis — that a discourse came first. By this, I mean that a set of miracle stories, a rhetoric of wondrous cures and divine intervention, was already attached to the place. The very existence of such discourse, orally preserved memory, or written testimonials attached to the cult place and its previous cult figure made necessary the Christianization of the place; the appropriation of the cult site (by placing the relics or attributing them to the place) is followed by the creation of the stories relevant to the saints. This creation of new rhetoric, a new set of miracle stories, can be modelled against the legends of the preceding pagan cult activities (as in Thecla's case), but they can also be based on the patterns of already well-known saints, as the figures of Cyrus and John may have relied on Cosmas and Damian. The process perpetuates itself, just as it happened in the temples of Asclepius: the stories are put into a framework, and a miracle collection gives an impetus for the fame and further popularity of the cult place, which in turn generates new stories — or even a new discourse, like the propagation of orthodoxy. Cameron's set of examples confirms my view on Christian incubation in the sense that these cult places and cult records were special and followed their own rules, both in the ritual and in the narrative. The close attachment of the stories to the cult place is one of the consequences of the unity and uniqueness of Christian incubation miracles.

CHAPTER 6

The Hagiographers

Who Makes the Incubation Stories?

The hagiographers' intrusions into their own stories not only make quite spectacular testimony for what they thought of themselves and how they wished to be seen, but they also show how well they knew their craft and what narrative and theological role they attributed to their own writing. Less openly, the hagiographers reveal a mixture of motivations and reasons for their work, sometimes personal matters and hatreds, and elsewhere more elevated convictions. Composing hagiography made one automatically a hagiographer, but inserting one's own self into the miracle stories as a character in the manner evident in incubation collections betrays a greater compositional talent and creative fantasy than is usually attributed to Byzantine hagiographers.[1]

In the midst of the shaping of the narrative into a compositional whole, a proper collection, we find the hagiographer — but not only them. The hagiographer, however conscious a composer with the most precise desire of giving birth to a text of literary value, did not rely only on their own literary taste and repertoire of expressions. Hence the question: Who shapes the miracle stories? The answer is the saint, the sick persons, as well as the hagiographer — and the traditional, internal rules of miracle narrative. This is because the patient of the Byzantine incubation saints, just like the sick supplicant who turned to Asclepius, was conditioned by the stories he heard about the cult that were often recorded and read in the sanctuary. The shaping of his dream was conditioned not only emotionally but also in a concrete way. In the previous chapter, I have discussed how the oral and written records in the cult place prepared the patients for what to expect in their dream and provided them with a narrative framework to articulate their experiences. In what follows, I will outline the impact of a narrative tradition in the formation of the miracle stories at the hands of the saints, patients, and, in greatest detail, the hagiographers.

To illustrate my point, I start with two examples from the incubation miracles, following Lennart Rydén, who on the basis of these two stories made an observation worth pursuing further. The first miracle is from the collection of Artemius (MA26): An elderly man afflicted with a hernia dreamed that they received from the saint the counsel to turn to a blacksmith for cure.

---

* Some parts of this chapter are excerpted by permission of the publishers from Csepregi, 'Who Is behind Incubation Stories?'.
1 For a discussion on the Byzantine hagiographer and his audience for a slightly later period, see Efthymiadis, 'The Byzantine Hagiographer and his Audience'.

The blacksmith objected to the idea of possessing any thaumaturgical gifts, perhaps even considering the sick man's request as a mockery. Yet the patient insisted, and when he visited the blacksmith's workshop for the third time for the remedy, the latter became so angry that he struck the man's hernia with an enormous blow of his hammer, and the sick man (naturally) recovered immediately. In Rydén's opinion, the story does not really have an anecdotic, composed character. To this miracle, Rydén paralleled the story of Cosmas and Damian, KDM24, that ends with the double recovery and marriage of the paralytic man and the mute woman, adding that he has the feeling that, in both cases, it was the saints who made the jokes, not the hagiographer or the patients.[2]

With this train of thought, we arrive at the questions of who created the miracle narratives, to what extent did they create the narratives, and in obedience to which mechanisms did they create it. The answer is given above, that it is the figures who shape the story: the saints, the patient, and the hagiographer. Developing this issue a bit further, however, it is important to touch upon the factor that is the most decisive element in the spontaneous taking shape of the events, as well as in the conscious formation of the story: the narrative tradition. By tradition, I intend several concepts. First, there is an almost automatic selection, which elevates an event in a self-explanatory way to a miracle. Laymen (often the patient or the eyewitness, but the readers as well) and the official representatives of the cult alike knew well what might render an event a miracle: if the wondrous intervention of the saint is experienced, if the sick is healed, the lost is found out, the sinner meets his punishment, etc. All of these events unmistakably reside within the saint's sphere of influence. Stories that do not conform to this scheme, however interesting they may be, narratable, or in their genre extraordinary, not only do not find their way into miracle collections, but not even their recipient regards them as miracle stories. I emphasize the working of this primary, natural filter, because further below, cases will be noted where the traditionally transmitted story is at odds with the requirements of any of the schemes (e.g. the patient dies instead of recovers). In such cases, a more cunning narrative technique becomes necessary, a sort of narrative twist to the story so that they could eventually find their way into the miracle collections. The requirements of the given genre or narrative scheme could certainly be controlled more directly by the authors and transmitters of the stories, on the basis of both style and content. Research on folk-poetry notes the phenomenon that is usually called the rule of self-correction, which is put into practice in the case of epic songs in an institutionalized context, when singers would discuss new versions at their assemblies and dismiss those which do not conform to the traditional style and traditional epic world.

---

2   Rydén, 'Kyrkan som sjukhus', p. 11.

After discussing briefly this primary role of the narrative tradition that shapes the text in its various chronological phases, we can return to the three formative agents of the miracle narrative. The first was the saint: the saint's actions, attributes, and gestures are strongly determined by the saint's own story, his or her *vitae*, the miracles the saint performed earlier, the saint's reputation, and the features and deeds communicated by iconographical representations. On the basis of all these, the saint's suppliant adopts a certain attitude towards the saint, characterized by personal expectations and anxieties alike. The most interesting of the patient's reactions to the saint are, of course, the cases when the patient's hesitation, incredulity, or opposition lead to the repetition of the wondrous dream-events, or even to a radicalization of them. These reactions were based not simply on the patient's conception of the saint; they may arise from his respect for the dream itself as means of divine communication, from his sceptical or credulous attitude, or from his preconceptions about the cult place or concerning Christianity itself.

At the other end of the cult experience, we find the (sick) worshipper who turns to the (healer) saint. In our case of incubation, however, this cult experience is mediated through dreams. This, in my opinion, means that the dreamer-patient obtains a greater role in the formation of the story than in other fields of Byzantine hagiography. Because the miracle itself, the encounter with the saint, takes place in a dream unlike various other manifestations of the Christian saints, it is visible only to the beneficiary of the dream. Here we do not have crowds of onlookers who witness the miracle. The bystanders could ascertain the healing of the patients and vouch for their previous condition, but the healer usually comes to a single individual in a dream-visitation. The hagiographer, even when they claimed to be an 'eyewitness', was forced to rely on the dream-narrative of the dreamer. The dream-experience and its narrativization were also deeply influenced by several factors: the personality of the dreamer, their faith, fears, expectations, and their own and their listeners' medical and theological knowledge.

The third and, for us readers, the ultimate figure in the process of moulding the religious experience into a meaningful narrative is the hagiographer. When we turn to the hagiographer, we see that his knowledge of the narrative rules of such stories also works on him. When hearing a story of a dream-cure, he could place it immediately into the schemes of incubation narratives. When he does this, he not only conforms to the story patterns, but he reflects on his own hagiographic endeavour as well. The hagiographer's project of collecting and authoring the miraculous cures of the saints is closely linked to his relationship with the cult place; he can be a beneficiary of the saint's cure himself, or official temple personnel, priest, or member of a lay sodality around the saint. His affiliation within these categories greatly contributes to his way of handling his sources, as we have seen in the previous chapters, as well as influencing his motivations for writing, like personal thanksgiving for healing or church propaganda. In what follows, I shall introduce the hagiographer's role and his person, not only as it emerges from the stories they wrote but with closer attention to his conscious self-presentation. In short, the question is this: What was the relationship of the hagiographer to the text?

The Hagiographer as Narrator, Author, Patient, Cult Personnel

The question above is better formulated if we ask, In what sense we can regard the hagiographer as either author, narrator, performer, compiler of the miracle stories, recorder of the text, or a creative composer of it? What is the image he would like to create for himself, what kind of storyteller/collector/virtuoso roles and analogies for such roles can be found in the miracle narratives themselves?

The (material) author of a narrative is in no way to be confused with a narrator of that narrative. In our cases of hagiographical writing caution is even more needed: the narrator of the miracles is set, and usually voluntarily sets himself, into the tradition of previous writers of saintly deeds. In this hagiographical tradition, authors and narrators alike are layered on each other — this is precisely what constitutes the hagiographic tradition. This layering of the narrators may emerge accidentally, in accordance with the formative rules of hagiography, but it may occur consciously as well.[3]

As with the continuing tradition of recording Christian miracle narratives, the recorder of miracles is already a familiar figure from the cultic and literary milieu of Greek Antiquity. We owe to Strabo the testimony that the miraculous cures in the Serapeion at Canopus were written down: 'Canobus [...] contains the temple of Sarapis, which is honoured with great reverence and effects such cures that even the most reputable men believe in it and sleep in it — themselves on their own behalf or others for them. Some writers go on to record the cures, and others the virtues of the oracles there.'[4] Recent research uncovered the world of this sort of priestly literary activity, choosing the Canopus temple scriptorium as a case study to illustrate how temple scribes worked. The role of temple scribes was by no means only recording; they were to search and interpret their sacred texts, and they were still efficiently functioning in the fourth century AD in the Canopus Serapeion, because from that period we have two important notices regarding their activity: first, that there was a veritable academy for studying sacred writings, surpassing even the one in

---

3 On types of narrators: Kazhdan, *Authors and Texts in Byzantium*; Booth, *The Rhetoric of Fiction*, esp. chs 6, 7, 8; on personal *versus* impersonal narration: Barthes's Introduction to his 'Structural Analysis of Narrative'.

4 *Geographica*, XVII. 801. Cf. Gil, *Therapeia*, p. 358, and for more: Duprez, *Jésus et les dieux guérisseurs*, p. 73.

Alexandria, and second, that contemporary Christians maintained that the scriptorium was a repository of magical arts.[5]

I have already mentioned earlier that at some places recording the cult experience in writing was compulsory. Even in cases like Trophonius's where the worshipper was supposed to write down his own experiences, it would be legitimate to suggest that the temple personnel was responsible for storing, rewriting, and sharing these records.

Vincenzo Longo addressed the difficulty in identifying the role of such miracle recorders:[6] in its original meaning, the Greek *aretalogos* denoted both the priest recording the wondrous deeds of the divine, and an official entertainer as well. The dichotomy of the term reflects the double-faced, both religious and profane, character of aretalogy itself. I am here more interested in the two-sided relationship between the hagiographer and his text, a process Derek Krueger called 'doubly generative'.[7] The effect the text made on its writer as a spiritual tool in shaping his personality and faith is more marked in the Christian context than, for example, in the Greek temple records, but it can be easily related to the relationship between scribes and holy texts (or magical artefacts, for that matter).[8] Claudia Rapp formulated another aspect of the hagiographer's role, which 'parallels that of the saint. Both, as it were, provide perfect models of sanctity, one through his writing, the other through his life.'[9]

In the modern analyses of the incubation miracle collections, scholars have primarily been interested in the hagiographer as a historical figure, and the author's self-representation in the incubation miracle tales was rarely investigated in the Greek context.[10] Thecla's hagiographer has been examined as a main character of ecclesiastical Realpolitik or as an antagonist of Basil of Seleucia,[11] or else the focus has been on his classical education, rhetorical training, literary and philosophical knowledge,[12] and his intimate relationship to the saint and to the cult had been often emphasized.

Our only hagiographer known by name, Sophronius, the future patriarch of Jerusalem during the Arab takeover, has received much scholarly attention.[13] As a hagiographer, he was member of the circle of friends in Alexandria which

---

5   See Frankfurter, *Religion in Roman Egypt*, ch. 6, 'The World of the Scriptorium', pp. 238–48.
6   Longo, *Aretalogie nel mondo Greco*, p. 19.
7   Krueger, *Writing and Holyness*, p. 2; cf. also his 'Early Byzantine Historiography and Hagiography'.
8   Frankfurter, *Religion in Roman Egypt*, p. 239.
9   Rapp, 'Byzantine Hagiographers as Antiquarians', p. 41.
10 Petsalis-Diomidis, 'Sacred Writing, Sacred Reading'.
11 Dagron, 'L'auteur des Actes et des Miracles de Sainte Thècle'.
12 Johnson, *The 'Life and Miracles of Thekla'*, ch. 4.
13 About Sophronius's person and about the identity of Sophronius the Sophist and Sophronius the Patriarch, see Vailhé, 'Sophrone le sophiste et Sophrone le patriarche'; Fernandez Marcos, *Los Thaumata*, pp. 163–64; about the identity of the two, see Schönborn, *Sophrone de Jérusalem* versus Ševčenko, 'La agiografia bizantina dal IV al IX secolo', pp. 137–40.

formed around John the Almsgiver, himself the author of a *Vita of Saint Tychon*.¹⁴ To this group we owe (besides the works of Sophronius, among them his first (lost) *Vita* of John the Almsgiver) also the *Pratum Spirituale* of John Moschus and the *Lives* composed by Leontinos of Neapolis.¹⁵ Sophronius wrote partly under this influence (and as a result of his stay in Alexandria and Menouthis) the *Laudes* and the *Miracula Cyri et Johanni* as well.

The collections of Thecla and that of Cyrus and John are unique among the incubation corpora in that they are literary works by named authors; the first was transmitted as the work of Basil of Seleucia, the latter in the oeuvre of Sophronius, hence they more or less escaped the usual rewritings and insertions of miracle collections. We find later additions, greatly changing the theological message of the miracles, in the Artemius material, a collection that is anonymous but can be related to a specific author. It has been suggested that the hagiographer of Artemius, on the basis of his medical vocabulary and his polemics against doctors, was an assistant in a nearby hospital who, as a member of the church personnel, was an adherent of the cult and who, thanks to his myriad details on the everyday life of the capital and on the church building itself, has much to reveal to the social and art historians. A recent hypothesis saw him hidden among the characters of the miracles. In the case of Cosmas and Damian we are dealing with colourful, multiple layers of hagiographic material that had been building on each other for centuries. From the flow of the narrative, there only occasionally emerges a — sometimes named — personal voice.

What interests me in the hagiographer is his figure in relation to his narrative, and the picture he consciously or involuntarily provides about himself. I am looking for answers for questions such as what ambitions, especially literary-creative ambitions, motivate the hagiographer and what are the narrative situations in which he puts himself forward or when he prefers to remain invisible. During the process of the creation of the hagiographer's persona, it may be surprising to discover that *reflection on the writing self* is manifest in the metaphors the hagiographer applies to himself.¹⁶ What he chooses to be the simile for himself is not only based on his temper and self-esteem but also intimately linked to the way he perceives his work as a collector, organizer, and redactor of stories, who may struggle in selecting from the plenty but nonetheless be searching out the best tales.

---

14   For more about him and about the circle of hagiographer-friends, cf. Delehaye, *L'ancienne hagiographie byzantine*, pp. 51–68.
15   Such as the *Life of Symeon the Fool*, the reworking of Sophronius's first *Life of Saint John the Almsgiver*, the *Life of Saint Spyridion*; cf. Mango, 'A Byzantine Hagiographer at Work'.
16   For the idea of the hagiographer reflecting on the writing self, a useful parallel is Herodotus; see Benardete, *Herodotean Inquiries*.

The Hagiographic Endeavour: The Case of Thecla's Hagiographer

Thecla's hagiographer depicted himself as a merchant of much-sought-after precious stones (a topos of Byzantine hagiography[17]), a metaphor which speaks to the value of the saint's narrated deeds. Another image of himself, as gold digger, reflects upon the difficulty of his task in obtaining these treasures, aware of the heavy chore of carrying away the layers of soil covering the precious material.[18]

Thecla's hagiographer, before embarking upon the saint's miracles and at the end of the *Vita*, already signalled his future project and spoke of the indispensable help of Thecla in this endeavour. Among his motivations in writing about the miracles, he mentions that some of these miracles happened to himself;[19] a further reason he gives was the indirect request of Thecla, which she communicated through one of her protégés, Achaius, a friend of the hagiographer (as Dagron called it: 'ami initiateur, sainte inspiratrice'). However, in the closing section of the corpus, the hagiographer addresses a much more personal request to Thecla. As if requesting this in exchange for his work, he beseeches the saint to rescue him from the anger and malevolence of a certain Porphyrius.[20]

If we examine closely when and under what circumstances the hagiographer appears in the forty-six miracles of the collection, we come to the following conclusion: the hagiographer comes into sight at proportionally distributed intervals in the corpus, almost with a regular rhythm. After the first mention of himself at the end of the *Vita* (which is at the same time an introduction to the *Miracula* and the justification for the undertaking of collecting the miracles), he appears in MT 12, 31, and 41. Each of these miracles forms part of a thematic group: MT 12 is the closure of the thematic unity that speaks about the bishops of Thecla's church (such as Dexianus, the hagiographer's contemporary, and Thecla's favoured bishop, Menodorus, bishop of Cilicia and Symposius, an earlier bishop of the sanctuary, MT 7–11). This section is closed by MT 12, in which the hagiographer first tells of his own miraculous recovery. It is underlined that just as the miracles of the collection are part of a longer series of countless miracle stories that record Thecla's deeds, this healing miracle of the hagiographer is similarly just one of the miraculous recoveries that Thecla performed in his favour. Putting aside the fact that, in this case, he does not give the patient's (i.e. his own) name and other personal information like in the rest of the stories, the miracle-narrative

---

17 MT 44; for its other occurrences, cf. *Vie et miracles*, ed. and trans. by Dagron, p. 405.
18 On Thecla's hagiographer as a historiographer (in the *Vita*) versus the researcher and social observer of the *Miracula*, cf. *Vie et miracles*, ed. and trans. by Dagron, pp. 22–23.
19 *Vie et miracles*, ed. and trans. by Dagron, pp. 280–81.
20 *Vie et miracles*, ed. and trans. by Dagron, pp. 16–18.

in its illness–dream–healing story-pattern does not differ from the other pieces of the collection. Naturally, he tells his story in a first-person narrative. But we may surmise that this innocent start to the healing miracle is just a prelude to the telling of a far more significant event shaped into a miracle: in connection with Thecla's healings, the hagiographer put himself into the role of a beneficiary of the miracle. When talking about himself, he starts another story, unconnected to his illness but which expresses more markedly Thecla's grace over him. This story narrates the hagiographer's confrontation with the new bishop, the successor of Dexianus who in this story is called a dishonest drunkard and became known in ecclesiastical history as Basil of Seleucia. The reader gets the impression that the hagiographer previously told his story of recovery not only to extol his own person, but to give credit to Thecla's wondrous intervention into ecclesiastical politics. In keeping with his effort to establish credibility, the hagiographer emphasizes that it was still a matter of Thecla's personal help towards him, particularly in his conflict as a priest against his bishop. According to the narration, the background of the events was Basil's episcopal election. As an omniscient narrator, he underlines the gravity of the way things happened by not speaking about it: '[the story of] how he became bishop, and how he got the church into his power, which is unworthy even to appear on stage in the theatre, I omit for now'.[21]

As I address elsewhere the significance of this miracle for theology and for ecclesiastical power relations, for the moment I would only call attention to the fact that, after having presented himself as a healed patient, the hagiographer depicts himself among the priests of Thecla's church. After this story, the miracle stories that are not connected so closely to the cult place and its personnel begin (MT13: 'There was once a military commander [...]'; MT14: 'There was once a man [...]').

The hagiographer's next appearance on the scene in MT31 is an emblematic representation of how he considers his own role as narrator and how he involves Thecla in that: during the writing of the miracles, the hagiographer was oppressed by fatigue and negligence. Yet Thecla appeared to him at this moment in the very place where the hagiographer usually studies his books, and at a time when the hagiographer was transcribing a draft version of a miracle written on a tablet.[22] Thecla started to read the already finished part and was greatly delighted by it. After this encouraging apparition, the hagiographer redoubled his efforts to continue the collection. I would again point out the context and the miracles among which this scene was described; I am convinced it is again a homogeneous thematic group. From MT26 onwards, Thecla appears in her

---

21 MT12.45–46: 'τὸ μὲν ἐπίσκοπός τε ἐγένετο καὶ τῆς ἐκκλησίας ἐκράτησε, τὸ μηδὲ σκηνῆς ἄξιον, ἀφείσθω τὰ νῦν'.
22 Cf. Dagron's remark about the technique of writing–rewriting–copying, *Vie et miracles*, p. 373, n. 1: 'les tablettes et le stylet servent à faire un brouillon, qui est ensuite recopié sur un quaternion de parchemin'.

quality of warrior-saint, including the account of when the saint protects her besieged city and her sanctuary. From MT 29, retaliation/punishment miracles follow, protecting those who are under Thecla's protection. It should be noted that here Thecla's attention is directed to those persons and things who are not only generally under her protection (e.g. the orphans of MT 35), but her attention is directed to people and things in direct connection with her cult (such as the cult objects of her sanctuary, the woman celebrating on Thecla's feast day, or the nun living at the sanctuary). The hagiographer did not accidentally write himself into the stories where Thecla was working for 'her own people'. His next, final appearance is in MT 41, the closing miracle of a well-defined thematic group, and at the same time, this appearance is a valuable reference to the kind of self-portrait that the hagiographer wished to record. MT 38, 39, and 40 each concern rhetoricians. These are brought about by Thecla's intervention on the hagiographer's behalf and on the occasion of the rhetorical contest organized in her honour. On the eve of the event, the hagiographer's ear became inflamed, which jeopardizes his participation in the contest; but Thecla aids him and he predictably wins the first prize.

Thecla's hagiographer always appears as the beneficiary of miracles and, moreover, as the protagonist of four detailed stories, two of which focus on his literary activity.[23] Although we are ignorant of his name, we learn far more about his personality here than in the cases of our other hagiographers. At the end of the collection, he reveals a hitherto concealed, and very much down-to-earth motive, for his embarking on writing the miracles. The hagiographer must have had a serious argument with a certain Porphyrius, whom he calls a dog, a pig, and a bastard. He appeals for the help of Thecla against this man and in order to quell his own wrath. Dagron suggested that this Porphyrius might have been the new bishop of Seleucia (succeeding Basil of Seleucia sometime after 468) and a successor of those bishops who lived under Thecla's protection (hence the prominent stories about them).[24]

The Hagiographers in the Collections of Cosmas and Damian

I have already addressed earlier how the consecutive, chronological order of the KDM sections was challenged by the London Codex itself, since the latter contains miracles from all the first five series, ranging from KDM1 to KDM33. To some extent, the miracles of the London Codex also undermine the distinction that Festugière made regarding the separate 'authorship' of the different sections. If instead of the 'author', we concentrate on the figure of the hagiographer, the most interesting part of this collection would be,

---

23 For the detailed structure of the miracles, see the next chapter.
24 *Vie et miracles*, ed. and trans. by Dagron, p. 16.

beyond doubt, Section III (KDM21–26), especially when compared to the respective stories of the London Codex. The self-display of the hagiographer's persona attests in the most exemplary way how a compiler-hagiographer styled himself into an author-hagiographer. He consciously shaped the description of his own presence in the text, first depicting himself as collecting miracles by hearing them in the church and then also displaying himself as a healed patient of the saints who makes a thanksgiving gift. Finally, he adds a third element: that the writing of the miracles was commissioned by a certain friend of his, called Florentius.

The hagiographer of the sixth part of the Cosmas and Damian collection (KDM39–47) is the only identified compiler of the corpus. He was called Maximus and was a monk of the monastery attached to the church. The community of monks, like the monastery-complex around the church of Thecla, was responsible for collecting and transmitting miraculous events. The acknowledged aim of our Maximus was twofold: to add new stories to the collection and to rewrite the already existing miracles in a higher literary style. He gives considerable information about his own hagiographical activity, especially in the preface of KDM40: he sees himself as far less insignificant and humble than the nameless hagiographer of the preceding miracle stories, the one who compared himself and his literary tribute to the poor widow offering two mites. Maximus calls attention not only to the truth of the miracles, but also to the proportioned structure of their narratives,

> since [...] Nature made for all living creatures that their limbs should be proportionate to the whole of their bodies; it is the same in my case: during the literary creation the parts of the narrative should necessarily be ordered proportionally, nothing can be superfluous or useless.

This last remark leads us further into the hagiographers' introspection, as in our collections, they usually do not stop at introducing their person in a simile. They consciously reflect their art of collecting, writing, and organizing the miracles. The ultimate achievement of self-display is when hagiographers write themselves and their enterprise into their stories, sometimes openly, at other occasions with subtle cunningness, using specifically their art of structuring and composing to hide themselves as hagiographers — and to come to the fore as narrative characters.

Sophronius

Sophronius started the *Laudes*, the short prelude to the miracle collections, with a classical image of Greek poetry, which — despite its loquacity — may recall to a modern reader Sappho's sixteenth fragment.[25] With the list of 'ἄλλοι

---

25 Sappho, *Poetic Fragments*, fr. 16. 'For some – it is horsemen; for others – it is infantry; | For some others – it is ships which are, on this black earth, | Visibly constant in their beauty. But

μέν [...], οἱ μέν [...] οἱ δέ [...], ἄλλοι δέ [...] ἕτεροι δέ',[26] Sophronius contrasts exultation by words: 'But for me, for whom words (*logos*) are dearer than my homeland. [...] I am convinced that the martyrs take their liking in that, as they themselves also declared the Word of God': "Ἡμεῖς δὲ οἷς λόγος ἐστὶν τῶν γηΐνων ὑλῶν τιμαλφέστερος. [...] ᾧ καὶ χαίρειν τοὺς μάρτυρας πείθομαι, ὡς Λόγου Θεοῦ χρηματίσαντες μάρτυρες'.

Sophronius was the most sophisticated of our hagiographers and the one who takes his literary mission the most seriously. He compares his role and his writing method to the activity of the physician — by this, perhaps, he means that he is placing himself nearest to the work of the doctor-saints: 'Probably just like the Asclepiadai do: mixing with honey the painful and the useful remedies that purge for those who need purgatives. I myself, therefore, imitate them by mixing to the previous, sweet miracles these following harsh ones, and attach these to the more pleasant things and make the end delightful' (MCJ32). Behind the simile, there may stand not only his self-styling in the medical profession that was nearest to the saints' healing function, but also the intellectual fascination of Byzantine medical science. Yet this ambitious simile is not the only one Sophronius uses to describe his own endeavour as a hagiographer. In another simile to illustrate the impossibility of his task to collect the miracles, he also depicted himself as Peter when he foolishly wanted to walk on the water. In the *Laudes*, he extends the water metaphor to his miracle stories, which he calls the few drops that can be numbered out of the vast sea of miracles. At last, in his own miracle story, he refers to his disease as Homeric blindness, where both the words 'Homeric' and 'blindness' are strong metaphors in themselves:[27] this man of erudition had to renounce, on the saints' command to his Homeric aspect, his commitment to pagan Greek culture in order to regain his eyesight, referring to both his physical capacity and the clarity of Christian orthodoxy.

In contrast to Thecla's hagiographer, who in order to secure his credibility, generally cited carefully his sources and his research work, or to the hagiographer of Artemius, who supported the veracity of his stories by giving geographical and chronological proofs, Sophronius wanted to put himself and his storytelling talent into focus. He did not even allow the indices we find in the miracles of Cosmas and Damian: the artificially created fiction of research, of listening to witnesses. Rather, he created an *ex nihilo* narrative strategy. He primarily emphasized his own compositional intentions and created the image of himself as the structuring mastermind. In the *Thaumata*,

---

for me, | It is that which you desire.' (trans. by Myatt); 'ο]ἱ μὲν ἱππήων στρότον οἱ δὲ πέσδων | οἱ δὲ νάων φαῖσ' ἐπ[ὶ] γᾶν μέλαι[ν]αν | ἔ]μμεναι κάλλιστον, ἔγω δὲ κῆν' ὄτ- | []τω τις ἔραται.'.

26 These words Sophronius also quoted at the Second Nicean Synod: cf. PG 87.3, col. 3387, n. 4.
27 How Homer stands as an ideological symbol of pagan culture in the early Byzantine Egypt is elaborated by Fournet, 'Omero e i Cristiani in Egitto secondo due testi agiografici'. A thorough interpretation of the Homeric blindness metaphor in Greek poetry and especially Neoplatonic philosophy — actually from Homer to Sophronios: Agosti, 'Le brume di Omero'.

Sophronius used alphabetical ordering and numerical proportions and was methodical in composing his own intrusions in the text. He put himself at the beginning and at the end of the collection, in this way dividing the circumstances of his own miraculous healing into two narratives. His own miracle story at the end of the collection (MCJ70) differs from the others not only in its exceptional length but because Sophronius, in order to produce the greater effect, places the obligatory narrative elements into a new position; the praise of his hometown, Damascus, is not sung by the hagiographer himself, but he gives the words to the apostle Thomas. As a patient, he is not just a patient, his illness is not only an illness, but Sophronius immediately assimilates himself to the blind Homer and makes the saints call him so. This is all the more odd, as Cyrus and John are not at all sympathetic to Greek learning, unlike Saint Thecla. Of course, Sophronius is careful to explain that the two 'authors', Homer and himself, are analogous only by the blindness. His literary aspirations evolve further when the appearing saints are described not simply as dressed like monks but that Cyrus appears in the likeness of the hagiographer's friend John (probably John Moschus) while Saint John appears as Peter, the *praefectus praetoriorum* of Alexandria. About the illness, we learn that it was *xerophtalmia*, and that Sophronius was visited by doctors, and he also specifies how a Byzantine eye-specialist made the diagnosis. A particularly interesting feature of the dream pattern is that Sophronius sees himself from outside his body (a phenomenon that originates in a new dream pattern that I shall analyse in Chapter 9). We see here many of the features that Sophronius shares with his fellow hagiographers of incubation miracles: he too was the beneficiary of a cure after the doctors had given up on him; he considers collecting and shaping the miracle stories both as an act of thanksgiving to the saints and as a literary activity during his stay in the church. And what is his personal stamp among these incubation hagiographers? Besides his virtuoso self-display as an erudite composer of the stories, we get a glimpse into how seriously Sophronius takes his war against the Monophysite Christians: one of the reasons for his hagiographic endeavour is to dress the saints as exponents of what he regards as orthodox, that is, Dyophysite Christology, in a largely Monophysite surrounding and to use all the context, vocabulary, and occasions the illness situations provide to formulate this message, with the conviction of being able to 'cure' these heresies, probably just like the Asclepiadai do.

The Hagiographer of Saint Artemius

Artemius's hagiographer is akin to Thecla's in that he establishes the credibility of the earlier miracles of his saint with the help of the miracles from his own generation and those directly preceding them, acquiring what miracles he could collect from still-living witnesses or from their children. In the first lines of the collection, he defines his role in a long simile, describing the ecstasy of one walking in a park full of gorgeous flowers, overwhelmed by the dilemma of which to choose. That this was a well-used motif is attested by the incubation collection of Saint Therapon, whose hagiographer also likens the hard task of choosing from the innumerable miracles of the saint to the dilemma of the traveller facing the beautiful flowers of a meadow.[28]

It is remarkable that although this corpus is the most medical in character, that is, detouring to the physical features of the illnesses (male hernia), the overture of this collection is the most aesthetic: 'Just as when someone enters a park and beholds the shapes of many delightfully beautiful trees and the variegated hues of different flowers uncloying in fragrance, to him everything seems praiseworthy. Then departing from there and coming to another place, he desires to report the spectacle of excellence to his neighbours also.'[29] It was supposed about Artemius's hagiographer that behind his figure so intimately at home with the special medical terminology and with the contemporary doctors of Constantinople, there could be a staff member of the Christitodoté hospital, perhaps one of the *hypourgoi* like the protagonist of MA22.[30] However, we should remember that medical knowledge and its vocabulary were in fashion among intellectuals in Byzantium,[31] and a life-long experience among the sick persons in the church could have also rendered the hagiographer well versed in these matters. In a footnote, Lennart Rydén proposed another hypothesis about the hagiographer's identity: In most miracles, the patients are all named, but the protagonists of MA18 and 22 are, as Rydén says, 'conspicuously' anonymous. In this middle-aged and experienced man who is an adherent to the cult by being a member of the All-Night Vigil Society, it may not be difficult to discover the hagiographer himself.[32] Recently, Stephanos Efthymiadis elaborated this hypothesis, and addressed in detail the two anonymous miracles. 'In writing Mir18', he argues, 'the author's main intention was not to make an objective report of a given miracle story, but rather to record reality through the emotional experience of the bachelor-hero.'[33] Efthymiadis sees in these two miracles a marked deviation from incubation conventions, namely that the two narratives do not involve healing but burglary. It partly takes place in a secular environment, and instead of being set in a dream proper, Artemius appears in person. Without questioning the plausible but difficult to prove attribution by Efthymiadis, I would only point out that, in view of the incubation stories in general, these miracles do not differ so conspicuously from others; we find several cases when the healers appear in the daytime, even outside their church, or care for

---

28 *Laudatio Therapontis*, ch. 14; cf. Haldon, 'Tortured by my Conscience', p. 271.
29 *The Miracles of St Artemius*, ed. and trans. by Crisafulli and Nesbitt, p. 77.
30 Grosdidier de Matons, 'Les *Miracula Sancti Artemii*'.
31 For references to primary sources (Procopius, Photius, Psellos, Anna Comenna, John Tzetzes) see Scarborough, 'Symposium on Byzantine Medicine', pp. x–xi.
32 Rydén, 'Kyrkan som sjukhus', p. 15, n. 5.
33 Efthymiadis, 'A Day and Ten Months in the Life of a Lonely Bachelor', p. 3.

the suppliants' lost and stolen property. Why these non–strictly incubation stories became incorporated into the collection and what narrative devices these stories used will be addressed in the next chapter.

For the purpose of the discussion of the hagiographer's self-fashioning, I would like to call attention to another of the observations Efthymiadis made. In his view, the hagiographer wanted to make the impression that some time passed between the two events, those of MA18 and 22, as the first seems to have happened to him in old age, the second much earlier. The protagonist of MA22 claimed to have been serving the saint from the age of ten, and in his devotion, Efthymiadis discovered 'the isolation and loneliness of the hero whose only friend turns out to be St Artemius'.[34] Taking Rydén's hypothesis a step further, Efthymiadis groups MA15 with the miracles hiding the hagiographer's persona, the main character of which was freely serving a man of prominence, still young, and similarly a member of the All-Night Vigil Society. All opinions, however, agree that our hagiographer must have been a learned man, with some medical knowledge and interest. The hagiographer, on the one hand, perceived his connection to the saint and his cult to be a special one, and on the other, unveils a particular talent for describing the busy social life of the capital, with a familiarity with its streets, churches and church personnel, factions, and key figures, be they actors, officials, or physicians.

At the end of this enquiry, we should ask, Is the incubation hagiographer in any way different from other hagiographers? In one particular aspect, I think, yes, he is. In many cases, he had firsthand experience with the practice of incubation and thus had a personal knowledge about the circumstances of the miracles about which he wrote. Many other hagiographers were beneficiaries of saints' miracles, but what I find important here is the experience of a miraculous healing and the elements that are associated with the incubation ritual: the community of sleepers, the time spent together, the space shared within the church, illness stories and dream narratives shared and exchanged, personal visual experience of the saint's dream apparition, and often the pain and desperation caused by the illness. Incubation hagiographers are in a special position because the hagiographers subjected themselves to the rules of incubation, not only when and if they underwent the ritual themselves, but also when they described it. Sophronius is a good example because he is the only one among our writers where we can compare his incubation hagiography with his other works. Another characteristic of incubation links the practice to the particular place, and although I do not see it as an exclusive privilege of the incubation hagiographers, we can sometimes identify the incubation hagiographers' special attachment to the cult place, which, strengthened by the face-to-face encounter of the incubation experience, may have created a strong bond between the saint and the hagiographer and between the hagiographer and the cult place.

---

34 Efthymiadis, 'A Day and Ten Months in the Life of a Lonely Bachelor', p. 12.

As for their conscious self-representation, it is not easy to summarize the overall impact that the incubation hagiographers made or wanted to make in the miracle stories. Thecla's hagiographer, a converted and learned Greek rhetor, dismissed the residuum of pagan cults but coloured his narratives with similes and literary references to Homer, Herodotus, Euripides, and Plato, thereby showing by example that Greek learning might fruitfully be used to praise a Christian saint. In my opinion, the hagiographer's personal stamp can be especially found in the urge to create a Christian *paideia*, a new narrative canon, hence his constantly thematized concern with the continuous dilemma of what material to include and what to dismiss. Like his contemporary and compatriot Theodoret of Cyrrhus, he wished to create, at least in writing, the Seleucia in which he desired to live: an educated city that values Greek eloquence. He places himself in it as its greatest rhetorician and makes Thecla the patroness of Greek literary learning blended with Christian faith. In a similarly personal manner, Sophronius wanted to communicate with his *Thaumata* that, like his Alexandrian friends around John the Almsgiver, he was a fighter for Chalcedonian orthodoxy.[35] In a Monophysite Egypt, Sophronius turned the saints into the mouthpiece of this conviction. In the centre of the corpus, he placed harsh punishment miracles performed on Monophysite Christians, and included scenes like the heretic's dream where the saints take the Eucharist in the orthodox way, make a public confession of the Chalcedonian creed, or order their perplexed patients to do the same as a condition of a cure. Sophronius's choice to make the saints into the defenders of orthodoxy was conscious, and I am inclined to think that this, alongside his own experience of their healing power, was his chief reason for making the whole collection. We can see further down-to-earth motivations for the hagiographic endeavour in the background of the other collections as well. Thecla's hagiographer, as he reveals in passing at the end of his corpus, had serious ecclesiastical trouble with someone, and he wished to mobilize Thecla and the whole cult with his learned commitment to it, in the hope he might emerge as a winner from this conflict. If behind Artemius's hagiographer there was the man who was robbed and who magnanimously and publicly forgave the thief, a fellow member of the All-Night Vigil Society, we may suggest that including himself anonymously in the collection of the miracles was a very telling gesture towards the church community to which he belonged.

---

35 On post-Chalcedonian hagiography using the Eucharist as a dogmatical and practical tool, see Menze, *Justinian and the Syrian Orthodox Church*, pp. 145–93, and Booth, *Crisis of Empire*, pp. 33–43; on Sophronius's theological system and his hagiographical agenda, Booth, *Crisis of Empire*, pp. 44–59 and 85–89.

PART III

Stories

CHAPTER 7

Compositional Structure in the Miracle Collections

> We must learn to treat hagiography for what it was, namely the literary equivalent of religious painting. When we gaze at the icon of St 'Abbacyros' in S. Maria Antiqua, we do not regard it as a real portrait.[1]

To be called aretalogy, it is not enough that a text records the miraculous deeds of divine beings; it is essential that it must also be a narrative. This involves both a structure and a specific literary demand. The *ex votos* in themselves are not aretalogy narratives, but the *Iamata* are. Despite how short their stories were, in their composition their aim was to secure the visitors' admiration, as Vincenzo Longo has written.[2] My point of departure for writing here about story and narrative will be the paradigm expanded by Adriana Cavarero: in contrast to the protagonist(s) of the *Iliad*, the Ulysses of the *Odyssey* seeks immortal fame not by his deeds but through the narratability of a story that is passed down through generations. Hence, Cavarero continues, 'The story is therefore distinct from the narration. It has, so to speak, a reality all of its own, which follows the action and precedes the narration. All actors leave behind a story, even if nothing guarantees that this story will get told later.'[3]

The compositional freedom of the narrator and the general malleability of the elements of the text are framed by the internal rules of the narrative, by *the logic of the narrative*.[4] In the case of the incubation stories, this means the order in which the events follow each other as well as the necessary occurrence of certain standard elements: the illness, the way to the healer, undergoing the ritual sleep, the dream appearance of the healer, and the given prescriptions, followed by the miraculous recovery. Though the sequence of this basic scheme is not alterable, there are occasions when some of the elements are missing — for example, there is no initial illness or the patient does not get healed — but the cohesive force of the narrative logic is so compelling that it bends the exceptions into the essential scheme, through narrative detours or explanations. For example, the lack of an illness can become either solved by a casual accident, or the concept of illness can be

---

1 Mango, 'A Byzantine Hagiographer at Work', p. 41.
2 Longo, *Aretalogie nel mondo Greco*, pp. 52–53.
3 Cavarero, *Relating Narratives*, p. 28.
4 I have borrowed the expression from Ligota, 'This Story Is Not True', p. 5; here, besides the *logic of the narrative*, he points out another tendency, quoting Herodotus: '"my logos has looked for digressions" [...]. Thus on the one hand the world coming to be known, on the other the story finding its way — Herodotus speaks of various *hodoi tón logón*, ways of stories, versions; he has to decide which to take.'

used in a symbolic manner (e.g. heresy as spiritual blindness). If the patient does not believe in the miraculous capacity of the healer, his story can be shaped into one of conversion, an exemplary test-case. Punishment miracles or conversion miracles call to life a new scheme, but they are still under the hierarchic structural unity of the healing-miracle context. To illustrate how the missing elements are transformed and receive their due place in the story, I will recall a tale from the *Iamata*:[5] A man, wholly sceptical, was lingering around the temple of Asclepius, by no means giving credit to the god's miracles. To unmask what he imagined as the trick, one night he climbed up a tree to peep into the incubation hall and learn what was going on in the sanctuary, what the believers regarded as miracles. Predictably, he fell down and got hurt; in the circumstances, what else could he do but turn to Asclepius, and divine intervention dispelled his doubts.

The protagonist of the story had to become ill to get in contact with Asclepius in his quality as Healer and for his story to become a narrative: becoming ill was the means, his chance to be part of the tale.

The Credible and the Incredible

Building up the logic of the narrative goes hand in hand with the narrator's aim to establish credibility. For the writers of miracles, the chief question is if there is any attempt to distinguish the historical from the mythical. Or on the contrary, we should ask, 'is there an attempt to mix them?'. The hagiographer's and generally the miracle writer's goal is to find the right proportion of these two elements: on the one hand, to fix the story into the historical context by giving dates, places, names, and particulars that nail down the event in reality; on the other hand, they are no less interested in elevating the most ordinary into the realm of the miraculous, thus often rendering the 'facts' special and fitting them into the pattern of divine intervention.[6]

Including the chronological and geographical references gives credibility not only to the event but also to the hagiographer; it attests that he knew his craft and was circumspect in collecting his material. Thecla's hagiographer writes: 'This is why I mentioned the persons, the places, and the names, so that there would be no doubt in the readers about these things but so that they might grasp from near and be persuaded about the truthfulness of what I am going to tell.'[7]

---

5 T423.10.
6 A remarkable analytic approach in determining hagiographic facts and fictions is offered by Pratsch, 'Exploring the Jungle'.
7 MT Prologue, 18–21: 'Διὰ τοῦτο δὲ προσώπων καὶ τόπων καὶ ὀνομάτων ἐμνημονεύσαμεν, ὥστε μηδὲ περὶ αὐτῶν τοὺς ἐντυγχάνοντας ἀμφιβάλλειν, ἀλλ' ἐγγύθεν ἔχειν καὶ ποιεῖσθαι τὴν περὶ ὧν εἰρήκαμεν ἐξέτασιν τῆς ἀληθείας.'

The hagiographer may also underline his own authenticity by showing that he knew intimately the *place*, so important in incubation narratives, by being at home in the sanctuary and in its surroundings. This last aspect is the most striking perhaps in the case of Artemius's hagiographer: he not only sets his stories into the everyday life context of Constantinople but also lists minute details about the Oxeia quarter and the interior of the church or the habitual participants of the saint's vigil. Thecla's hagiographer is more focused on the exactness of the dates and on naming and describing the characters of his tales; Sophronius also links some of his stories to living and well-known persons of his day, like John the Almsgiver, Peter the prefect of Alexandria, or other sanctuary personnel that he describes in detail.

Besides the factual background of the narrative, we can occasionally gain a glimpse into a device of realist fiction, what Roland Barthes called *l'effet de réel*, reality effect, where an often superfluous detail points to an external reality.[8] The most obvious element of such reality-fiction is the insistence on testimonies, on direct sources and the living descendants of the beneficiary of the miracle. To this type belongs the hagiographer's own involvement in the event or his described presence at the telling of the event, just as one of Cosmas and Damian's hagiographers had pictured himself and his informant as fellow pilgrims and participants of the *pannychis*, while probably basing his work on a written miracle-catalogue.

When Thecla's hagiographer meticulously informs us about his testimonies, he is seeking to establish his own credibility by way of presenting the reader with the steps of his research, his journeys, his asking around. Yet not only is this search like the one his model Herodotus represents, but there emerges what was missing from the Herodotean narrative: 'the interface, what to the modern historian is, in fact, his world, *le métier de l'historien* in both senses, but rather more in the concrete sense, the historian's study, the books, the documents and other artefacts that constitute the material he works on. […] It is writing with its system of spatial and temporal lags that opens the possibility of, makes room for, an intervening layer, the layer of records and remains.'[9] This layer is provided by the hagiographer's narrative, by listing the historical dates, historical persons, and events and embedding them into the context of the story. However, it is not only the rhetor Isocasius or Basil of Seleucia or the Arian controversy that play a role in the miracles, but references and analogies enter the miracle also from the legendary world of Thecla, such as the figure of Paul, who appears in MT26 as a secondary reference, in no way connected to the logic of the story. Like her legendary past, Thecla's relationship with Paul sustains the veracity of her present miracles. The hagiographer equally exploits the pre-Christian credibility of

---

8 Barthes, 'L'effet de réel'.
9 Ligota, 'This Story Is Not True', p. 5.

the cult place by stressing that Thecla overcame those Greek deities whose previous activity was attested by everyone.

Parallel to this, there is another conscious tendency: emphasizing that the narrative is a literary-artistic fiction underlining the epic features of Thecla's deeds. Among the literary models of the hagiographer, there are Homer and Euripides, as witnessed by the numerous quotations, inserted half-sentences, and adjectives that are used for the protagonists in order to turn the stories into something mythical, a poetic artefact rather than a device to draw the reader closer to the objective reality depicted in the story.[10]

The parallel existence of these two tendencies and their interconnectedness on the narrative level may originate from the characteristic of the miracle itself: a phenomenon that in the world of reality needs verification and proofs by means of reality. But at the same time, the truest element emerging from the essence of the miracle is the tale, the legend, the divine, the heroic, which is hard for the senses to grasp. This double character, however, can well radiate from the hagiographer's intellectual attitude: he was one of the last remaining examples of the class of ancient rhetors of classical learning that was near to extinction, for whom literature obviously starts with Homer and in whose eyes grasping the divine and extolling the beautiful, even if it be Christian, is done by means of the best of the ancient literary tradition. Besides all of his aesthetic and authorial consciousness, he had chosen the task of establishing credibility and safeguarding the authenticity of Thecla's miraculous activity and that of the cult site. But at the same time, another effort is also visible: to establish some elements of the new Christian *paideia*. In my opinion, this is why the references to classical authors are so frequent; naming his classical examples and identifying his quotations does not show the hagiographer as a second-rate intellectual. In view of the newly converted hagiographer's intention of establishing Christian *paideia*, not so much on his personal level but for the surrounding Christian community, this selection and references to Greek authors becomes an educational programme as well. Homer, Euripides, Plato, and Herodotus became watchwords indicative about what could be retained and reused in Christian hagiography.[11] Almost two centuries later, Sophronius had been doing something similar, with more nuanced narrative tools and references, but his intention must have been rather to show off his learning and literary virtuoso style, and he was less interested in safekeeping

---

10 Thecla flies over the sky on a flaming chariot (MT26); her coming is described as flying in a number of miracles (MT11, 12, 35, 46), in MT11 with a Homeric simile; cf. *Vie et miracles*, ed. and trans. by Dagron, p. 97. A dialogue between a Greek rhetor and Thecla uses a Homeric line of dialog between Achilles and Thetis (MT38); Thecla's favourite bishop is paralleled to Diomedes (MT3); the country of the temple robbers is called Laistrygonia (MT28). For all the Homeric references, see *Vie et miracles*, ed. and trans. by Dagron, p. 157.

11 For more on the subject, see Ševčenko, 'A Shadow Outline of Virtue'; Privitera, ed., *Paideia Cristiana*; Cristante and Ravalico, eds, *Il calamo della memoria*.

a past tradition that was no longer his own, but had instead become a part of the education of men of letters.

In connection with writing about the miraculous, Fernandez Marcos has stated that Sophronius was surprisingly credulous, bereft of critical spirit.[12] I have already noted the limitations of this remark; Sophronius aptly applied the rules of miracle narration, which has nothing to do with his personal beliefs. He himself, like all hagiographers and in fact all miracle-tellers, becomes the 'measure of the miraculous'. This *mesure du thôma*, in François Hartog's analysis of Herodotean storytelling,[13] has an important role in the building up of the narrative: the reader (listener) expects the miraculous, and when the narrator starts telling the extraordinary, he steps out from the narrator–reader (me and you) bipolarity and creates another one, us (I and you, my readers) and they. That is, by being the measure of the extraordinary, the narrator establishes the grouping based on considering what is miraculous: for me and for you it is unheard of; for them, their habitual custom.

When applied to the Christian miracle narratives, the *we/they* opposition, defined by the miraculous, receives another dimension: *we* narrator and readers, all of us, who believe that this story is a miracle versus *they*, those who do not share this common thought world of the miraculous. In the case of incubation miracles, this latter category includes those who regard healing as a result of medical knowledge or attribute the recovery to agents other than the physician-saints, or who are otherwise reluctant to acknowledge the events as divine intervention.

Compositional Structures and Individual Characteristics of the Collections

One of the basic elements of the stories telling the lives of saints and miracles is the *expansion* of the chronologically and geographically fixed character of the miracle into the timeless and spatially unbound possibility of the miraculous. There are countless tools in the miracle narratives to achieve this expansion: the anonymous character of the beneficiary of the miracle, the long-distance miracles, the intermediary roles of images, words, gestures, dreams, and remembrances. While on the structural level, such an expansion means the embrace of repetition, circularity, the numerous occurrence of the same miracle-type, and the working of the same miraculous cure on several patients, they include also the function of portable objects, empowered by

---

12 Fernandez Marcos, *Los Thaumata*, p. 171.
13 Hartog, *Le miroir d'Hérodote*, pp. 243–45. Further, Hartog elaborates more on this concept: 'Traduction de la différence entre là-bas et ici, le *thôma* produit finalement un effet du réel: il dit, je suis le réel de l'autre; là-bas en effet les choses, les *érga*, ne peuvent être que *thômasta*' (p. 249).

the *dynamis* of the miracle-worker (such as the holy wax, a piece of soil, ash, oil, water from the cult site), or the forms of personal devotion, which are not linked to the cult place but still have the potential to evoke the miracle. That the universality of the miracle is embedded not only in the universally held theological background but also in the characteristics of the miracle narrative itself has been best summarized by Michel de Certeau:

> In these diverse ways the hagiographical account breaks the rigor of daily life by freeing the imagination, introducing once again the repetitive and the cyclic into the linearity of work. […] We encounter here a *poetics of meaning* that cannot be reduced to an exactitude of facts or of doctrine without destroying the very genre that conveys it. In the shape of an exception and a deviation — that is, through the metaphor of a specific instance — the discourse creates a freedom in respect to daily, collective, or individual time, but in a non-place.[14]

This observation as a basic framework of hagiography and de Certeau's expression the *poetics of meaning* are worth keeping in mind during the analysis of the incubation collections. I shall later return to the question of how these collections conform to this paradigm of universality.

Compositional Structures in Thecla's Miracle Collection

Thecla's entire collection consists of forty-six miracle stories. If viewed in their entirety, the stories reveal a very conscious and artistic arrangement, which is manifested primarily in the creation of thematic groups, the skilful distribution of these groups, and the variety of the subsequent topics. The order inherent in the collection has already attracted the attention of scholars: first Rademacher outlined the compositional units of the stories, and later Festugière reflected upon his results.[15] It is worth revisiting and comparing their methods of analysis, even knowing that neither of the two was able to work on the entire corpus, since they knew only the version with a large lacuna.[16] Thus, they analysed only twenty-eight plus one (?) miracles. Rademacher, for the stories that were found next to each other in the incomplete corpus, established the following grouping: MT1, the first miracle, is followed by four miracles concerning women; then come seven punishment miracles,

---

14 De Certeau, 'A Variant: Hagio-Grafical Edification', p. 274.
15 Rademacher, 'Die Wunder Theklas'; *Sainte Thècle, Saints Côme et Damien*, ed. and trans. by Festugière.
16 The lacuna in manuscript gr. 1667 that served as the basis of the edition is between Miracles 1 and 18; the copyist still marks the miracles with the original numbering (MT1, 19), but even this telling sign disappears in the next generation of manuscripts. Thus, the continuously numbered thirty-one miracles form the basis of Pierre Pantin's edition in 1608, on which the *Patrologia Graeca* would also rely; cf. *Vie et miracles*, ed. and trans. by Dagron, pp. 140–44.

and again seven miracles of 'benevolence', and the collection terminates with four further miracles on women. In this way, with the 'help' of the missing stories, it was tempting to formulate the hypothesis that we are dealing with an utterly conscious, thematic planning, a collection symmetrical both in its numerical proportions as well as in its topics (4+7+7+4). Festugière, similarly ignorant of the missing parts, judged the hypothesis 'tout à fait artificielle'.[17] The discovery of the lost parts naturally alters the picture, yet, having done away with Rademacher's numerical neatness and exaggeratedly harmonious plan, it is all the same difficult not to see a willed thematic grouping and well-structured units, selected and arranged with care. In his preface written to the French translation of Thecla's miracles, Festugière himself was also hesitant about how to judge the artistic-literary awareness of the hagiographer. For he had in mind, against the picture provided by the collection, a great number of examples from early Byzantine hagiography, with all of their casualties, multiple redactions, and different traditions of transmission, that is, with the most characteristic features of the hagiographical type: 'ils ne sont pas là en vertu d'un dessein préconçu et d'un raffinement d'artiste; [...] chaque chapitre, sauf exception, a amené l'autre, tous les miracles ressortissant à un même sujet forment une sorte de petite unité dans l'ensemble'.[18] When summarizing his impression on the composition of the collection, Festugière returns to a metaphor that he liked to employ on previous occasions as well:

> En résumé, à lire Basile [that is, Thecla's hagiographer] ligne à ligne, on n'a pas du tout l'impression d'un cadre rigide imposé du dehors, amis tout d'abord, à première vue, d'une ordonnance assez lâche où les miracles sont enfilés comme des perles. Bientôt pourtant, dans l'enfilage, des groupes se distinguent, qui forment chacun une unité. Et ces groupes se relient, soit par ressemblance soit par contraste. Tout l'art consiste alors à conduire doucement de groupe à groupe, ou à ménager les contrastes. C'est là qu'est le vrai raffinement, la vraie 'Künstelei'. Non pas dans une sorte d'architecture à pavillons symétriques, très éloignée du génie grec, mais dans la ποικιλία.[19]

As I earlier addressed in the chapter on the hagiographer, Thecla's writer unveils to the reader the process of his research, his taste for selecting the stories and arranging them, highlighting his personal role in shaping the composition. At the beginning of MT 28, he lists the consecutive steps of his activity, underlining that he did not find the miracle stories together ('μήθ' ἅμα πάντα, μηδὲ παρ' ἑνὶ πάντα, ἀλλὰ μηδὲ ἀθρόως πάντα εὑρεῖν'), and that not only did the gold digger's searching require endurance, but the artful arrangement of the pieces was no small task either:

---

17 *Sainte Thècle, Saints Côme et Damien*, ed. and trans. by Festugière, p. 25.
18 *Sainte Thècle, Saints Côme et Damien*, ed. and trans. by Festugière, p. 28.
19 *Sainte Thècle, Saints Côme et Damien*, ed. and trans. by Festugière, pp. 31–32.

> I was collecting the miracles methodically, which, with time passing, had been mixed up, had fallen into oblivion and had faded somehow, running in all directions away from the criteria of memory, order, place, and stories. But nevertheless I must tell that story, which I have found only with difficulty, searching for it with so much fatigue.[20]

The hagiographer thus was in the possession of *taxis*, the force of a form-creating order. Hence it seems legitimate to try to establish a new thematic grouping of the miracle collection, in part following Gilbert Dagron,[21] but also taking into account the conclusions of both Rademacher and Festugière. Dagron's categories are occasionally replaced by my interpretations, in the following way:

Introduction
    1–4: Victory over ancient pagan deities (Thecla and her immediate cult place)
    5–6: Saving Seleucia and Iconium (the place of the cult in a larger context)
    7–12: Priests related to the sanctuary (5)
    7–8: Dexianus (a contemporary, Thecla's priest already under Symposius)
    9, 9b: Menodorus
    10: connecting link, Symposius
    11: a relative or compatriot of Symposius
    12a, 12b: the hagiographer vs. Basil, bishop of Seleucia
    13–15: noblemen
    15–16: journey by sea and journey by land
    18–21: women
    21–22: theft
    23, 24, 25: eye complaints
    26, 27, 28: Thecla as warrior
    26: Thecla appears on her feast day in the sky, upon a flaming carriage; similarly protects the town of Dalisandrus during a siege
    27: protecting the town of Selinunte during a siege
    28: protecting her own sanctuary
    28, 29, 30: protection of her sanctuary and cult
    29–35: punishment, protection of her people
    29: revenge, protection of her cult and feast
    30: revenge, protection of her cult
    31: the hagiographer; Thecla appears and encourages him
    32: punishment of Dexianus
    33: punishment of Orention (woman-affair)
    34: punishment (woman-affair)

---

20 *Vie et miracles*, ed. and trans. by Dagron, p. 362.
21 *Vie et miracles*, ed. and trans. by Dagron, pp. 29–30.

35: punishment, for stealing money from orphans
36–37: healing spring
38–40+41?: Greek rhetoricians
38: Greek rhetorician, who converts
39: Greek rhetorician, refuses to convert
40: Greek rhetorician, suppliant of Sarpedonius, refuses to convert
41: healing of the hagiographer, who can be classified as a converted Greek rhetorician
42, 43, (44), 45, 46: women
Epilogue

Thecla's corpus is the most structured of the miracle collections; the thematic groups, the connecting themes, and the reappearing figures are well elaborated (in my judgement) in sharp contradiction to Johnson's statement that 'the *Miracles of Thekla* are more casual in their approach to collection, arranging their material with no real structure or overarching argument'.[22]

The phenomenon that several miracles can happen to the same person (Dexianus, Symposius, or the hagiographer) is not unknown from the other miracle collections either. It may betray that we are dealing with a person or persons close to the hagiographer, perhaps a personal acquaintance of him.[23] It can similarly point to a markedly oral source (hearsay, personal connections, witnesses, survivors, temple personnel), in which tradition it is possible that information accumulates in such a way as to form narrative groups centred on single figures.

Are there any elements in Thecla's corpus that differ substantially on the basis of thematic grouping from the four other collections? The first striking feature is the repeated triple appearance of the hagiographer, at more or less identical paces, in three different groups of the beneficiaries of the miracles. The second characteristic, which becomes conspicuous not so much on the basis of the thematic classification but more by observing the participants of the miracles, is the detailed description of the figures. This means that there are no anonymous characters: the figures are strongly characterized, so that the reader knows he is dealing with individuals. Even in the rare cases of unnamed protagonists, it is underlined to what places or professions they belong. The characters without names are from Cyprus or Eirenepolis; though it is well known from the *miracula* literature that the geography of the sacred has a well-defined range, here it is even more true that the scenery of the miraculous remains well within certain limits. This contrasts with the geography of Sophronius, for instance, where the hometowns of the beneficiaries of the miracles range from Damascus to Rome. Neither the extension of the real geographical borders, nor the creation of a *non-place*, commented upon by

---

22 Johnson, *The 'Life and Miracles of Thekla'*, p. 196.
23 Familiar also from the miracles of Artemius (e.g. MA19–20).

Michel de Certeau,[24] are typical of the Theclan corpus. In accordance with the closed geographical space of the narratives, their time is limited as well.[25] But how can this time 'be closed', or taken under control, particularly the event of Thecla's 'mythical' death, her disappearance between the opening rocks, the starting point of the cult? The most important factor is that the hagiographer consciously frames his narrative within the context of both that time and space that can still be grasped by the memory of the preceding generation. This compositional method or redactional attitude is the most authentic way through which the cohesion of the narrative is obtained. For the sake of comparison (and counter-example), it is enough to recall the commonplaces generally familiar from hagiography, which claim that the truth of the miracles is firm as a rock. Instead of reiterated affirmations, Thecla's hagiographer prefers other methods. First, he puts emphasis on the documented pre-Christian activity of the cult place; hence Thecla's appearance was by no means an *ex nihilo* legendary event, but involved the transition of the cult place, with its healing function, from Sarpedonius the previous healer to the new Christian owner. And who could doubt the credit of the cult predecessor? The presence of those figures, who turn initially to Sarpedonius and expect miracles from him — and occasionally also attribute them to him (MT40) — even when their story does not end with conversion or the acknowledgment of Thecla, authenticates the cultic continuity and thus the legitimacy of the takeover. Furthermore, the hagiographer used another tool to bring the mythical nearer and to revive the unverifiable past miracles of the saint: he included in the stories (which are well dated, geographically specified, and elevated to the authenticity of a document by the inclusion of the dates) the name of the bishops and witnesses. Into the midst of all these, he inserted that miracle of Thecla in which she rides on her flaming chariot from Seleucia to Dalisandrus, the story that brings her the closest to the deities of Greek religion (MT26).

Compositional Structure in the Miracles of Cosmas and Damian (KDM-CL)

The formation of the miracle material of Cosmas and Damian is more complex for two obvious reasons: first that we are dealing with the accumulation of stories over centuries, and second then that we have two separate collections, in part addressing the same story-material but with different literary ambitions. The more diffused miracle collection, edited by Deubner (KDM) on the basis of the presence or absence of prologues at the beginning of the sections, as well as on indications of time, was divided into six series: (I) Prologue, KDM1–10; (II) without prologue, KDM11–19, with KDM20 added; (III) Prologue,

---

24 De Certeau, 'A Variant: Hagio-Grafical Edification', p. 281.
25 On the geography of the sacred and the circularity of a closed time, cf. again de Certeau, 'A Variant: Hagio-Grafical Edification', p. 280.

KDM21–26; (IV) without prologue, KDM27–32; (V) Prologue, KDM33–38 (which are much later than the previous ones); (VI) Prologue, KDM39–47 + epilogue, by Maximus the deacon probably at the end of the thirteenth or beginning of the fourteenth century.[26]

From external evidence, we can be certain that, by the beginning of the seventh century, miracles from series I–III were circulating.[27] There is also evidence that stories from series I–IV were known, probably by the ninth century, as far as in Egypt. This evidence comes from the London Codex, which contains twenty-one miracles present also in the KDM corpus. If we disregard the later fifth part as well as the thirteenth-century part of Deubner's collection, and if we accept that from the London Codex is missing roughly ten miracles because of the missing folios in the middle, but we include the *in vita* miracles, then we end up with twenty-four miracles present in both collections, and fourteen miracles unique to the London Codex.

Interestingly, the first two miracles of the Codex are *post mortem* miracles that took place in Pheremma, at the church built upon the tomb of the saints. These stories in the Deubner-version figure as *in vita* miracles.[28] There are no organizing principles in either of the two collections such as were used in the other miracle-corpora: no extraordinary beginning with a special miracle, no thematic grouping or link between the stories through reappearing characters (features familiar from all the other three collections), no patients in consecutive miracles with the same name, same illness, or same provenance (the only possible exception in the KDM is that non-Christians and the figures of the Jewish woman and the two pagan Greeks figure only in the first series). This has the result that the collections of Cosmas and Damian do not seem to be 'finished' in the same way as the three other composed and arranged miracle corpora but present the miracle material as open to endless additions.

The parallel stories of the two collections are the following:

    CL1 – *in vita* miracle in Deubner, the farmer who swallowed a serpent

    CL2 – *in vita* miracle in Deubner, about the wife of Malchus

    CL 5 – KDM 1

    CL 6 – KDM 3

    CL 7 – KDM 33

    CL 9 – KDM 6

    CL 11 – KDM 25

    CL 13 – KDM 11

---

26 The division was first established by Deubner, reproduced in *Sainte Thècle, Saints Côme et Damien*, ed. and trans. by Festugière, p. 87.

27 On the basis of the already mentioned testimony of Sophronius in the *Thaumata*, who knew KDM2 and KDM24.

28 CL1, the farmer who swallowed a serpent, and CL2, about the wife of Malchus.

CL 14 – KDM 27
CL 21 – KDM 17
CL 22 – KDM 20
CL 23 – KDM 9
CL 24 – KDM 19
CL 25 – KDM 13
CL 26 – KDM 23
CL 28 – KDM 28
CL 29 – KDM 31
CL 30 – KDM 32
CL 33 – KDM 21
CL 34 – KDM 22
CL 35 – KDM 26
CL 36 – KDM 29
CL 37 – KDM 30

At the beginning, there is already a noteworthy shift: the CL starts by telling posthumous miracles that took place in Pheremma, in the church built on the saints' tomb (CL2–3). In CL5, however, the text speaks of a harbour. This harbour cannot be in Pheremma (near Cyrrhus, in Cilicia), yet the text does not mention Constantinople (as it often does later). We are probably dealing with a shift to the miracles taking place in the capital, which escaped the attention of the compiler/narrator. Furthermore, CL16 bears the title 'About another paralytic', but since the preceding miracle was not about a paralytic, it may be legitimate to suppose that the compiler was selecting from a larger (or differently arranged) collection.

If we set the stories present in both corpora side by side, there are some general tendencies that can be noticed. In the Deubner-corpus, the social position of the patients gains an increased emphasis. For instance, characters vaguely defined in the London Codex become in the KDM representatives of the imperial court or of Byzantine aristocracy through embellishments and additions to the core of the stories. We encounter the following professions in the KDM: palace officers 3–4, 16, 21 (39, 40); nobles 24, 26; merchants 10; clergy or relatives of clergy 12, 22, 23, 27 (38). The same phenomenon of enhancing the patient's social standing can be observed in transforming the simple character of CL13 into the protagonist of KDM11 who also had servants around him; on other occasions, the KDM speaks about the sick man's own physicians. In the same vein, priests of the London Codex are given higher ecclesiastical rank in Deubner's corpus, or appear as secondary characters as in KDM22 where the deacon of the church, missing in CL34, was added to the story.

In the KDM, the symptoms of the illness are treated in more detail, as are the circumstances of the patient's stay in the church (e.g. in KDM33 we read that the patient suffered for two years, while there is no mention of this detail in CL7). KDM also more frequently attributes the illnesses to demons: the illness of the woman in CL28 becomes an illness caused by a demon in KDM28, just as in CL7, an unspecified cause turns out to be a demon-caused illness in KDM33. Demons or the machinations of the devil figure in KDM4, 12, 28, 27, 33, 36; in contrast, a demon is mentioned only twice in the London Codex (CL15, 33), but even in these cases, the demon is not the cause of the illness (he just urges the patient to leave the church when the saints do not appear quickly enough).

The importance given to the sanctuary itself underwent a similar change: unlike the simple references of the London Codex, the KDM dedicates more attention to the spatial descriptions of the church interior, just as we find in the contemporary collections of Artemius and of Cyrus and John.

Most of these tendencies can be observed if we compare them to the development of the miracle in CL26, a story that became very much enlarged as it found its way into KDM23. The London Codex defines the protagonist simply as a priest, whereas the KDM describes him as a priest of high rank from Constantinople, who is actively engaging in ecclesiastical matters. Ordinary doctors of the CL became the patient-priest's own physicians; moreover, when their treatment fails, he calls for the chief physician of Constantinople. In line with the tendency of the KDM story to become more and more complex, new additions include the description of the various medical treatments and the exact localization of the patient in the church building; where the London Codex speaks of two illnesses afflicting our man simultaneously, the KDM writes about two consecutive illnesses which necessitate two separate miraculous interventions. At the end of the KDM story, the saints teach the patient a special prayer that would protect him from illness in the future; after this detail, the hagiographer describes the healed man as his close acquaintance.

The latter aspect is a major narrative difference that can be observed in the case of CL33 – KDM21 as well. The miracle is recorded in the London Codex just like any other one in the collection, while in the KDM it is presented in a way that the healed patient tells his story to the hagiographer. As I noted earlier, this is the first of the miracles from the set of KDM21–26 where all the stories were described as collected by a patient who heard them from his fellow pilgrims while in the church. In this artfulness, I see an indication that the London Codex was earlier than the collection of the KDM — at least insofar as the composition is concerned (not necessarily the circulation of the individual miracle stories).

Despite its tendency for economy of wording, the London Codex may occasionally offer more information. Perhaps some of these details generated less interest in the KDM hagiographers; but more likely, the core of the London Codex stories had lived a life of their own before it became recorded in the way known to us, and during this formative process, it became enriched with elements important for that actual community and audience. The anonymous converting pagan of KDM9 is called Dioscuros in the parallel miracle of CL23. This is the miracle in which the pagan addresses the saints as Castor and Pollux, and the story that Deubner regarded as the key for identifying Cosmas and Damian's cult-predecessors. Maybe not initially but surely by the sixth century, at a time when the features of the popular pagan deities were still known, Cosmas and Damian were called not just brothers but twins. In the latest section of the KDM there are several miracles averting shipwreck. Can it be that the Dioscuri were created just to be a part of the story, to characterize the pagan's error? Is it possible that Castor and Polydeices actually had nothing to do with the cult but only with the miracle-narrative? One could plausibly argue that the patient's omitted name, Dioscuros, recalled in the hagiographer's mind the Dioscuri. Yet the same argument works backwards as well: the pagan received the name Dioscuros because he was invoking the Dioscuri.

Additional information can sometimes be clearly exaggerated. In CL6, we learn that the sheep who turned out to be the means of the cure was called Cosmas. However, it is added that he was called Cosmas not so much because of the saints, but because his previous owner was called Cosmas (a detail missing from the KDM). Similarly, CL17 mentions that the sick person saw the saints in a dream, in the form of two priests of the church, who were called Cosmas and Damian in the saints' honour, but in fact they were Saints Cosmas and Damian. Characterization is likewise overstated in CL18, with two men as patients, both of them with a cataract on their eye, both called Thomas, but one of them is rich and the other one is poor.

Elsewhere, the elaboration of details is more meaningful. In the same story told in CL22 and KDM20 about a father and his sick son, the father is anonymous in the KDM and we learn only that he was a deeply faithful Christian. The CL is more discursive: here, the man has a name, Seurianos, and we read that he 'governed the province of the people of Arcadia'. Arcadia was a division of Egypt, and in the first report about the codex, Rustafjaell explains that,

> in a manuscript written in Egypt we should naturally expect the scribe to claim honour of the relics for his own country, and, if the text is sound, it is possible that some Egyptian locality lies hidden in it. But without further evidence it is difficult to come to any safe conclusion. The text certainly bears other traces of its Egyptian origin [...]. But an Egyptian colouring is given to miracles, which in Deubner's text might be referred to Constantinople.[29]

---

29 Rustafjaell, *The Light of Egypt*, p. 97.

Concerning the discrepancies in the same stories told in CL21 and KDM17, Rustafjaell remarks that 'the change points definitely to a Jacobite country'.[30] A further local feature may be the description of the protagonist of CL2, who in the London Codex is characterized as a member of the *philoponoi*, an element missing from the parallel version of the KDM story (4).

More conspicuous is the meticulous attention paid to the patient's theological position. I will compare CL35 with KDM26 to highlight how the above-described general alterations work. I quote the miracle itself (CL35):

> Afterward, there was a sage and saintly woman with a terrible disease in her breast who arrived at the port of salvation, namely the church of saints Cosmas and Damian. The deacon of the church in the imperial city, a pious man, was in the habit of going to the church on Fridays and praying there in the evenings and at night until Saturday. And while the woman was incessantly asking the saints for healing, the deacon, as was his custom, came to pray on the night before Saturday. As soon as he lay to have a bit of rest, the saints appeared and said to him, 'Say to the woman with the breast disease, "You have been released regarding your breast. Go home in peace, and you will find healing."' The priest woke up in the middle of the night and, coming to his senses, thought, 'How can this be the message of the saints, by which the woman indicated will be healed? How can I provide proof of the healing? If I go and say to the woman, "You are delivered from your affliction," she will probably ask me and say, "Man, I am in the grip of sickness. You deceive me with empty words you never heard from the saints."' Thinking these things to himself, he began to pray. The saints appeared and again ordered him to say the exact words to the woman. But he felt it was a delusive dream and that the saints' words were just empty chatter, so after prayers, he lay down and slept. For the third time, the saints appeared and, threatening him, said, 'Go and immediately tell the woman what we have told you. To convince both you and her, the woman who feels pain in the side of her breast should search under her mattress and find the medicine, which, if she anoints herself with it, will soon rid her of the trouble.' So when the morning dawned, the deacon went and said to the woman, 'You have been freed from the illness that has been afflicting you.' Looking at him with a strained look, the woman said to him, 'It is not becoming of you to mock somebody in such distress with deceitful words. For you know that, like many others before me, for some reason, the saints are not releasing me now, even if they want to heal me.' And he replied: 'I do not say these things of my own accord, but I have come here at the command of the saints to say them. And the medicine that will cure your illness you will find under your mattress, as I have been ordered to tell you.' She hurriedly started to

---

30 Rustafjaell, *The Light of Egypt*, p. 97.

search and found the medicine under her mattress. No one knew what it was or what was the fragrance it emanated, filling the place. Immediately anointing herself with it, she quickly got rid of her troubles. She went home, thanking saints Cosmas and Damian and praising Christ, who had given such grace to his saints.[31]

In this story, the main character is the woman with a pain in her breast, about whom we learn that she was wise and pious and she came from somewhere else to Constantinople. The narrator of the KDM shapes this figure into a high-society aristocrat woman, almost unapproachable because of her social position. In the CL story, the meek deacon of the church acts as intermediary. It was a familiar motif from ancient and Christian incubation miracles that the priests or the temple personnel became the mouthpiece of the healers, often as the (healthy) recipients of the curative dream. In the Deubner collection, the story undergoes radical changes: the man is at the centre of the story, who at this time is not a simple deacon of the church but a heretic — a heretic priest in a high ecclesiastical position of his own (heretical) sect. That the saints address the dream to him is not only a test of faith in them, but it is also an attempt to make the heretic acknowledge the truths of orthodoxy and convert him. Hence, to the more or less similar narrative events, a fundamentally different theological background was added.

Reginald Grégoire wrote that the hagiographic text is at the same time *existentialist*, that is, decisive for a history of a community; *political*, as it denotes a framework of the system of social networks; and *structural*, because of the narrator-redactor.[32] The further comparison of the two versions of Cosmas and Damian's miracles would allow us to see the change that took place in the collective memory of the cult, and compare the old and new functions (political, ecclesiastical, and cultic) that the miracle records had in two different communities, a task that I leave for Chapter 10.

Compositional Structures in Sophronius's Thaumata

Scholarly attention to Sophronius's writing technique has mainly focused on his style and rhetorical repertoire.[33] Besides Sophronius's stylistic brilliance and prose rhythm, scholars commented on the hagiographer's compositional vanity, which manifested itself in his 'self-confident linguistic exuberance',[34]

---

31 *Cosmae et Damiani*, ed. by Rupprecht, pp. 46–47.
32 Grégoire, *Manuale di agiologia*, p. 238.
33 On his style, see Agosti, 'Le brume di Omero', also Booth, *Crisis of Empire*, p. 46; his Syrian background and possible bilingualism are among the influences that shaped his style: cf. Allan, *Sophronius of Jerusalem*, p. 16. On his rhetorical repertoire, see Duffy, 'Observations on Sophronius' Miracles'.
34 Duffy, 'Observations on Sophronius' Miracles', p. 73.

on the ambivalence between his faith and his commitment to classical Greek authors, and on the tension between his 'highbrow style' and his hagiographical intent to popularize Chalcedonian theology. In a similar manner, scholars commented on Sophronius's opposition to the dogmatic medicine of the iatrosophists and to pagan superstition.[35]

In the collection, there are different types of narratives; short, condensed stories alternate with extremely detailed descriptions. The concise, shorter miracles were probably based on the votive records or some sort of miracle inventory at the sanctuary — despite the hagiographer's silence on any such records. Sophronius might have obtained the material for the longer stories from oral sources, from the dreamers themselves. The length of such stories was often six or seven times larger than that of the votive-type narratives. In discussing the hagiographers' personal stamp, I have already pointed out Sophronius's predilection for alphabetical and numerical ordering. The overall structure of the collection of the seventy miracles is as follows:

    1–35: Alexandrian patients

        1: first miracle with **A**mmonius from **A**lexandria
        8, 9, 10: Christodoros's family
        10–11: three sick children called Mary, daughters of church personnel (they reappear in 60, 67)
        13, 14, 15: alphabetical connection[36]
        19, 20, 21: female patients
        24, 25, 26: female patients
        24: two stories, a rich and a poor woman, both called Julianna
        26–27: protagonists called Theodora and Theodoros
        28: two stories: a rich and a poor man
        29, 30, 31, 32: punishment miracles to pagans
        33–34: women, not ill, on pilgrimage, miracle happens on their way

    36–50: Egyptians and Libyans

        36, 37, 38, 39: Monophysite heretics, Communion
        46–47: cures by bath

    51–70: Foreigners

        54–55: illness caused by magic, remedy: pork
        55–56: patients from Cyprus
        70: cure of Sophronius

---

35 On all these arguments, see Agosti, 'Le brume di Omero'.
36 Duffy, 'Observations on Sophronius' Miracles', pp. 72–73.

For the main structure of the corpus, Sophronius himself gives the following explanation: he deliberately included seventy miracles because, he writes, seven is a magical number and zero is the perfect number.[37] This corpus is divided into three parts: thirty-five are dedicated to Alexandrian patients, fifteen to Egyptians and Libyans, and the last twenty to foreigners. The last among the miracles of the foreigners, and the concluding miracle of the collection, is Sophronius's own miraculous recovery. MCJ1 starts with the story of Ammonius from Alexandria, yet this alphabetical order is not continued through the corpus; instead, we shall find examples in which stories are linked together on the analogy of the patients' names. Within this larger grouping, the most striking are the miracles placed in the middle of the corpus, most importantly MCJ36, which inaugurates the punishment miracles performed on Monophysite heretics and hence most markedly expresses the saints' (i.e. the hagiographer's) Chalcedonian position.

Sophronius — unlike Thecla's hagiographer — did not work in consecutive thematic groups. He established his three major units based on the provenance of the patients, but besides this, there are small story-islands among the miracles: a few stories are linked together by a sometimes stated or sometimes implicit connection. Sophronius is at his best when it comes to the internal structure of the individual miracles. The first of his story-islands, in which the stories are strongest in their interrelatedness, contains the stories ordered around the *oikonomos* of the church, Christodorus. Due to its concentration on a single individual, it is also unique in the collection. Sophronius presumably knew him well, and he was perhaps a source of many of the miracles. It is impossible to determine why he acquired his distinguished position, perhaps because of his importance in the sanctuary or because of his closeness to the hagiographer. MCJ8, 9, 10 record the miraculous cures of Christodorus, of his wife, and then of his daughter, but as a secondary character, he appears near the end of the collection, in MCJ67. In this case, he appears not as the patient but as the beneficiary of the dream-recipe that has to communicate to another man, a sick suppliant. Out of this first story-island, a second is born, linked by the analogy of names. Christodorus's daughter is called Mary; she was complaining about her tooth and ear, and her parents turn to the saints on behalf of their child.

Within the same miracle (MCJ10), another story follows, again about a girl called Mary, with similar pains in her ear. The next miracle (MCJ11) remains on

---

37 Cf. the explanation of Fernandez Marcos, which I already quoted in connection with the *libelli miraculorum*: Augustine in the *De vera religione* tells how he collected and arranged miracle stories. He also mentions that he recorded seventy such miracle stories, some of which were read aloud during the liturgy in the church in Hippo. Fernandez Marcos's hypothesis is that Sophronius might have been influenced by this fact to choose seventy stories (*De vera religione* 25. 47, cf. Fernandez Marcos, *Los Thaumata*, p. 158), although I do not find this explanation probable. Sophronius was not reticent and loved to show off, and he would no doubt have referred to Augustine if he had been his example.

the same theme, with its protagonist also called Mary, who was the daughter of a certain John, who was the deacon of the church at Sophronius's time. Just like Christodorus, this John the deacon also reappears later, in MCJ60.

After diverse miracle-stories, the next thematic units are of MCJ19, 20, 21 and 24, 25, 26, all with female patients. Within these groups, Sophronius establishes another connection: in MCJ24, he tells two stories, about a rich woman and a poor woman, both named Julianna. The protagonist of the closing miracle about women (MCJ26) is Theodora; the likeness of names leads to the male protagonist Theodoros of the following miracle (MCJ27), with Sophronius himself underlining the name analogy as his basis of structuring the stories. In the next, MCJ28, mirroring the double miracle of the rich and poor Juliannas, we again have a double story: a rich and a poor man recover by the same miracle, with the help of one to the other — a motif familiar both from Artemius and from the miracles of Cosmas and Damian as well.

This group is followed by a set of stories that the hagiographer himself marks as a thematic unit, MCJ29, 30, 31, 32, as being punishment miracles. Besides being punishment miracles and falling at the same time into a larger structural division (that is, miracles to Alexandrians), this group has an additional characteristic: all the protagonists are pagans, either acknowledging this proudly (as the famous Gesius in MCJ30) or as Christianized, recalcitrant pagans (as MCJ31). There is one important remark on Sophronius's structural organization at the end of MCJ30: he writes that there are miracles of Saints Cyrus and John which were also performed by Cosmas and Damian, such as the one with the paralytic man and mute woman, or the story of the Jewish woman with cancer. These appear similarly in Menouthis, but Sophronius writes that he avoided including them on purpose. Instead, he says he wished to concentrate only on those events that are unique to Menouthis. Besides the fact that the two miracles Sophronius recalls here would not have had a thematically relevant place in this group because they are not punishment miracles, it is worth noting that the two mentioned miracles of Cosmas and Damian do not figure in the (truncated) London Codex, hence Sophronius probably knew the more widely spread collection of the saints (the KDM).

At the end of MCJ32, he writes that this is the end of the section dedicated to the miracles that happened to the Alexandrians, but then continues before he closes this section definitely at the end of MCJ35. Was it the case that the hagiographer, having in mind the would-be unity of the seventy miracles of the collection, wanted to complement the first, coherent part? Additionally, the miracles attached for this purpose, MCJ33 and 34, reveal similarities: both concern two women who were initially not ill but were making a pilgrimage to the church in order to honour the saints, and an incident happens to both of them along the way.

MCJ36 inaugurates the second larger section of the collection, the group of fifteen stories that record miracles that happened to Egyptians and Libyans. It would be interesting to know whether the patients coming from different parts placed their votive tablets randomly, or if there were separate sections on the church wall for the Alexandrians, foreigners, etc., or if this grouping was arbitrary and Sophronius searched himself for miracle stories linked by provenance.

This is the section where Sophronius's conscious composing can be best observed. It manifests itself in the selection and elaboration of stories at the crucial strategic points of the corpus. We should not forget that Sophronius, unlike most hagiographers, knew in advance how many stories he wanted to collect; thus it is reasonable to imagine that, in the centre of the corpus, there are placed those narratives which characterize the entire collection, or even his whole endeavour, with an explicit theological message.

The miracles opening the second half of the collection (36, 37, 38, 39) all focus on various (Monophysite) heretics, on taking communion in an orthodox way as the condition or means of cure, and in all cases, they confront the opposing principles of faith.

In the closing miracle of this group, MCJ39, Sophronius, just as he often does, tells two stories under the umbrella of one miracle. While in the other cases there was some slight connection between the two narratives (if nothing else, the protagonists being both patients of the saints), here he uses a particular way of tying the different stories together: MCJ39 is about a paralysed heretic, who by no means wants to accept the teaching of Chalcedon, the creed that the saints emphatically confess. The physician-saints heighten the man's pains, in this way forcing him to receive communion in the orthodox way. After repeated protests, the patient finally gives in, and in the end, he accepts the correct faith and is healed. This event reminds Sophronius of the church servant called Menas, who is not sick at all and is a heretic. In his dream, Menas witnesses that the saints receive the Eucharist (!) in front of him, and then they whip him and warn him that he would be allowed stay in their church as a servant only if he turns away from his erroneous beliefs.

After some stories on diverse themes, MCJ46–47 forms the next smaller unit: MCJ46 incorporates two stories where, for the cure, both of the patients have to take a bath in the water of Siloam in Jerusalem; taking a bath is similarly the cure in MCJ47.

Before the section on Egyptian and Libyan patients ends with MCJ50, Sophronius in MCJ49 corrects himself, saying that because this miracle is a punishment story, its place should be among the thematic punishment miracle-group in the Alexandrian part. This attests that, when recording his stories, he did not lose sight of the compositional units that he himself created.

The third and last larger unit, MCJ51–70, narrates the miracles that happened to foreigners. Similar to the head of the previous greater section, the opening story of this unit is also a prominent one. The beneficiary of the miracle in MCJ51 is a priest, and Sophronius argues that because he is a leader in the church, his story merits a leadership position amongst the subsequent miracles. In line with the protagonist's leadership, the miraculous event is just as extraordinary: from God, the saints are granted their petition that the dying abbot should return to life, and in addition, he receives twenty more years of life. MCJ53 tells two miracles: the first miracle concerns a certain master; the second concerns his servant. It may be plausible to suppose that such double healings were recorded on the same *ex voto*.[38] MCJ54 and 55 address maladies caused by a demon, and in both cases the means of the cure is pork, and in both stories there is a character for whom swine is a religious taboo.[39] MCJ55 links further to MCJ56, as the patients are in both cases from Cyprus. In the subsequent miracle stories, there are no similar thematic connections.

I have formulated the hypothesis that Sophronius's chief compositional talent can be best observed in the individual stories. What he skilfully adds to the raw material — name, provenance, illness, and miraculous events — occasionally follows, to a great extent, the form criteria of saints' *Vitae*, some elements of which rely on the encomium tradition. MCJ54 is probably the most representative in this respect, and its close analysis may sufficiently highlight my point.

MCJ54 concerns Isidorus the epileptic. Sophronius starts his narrative with a *laudatio* of elevated tone about the town of Damascus (the hometown of the hagiographer as well) which is followed by a compact genealogy of the patient: Isidorus's father was Dionysius, a nobleman from Damascus, whose forefather was the famous philosopher 'Nicolaus, the tutor of Herod and teacher of the children (?) of Antonius and Cleopatra', from whom twelve generations of scholars originated. As a child, Isidorus was chased by a demon in the bathhouse, an event that Sophronius describes profusely. After the child fell down onto the pavement, his tutors carried him out of the bath but did not attach great importance to what happened, regarding it to be caused by the usual weakness from the hot vapours of the bath. Yet they soon turned to doctors, who diagnosed the illness as *epilepsy* caused by melancholic humours. At this point, the whole family embarked upon the pilgrimage to the church of the saints: the father with his son and his wife. His wife was called Julia, and she was — by some Hellenic (i.e. pagan) error — the worshipper of Adonis. For this reason, she could not eat or touch swine, a fact that she concealed from her family. The curative method recommended by the saints was that the mother should smear the child from head to toe with pork fat. And while in most incubation stories, both pagan and Christian, the recovery and thanksgiving would now follow, Sophronius's narrative is far from ending. The mother had to overcome her religious taboo and apply the fat, something the demon could not stand and thus — as if castigated by some divine force — left the boy's body. Moreover, the child obtained a life-long protection from demons, and the prescription served to correct the mother's erroneous beliefs.

---

38 Just as Aelius Aristides wrote in detail about the experiences of his servants with Asclepius, or the master of the slave in Epidaurus dedicated as votive gift the object of the miracle concerning both of them (T423.10).
39 I wrote about this in detail in Csepregi, 'Pork as a Wonder Drug'.

The basic elements are identical with those from incubation stories and from sources that received a more or less elaborate literary form: name, hometown, occupation, illness, curative dream. But Sophronius, in my opinion, not only enlarged these elements and added colours to them, but his way of adding material and the parts of the narrative shaped in this way results in the structure of the miracle resembling that of the saints' *Lives*. In turn, the compositional elements of the saints' *Lives* reach back to the ancient genre of the encomium.

Hippolyte Delehaye has analysed those analogies and rhetorical similarities that, in the panegyric literature of the martyrs, follow the ancient encomium model.[40] I would extend his remarks to the analogies between the structure of the encomium and of the miracle narrative (especially in the *Thaumata*) and the hagiographical reverse of this structure. At the end of the third century AD, Menander (whom Delehaye refers to as 'the par excellence theoretician of rhetoric') in his Περὶ ἐπιδεικτικῶν, listed the following elements as indispensable parts of a proper encomium:[41] The essential element of the *prooimion* is the αὔξησις, that is, the narrator's apologies in the face of the greatness of the task, the extraordinary character of his subject, and his own humble qualities; finally he starts the ἐγκώμιον in the strict sense, commencing with his hero, listing his birthplace, his ethnic group, often praising the city in question (πατρίς, πόλις, ἔθνος), then the hero's family, his γένος and occasionally the circumstances of his birth, the preceding or accompanying miraculous events (τὰ περὶ τῆς γενέσεως), the physical characteristics of his hero, his childhood and upbringing (τὰ περὶ φύσεως, ἀναστροφή, παιδεία), detouring to his lifestyle and activity (ἐπιτηδεύματα), until he arrives at the narrative of the hero's deeds (πράξεις).

It is notable that the narrative units of Sophronius's incubation miracles coincide with those of the encomium. In the centre of his narrative, however, we do not find the saint but the supplicant patient. It is the patient's life-story and his microcosm that unfold from the formulaic beginning of the narrative, in which the obligatory requirements of the ancient Greek healing miracles (the sick person's name, hometown, profession, illness, and recovery) evolve into little story-mosaics. In addition to the patient's characteristics, some remarks on his faith are often added: how zealously Christian they were, or how their erroneous beliefs manifested themselves, and sometimes references to his antecedents can also be found, as in the just described MCJ54.

Of course, the identical skeleton of the narrative pattern adapts itself to the protagonist of the narrative, who is an ordinary man or woman, hence the wondrous circumstances of birth, where a deep theological message occurs, are missing. Their physical characteristics are partly or entirely replaced by

---

40 Delehaye, *Les passions des martyrs et les genres littéraires*, pp. 141–47.
41 Similar to him is the Alexandrian Sophist Theon (first century AD), in his Προγυμνάσματα, in the chapter 'Περὶ ἐγκωμίου καὶ ψόγου', for the English translation of which, see Kennedy, *Progymnasmata*.

the description of the bodily symptoms of the illness; childhood and growing up are often marked by the motif of the long-lasting illness, which the patient suffers from his childhood. In the place of the praxis are all those activities which connect the protagonist with the saints: his learning about the healers, his disappointment in medical doctors, his journey to the saints, his acts of devotion or incredulity, his relationship with his fellow-pilgrims, the practice of incubation and all the details relating to his stay in the sanctuary, and most importantly, his encounter with the saints and the acts, gestures, and tests he has to perform in order to receive the cure.

In Sophronius's case, the clash of the two literary genres mirrors his being at home to some extent in both traditions, which melt into an ideological and textual framework of praising the saints of the place and through them, Christ's works. Sophronius's compositional technique may be the result of his two storytelling milieus: On the one hand, his stay in the monastery, the audiences and authors of saints' *Lives* he met there, and his friendship with Saint John the Almsgiver and John Moschus. This pair also wrote hagiography and might have had a strong impact on Sophronius's compositional technique and the way that his miracle story structures drew on the patterns of encomium (and its Christian transformation, the saints' *Lives*). On the other hand, Sophronius knew the miracle collections of Saints Cosmas and Damian and of Saint Menas, and as he attests, the incubation miracle stories of Isis (and perhaps those of Serapis), and he was well versed about how incubation miracle narratives are built up. The result was a rhetorically overflowing extension of both narrative traditions.

Compositional Structure in the Miracles of Saint Artemius

The miracle collection of Artemius is easily definable in terms of time and space. It is evidently the work of a single hagiographer, likely with a later additional *morale* at the end of some stories. The forty-five miracles have been divided differently by various scholars. Kougeas distinguished two parts: first, the older miracles of MA1–17, while the second part he divided into further smaller groups, written at different times, MA18–20, 21–44, 45.[42] Delehaye echoed this division,[43] while Marco Dorati refined it by stating that the two parts may well be the work of a single hagiographer but represent two different phases.[44] The first part of the collection, MA1–16, is characterized by shorter stories and a dry and rather technical tone with few details in the narrative. The miracles of the second section, MA17–45, contain longer and

---

42 Sokratis Kougeas, review of Papadopoulos-Kerameus's edition, *Laographia*, 3 (1911), 277–319, summarized also by Haldon, 'Supplementary Essay', p. 35.
43 Delehaye, 'Les recueils antiques', p. 33.
44 Dorati, 'Funzioni e motivi', p. 113, n. 86.

more elaborated tales and are characterized by a richness of motifs describing complex situations, which Dorati calls *veri e propri racconti*. In this part, we find the formulaic closures and transitory summaries in the miracles, as well as the repeated appearance of the same characters (in MA18, 22; MA19, 20; MA38–40 and 43).

Lennart Rydén described the individual miracles of the collection as episodes: like those of a film series, with the same main characters and with essentially homogeneous story elements. Nowhere do we hear about any such compositional ambitions to order the miracles into thematic or otherwise linked groups as in Thecla's stories. The sense of a compositional whole as with Sophronius's collection is equally missing, and there is no numerical organization or classification of patients. In the *Thaumata*, the non-consecutive island-like miracle groups form at least an archipelago if not a terra firma; in the case of Artemius, we can indeed speak only of islands. The saint's medical specialization in cases of hernia (although there are a few other types of miracle working) excludes a grouping of the patients on the basis of their illness. Neither does the hagiographer exploit the other possible methods of classification, such as provenance or the personal characteristics of patients. I found three smaller miracle groups in the collection in which the related narratives concern the repeated experiences of a single individual: MA19–20 tell the miracles concerning a man named George, and MA38, 39, 40 are another unit with another protagonist called George (different than the previous one). The peculiarity of this group of three miracles is that it unfolds the *miraculé*'s life over several decades: we meet George as a child with his money changer parents, who learns the craft of scales and exchange rates, yet at the age of nine, George comes under the spell of the church of Saint John the Baptist (the one that hosts Artemius). He becomes a reader in the church, but his parents drag him home; he falls ill, and thereafter he enjoys the special patronage of Saint Artemius. This attracts him to become a monk, and as such, we encounter him years later in the next miracle. After another struggle with his parents, at the age of twenty-two he becomes an ordained priest in Constantinople. In the meantime, we learn about his years spent previously on the island of Plataiai: the third miracle takes place there, when George is still an eighteen-year-old deacon. About him, we can only suspect that the hagiographer knew him in person and was perhaps one of his informants. About the other George of MA19–20, however, the hagiographer says explicitly that at the time of the recording, the protagonist 'still survives, proclaiming and recounting the glory of the martyr'.

The experiences of George in MA19–20 are surrounded by the two other miracles with an identical protagonist; in this case, the miracles do not follow closely on each other, but they are structured in a frame: the anonymous man who received help in MA18 reappears in MA22: 'it happened at some point that the very same victim of burglary about whom we have just spoken'.

There is another pair of miracles, connected only by a formulaic phrase and perhaps by the analogy of names: MA16–17. In MA16, a man called

Sergius from Alexandria cries out for Artemius in this way: 'Saint Artemius, you were Doux and Augoustalius in my native land of Alexandria; cure me along with the many!' In MA17, a senator called Sergius sends a sick relative of his to Artemius; to accompany and entertain him while in the church, he also sends an actor from Alexandria. As a result of a punishment miracle, the Alexandrian actor develops hernia, and he shows it to another patient with a following words: 'See how it is! The saint who allegedly became Doux and Augoustalius of my country sent me this man's hernia!' Elsewhere, this sort of linking is not characteristic of the hagiographer — can it be the case that the phrase remained in his mind from the previous miracle and he unconsciously builds it into this story apropos of the other Alexandrian?

The hagiographer's style has attracted scholarly attention on two fronts: First, to a lesser degree, observations have been made on Sophronius's language and vocabulary.[45] Second, greater concern has been reserved for the literary value of his work and for how it reflects everyday life in Constantinople. Most episodes in the collection are told with an unusual enthusiasm, as Lennart Rydén has remarked, and pose the question whether such literary merits of the text, its entertaining and exciting characteristics, were due to the hagiographer's artistry or were inherent in the saint's legendary material. In the latter case, Rydén argues that the hagiographer realized and respected the literary values of the stories and did not enhance them with superfluous additions. If the first hypothesis is true, which Rydén considered the more likely case, then the hagiographer pondered the possibilities of the material and transmitted them by elaborating the spectacular events and doing so with a considerable degree of humour. Considering together the stories and their language, Rydén calls the hagiographer's way of storytelling open and apparently inartificial, which was probably viewed as inartistic by Byzantine intellectuals.[46]

---

45 Grosdidier de Matons, 'Les *Miracula Sancti Artemii*'; Lopez Salva, 'Observaciones lexicales'.
46 Rydén, 'Kyrkan som sjukhus', pp. 12–13.

CHAPTER 8

Narrative Techniques and Variants of the Dream Stories

Comparing the same miracles of Cosmas and Damian in two different narrative sources leads me to examine the construction of individual stories. In the last thirty years of Byzantine scholarship, a growing attention has been paid to the narratives techniques and story-units of Byzantine hagiography.[1] This interest is not without precedence in incubation studies either: Otto Weinreich examined the rhetorical topoi and folklore commonplaces already in the ancient Greek incubation-material.[2] There are some narrative elements that are characteristic of the Christian records of dream healing, some of which can be found in both the ancient Greek and Christian dream-tales.[3] These recurrent story patterns, themes, and motifs partly come from the inherent rules of miracle writing, and partly attest the peculiar skill of the hagiographer, but studied closely, they may also help to understand what made incubation stories unique.

One of the most seminal works on narrative structures was Vladimir Propp's analysis of Russian folktales, written in 1927.[4] He put together five groups of elements that 'define not only the construction of a tale, but the tale as a whole', namely,

1. The functions of the *dramatis personae*;

2. Conjunctive elements (*ex machina*, announcement of misfortune, chance disclosure — mother calls hero loudly, etc.);

3. Motivations (reasons and aims of personages);

4. Forms of appearance of the dramatis personae (the flying arrival of dragon, chance meeting with donor);

5. Attributive elements or accessories (witch's hut, or her clay leg).

---

1 An excellent bibliography is Høgel, 'Literary Aspects of Greek Byzantine Hagiography'.
2 Weinreich, *Antike Heilungswunder*, pp. 175–201.
3 For example, navigation metaphors are frequent in the Christian incubation-miracle narratives, especially in the miracles of Cosmas and Damian, for the whole process of the ritual. The illness is a 'sea of troubles', the healing sanctuary is the 'harbour of health', Cosmas and Damian succour in shipwreck, and the saint appears as captain of the ship. The explanation may not be, as supposed earlier, their association with the Dioscuri, protectors of the shipwrecked, for it was a common motif in the incubation stories of Lebena and Epidaurus as well. Girone, *Iamata*, III. 1; 3a; IV, 1, and Herzog, *Die Wunderheilungen von Epidauros*, C56, C63.
4 Propp, *Morphology of the Folktale*.

He also identified thirty-one narrative units in the construction of most of the stories. Propp's influence has been enormous, particularly in biblical studies; Gerd Theissen and George Tinker applied Propp's analysis to the healing miracles of the New Testament. Theissen identified six major themes of the miracles (which he termed exorcism miracles, healing miracles, epiphanies, rescue miracles, gift miracles, and rule miracles), with their attendant characters of the miracle-worker, the sick person, the demon, the crowd, the opponent, and the disciples. Altogether, he distinguished thirty-three motifs in the miracle themes, from the coming of the miracle-worker to the spread of the news of the miracle. Regarding healing, Theissen subdivided further the means of healing into (1) the healing touch, (2) the healing word or presence, (3) the application of medicament, and (4) healing associated with the performance of a prescribed act.[5]

While Theissen concentrated mostly on healing, Tinker viewed the stories in their entirety and established the following compositional categories:

1. The problem is introduced (the sick or maimed person).
2. Tension is built up (resistance is introduced or a difficulty is heightened).
3. The healing moment is described.
4. The healing is demonstrated.
5. The reaction of the crowd is described.

First, Festugière analysed literary commonplaces and folklore motifs in Greek Christian hagiography.[6] Afterwards, this was followed by half a century's disinterest in the subject. Recently, similar to the study of Byzantine hagiography as literature, its themes and topoi came to the forefront of scholarly research (in the articles of Dickie and Delierneux and more extensively in the monograph of Thomas Pratsch on the Middle Byzantine *Lives* of saints).[7] Giulio Guidorizzi extended the application of the Proppian model to Byzantine hagiographical texts.[8] By identifying the figures specific to the incubation context, I can use these categories for almost all the characters and objects that feature in incubation healing stories:

A. Helpers — (1) outsiders (includes priests, doctors, other incubants in the church); (2) close acquaintances (includes family members, friends); and (i) deliberately or (ii) involuntarily

---

5 Theissen, *The Miracle Stories*, pp. 47–72.
6 Festugière, 'Lieux communs littéraires'; for more specific case studies, see also Derouet, 'Les possibilités d'interprétation sémiologique'.
7 Dickie, 'Narrative Patterns in Christian Hagiography'; Delierneux, 'L'exploitation des topoi hagiographiques'; Pratsch, *Der hagiographische Topos*.
8 Guidorizzi, 'Motivi fiabesche nella agiografia bizantina'. The application of the Proppian model and its variants with followers and critics working on Western medieval hagiography is best described, with rich bibliography, by Goodich, 'Filiation and Form'.

B. Obstructing figures (e.g. doctors — can be both helpers and obstacles)
C. Companions, fellows (fellow supplicants, other patients)
D. Helping objects, obtaining these objects (mostly curative objects, medicine, or supernatural remedies)
E. Obstructing objects or phenomena and hindering circumstances (objects causing illness; unbelief, delayed appearance of the healer, not recognizing him)
F. The way (to the sanctuary, to the healer; also in a symbolic sense)

Although it may seem interesting, the applicability of the Proppian pattern to healing miracles is more due to the richness of the pattern itself than to its particular relevance to the hagiographic material. Yet it raises an important question for the healing narratives: Who is the real protagonist of the story? Unlike most stories of saints' miracles, where the central character is beyond doubt the celebrated saint, the narrative of incubation healings concentrates on the sick persons. We learn the most about the patient from the stories; all of the episodes focus around them and not so much around the healer. Taken as a whole, only the miracle collection has the physician-saint in its imaginary centre as the ultimate source of all single miracles, but the individual stories concentrate always on the patients.

It proves more useful to turn to Barthes's classification of narrative elements and to distinguish in the miracle stories what he calls *cardinal units* or *nuclei* of the story and *sequences*. This brings us back to the concept of defining characters by what they do, and not by who they are.[9]

The cardinal units of incubation miracles are similar in the Asclepieian-type miracles and in the Christian incubation narratives:

1. Patient's name-provenance-profession;
2. The illness;
3. The way to the sanctuary;
4. The incubation dream, apparition of the healer;
5. The advice for cure given, or the miraculous cure (in dream or awake);
6. Recovery;
7. Recognition and declaration of the miracle.

In contrast to Theissen's and Guidorizzi's models, these core elements are chronologically consecutive in the incubation stories. When the miracle narrative must necessarily limit itself to an epigraphic *ex voto*, because of its space limits, these elements are present in their barest narrative form.

---

9   Barthes, Introduction to his 'Structural Analysis of Narrative'.

However, when there is the possibility to expand the story directly, around these nuclei of incubation miracles, a few other circumstances can be added:

1. Personal characteristics of the patient;
2. Details, symptoms, and sometimes the *cause* of the illness;
3. The way to the sanctuary which may include previous failure in seeking a cure (at doctors), may be realized on the initiative of someone else (family, friends, or the spread of the healer's fame), can happen at the healer's initiative (invitation dream);
4. Variants of incubation-dream: when someone else incubates on the behalf of the patient; when the dream is delayed; when the healer comes in the daytime; when the dream is dismissed as *phantasia* or dreams are repeated; when healers are not recognized;
5. Precondition of cure; punishment;
6. Partial cure, restoration of initial state after punishment;
7. Punishment remains.

These units follow each other in a precise order, according to a natural course of events and in narrative order as well. For these patterns, it holds true what A. B. Lord says about the units of oral poetry, that they follow a narrative logic and are freely adaptable:

> Although the themes lead naturally from one to another to form a song which exists as a whole in the singer's mind with Aristotelian beginning, middle, and end, the units within this whole, the themes, have a semi-independent life of their own. The theme in oral poetry exists at one and the same time in general and also for any individual singer's forms of it. His task is to adapt and adjust it to the particular song that he is re-creating. It does not have to have a single 'pure' form either for the individual singer or for the tradition as a whole. Its form is ever changing in the singer's mind, because the theme is in reality protean; in the singer's mind it has many shapes, all the forms in which he has ever sung it, although his latest rendering of it will naturally be freshest in his mind. It is not a static entity, but a living, changing, adaptable artistic creation. Yet it exists for the sake of the song. And the shapes it has taken in the past have been suitable for the song of the moment. In a traditional poem, therefore, there is a pull in two directions: one is toward the song being sung and the other is toward the previous uses of the same theme.[10]

Naturally, the length of the miracle narratives imposes a framework on this free-flowing compositional creativity. In what follows, I shall analyse some of those units that are additional to the main pattern and better reflect the variations of the basic miracle-theme.

---

10 Lord, *The Singer of Tales*, p. 94.

The first among such episodes that can be elaborated in accordance with the hagiographer's taste and motivation is the formation of the work itself. Although I addressed the hagiographers' motivation in Chapter 6, I would still like to call special attention here to the topos of the saint appearing to the hagiographer and helping him in writing. Just as in the Byzantine miracle collections, in the pagan testimonies such direct divine cooperation is frequently mentioned. A popular frame of this motif and one not confined to incubation is the dream of the aretalogos-hagiographer, in which the divine being appears and encourages (or orders) the future narrator to record their stories. Among the Greek examples are the Imouthes-Asclepius aretalogy[11] and the story of Thessalus the physician;[12] whereas the vision of Thecla's hagiographer fits nicely with the Christian examples:

> I was neglecting my work, of writing down the miracles, I was lazy to take up the tablet and the pen, as if I had given up my research and the collection of the miracles. I was in such state of mind [...] when I saw with my very eyes that St Thecla sat by my side, in the place where I used to consult my books. She took my notebook from my hand in which I have transcribed the last miracle. And behold! she starts reading it and takes pleasure in it and indicates to me with a smile that she likes what I have written hitherto and that I should continue this work, and not leave it incomplete, until I succeed in understanding what others know and in learning all from them with the utmost care. After this vision I was seized with terror and zeal to pick up my tablet and pen and carry out everything she ordered. (MT 31)

Similar to Thecla's hagiographer, Cyril of Scythopolis also benefited in sleep from the encouragement of his subject, Saint Euthymius, who appeared to the despairing hagiographer with an apple dipped in honey, which he brought to Cyril's mouth to provide him with sufficiently sweet eloquence.[13] In the same way, Sophronius was also greatly helped by the saints: in the *Laudes*, he tells us that Cyrus and John often appeared to him and read what he wrote, and even corrected his errors. Moreover, when ink or paper was missing, the saints provided it for him, and just like Thecla, their faces radiated with joy when they found the text enjoyable, whereas they reprimanded the hagiographer when he was negligent.[14]

---

11 Oxyrynchus Papyrus XI, 1381 (= T331).
12 See Festugière, 'Lieux communs littéraires', pp. 126–29, who quotes Byzantine examples as well. For another common motif analysed by him, the rediscovery of a lost manuscript, see his *La révélation d'Hermès Trismégiste*, parts: 'Les fictions littéraires du logos de révélation' and 'Révélation par la découvert d'un livre ou d'une stèle'.
13 Cf. Rapp, 'Byzantine Hagiographers as Antiquarians', p. 40; the *Life of Euthymios* is in Price, *Cyril of Scythopolis*, pp. 1–92.
14 Sophronius, *Laudes*, PG 87.3, col. 3383.3.

Wordplay, Riddles, Enigmas

Riddles did not come primarily from the narrators' playfulness but had deeper roots that linked dream cures with dream divination. Though the Christian saints may also foretell the future (e.g. KDM26), the close relationship between incubation healing and giving oracles manifested itself in those dream-recipes where the remedy is told in the form of wordplay or a riddle.[15] When Alexander the Great was besieging the town of Tyre (Tyros), he saw in a dream that he was chasing a satyr for a long time before capturing it. His dream interpreters were happy to inform him that the satyr (*satyros*) was the promise of a successful siege, for *sa – tyros* means 'Tyros is yours'.[16] Predictably enough, people in the besieged city had dreamt that their protector god, Apollo, would depart and side with Alexander; therefore the citizens nailed the god's statue down to prevent his leaving.[17]

There are similar wordplay counsels from Asclepius, where the figure of Pallas Athena stood for taking Attican honey,[18] or when Asclepius offered his fingers to be eaten and hence the sick man could deduce that fingers, *daktyloi*, indicated the eating of dates, *daktyloi*.[19] As the examples show, solving the riddle to find the indicated recipe could come about by playing with the word or through analogies between the image seen in the dream and its further indications. Steven Oberhelman saw the fourth book of the Hippocratic *Regimen* (*On Dreams*) exploiting the same analogy-principle, pairing the visual representations of the dream with symptoms of illnesses.[20]

Christian hagiography also exploited the same sort of wordplay, in which the name of a figure appearing in a dream is itself an instructive allegory. In one of Saint Demetrius's miracles, Saint Eutaxia (whose name meant 'Good Order') appeared and was never supposed to leave the saint and his city.[21] Similarly allegorical advice was given as a recipe to a patient of Saints Cosmas and Damian in a dream. In a miracle that figures both in the London Codex (CL6) and in the KDM corpus (KDM3), a sick man was told that his remedy would be to burn and drink the 'pubic hair of Cosmas'. He was quite astonished by the apparently unholy order and kept wandering about in the church, pondering the solution of this riddle. Suddenly, he heard one of the church servants call by name a sheep which was given as a thanksgiving

---

15 Oberhelman, 'The Interpretation of Prescriptive Dreams'.
16 Artemidorus, *Oneirocritica*, 4. 24.
17 Plutarch, *Life of Alexander*, 24, 3; for more cases of gods or their statues appearing in dream when a Greek city suffered hardships, see Stewart, 'Ritual Dreams and Historical Orders', pp. 340–41.
18 Aelius Aristides, *Oratio*, XLVIII. 40–43 (= T449a).
19 Artemidorus, *Oneirocritica*, 5, 89 (= T449).
20 Oberhelman, 'The Interpretation of Prescriptive Dreams', p. 420.
21 *Miracula Demetrii*, 76–87 (in *Les plus anciens recueils*, ed. and trans. by Lemerle, vol. I; cf. Delehaye, 'Les recueils antiques', pp. 63–64 and p. 72).

gift to the saints, and which was also called Cosmas. Illuminated, he called for a barber and they cut and dissolved the pubic hair of the sheep Cosmas in water; as he drank the liquid, he immediately became well. Even before we learn of the solution, the narrator at the beginning of the miracle draws a parallel between Christ, the source of the saints' healing power, and the actual means of the cure in terms of the spiritual and the real lamb. Another wordplay-recipe for a cure was given by Cosmas and Damian (KDM6) when they advised a patient not to eat food that began with the letter A.[22]

Precisely because of the riddles' prophetic-pagan connotations, Thecla's hagiographer made a point of claiming that the saint did not work with riddles and enigmas; they were methods that, according to the hagiographer, belonged to the traps of Greek daimones. Nevertheless, when it came to the interpretation of one of his own dreams, he could not avoid dealing with the inherent symbolism of it. In MT12, the hagiographer was suffering from anthrax, and his doctors told him that his finger must be amputated. Full of fear, he fell asleep and saw himself being asleep in the atrium of the church, where wasps attacked him. Thecla entered, and having taken off her shawl from her head, she started to chase away the wasps from the hagiographer's body, brushing them away with her hands and trampling them with her feet. In the same miracle, another, more enigmatic dream foretold the hagiographer of his excommunication. In this dream, prior to receiving the actual sentence, he saw a dwarf, a short black boy (who was, it seems, a real figure of the town), offering the hagiographer a dirty black coin. He reluctantly took it, and the next day, with the news of his excommunication, interpreted the aforementioned character as the bishop, Basil of Seleucia, and the dirty coin as given to him instead of the Host. Although Thecla's hagiographer dismissed the enigmatic man as a pagan, due to the content and narrative of the dream, the hagiographer could not entirely erase the man's association with Basil from his mind.

Sophronius, in contrast, states that the saints found pleasure in the riddles, and labelled the saint as the ones 'who dispelled my Homeric blindness with ingenious dreams full of riddles, because they took pleasure in such things';[23] but oddly enough, he did not record any actual dream riddles.

On the borderline of the enigmatic, there are those curative means that incorporate theological (Trinitarian) symbolism: three Muscat seeds (KDM21), three beans taken to be in the name of the Father and Son and Holy Spirit (KDM38), or the three jujube berries as a symbol of the Trinity in Artemius's collection (MA45), and the mute lady's miracle cure while singing the Trisagion (KDM7). More complex is the dream of a pagan in KDM10, who, while asleep in the church of Cosmas and Damian, saw three children

---

22 Festugière identified the food beginning with *a* with barley (*alphita* in Greek); *Sainte Thècle, Saints Côme et Damien*, p. 107, n. 21.
23 Sophronius, *Laudes*, PG 87.3, col. 3383.9.

eating bread and was unable to take his share, in spite of his desire. This source tells that a pagan's witnessing of the Eucharist counted as a profanation of the mysteries and the Church punished her with death, and the hagiographer regarded even this symbolic witnessing in her dream as such an offence.

Healers often gave numerical clues adjacent to riddles when indicating how to find some curative objects or persons — I will describe such clues below when I am addressing these categories. Numerical indications were also given when some part of the ritual was repeated: the saints appear three times, the miraculous cure happens on the third day.

While the description of the events of a saint's life is determined by a chronological sequence, with the miracles the hagiographer had the task to establish some framework not based on a linear-logical development. Sometimes, there is a deliberate attempt to connect the stories into a sequence by means of transitions that link them to consecutive miracles[24] (most 'chronological' are those miracles of Artemius where events happened to the same person at different stages of his life, such as MA38, 39, 40 or MA19–20). But more often, the narrator retold the saints' intervention to different people, restarting, developing, and concluding the miracle story again and again, 'le récit miraculeux est volontiers haletant, répétitif comme une incantation, chronologiquement disloqué, tenu à bout de plume par un enquêteur et témoin qui ne se veut jamais simple auteur'.[25] Sophronius expressed the essential repetitiveness of the miracles by explaining that he has placed the poor patient of MCJ18 following the rich one of MCJ17 'as in the marketplace'.

Repetition and one-dimensional characters in these miracles are not confined to the narrative only. The essence of miracles is that they can happen repeatedly to different people. The repeatability of the miracle and the repetition of elements within it suggest the possibility that these miracles will reoccur.[26] A topos familiar from ancient aretalogy is that a miracle witnessed or recalled refers to miracles left untold: At the end of the *Life of Iamblichos*, Eunapius wrote that in following one of his miracles, his disciples did not dare to put

---

24 For how this was achieved in Thecla's corpus, Dagron has illustrated in *Vie et miracles*, p. 153; see also Johnson, *The 'Life and Miracles of Thekla'*, p. 116.

25 *Vie et miracles*, ed. and trans. by Dagron, p. 152; 'La nécessité miraculeuse n'apparaître que si l'on retire un peu de sa logique propre (ou de son illogisme fondamental) à l'enchaînement des faits'.

26 'Lo schema oggettivo che inquadra le esperienze soggettive dei singoli malati fa di esse non più una serie di avvenimenti unici e irrepetibili, ma un manifestarsi di fenomeni ricorrenti e ordinari, quasi di "routine", di cui tutti i fedeli, presenti e futuri, possono beneficiare. Ciò è in linea con le esigenze propagandistiche di un tempio come Epidauro, ma anche con le convinzioni di un devoto come Elio Aristide: l'oggettivazione delle esperienze individuali vissute attraverso la pratica incubatoria, sottratte al singolo e consegnate alle forme di una tipologia fissa, diviene una garanzia della ripetibilità dei miracoli, e di conseguenza della possibilità per tutti i fedeli, presenti e futuri, di beneficiarne.' Dorati and Guidorizzi, 'La letteratura incubatoria', p. 361.

the thaumaturgic power of their master to the test, because on the basis of one miracle, they gave credence to all other ones.[27]

In the eyes of the believer, reader, or patient, references to biblical healings do not only recall the activity of Jesus and connect the saints' workings to that of Christ on a theological level, but they also establish an analogy between the healing miracles. This analogy between the cures of the saints and those of Christ is present in both the narrative's structure and its events, showing the possibility of an infinite repetition of the healing miracles of Christ. This analogy simultaneously promises and proves the possibility of repetition. In this aspect, repetition focuses on the individual; it has, however, a role for the community as well. Reginald Grégoire has analysed this communal role stating that, on the narrative level, all miracles are a result of a communal consciousness. The repetition of miracle motifs reflects the fact that the communal consciousness expressed an already cohesive communal experience. In the miracle, Grégoire identifies the strengthening factor of the community's reality, repeatedly confirming the identity of the healed patient, the healer, and the surrounding community as well as their entwined relationship.[28] All of these characters define each other, and the miracle defines all of them and their interconnectedness. In other words, they create each other, and the miraculous cure transforms the participants into the characters of healed patient, healer, and witnesses. Grégoire nicely shows how these three identities become two by the end of the miracle narrative: the miracle-worker and the community of his believers.[29] At the beginning of the narrative, the patient is distanced from the community; he receives individual characteristics through his name, origin, and the singularity of his illness (i.e. he has one illness that needs to be cured). At the end of the story, the patient, as one who has experienced the thaumaturgic capacities of the healer like the many others around him, becomes reintegrated into the community. What rendered him unique, his leprosy, blindness, etc., disappears by the end of the narrative. Thus, on the one hand, he returns to his own normal context. On the other hand, he cannot be again the same as before the miracle, but will become a part of those believers who are not simply Christians, but those who have personally experienced the power of that particular healer. At the end of the miracle, the customary thanksgiving formula is altered: it says that thanksgiving is due not to the saints, but to Christ working through them and thus makes the healers themselves also beneficiaries of Christ's grace, uniting the whole Church, the community of the living and the dead as followers of Christ, the *Solus Medicus*.

---

27 Eunapios, *Vita Iamblichi*, 459, l. 52; cf. Festugière, 'Lieux communs littéraires', p. 134.
28 Grégoire, *Manuale di agiologia*, p. 301.
29 Grégoire, *Manuale di agiologia*, p. 302.

Repetition, within the unity of each story and in the entire miracle collection, had an almost liturgical function. In the same way as the consecutive narratives point to the future repeatability of Christ's past miracles, the repeated motifs in the miracles confirm the reality of the told and retold stories.

Dialogue

Dialogues are a common feature in both ancient and Byzantine incubation miracle records; their persisting presence invites for a closer look. In an encounter between doctor and patient, dialogues play a critical role. Dialogues in the dream encounter represent and re-create a real-life meeting and exchange of words. Both ancient and Christian healers initiate a dialogue, often asking what a physician would ask. Asclepius would frequently address questions to his patients in order to establish familiarity, and we can often see his worshippers in intimate conversation with their deity. If we look at the questions Asclepius asks, we see that his concern and human tenderness are prominent. His directness is manifest also in the individually tailored cures, the way Asclepius questions the patients to learn also about their passions and individual weaknesses. In accordance with these answers, he prescribes the cure, but they also render the treatments unique, illustrating the uniqueness of the patient and their illness in the eyes of the god. From a childless woman, he asks whether she would like to have a boy or a girl (T423.34). Sometimes, Asclepius questions his patients to reveal and dispel their incredulity (T423.3) or to unmask a liar (T423.7); the most interesting cases are those with direct speech: 'Euphanes, a boy from Epidaurus. Suffering from stone he slept in the temple. It seemed to him that the god stood by him and asked: "What would you give me if I cure you?" "Ten dice," he answered. The god laughed and said to him that he would cure him. When day came he walked out sound' (T423.8),

The dialogues during the ritual encounter with the healing god also give an opportunity for the patient to react and counteract (like a certain Polemo to Asclepius, when ordered not to drink anything cold: 'My good sir, what if you were doctoring a cow?'[30]).

The Christian healers also initiate a dialogue with their patients, very much like a doctor would. In Saint Artemius, we witness an almost permanent formula with which he addresses his worshippers: 'What do you have?' or 'Lift up your robes!' (MA2, 5, 11, 20, 28, 40) When the saints cure in pairs like Cosmas and Damian or Cyrus and John, it often happens that the miracle story records their dialogues between each other, sometimes even discussing their patients (I write in more detail about this in the next chapter).

---

30 Philostratus, *Vitae Sophistarum*, I. 25.4, Polemo c. AD 100 (= T433).

It is interesting that the dialogue form survives when the dream is told and then, in turn, written down, even if it has to be done in the most space-saving way like on the votive inscriptions. There is a necessity and demand that the dreamer should retell word-by-word his experience. This is not the personal character or intimacy of healing or of cult experience. The role of dream-dialogues and the importance of reconstructing them are rather different, generic to the dream-experience itself and the timeless custom of 'recalling' it as closely as possible to the details of the actual event. When the dream becomes a narrative, the encounter between the two parties repeats itself, with the help of the recalled or re-created dream-dialogues. With the direct speech, the story comes alive; the experience becomes authentic. I venture to say that the persistence of dialogues in incubation stories also bears the impact of the real-life experiences between the patient and doctor and represents the careful repetition of 'what the doctor said', not only in terms of the recipe, but in reproducing the authentic diagnosis.

Finding Objects

In Asclepieian incubation stories, it is a familiar narrative element that directions may be given in the dream for finding objects that ensure the cure. The god may specify the location of a lost person,[31] of lost treasure,[32] but may also turn the search for the object into the cure itself. An example of this is when the blind man was told to search for his ointment bottle, the location of which was indicated precisely by Asclepius, and when he was about to find it, his eyesight returned.[33] The Christian incubation healers are likewise concerned about giving indications in dream for the suppliants to find curative objects or, alternatively, the object that caused the illness. The Christian incubation stories are longer and often more complex than their pagan antecedents, and this fact facilitates the combination of motifs in the narrative. Thus, finding a lost treasure in Thecla's collection overlaps with her general care for women (MT21: finding the stolen wedding-belt), her never failing vindication of violations of her cult place, as well as the power of her all-seeing 'divine eye' (MT22). In the key case of Artemius (MA18), finding the stolen objects unwraps a series of events that allow us a glimpse into the everyday life of the church and into personal tensions among the saint's followers.[34] In all these three cases, it is important that the saint identifies the culprit. In the Artemisian miracle, such elements become entwined with

---

31 Epidaurian Stele B, 24 = T423.24.
32 Epidaurian Stele C, 3 = LiDonnici, 'Tale and Dream', pp. 104–15, where the localization is in the form of an enigma.
33 Epidaurian Stele C, 22 = LiDonnici, 'Tale and Dream', p. 128.
34 For a detailed analysis of the miracle, cf. Rydén, 'Kyrkan som sjukhus', p. 16, n. 5, and Efthymiadis, 'A Day and Ten Months in the Life of a Lonely Bachelor'.

the story, as do the recognition of the stolen objects and the saint's order of forgiveness for the thief.

Another framework regarding the finding of objects is when the healer indicates the means of the cure. This can be something miraculous, but it can also be a completely simple object, viewed and used by a hopeful patient because the saints had indicated the object. Thus in the London Codex, Cosmas and Damian in a dream gave a walking stick to a paralysed man, encouraging him to try and move his legs and hands while supporting himself with the cane. When the man awoke, he found the walking stick on this mattress, and believing the dream provided guidance, he practiced with the stick and became well (CL16).

A variant of this motif can be found in which someone besides the sick person directly receives the dream-indication. In such cases, the finding of the curative object can also serve as proof for both parties, as in KDM26 (CL35), where Cosmas and Damian appeared to the incredulous heretic and indicated the means for a noblewoman's cure, which was hidden under her mattress.

A further form of this narrative unit comes from the borderline between magical beliefs and religious rituals: finding the object that caused the illness not in the medical sense, but by way of sympathetic magic. MCJ35 contains a folktale-like motif about an object fished out from the sea. It tells the story of a certain Theophilus who fell victim to sympathetic magic, and his hands and feet became paralysed. In his incubation dream, the saints advise that he should carry himself to the sea and find a fisherman who is casting his net into the water. Theophilus should pay the fisherman, so that he would cast his net *for him*, and what he catches will become the sick man's remedy. The object fished out is a small wicker basket, locked with a key and sealed with pieces of lead. The fisherman thought that the price paid by the sick man was insufficient for the curious object. They quarrel and as a result, they go to the dispensator of the church, who asks to examine the casket more closely. With difficulty, they open it and find inside a horrible sight: a small, metal human figure in the form of Theophilus with its feet and hands pierced with four nails, one for each limb. As they extract the nail from the right hand of the figurine, the man's right hand becomes healed; and so it continued with all his paralysed members.[35]

A similar magical machination caused the illness of Theodorus of Cyprus in MCJ55. The saints prescribe him a rather magical cure, and at the same

---

35 Dickie, 'Narrative Patterns in Christian Hagiography' analysed some of the miracle stories of Symeon Stylite the Younger and concluded, 'The form in which stories about saints healing the effects of magic-working are told has not been studied. There is a standard narrative pattern to many of them. It must go back well into the fourth century, but in this case what the prototype is for the story-pattern is a mystery. The same is true of stories about the opposition a saint encounters and the charges made by his fellow-clerics about his miracle-working being nothing but sorcery: they too have a characteristic form' (pp. 86–87). See also Festugière, 'Types épidauriennes de miracles dans la vie de Syméon Stylite le Jeune'.

time, they reveal to him that the object that caused his illness is hidden in his house. Hence, he sends a servant back to Cyprus, and on the spot indicated by the saints, under the threshold of his bedroom, they find the noxious object. Although the object is not described with the same precision to detail as the description of the *defixatio* figure, it served to identify the culprit, and its removal contributed to the effectiveness of the saints' remedy.

In the two cases above, the objects were harmful ones and finding them was a voluntary act, but the saints may make their patients find curative objects as well, even without the patients having sought their help. I use the term 'parallel object' for something that first seemed to be something else but turned out to be the object of the miraculous cure. Artemius once appeared in dream to a sick man and gave him a gold coin to buy a drink, and the man, awakening, felt to his joy that he was still grasping the coin in his hand. When he examined it closely, he recognized that it was a wax seal bearing the image of the saint which, when melted, cured his hernia (MA16). Thecla too sent to a dreamer the image of a precious stone of every colour that had miraculous powers to heal, but when the man woke up, he found nothing like it. In the meantime, his relative was on the way to see him, and on the road he found a beautiful pebble, which our man identified as the one sent by Thecla (MT38). Elsewhere in a dream, Saints Cyrus and John gave a fig to a sleeping patient that would cure him. After his initial disappointment of not finding it upon waking, the man tells his dream to his wife, and while listening, she just catches sight of the fig next to them (MCJ5). Dorati and Guidorizzi put these cases of finding objects into a larger category, that of real testimonies of the dream experience, a category that would encompass all sorts of proofs of divine intervention (blood, scars, and other physical signs) together with everything the healers indicate in dream and which exists in reality.[36]

Outsiders as Helpers and Healing Outside the Sanctuary

Just like indicating objects, healers may foretell in dreams the precise place and time where and when the person whom the patient needs can be found (e.g. Thecla in MT9). They describe him in detail, telling the dreamer their name, profession, and address (MA26, KDM18). They may also send a numerical clue: the first man you meet when passing the gate towards the sea (MCJ18), the fourth camel by the well (MCJ13), etc. Alternatively, the healers can appear in dreams to both parties, and the mutual exchange of their dream experiences makes recognizing each other possible.[37]

---

36 Dorati and Guidorizzi, 'La letteratura incubatoria', pp. 362–63. They related the motif of the precious stone/pebble found in Thecla's miracles to Bellerofon's dream in Pindar (*13th Olympic Ode*) who saw Athena in dream giving him a golden horse-bit, which he duly found in his hands.
37 CL15, CL18, KDM39.

The strangers' involvement in the miraculous cure had important precedents in ancient Greek ritual healing as well. A record in the Epidaurian *Iamata* tells the following story:

> Nicanor, a lame man. While he was sitting wide-awake, a boy snatched his crutch from him and ran away. But Nicanor got up, pursued him, and so became well. (T423.16)

We find similar stories about Saint Artemius, where he acted through a bath boy or even disguised himself as a bath boy.

A further version of the outsider-helper theme is that of healing on the road, such as when the miraculous cure happens on the way from the sanctuary, usually after unsuccessful attempts at incubation in the temple or church. The *Iamata* example tells the following story:

> Sostrata, a woman of Pharae, was pregnant with worms. Being in a very bad way, she was carried into the Temple and slept there. But when she saw no distinct dream she let herself be carried back home. Then, however, near a place called Kornoi, a man of fine appearance seemed to come upon her and her companions. When he had learned from them about their bad luck, he asked them to set down on the ground the litter in which they were carrying Sostrata. Then he cut open her abdomen and took out a great quantity of worms — two washbasins full. After having stitched her belly up again and made the woman well, Asclepius revealed to her his presence and enjoined her to send thank-offerings for her treatment to Epidaurus. (T423.25)

Here we cannot be entirely sure whether the man of fine appearance was Asclepius or someone else who healed in his name. In the Christian collection, we find the same theme: the healing on the road (KDM1, 18, MMenas 12, MCJ37), with the similarly double nature of the healer. In some cases, as in KDM1, the men who miraculously cure the man turn out to be the saints in disguise, while in other cases, there are outsiders who perform the miracle on the saints' behalf.

Although Asclepius occasionally performed healing at a distance, just as in this case of healing on the way *back* from his temple, this type of miracle-working was more characteristic of the Christian healers, as a result of a new conviction that there are tangible, transportable objects transmitting the thaumaturgic effect of the healer. Some stories even point to what would be the new paradigm in the Middle Ages, when invoking the saint will suffice. But because in incubation ritual the place itself, going there, and being there are overwhelmingly important, both in pagan and in Christian contexts, the readiness to go the sanctuary — even if the cure arrives before or after incubating — gained more emphasis.

From Asclepius's cases we find a healing just at the point of arrival, with the readiness to incubate:

A voiceless boy. He came as a suppliant to the Temple for his voice. When he had performed the preliminary sacrifices and fulfilled the usual rites, thereupon the temple servant who brings in the fire for the god, looking at the boy's father, demanded he should promise to bring within a year the thank-offering for the cure if he obtained that for which he had come. But the boy suddenly said, 'I promise'. His father was startled at this and asked him to repeat it. The boy repeated the words and after that became well. (T423.5)

In all these cases, it is emphasized that the patient had been at the sanctuary; in both the classical and Christian cases, the importance of being at the sacred site is equally confirmed. Closely linked to the sanctuary, these stories also push the saints' thaumaturgic activity outside the sanctuary's boundaries (similar to the dream visits at the patient's home, which I discuss below).

Among the Christian miracles, we read of a Libyan camel driver who suddenly became deaf and set off on his journey to visit Saints Cyrus and John in Menouthis. After passing the city's first gate, his ears started to open, and his condition gradually improved as he came nearer to the church. When he entered the sanctuary, he was completely cured; he gave thanks to the saints and left (MCJ45). Like other sacred places, incubation sites also had this characteristic of being at the centre of their own concentric thaumaturgic power.[38]

The outside helpers are often involved without their knowledge or even against their will. Additionally, they claim to possess no medical knowledge, a statement that sharply contrasts with their role in the narrative. Such stories often make a hostile or ridiculous pun on Byzantine surgeons and underline that the doctor-saints act with non-medical methods. For this reason, I address these cases in more detail partly in the next chapter, under the label 'Non-doctors Performing Miracle Cures' (including animals used in miracle cures), and partly below, under 'Dream Versus *Phantasia*'. Sometimes the saints use these outsider helpers to teach a lesson, to make the patients overcome their distrust, or to bring together people from different social standings. Some stories that will be discussed below are a poor man who was instructed by a saint to feed a rich man (CL18), a rich lawyer who was to be shaved by a paralytic butcher (KDM34), or an aristocrat who dreamed that the saints instructed him to turn to an actor and receive his slaps in order to be miraculously cured (KDM39). While these miracles require a helper, they can also be referred to as punishment miracles.

---

38 On the concentric nature of the sacred space, see Wacht, 'Inkubation', cols 181, 207 ff.

Punishment Miracles

Punishments always concern a ritual offence or an act that is interpreted as a ritual offence. The punishment in incubation narratives stays within the framework of illness: it can be the initial illness, the healer's refusal to cure, forcing the once miraculously healed illness to return, or in extreme cases, death. Punishment miracles in Asclepieian incubation stories were already in the focus of attention of Herzog and LiDonnici. Both of them addressed their presence in the miracles from the point of view of the sources. Herzog held that the punishment stories were inserted by the official cult propaganda.[39] By contrast, LiDonnici argued that if the punishment were followed by the patient's repentance and making amends, and then further followed by the healer's forgiving (manifested by his healing or the restoration of the original situation), it is more likely that the patient in question made the recording.[40]

If we examine the punishment miracles, the miracles themselves reflect important characteristics of the cult and of the cultic healer. In the general cultic background, we see Asclepius punishing those who are opposed him: those who do not believe in his power or who are reluctant to pay the offering that they agreed to initially. Thecla is particularly determined to avenge wrongdoing to those under her protection: the sanctuary and women especially. Compared to the other incubation saints, Thecla is the quickest to punish with death — a phenomenon indicative about her wider sphere of operation. (It is not surprising that these three death-punishment miracles form a thematic group (MT33, 34, 35) within the collection, just as the punishment miracles of Cyrus and John are grouped together.) In passing judgement over those who commit a sin against herself or those under her protection, Thecla, not unlike Pallas Athena or Artemis, bears traces of the attributes of an autonomous divine being; this is evidenced by the death that she most often inflicts by her own decision. An example of this can be found in the miracle in which the temple-robbing brigands meet their death (MT28). Here, the enraged Thecla is described in terms of an *imitatio Christi*, and her act is paralleled to the judgement of death for the impiety of Sodom and Gomorrah. Thecla can also appear as an intermediary, taking the initiative but eventually turning to Christ for the final authorization. On one occasion, Thecla visited a man in a dream, somebody who had embezzled the money of orphans; Thecla angrily informed him that she has pleaded the case before Christ and was told that the dreamer had been sentenced to die within a week, an event that duly took place and was recorded in the narrative (MT35). Thecla herself can also use an intermediary, as she did in the case of a man who had desired a woman he had seen at Thecla's feast. In punishment for the man's arrogance for even daring to ask the saint's intermediary to obtain her, Thecla carried

---

39 Herzog, *Die Wunderheilungen von Epidauros*, pp. 56–57.
40 LiDonnici, *The Epidaurian Miracle Inscriptions*, p. 40, n. 3.

out his death sentence through a demon that attacked the man with such a horrible illness that he died within three days in the midst of spectacular sufferings (MT33). Similar death awaited those two thieves who not only robbed a gold treasure of Thecla but seduced one of her virgins as well. The hagiographer at the beginning of the miracle explains the aim of the detailed description of the sacrilege and the punishment: he wished to include this frightening miracle in order to turn the readers away from impiety, sacrilege, and any conduct that is unworthy of the martyr — and above all because his concern was to tell stories that were *useful*.[41]

Saints Cosmas and Damian are the most concerned with general shortcomings: they often punish non-Christian pagans (by not healing them unless they convert), but there is a story where they punish a believing Christian who has a passion for horseracing (KDM11). In this story, the punishment becomes the vehicle of the miraculous cure and at the same time of the inducement for abandoning the vice. In other cases, they may cause an illness and then cure it in order to manifest their grace on the incredulous (KDM16, 37), or they may simply inflict an illness for a serious ritual offence and never cure it (KDM43).

Cyrus and John have an eye mostly for theological-dogmatic concerns. They punish harshly only in the case of pagans and heretics, that is, non-Chalcedonian Christians, by inflicting pain, violence, or rendering the patient ridiculous.[42] Similar to punishment and largely used by Cosmas and Damian and by Artemius is the cure through the teaching of a lesson: the rich must give money away, only the chaste wife can cure the jealous husband, etc. It is interesting that it is most frequently in punishment miracles that social barriers dividing the patients disappear — at least in the narrative.

One type of punishment miracle no doubt belongs among those recorded by the authorities of the sanctuary: punishment by death. The death of a patient in itself can be interpreted as a failed miracle; as such, it calls for a shift in the narrative. This new point of view in the story transforms the customary illness-miracle-recovery pattern into a punishment miracle, viewed, written, and interpreted by others. In such cases, the message of the divine miraculous power often shifts onto theological grounds and reminds the audience that there are some minimum requirements in order to be healed (or spared). Emblematic is the case in MCJ32, of a pagan who pretended to be a Christian, even to the point of taking the Eucharist in his efforts to disguise himself. He was immediately seized with convulsions, and three days later he died. In a different way, a witness, who in turn becomes the true protagonist of the

---

41 MT34. On this sort of moral-edifying concern (using the examples of our sources), cf. Maraval, 'Fonction pédagogique' and Déroche, 'Pourquoi écrivait-on des recueils de miracles?'.

42 MCJ12, 13, 28, 29, 30, 31, 32, 36, 37, 38, 39, 49, 67, analysed in detail in Fernandez Marcos, *Los Thaumata*, pp. 180 ff.

miracle, can tell a punishment miracle and the dead or non-healed person becomes a catalyser of the miraculous event.[43]

In a punishment miracle in Thecla's collections (MT33), a lustful man sees the saint in a dream, encouraging him to take the woman he saw during the saint's feast. This dream, of course, was the result of the man's own passion, but since it was exactly what he wanted, he took it for a divine apparition. He is duly punished. However, this story evidences something far more interesting: that different sorts of dream-sights can be combined in the story, a true dream in contrast to the false *phantasia*.[44]

Dream Versus Phantasia

The role of telling the miraculous event and its relationship to sight is all the more important as the dream-miracle is visible only to the beneficiary of the miracle. In order to verify that the miracle actually happened, or sometimes in order to verify that the miracle could happen, the dreamer has to retell the dream in his own words. Prior to this, the dreamer should reconstruct in his mind what he saw and heard, that is, he needs to create a meaningful and narratable story. It is a recurrent motif that the first test of the dreamer's faith is whether he or she narrates the dream, or in other words, whether he regards it as a true dream. On some occasions, the patients are convinced they have seen not a real dream but a *phantasma* or *phantasia*.[45] The *phantasma* is a deceiving apparition, lying and without authenticity, which is not worth being told openly, and a character acts upon the assumption that it is real. The following eighteenth miracle of the London Codex illustrates a sick man's hesitation when the dream prescribes something unheard of.

---

43 In KDM12 the hagiographer of Cosmas and Damian made an outsider the protagonist of the story, another patient (Martha). During the ritual dream, she witnessed the death of her neighbour; the saints appeared before her eyes and gave a small tablet with a message (πιττάκιον) to the elderly woman who was lying next to her. When Martha woke up, she reproached the divine physicians for neglecting her while caring for her neighbour. Soon she noticed that funerary preparations were taking place in the church and learned that the woman next to her had died. She fervently prayed to the saints: 'Good masters, great doctors, I want to leave, do not approach me for a while! I beseech you that you would heal me, I do not need this sort of departure!' The following night the saints rebuked and then finally healed her.

44 'L'hagiographe joue parfois sur la triple origine des rêves; ainsi lorsqu'un jeune débauché, tombé amoureux d'une femme aperçue à la messe, voit la nuit suivante Thècle lui en faire don (mais il s'agit bien sûr d'une maladie qui le dévorera.) Ici se mêlent dans la même représentation onirique stimulus physique, fantasme démoniaque et avertissement divin, mais par rouerie, pourrait-on dire, et sans que la maîtrise du songe échappe à la sainte.' Dagron, 'Rêver de Dieu et parler de soi', pp. 41–42.

45 For example, MT33, KDM2, 3, 12, 39, CL35 (KDM26), MCJ18.

Thomas was blind because of a cataract and thus unable to practice any craft. He lived in extreme poverty. He arrived at the church of Cosmas and Damian, and to these wise physicians he complained both of his illness and of his poverty. The servants of God ordered him as follows; if you want to regain your health, borrow from someone twenty *nomismata* and buy birds. The servants also appeared to the future moneylender and instructed him to give twenty *nomismata* to the man who would come to him, and they described the personal characteristics of Thomas. The next day, when Thomas reached the indicated man's house, he became ashamed of the whole matter, and it took him considerable time to find the courage to tell the man about his dream-apparition of the saints and their prescription. The other man in turn also revealed his own dream (recognizing Thomas even before he told his dream), and thus they signed a surety that eventually led to the miraculous cure.[46]

The reasons for doubting the authenticity of the dream and for relegating it to the realm of *phantasma* could be that the saints order something blasphemous, an act that would disregard social and financial differences, or would expose the patient to ridicule. Two examples from the KDM best illustrate this: Cosmas and Damian advise a lawyer of high standing to look for a certain paralysed butcher and have himself shaved by the butcher's trembling hands. When the butcher tries to excuse himself from the task, the lawyer angrily thinks, 'he saw a chimera, not a real dream-sight' (KDM34). In another miracle (CL35 = KDM26), the deacon, who is instructed by the saints to tell a sick incubant woman to go home because she would be healed, is also confused and thinks that 'he only saw a deceiving dream apparition (*oneirwn phantasian*), and the saints' talk just empty chatter'.

Harsher is the saints' command and more unlikely is the dream's truthfulness in KDM39: in his dream, a patrician saw the saints ordering him to receive slaps from a sick actor in the church in order to be healed. He thought that it was not a true dream but, as Festugière translates, 'une tromperie et une dérision, inventée, pour l'outrager et le couvrir de ridicule, par un démon jaloux et qui en voulait à son honneur'.[47]

The reality of the dream and its truthfulness had serious criteria in Antiquity.[48] The importance of narrating dreams was certainly not limited to miraculous or healing dreams only. As the word *opsis* shows, which denotes

---

46 For more on the same motif, cf. Nelson and Starr, 'The Legend of the Divine Surety and the Jewish Moneylender'.
47 *Sainte Thècle, Saints Côme et Damien*, ed. and trans. by Festugière, p. 194.
48 Recall the distinction in Homer (*Odysseia*, XIX. 562–67) between the true and false dreams that come through the gates of horn (*keras*) and ivory (*elephas*), which he links to the verb kraino (fulfil) and *elephairontai* (deceive). The concept persisted through the whole classical and Hellenistic period from Plato and Vergil to Geza Roheim's *The Gates of Horn and Ivory*; cf. Amory, 'The Gates of Horn and Ivory'; Del Corno, 'I sogni e la loro interpretazione nell'età dell'Impero'; Kessels, *Studies on the Dream in Greek Literature*; Lévy, 'Le rêve homérique'.

seeing, sight, and dream equally, the dream was part of the visible world. In the realm of Herodotean dreams, for instance, the dream-experience is an *autopsia*,[49] that is, the event seen in dream makes the dreamer a direct and authentic eyewitness.

The very act of defining whether a dream is real or not may have a role in shaping the narrative. For example, dreams seen at certain hours (midnight or midday), with special clearness (with recognizable persons appearing), or repeatedly, as dreams often repeat three times, seem more veridical.[50]

The Role of the Dream in Building Up the Story: Variants of the Dream Theme

Recently, a new scholarly interest has manifested itself in the structuring role of dreams in narratives.[51] What earlier Husser noted regarding the role of dreams in Old Testament narratives can be used most fruitfully for analysing incubation miracles as well:

> Dreams also appear to be a compositional technique particularly well suited to the structuring of a narrative text. They do so in the following two ways: Integrated into the situation described at the outset, the dream henceforth serves as the common thread, unifying the different elements in the narrative and bringing it to its conclusion. The plot is developed between the dream, which forecasts the outcome, and its realization, expected at the end of whatever peripeteia the author cares to imagine. [...] Another way in which dreams may structure a text is by permitting and indeed provoking the symmetrical organization of the text. Organized around an axis corresponding to the awakening of the dreamer, the narrative takes the form of a diptych, the panels of which often mirror each other word for word: the scene experienced in the dream will be lived out again in the wakeful world, for the dreams act as an initial prophetic element or instruction given to the hero of the story.[52]

In the incubation corpora, we find the several variants of the dream narrative that often intersect with each other, just as with the narrative units mentioned before. In what follows, I would like to illustrate what are the most frequent ones and how they work to shape the miracle narrative.

---

49   Hartog, *Le miroir d'Hérodote*, pp. 278–79.
50   Dagron, 'Rêver de Dieu et parler de soi', p. 41; examples are in his n. 19.
51   Cf. Merola and Verbaro, eds, *Il sogno raccontato*; recently a research programme was organized by Remo Cesarini at the University of Bologna: 'Il Sogno raccontato nella letteratura'.
52   Husser, *Dreams and Dream Narratives*, p. 103, and the whole of ch. 6.5 'The Literary Function of Dream Accounts'; cf. also Husser, *Le songe et la parole*.

Dream to Another / Narration of a Third Party / Double Cure

As we could see above in the cases of outside helpers, within the context of the incubation ritual, the healer might not appear directly to the sick patient in question, but to another person, who became the recipient of the dream involuntarily. This arbitrary appearance of the gods or, more frequently, of the saints often served to test the faith, both of the incubants and of the persons involved. Within the sanctuary, the beneficiary of the dream could be a fellow pilgrim, a neighbour sleeping next to the sick, the accompanying doctor or friend, or the temple personnel.

Dreaming to another patient often adds the motif of the double cure to the incubation narrative.[53] This story below (CL35/KDM26) has four motifs that can be found in numerous other incubation miracles, separately or partly together: the narration of the third, dream to another than the incubant, double cure, and finding an object. In CL35, we read about a woman with breast pain, who practiced incubation in the church of Cosmas and Damian in Constantinople. Cosmas and Damian, however, appeared in dream to the deacon of the church who fell asleep after his customary evening prayer. The saints urged the deacon to tell the woman that she would be healed and can go home. The saints had to appear three times because the deacon was reluctant to communicate the message, not having any proof of it. At last, the saints, in order to persuade both of them, instructed the deacon to indicate a healing ointment (*pharmakos*) hidden under the woman's mattress, which she eventually found, anointed herself with it, and was miraculously healed. The story has a slightly different version in KDM26; the focus shifts more to the man who receives the dream, who becomes in the story an incredulous heretic, and the sick woman is described as a noble lady. The heretic here becomes the main target of the saints' attention; he is the one who needs to be convinced about the saints' miracle-working power.

The inclusion of the outsider witnesses can be noted in several other early Christian miracle narratives. Occasionally, such a story could become so popular that it became attached to three different collections of saints (like the one of the paralytic man and the mute woman).[54] Here the presence of the third person as a narrator can be explained by the impropriety of the events; it is unlikely that any of the parties would have gone around repeating it. The story goes that Saints Cosmas and Damian appeared to the man who was seeking a cure through incubation. They told the man that in order to be cured, he had to approach the woman lying nearby, a lady who was mute. After repeated dream visits, the man took courage and crawled to the woman, who started to scream out of terror, whereupon the paralytic leapt up and

---

53 For example, KDM24, 25, 26, 34, 39.
54 KDM24, the miracle was also confirmed among the deeds of Saint Menas (MM5) and Cyrus and John as well, and Sophronius also knew it.

ran away. The 'third party', being the one who slept between them, closes the story with the narration of the double miraculous cure and the subsequent marriage of the paralytic man and the mute woman.

A story that closes Thecla's collection (MT 46) provides the view of an outsider of the miracle, parallelly presenting the beneficiary of the miracle and the saint. Moreover, her testimony serves as proof about the reality of the miracle. A lady, a sort of desperate housewife, comes to seek Thecla's help after having renounced her husband, her children, and her home and was assured that Thecla would sleep next to her, holding her in her arms. She goes to sleep at her incubation place, shared with another woman, Susanna. And instead of a dream story, we hear Susanna's account, in which she awoke and wondered how a third person would fit in their bed, saw Thecla flying between the two of them, and without rising from her bed like a sleeping person would do, slipped back into her chamber where she was said to have been sunk into the ground. I find it quite extraordinary that the closing piece of the collection is not a dream but the ritual of sleeping in the church as seen from the outside, by a witness who became the hagiographer's firsthand source.

The Incubatio Vicaria, Dreaming by a Proxy

In both the Greek and the Christian records of ritual sleep, there are variants of the incubation cult practice. These alternations can be due to exceptional circumstances, or on the contrary, to local cult versions that happened regularly within their territory. One important and well-spread variant was practising temple sleep by proxy, the *incubatio vicaria*, when it was not the patient but an intermediary who went to sleep and communicated in the dream with the healer. This version of the ritual produces an alternative narrative unit in the records as well, with the inclusion of a third person who dreams on behalf of the patient.

Most often, a proxy was sent due to the patient's condition, often being too ill or too young. It could also take an institutionalized form, as attested by a curious record from Strabo, who describes a cult where the worshipper had to make the pilgrimage, yet practising incubation on his behalf was the privilege of the priests:

> On the road between the Tralleians and Nysa is a village of the Nysaeans, not far from the city Acharaca, where is the Plutonium, with a costly sacred precinct and a shrine of Pluto and Core, and also the Charonium, a cave that lies above the sacred precinct, by nature wonderful; for they say that those who are diseased and give heed to the cures prescribed by these gods resort thither and live in the village near the cave among experienced priests, who on their behalf sleep in the cave and through dreams prescribe the cures. These are also the men who invoke the healing power of the gods. And they often bring the sick into the cave and leave them there, to remain in quiet, like animals in their lurking-holes, without food for many

days. And sometimes the sick give heed also to their own dreams, but still they use those other men, as priests, to initiate them into the mysteries and to counsel them. To all others the place is forbidden and deadly.[55]

When elsewhere Strabo wrote about the practice of Jews sleeping in the sanctuary in order to receive portents in dream, he recorded Moses' order that 'people who have good dreams should sleep in the sanctuary, not only themselves on their own behalf, but also for others for the rest of the people'.[56] Strabo remains our source for the information that sending a substitute was an option in the incubation practice at the sanctuary of Serapis in Canopus.[57] Incubation by proxy was practised when the sick person was unable to perform incubation — in cases of small children, for example; hence parents were often recorded as incubating on behalf of their child. A similar process was necessary if the patient was too ill to reach the shrine or in extreme cases even unconscious. An example from Epidaurus describes the procedure in the following way:

> Arata, a woman of Lacedaemon, dropsical. For her, while she remained in Lacedaemon, her mother slept in the temple and saw a dream. It seemed to her that the god cut off her daughter's head and hung up her body in such a way that her throat was turned downwards. Out of it came a huge quantity of fluid matter. Then he took down the body and fitted the head on to the neck. After she had seen the dream she went back to Lacedaemon, where she found her daughter in good health; she had seen the same dream.[58]

In the Christian cases of dreaming by proxy, the reasons given are various. Most often, the patient is too ill to travel, or for example, we are told that the patient had too many sins (KDM32); parents often dream on behalf of their children, and we also hear of a husband sleeping on behalf of his wife in childbed.[59]

Invitation Dream

More common than the substitution-incubation was for ancient and Christian dream-healers to send an invitation dream. The arrival at the cult place was often preceded by the healer's previous appearance, in which he might have

---

55 Strabo, *Geographica*, XIV. 1. 44; cf. Dillon, *Pilgrims and Pilgrimage*, pp. 152–53, listing other entrance taboos to shrines.
56 Strabo, *Geographica*, XVI. 2. 35.
57 'The temple of Serapis [...] is honoured with great reverence and effects such cures that even the most reputable men believe in it and sleep in it — themselves on their own behalf or others for them.' Strabo, *Geographica*, XVII. 1. 17.
58 Stele B. T423.21.
59 I counted the following cases of a dreaming by proxy: in Cosmas and Damian: KDM6, 20, 26, 28, 29, 32, 36; in Cyrus and John: MCJ10, 44 (when the patient is said to be too ill), 54; in Artemius: MA4, 24, 28, 42, 43, 45.

called the patient's attention to the existence or relevance of the cult site. The occurrence of the invitation dream mostly was a promise of the cure. On rare occasions, however, it could be the very precondition of approaching the ritual healer: nobody was allowed to enter the shrine of Isis at Tithorea unless invited by the goddess in a dream beforehand.[60]

The description of the invitation dream has a twofold role in the story, both on the level of the cult experience and on the narration; the invitation dream introduces the healer before the miraculous intervention. It brings the healer closer to the patient and prepares the dreamer and the readers alike for what to expect. The invitation dream serves for the healer to identify himself, to reveal his bodily appearance to the dreamer and to attest his or her medical, that is, wonder-working competence.

Dream at Home

A variant of the invitation-dream theme is when the sick receives the dream visit while at home, either following an invocation or being visited by the healer without asking for it.[61] In addition to their ritual context, these events are also incubation experiences because the requisites of incubation are present: These people wanted to go to the saint in order to sleep in their church and become healed through a dream epiphany. For various reasons, they could not go the church itself, but they were prepared for seeing the healer spiritually. Yet there is no need to force every single story under this label. Just as with Asclepius, there were simply cases when the miracle-working power of the healers was presented in a different way. This does not diminish the fact that we can legitimately view these collections and figures as connected to incubation.

Another common variant of the dream invitation is when the patient initially sought a cure from doctors and was deeply discouraged before the proposed operation. Thecla's hagiographer tells us (MT12) how the saint appeared to him in a dream when he was scared because of the imminent amputation of his finger. Similarly, Cosmas and Damian appear to a sick woman's husband who was worried for his wife's life the night before the surgical intervention (KDM28).

---

60 'For the Tithoreans deemed it not lawful to dwell round about and there is no admission to the shrine except for those whom Isis herself has favoured with an invitation in a dream. The same is done also by the underworld gods in the cities on the Meneander: they send visions in dreams to whomsoever they wish to enter their shrines.' Pausanias, *Guide to Greece*, x. 32. 13; cf. Nock, *Conversion*, pp. 153–54; and Dillon, *Pilgrims and Pilgrimage*, p. 152. Compare with the practice at Lebena: 'A Lebena, prima che il malato fosse ammesso alle cure nell'*adyton*, era necessario un consulto presso il santuario: consulto che poteva avvenire anche in assenza del paziente' through the intermediary of a family member or a friend. Girone, *Iamata*, p. 82.

61 For example, in MA11, 13, 39, 40, or KDM13, 47.

Another aspect of the dream invitation is that the healer (pagan or Christian) not only proves his sphere of influence and power over the dreamer's illness, but at the same time, they define the territorial limits of his capacity. The invitation to the cult place, as Dorati and Guidorizzi have underlined, at the same time means that the healers do not heal anywhere. Their power has a spatial field of force, and the patient must get within this sphere.[62]

For an analysis of the cult experience itself, the invitation dream sheds light on the psychology of the dreamer: his inner preparation, his doubts and anxieties as well as his hopes about the miracle, and also his expectations about the healer. The dream invitation, already a miracle itself, always promises a further miracle. For the sick man, it emphatically promises the miraculous cure, thus preparing the ground for removing what within himself may actually block his chances of recovery. In a certain sense, the dream invitation is an oracle: a narrative unit and a part of the ritual experience that recall repeatedly the strong connection of healing and divination in incubation, fading in its Christian practice.

In the lack of other intermediaries, the appearance of the healer bridges the gap between the patient and the sanctuary. That is, if the patient lives too far away or if he has no friends or family members to advise him to go to the sanctuary, the invitation dream solves this difficulty. Moreover, it also bears testimony that not only may the suppliants choose the object of their devotion or source of hope but the holy healers can also select their patients.

These versions of the incubation ritual, such as dreaming by proxy or receiving an invitation dream, confirm two important aspects of incubation in general, a thesis that is at the core of this book. First, these phenomena are at the same time a narrative unit and variant/detail in the story and an element of the cult practice/experience; they attest that the incubation ritual and the way of telling go parallel, in both the Greek and Christian stories. Second, being at the very place was the most important characteristic of temple sleep, pagan and Christian alike.

---

62 'In questo dobbiamo certo riconoscere un'affermazione della centralità dello tempio, ma possiamo anche leggere, nella crescente importanza del motivo, una sorta di compromesso tra una sfera d'azione che s'è sempre più espansa nel corso del tempo, di pari passo con il sempre crescente prestigio di divinità come Asclepio, e una funzione guaritrice che non s'è mai del tutto sganciata dagli originari limiti territoriali delle potenze legate all'incubazione, che possono operare solo nel territorio cui sono vincolate.' Dorati and Guidorizzi, 'La letteratura incubatoria', p. 354.

CHAPTER 9

Doctors and Miracles

Doctors and Medicine in Early Christianity and Byzantium

The relationship between Christianity and healing has been widely discussed, but it was only recently that Gary B. Ferngren gave voice to a well-formulated new argument: Christianity became a healing religion in great part as an answer to the Asclepieian (Isean, Serapieian, and similar) healing cults, in order to fulfil a social demand addressed towards the immensely popular healing cults of pagan deities.[1] This view does not regard healing as an inherent essence of Christianity from its start.[2] In this context, miraculous healing is to be interpreted primarily as miracles, and as miracles they represent signs, not aims in themselves: 'they represent the external aspect of salvation, the physical manifestation of a new spiritual order'.[3]

That the healing ministry of the Church was incorporated into a theological framework and became an important element of the self-definition of the Church presupposes a nuanced attitude towards lay medicine and professional doctors in general.[4] Healing was a charismatic gift, and the power to heal was given to Christian elders according to James (5. 13–18). This consequently presented the faithful as obliged to consult first (or for the zealots, solely) the holy men or healing relics. This priority of spiritual healing always served as a test of faith, yet the enmity of the Church towards medical science is far from being true. Within the attitude of the Church to medicine, two factors are to be distinguished: medical science and physicians. The judgement over medical healing in the early Church partly represented the standard of the Jewish tradition, which had itself undergone a radical change. In the Old Testament, there is a decisive turning point in the Book of Sirach (38. 1–15); the physicians, so far showed almost exclusively in a negative light, became regarded as tools of God. The explanation of this new attitude was that Judaism was captured by its fascination with the Greek medical tradition in the Hellenistic period, and as a result, it re-evaluated its conceptual framework concerning curative methods, the art of healing, and healers as well. The chief

---

1 Ferngren, 'Early Christianity as a Religion of Healing' and more in detail in his book: Ferngren, *Medicine and Health Care in Early Christianity*.
2 That Christianity was from the start a par excellence religion of healing was perhaps most influentially expanded by Harnack, *The Expansion of Christianity in the First Three Centuries*, I, pp. 121–51; for a similar view, cf. Case, 'The Art of Healing in Early Christian Times'.
3 Ferngren, 'Early Christianity as a Religion of Healing', p. 3.
4 See more in Bernard, *The Healing Ministry in the Church*; Schadewaldt, 'Die Apologie der Heilkunst bei den Kirchenvätern'; Kelsey, *Healing and Christianity*; and more recently Dörnemann, *Krankheit und Heilung in der Theologie der frühen Kirchenväter*.

difference of the two theological worldviews within which the earlier and later Old Testament traditions interpreted medicine was that, on the one hand, with time 'medicine comes to be viewed as a positive contribution to human welfare', while on the other hand, it was starting to regard 'human suffering as the work of Satan and of his cohorts'.[5]

The basic thesis that definitively shaped the standpoint of the early Church was that, since the material world itself is God's creation, the body does not merit scorn; hence, the remedies of nature together with medical science are the results of God's loving care.[6] There were a few exceptions who did not share this view, Arnobius, for instance, but his rigid enmity towards medicine was in all likelihood founded in his personal conviction, not in a traditional theological heritage.[7] Darrel W. Amundsen, who dispelled the false notion about the negative approach of the Church towards medicine, speaks of a 'double standard', namely that monks viewed bodily cures with more severity because they profited from its benefits less frequently and only in the case of an emergency when the previous prayers and spiritual healing were to no avail.[8] Yet in the light of the sources, even Amundsen's hypothesis can be challenged; the monastic community could view bodily healing also from a moral-allegorical angle. This interpretation was provided by Roberto Fusco, when analysing the spiritual atmosphere of hagiographical literature which discusses (among other things) healing and the early Christian approach towards the ancient medical tradition.[9]

One element of the ancient Greek heritage that early Christianity judged positively was its complex of similes, borrowed from medicine and indirectly from Greek philosophy, giving positive metaphorical value to the physician who unselfishly helps the sick, undertakes unpleasant tasks, in order to administer a cure. The borrowing of ideas and vocabulary between medicine and philosophy was by no means unidirectional. Medical literature did not only receive the repertoire of philosophical argumentation,[10] but shared definitions of the disciplines were also born: 'philosophy is the medicine of souls' — 'medicine is the philosophy of the bodies'.[11] Accordingly, the philosophers who were

---

5   See Kee, *Medicine, Miracles and Magic*, ch. 1, 'Healing in the Old Testament and Post-Biblical Traditions', for all the biblical references for Yahweh as healer, Yahweh and the physicians, physicians as agents of God, sickness and the demonic.
6   D'Irsay, 'Patristic Medicine' and D'Irsay, 'Christian Medicine and Science in the Third Century'.
7   Cf. Temkin, *Hippocrates in the World of Pagans and Christians*; on the basically positive attitude of the Church: Amundsen, *Medicine, Society and Faith in the Ancient and Medieval Worlds*; for an extensive bibliography, see Ferngren, 'Early Christianity as a Religion of Healing'.
8   Amundsen, 'Medicine and Faith in Early Christianity'.
9   Fusco, 'La cura del corpo nella tradizione monastica bizantina'.
10 'It is in the first place the influence of the philosophical teaching routine that is noticeable in the prolegomena to the separate writings of Hippocrates and Galen'; the fifth-century AD medical writer Palladius applies also the four dialectical methods (division, definition, demonstration, and analysis); cf. Westerink, 'Philosophy and Medicine in Late Antiquity', pp. 170–71.
11 Westerink, 'Philosophy and Medicine in Late Antiquity', p. 173.

assisted by the spiritual office of ethics became the *medici animarum*.[12] The history of these analogies reaches back to Greek philosophical borrowings from medicine, ideas that were to arrive into Christianity through the intermediary of philosophy. The idea that philosophy itself is medicine draws back to the Cynics; in its purest form, Diogenes of Oinoanda expressed it in the second century AD, applying the same vocabulary from the inscriptions to praise the merits of excellent doctors.[13] In sixth- and seventh-century Alexandria, the similarity between the figures and disciplines of the doctor and the philosopher became more prevalent.[14]

In addition to these shared ideas and terminology of the disciplines, I have in mind other concepts taken over by Christianity from Greek medicine, both scientific and ritual, such as the causality between sin and illness.[15] In close relation to this idea, we find viewing illness as pollution, uncleanness, and healing as cleansing.[16] In the latter case, the vocabulary originated from religious terminology and was taken over by medical language; from there, it found its way into philosophy.

There was no expression with a wider range of influence and that was more decisive in the shaping the theological judgements over medicine than the contemplation of Christ as physician.[17] The phrase *Christus medicus* first appears in a letter written by Ignatius of Antioch before 117,[18] yet the term owed its lasting popularity to Augustine.[19] This metaphor was influenced by Greek medical tradition to such an extent that the medical writer George of

---

12 Cf. Amundsen, *Medicine, Society and Faith in the Ancient and Medieval Worlds*, p. 133; Ludwig Edelstein was the first to point out the significance of medical analogies in his 'Greek Medicine and its Relation to Religion and Magic', p. 206.
13 Diogenes of Oinoanda, Fr. V. col. II. in Festugière, *L'idéal religieux*, p. 74: 'ἰατρεῖον ἐστιν, ἄνδρες, τὸ φιλοσόφου σχολεῖον. οὐ δεῖ ἡσθέντας ἐξελθεῖν, ἀλλ᾽ ἀλήσαντες'. The *soter* philosophy was dear to the Epicureans. Festugière suspects that there was also a wordplay involved in another fragment of Diogenes of Oinoanda (Fr. II. col. V): Ἐπίκουρος – ἐπικουρεῖν. About the 'delivery' offered by Epicuros, cf. Cicero, *Tusc.* I. 48; *De Finibus* I. 44; and Lucian, *Alexandros*, 61. On an inscription dating to AD 121 Epicuros himself was called *soter*, while the wording of Lucretius (III. 1043) is identical to the praise of that deliverer, who protected Thebes in Egypt during the epidemic of 42 BC (still Festugière, *L'idéal religieux*, p. 74).
14 Westerink, 'Philosophy and Medicine in Late Antiquity', p. 169.
15 Parker, *Miasma*, ch. 8: 'Divine Vengeance and Disease'; von Siebenthal, *Krankenheit als Folge der Sünde*; and in the rather poor article of Mazzini, 'La malattia e metafora del peccato nel mondo antico, pagano e cristiano'.
16 See esp. Parker's *Miasma*, referred to above, and Moulinier, *Le pur et l'impur dans la pensée des Grecs*; Bevan, *Hellenism and Christianity*, ch. 8, 'Dirt', pp. 145–56; for healing sickness and sin: Remus, *Jesus as Healer*, p. 32.
17 In more detail, see Dörnemann, 'Einer ist Arzt, Christus'.
18 'Εἷς ἰατρός ἐστιν [...] Ἰησοῦς Χριστὸς, ὁ Κύριος ἡμῶν'. Ignatius of Antioch, *Ad Ephes.* 7 (PG 5, col. 650); cf. Schouten, *The Rod and the Serpent of Asklepios*, p. 67; Dumeige, 'Le Christ médecin dans la littérature chrétienne des premiers siècles', p. 118; cf. also Schipperges, 'Zur tradition des "Christus Medicus" im früchen Christentum'.
19 For example, *De doctrina Cristiana* I. xiv. 13; cf. Arbesmann, 'The Concept of "Christus medicus" in St Augustin'.

Picida calls Christ a second (and rather neglected) Galen.[20] In Jerome, Jesus is called 'verus medicus, solus medicus, ipse et medicus et medicamentum, verus archiater, quasi spiritualis Hippocrates'.[21]

The Church, besides its role in spiritual and thaumaturgic healing, took a prominent part in the establishment of institutional health care as well.[22] In the wake of social demands and the newly found theological tenets of healing,[23] the first hospitals were born out of monastic and ecclesiastical foundations. The emergence of such early institutions of charity was backed by the decree of Constantine the Great, who in 332 set aside part of the incoming taxes for these purposes of the Church; during the reign of Theodosius I (379–395) there were already a number of charitable organizations functioning in Constantinople. Among the *xenones* and *xenodocheia* mentioned by Leontinos, bishop of Antioch (344–358), it is highly probable there was a hospital as well, yet the first firm evidence for the founding of a proper hospital dates to the 370s and comes from Basil of Caesarea, himself a trained physician who ensured the professional quality of the personnel. His example was soon followed by Eustachius in Pontus and John Chrysostom as the bishop of Constantinople (398–404) with his hospital-foundation. As historians of medicine often underline, hospitals in Byzantium resembled far more a modern hospital than the wretched dwellings known from the medieval West. Besides having trained doctors and nurses, the Byzantine hospitals also fulfilled a many-sided role: a 'combination of medical centre, poorhouse, old folks home, hotel and meeting-place'.[24] By the fifth century, hospitals were functioning in Hippo, Ephesus, Ancyra, and the influence of the hospital of Basil can be suspected around the foundation of the first hospitals of Jerusalem.[25]

---

20 George of Picidia, *Hexaemeron*, I. 1588, in Nutton, 'From Galen to Alexander', p. 4.
21 Peace, 'Medical Allusions in the Works of St Jerome'. Peace, however, seems to be mistaken: the *quasi spiritualis Hippocrates* in the Letter to Pammachius against John of Jerusalem, does not refer to Christ.
22 About the Christian *xenones* and *nosocomeia*, about the fourth- to seventh-century sources of treating the sick, and also about the hospitals of Byzantine cities, cf. Miller, *The Birth of the Hospital* and his 'Byzantine Hospitals'; Harnack, 'Medicinischen aus der altesten Kirchen geschichte', pp. 35–40; Nutton, 'From Galen to Alexander' and recently his *Ancient Medicine*; in the outline of Byzantine hospitals above I follow Miller and Nutton.
23 At the end of the third century AD, several social and political boundaries changed and a new system of authority and power-networks emerged. The old role of patronage by the former pagan aristocracy, which included attending to sick household members as well, was altered, leaving its impact on local-regional health care. Their immediate role in this area was taken over in the eastern Mediterranean by bishops such as Gregorios Thaumaturgos, Cyprian, or later Basil the Great. On the social aspects, see Constantelos, *Byzantine Philanthropy and Social Welfare*, esp. pp. 152–221.
24 Nutton, 'From Galen to Alexander', p. 9.
25 At the end of the fifth century, a monk called Theodosios, originating from the vicinity of Caesarea, had three buildings built near Jerusalem: one for sick monks, one for poor patients, and one for well-to-do laymen who needed medical care. A few decades later

In the following century, hospitals reached the smaller towns of Egypt just as they were established in Antioch or Edessa. The activities performed in the hospitals became so well known and so quickly part and parcel of the theological vocabulary inspired by practical life that a contemporary of Chrysostom, the ascetic writer Neilos of Ancyra, in a metaphor likens the world, its sinners, and Christ working for their salvation to a huge hospital, a *nosokomeion* in which the sinners are the patients and Christ is the doctor on duty for their souls. Just like a good physician, he does not offer the same remedy to all, but examining each patient, he adjusts the treatment to the spiritual requirements of the sinner.[26]

By the fifth to sixth centuries AD, in addition to city walls and splendid churches, hospitals joined the criteria of what marked urban culture (in Constantinople alone there were five hospitals by this time, with a specialized eye-surgery department in one of them). In these places, doctors could belong to the highest elite of society.[27] Soon, specialists, professionally trained doctors, replaced the benevolent Christian volunteers, and the traditional medical knowledge of Antiquity became incorporated into the Christian art of healing.[28] In Rome and in Constantinople, a 'prince of chief-physicians' (*comes archiatrorum*) was appointed to the top of the medical hierarchy, and in a seventh-century *Life of Theodore of Sykeon*, the saint is called 'the doctor-disciple of the real Chief Physician, Christ our Lord'.

This is the milieu in which the wondrous healings of the Byzantine incubation saints receive their form as miracle collections and whose cults flourished primarily in the vicinity of the two centres of medical practice: near Alexandria and in Constantinople.

---

the emperor Anastasius himself had a large hospital built in Jerusalem, on the initiative of Saint Sabas.

26 S. Nilus of Ancyra, *Epistles* III. 33. PG 79, cols 248–49; cf. also Miller, 'Byzantine Hospitals', p. 55; The Latin text is in Nutton, 'From Galen to Alexander', pp. 9–10; 'Sed magnus animarum nostrarum medicus modum, quo absconditis medicinam afferat, optime callet. Ne itaque indigneremur, neque animum despondeamus, neque inique feramus, quae nobis, uti addecet, infert Dominus. Multi namque in hujusce aevi valetudinario degunt infirmi sauciique, nec una eademque omnibus mensa conducit: diversa etenim omnibus et circuitus temporum, et dietam medicus indicit. Hic, ait, male sanus melle saepius consoletur; alius absinthii amarore tristetur; alius insuavi elleboro communicet; alioque modo alteri providet et medicinam affert. Eadem ratione Deus singulis nostrum conducibilia ordinat.'

27 Cf. Baldwin, 'Beyond the House Call' and Blockley, 'Doctors as Diplomats in the Sixth Century AD'.

28 For this transfer of medical knowledge, see the contributions in Zipser, ed., *Medical Books in the Byzantine World* and as well as a fresh summary, Zipser, 'Medicine, Byzantine'.

Dreaming about the Saints as Doctors: A Medical Gesture in the Miraculous Dream

By virtue of its visual quality, the dream may more accurately reflect the image-creating fantasy of the dreaming community than conscious iconic representations, and it can mirror its slow, culturally dependent transformations as well. The visual world of the sleeping patient is shaped by the impressions of their waking state. The culturally dependent character of dreams has interested a number of scholars; for Late Antiquity, E. R. Dodds best revealed the changes in the cultural experience of dreams. Additionally, I. Hahn provided a social and cultural background based on dreams: he analysed Artemidorus's *Oneirocritica* and indicated the dreamers' social and financial concerns about the surrounding reality, their family issues, their fears, and their individual and communal experience.[29]

What happens in the context of the dream experience allows us a glimpse into the dreamer's psyche, his visual world, and the iconic language, the *imaginaire* of his time. No doubt, the iconographic representations inside and around the temple made a great impact on how the healer appeared in the dream, on his attributes, his clothes, etc., both in Greek and in Christian incubation. The influence was so strong, and to such a great extent, that it led to a personification of a depicted figure that the man of Antiquity might dream with the cult image itself, which according to the ancient dream-interpreters, was equivalent to the deity's own epiphany.

The personal feature of the incubation experience conforms to the earliest recorded dream-patterns of the Greeks: in the dream, persons appear in their entirely bodily appearance. The basic lines of the ancient dream-scheme differ from the events of incubation in that the non-incubation-dreamer (in the dreams known mostly from literature) is a passive spectator, even if the dream-figure addresses him. In contrast, the incubation participant becomes actively involved: the healer not only addresses him, but also enters into a dialogue with him, asks about his symptoms, jokes or bargains with him, or even makes the cure dependant on the patient's decision (Asclepius in one case asked a barren woman if she wanted a boy or a girl). In this active and personal involvement in the incubation dream, I see the imprint of the patient–doctor relationship as experienced in the real world. Independently of the healer's medical or miraculous repertoire, in the sources of incubation, from the early stage the cure of the sick is immediate; in the wake of the dream, they most often leave the temple healed. A few centuries later, the methods of divine cures experienced in dream, along with the time span and circumstances of the miracle, had undergone a significant change while the ritual of incubation fundamentally remained the same. The first change took place when the immediate miraculous cures had been superseded by

---

29 Hahn, *Traumdeutung und gesellschaftliche Wirklichkeit*.

the prescriptions given in the dream: the complex therapies of Asclepius, his advice for concoctions, poultices, baths, gymnastics, diets, all of which led to a cure only with time, yet they were regarded as by no means less miraculous.

Several miracles of the Epidaurian corpus may well illustrate the relationship between the worshipper and the deity, shaped to some extent by the real encounter of the patient and the doctor: 'Gorgias of Heracleia with pus. In a battle he had been wounded by an arrow in the lung [...]. While sleeping in the Temple he saw a vision. It seemed to him the god extracted the arrow point from his lung. When day came, he walked out well, holding the point of the arrow in his hands' (T423.30). Thus, Asclepius appears and performs the cures, sometimes giving orders to his assistants to hold the patient firm or lift and carry his bed. Six centuries later, in Pergamon, Aelius Aristides, a resistant hypochondriac who was well versed in the varieties of ailments, recorded the god-sent dream-prescriptions, which were probably greatly influenced by his own medical knowledge as well as his fears of certain therapies. Yet there is more in his tales than the subconscious outlet of a pharmacomaniac; according to Aristides' account, in Pergamon around the temple, there were trained physicians whose role was to interpret and, if needed, prepare the god-sent prescriptions. However, we should not see in this the only key to all therapeutic success. We learn from Aristides that, on the insistence of the dreamer, these doctors carried out the dream-treatment, even if it was contrary to their medical opinion. The doctors' presence and, based on the sources, the immeasurable impact of the medical craft on cultic healing certainly indicated a new field in temple cures. Scientific medicine could also shape the content of the dream: Aristides once dreamed that two physicians were discussing his treatment. One raised the question with his colleague: What does Hippocrates suggest? The other's answer was that the patient should run a distance of ten *states* to the sea and then jump into the water. When he awoke, Aristides asked the doctors' opinion about this.[30]

Discussing therapy (be it a 'medical' or miraculous treatment) recurs in the early Christian dream-healing narratives as well.[31] Here the scene is complicated (or simplified) by the fact that we are not dealing with separate physicians involved in ritual healing but with doctor-saints; moreover, these were the two most prominent incubation cults with a pair of physician-saints working together. It is not surprising that the pair of physician-brothers, the saints Cosmas and Damian or Cyrus and John, occasionally discuss with each other over the patient about how to proceed. The dialogue-form becomes a new element in the motif-repertoire of incubation narratives. This does not produce a change in the dream-pattern, even if in the background of these overheard dialogues is the earlier experience of the sick with practising

---

30 *Hieroi Logoi*, 5, 49–52.
31 Cf. Zeppezauer, 'Warum wirken Wunder?'.

physicians. Instead, there is no change concerning the face-to-face encounter of the dreamer and the healer appearing in the dream; the sick meet their healer in person and in private, with the exclusion of the other patients.

As a result of the Church's newly found theological and social self-definition that now included the cure of the sick, the first monastically or church-founded hospitals were born in the fourth century. Hospitals spread quickly, and the activity within them became well known. Earlier, I cited Sophronius's simile for his hagiographical activity, whereby he selects stories just as doctors mix the painful with the useful (MCJ32), and later I cited Neilos of Ancyra's metaphor for Christ as an on-duty physician in a hospital.

More importantly, the tools and scenes of medical cure became an essential part of dream-events,[32] and much attention was paid to the treatment of scars (Cosmas and Damian often gave separate instructions for the follow-up care). In the same way, the representatives of medical science, doctors, became active characters in their miracles. The saints may carry the patient in dream to a nearby hospital in order to operate on him there; they handle the scalpel skilfully, and they are experts in techniques of bandaging. Likewise, the divine healers often involve physicians in the process of miraculous healing, either showing the cure to them or making them witnesses of the miracle, spectators to the inadequacy of their own science.

The gestures of scientific medicine left deep marks in a more specific way in the thought world of the sick. In a miracle of Saint Artemius, we read an account of how the saint is 'accustomed to make his rounds as if he were a chief physician in charge of a hospital, just as many have often been convinced by experience' (MA6). Without hesitation, the hagiographer connects the divine and real-life medical motifs, appealing to the everyday experience of the patients, both in hospitals and in the sanctuary. The peculiarity of the miracle is that the medical round, familiar from physicians practising in hospitals, comes to be included in the habitual gestures of the healer-saint. Yet here it is only the hagiographer, an *external* narrator, who shapes the story in this way. A similar outsider view of incubation is given in Aristophanes' *Ploutos*, where the narrator of the miracle is not the patient but his companion who spent the night in the incubation hall awake and peeping, and saw the divine healer going from one sleeper to the other.

The term Artemius's hagiographer uses here was in fact a *terminus technicus* of Byzantine hospitals for the physicians' medical round (*parodos*), and in this context, it is present in a further miracle in connection to the real Chief Physician (MA22). The word *episkepsis* appears in the miracles of Cyrus and John five times with the same meaning, to record the visit of the saints as

---

32 For example, in the KDM there are scalpels (19, 30, 42), needles (11), tampons (23), a medical lancet (47), an operating room with a pharmacy (30); and methods applied by the saints include fastening bandages (17, 23, 27, 30), massage (22), irrigation (23), and the removal of accumulated blood or pus (1, 13, 20).

part of a medical round (MCJ2, 9, 27, 34, 53).³³ On one of these occasions, the hagiographer even indicates the position of the saints among the allopathic and homeopathic medical schools: 'sanctis non contraria contrariorum secundum terrenos medicos remedia facientibus, sed similibus similia medelis sanantibus' (MCJ27).

In MCJ33, the saints doing their medical rounds appear to the Alexandrian(!) patient as a doctor of high rank and his disciple. The way the dreamer formulated or recalled this scene allows us to suppose that medical teaching in Alexandria included such a practice, and professors really took their students to visit the sickbeds. Similarly, in MCJ60, the patient from Constantinople (the other chief centre of medical training after Alexandria) is visited in his dream by doctors accompanied by young men, most probably their students. Both pieces of information complement the picture given by the eminent sixth-century physician Alexandre of Tralles, who puts emphasis on *peira* — bedside experience.³⁴

If the dreamer sees the healers as making their medical rounds, it means that, as a patient, he cannot be the only one present. It is here that one can grasp a cultural shift in the imagery, unknown for dreamers in earlier centuries; in their own dream, the dreamer witnesses the presence of other sleepers and observes the cure of others or their contacts with the saints.

This new awareness in the dream of the presence of other patients as a result of the medical visit may be considered to constitute a new motif. Cyrus and John appear in a dream to reproach the dreamer: 'Why do you shout so loudly and do not let those others sleep who are here with their illnesses? Do you think you are the only one here to have an unbearable dream?' (MCJ21). In another story of Cyrus and John, we read about a woman who was beyond hope. In her dream, she saw the saints performing their habitual medical rounds, and she saw them pass her by, without stopping at her bed. When she started to question the saints, still in her dream, why they did not pay attention to her, they sent her home to die (MCJ62). A similar scene is described among the miracles of Cosmas and Damian, in which a sick person sees in a dream that the saints are administering something to her neighbour. When she reproached them for neglecting her, the saints explained to her that they had allotted death to her neighbour, instead of a cure (KDM12). Elsewhere, witnessing others in dream can be a tool for formulating a theological message regarding conversion to Christianity or orthodoxy; in KDM9, a pagan sees in his dream that Cosmas and Damian 'had been doing their habitual rounds. When they reached the place where the pagan was lying, they turned aside and continued taking care of their other patients.' As the same course of events happened repeatedly, the sick man started shouting in his dream, begging not to be neglected. The same seemingly uncaring attitude is present in a story

---

33   *Sainte Thècle, Saints Côme et Damien*, ed. and trans. by Festugière, p. 223.
34   Duffy, 'Byzantine Medicine in the Sixth and Seventh Centuries', p. 23, p. 25.

of an Arian heretic, where the saints during their repeated medical rounds loudly diagnose the sick man and discuss what might be delaying his cure, which was, of course, his reluctance to convert to orthodoxy (KDM17).

In the shaping of the dream-pattern in ancient Greek incubation, the fact that it reflected a patient–doctor relationship played a decisive part, incorporating all the intimacy and personal character of that relationship. If the dream pattern has changed slightly in the course of centuries, this was due to the fact that it followed medical practice, which itself underwent significant changes. Likewise, into the dream *imaginaire* that formed around the healer, chief physicians, specialists, and professors with their medical students crept in, and alongside the medical rounds, the other fellow-patients as well.

The appearance of this new dream-pattern in Christian incubation narratives indicates how the knowledge of the waking world exercised an influence over the dream experience. In order that the other patients could emerge in the dream, and in order that the dreamer could contemplate the church as a hospital as if seen from the outside, it was not sufficient to go through the incubation ritual within a community and be enclosed for the night with many others who were seeking a cure. To shape the dream pattern into a meaningful new form, the imaginative force of the individual (or that of the community) needed the element well known to most patients from the working of a hospital, and thus the medical rounds of physicians were incorporated into the saints' activity seen in dream. Yet this was more than the visual domestication of a familiar medical practice. If we compare the images that the patients of classical and late antique Greece and the Byzantine Christians formed about a healer (in other words, what made them consider a healer to be a professional, whether it was the god of health or a saint), we can see that in the representations of ritual healers, their skill in surgery or in prescriptions played a great part because these attributes were thought to express their authority and medical expertise.

In this context, it was not only the thought world of the individual patients that influenced how the healer should look, but also the demands and ideas of their community influenced how a doctor should act. Incubation stories are precious sources to detect such influences because their medium was the dream, in which the patient could visualize their knowledge and expectations. Otherwise, these shifts in imagery would have been impeded by what the patient might actually experience. The manifestation of a doctor's visit in incubation healing and the change it showed in the dream pattern tells us something that usually remains hidden in communal imagery.

Medical Doctors in the Miracles

In the *Lives* of the saints and in the *miracula* literature, the reader is occasionally astonished by sharp invectives against medical science. Yet this is not a theological-ecclesiastical standpoint. On the one hand, it is inherent in the genre, a topos on the efficacy of the saint over his rival healers, and an enmity largely dependent on the personal experiences of the hagiographer. On the other hand, it is more directed against the physicians themselves than against the methods of lay medicine, which were, we should bear in mind, often employed by the doctor-saints as well.

Rivalry among healing methods was nevertheless an integral part of the division of the healing market, and accordingly, the hagiographer occasionally expressed his esteem for the representatives of the medical profession; rather, it would be more precise to say that the hagiographer often established a subtle distinction for illnesses within and beyond the doctor's competence. The presence and the role of physicians in Christian hagiography were greatly altered by the changes of hagiography itself,[35] while the non-hagiographical records depicted them from a different angle: doctors as diplomats, imperial envoys, politicians, and leaders within the social-ecclesiastical elite.[36]

The question of the healing procedure obviously raises the issue of medical methods in the repertoire of the ritual healers. This has been a well-researched topic, especially because these miracle collections give a detailed set of data about illnesses and cures.[37] In the miraculous stories of the physician saints, it is worth paying close attention to the presence of physicians themselves, their hagiographical, theological role, and the image of the medical profession at the time.[38] An issue hardly ever discussed but also deserving of attention would be the opinions held by doctors or put to shame, yet this does not mean that there was a real animosity between the Church and physicians. Hagiography, from this point of view, is an unreliable source, as doctors often had well-defined *narrative* roles.

The Doctor's Narrative Role

Doctors as alternatives to ritual and religious healing are natural counterparts to the physician-saints in the miracle stories. I am convinced that a great part of the doctors' role and their opposition to the saints were exaggerated for the sake of the narrative and must be interpreted so, without necessarily

---

35 Kazhdan, 'The Image of the Medical Doctor in Byzantine Literature'.
36 Cf. Baldwin, 'Beyond the House Call'.
37 See e.g. Magoulias, 'The Lives of the Saints as Sources of Data for the History of Byzantine Medicine'; and a critique of his approach by Patlagean, *Pauvreté économique et pauvreté sociale*, p. 103; Lopez Salva, 'Afecciones orquíticas y curaciones oníricas en el templo del Precursor de Oxeia'; Rosenqvist, 'Miracles and Medical Learning'; Talbot, 'Healing Shrines in Late Byzantine Constantinople', pp. 17–22, and her 'Two Accounts of Miracles at the Pege Shrine in Constantinople'.
38 As analysed, for example, by Ashbrook Harvey, 'Physicians and Ascetics in John of Ephesus'; Horden, 'Saints and Doctors in the Early Byzantine Empire'; cf. also Kazhdan, 'The Image of the Medical Doctor in Byzantine Literature'; Seiber, *Urban Saint in Early Byzantine Social History*, p. 88; and Constantelos, 'Physician-Priests in the Medieval Greek Church'.

envisaging a real conflict between the two parties. In addition to this narrative role, doctors also highlight some aspects of their contemporary social reality; thus, they offer a convenient model for the shift from the narrative to social background in my analysis that will be discussed in the next chapter. The picture we gain of physicians is a multifaceted one: they can be depicted as rivals, as those challenged and put to shame by the holy healers, or they represent the mundane world to whom the sick first turned before they discovered the true source of *soteria*, physical and spiritual salvation. In the miracles, doctors were perceived not only and not even chiefly as negative figures. Occasionally, they were depicted as cooperating with the saints, and their medical knowledge and their means to carry out surgery is even praised occasionally. As far as purely bodily health is concerned; when doctors fail, it could also be an indicator that the malady is a result of something not merely physical.

Even the hagiographers, the persons closest to the saints and the most knowledgeable about their healing capacity, did not hesitate to turn to doctors. These doctors may fail to combat the illness, but this action demonstrates that we cannot speak of a clear-cut animosity. Thecla's hagiographer tells us in MT12 that he first went to doctors with anthrax on his finger. Only when the doctors proposed to amputate it did he decide to seek help from the saint. Similarly, Sophronius sought first the Alexandrian doctors' advice regarding his diseased eye, and because they could not help he turned to Saints Cyrus and John.

Doctors, however, are also narrative characters; they are depicted in different roles in the miracle stories. I identified the following typology that incubation hagiographers used: (1) doctors as patients; (2) doctors as exponents of Greek (pagan) learning; (3) doctors put to shame by the saints for their mock cures; (4) non-doctors acting in the healing role, as the saints' instruments to the cure; and (5) doctors in a non-healing role.

At the intersection of the doctor as patient and as representative of Greek learning, the most illuminating case is the story of Gesius in MCJ30. Here, the lesson of Cyrus and John was directed against Greek religion and philosophy together with medicine, personified by the most remarkable Greek physician and scholar of the end of the fifth and beginning of the sixth centuries.[39]

Gesius of Petra was a physician resident in Alexandria who was believed by both pagans and Christians to be an excellent teacher, doctor, and man. He gave shelter to a persecuted Neoplatonist called Heraischus, who died there

---

39 The Gesius references are in Nutton, 'From Galen to Alexander', p. 6, n. 43: Photius, *Bibliothéké*, 352 B; Suda s.v. 'Gesios'; Temkin, *Hippocrates in the World of Pagans and Christians*, p. 169; according to Baldwin, Gesius was converted to Christianity: Baldwin, 'Beyond the House Call', p. 18 and n. 40; for the opposite view, see Nutton, 'From Galen to Alexander', p. 6, and R. Herzog on Gesius: 'Der Kampf um der Kult von Menuthis', pp. 122–23. Further references are in Nutton, 'From Galen to Alexander', p. 6, n. 22, among them Meyerhof, *Von Alexandrien nach Bagdad*, p. 396; his correspondence is in Zacharias Scholasticus's *Ammonios* (= PG 85, cols 1012f; 1060ff.

and was buried by Gesius. He was a friend of two Alexandrian students who later became Christian professors in Gaza, Aineas and Procopius (the latter the brother of Zacharias Scholasticus), and they exchanged letters. Ammonius in his *De opificio mundi* paid tribute and homage to Gesius. Damascius also praised him as teacher and physician. Gesius wrote a compendium on Galen, in sixteen books, which was still in use in the tenth century. He attributed the miraculous cures of Cyrus and John to the treatments prescribed by Hippocrates and Galen and claimed that they were not supernatural or miraculous. The saints retaliated with a theatrical punishment miracle. Gesius's back, shoulders, and neck came to ache, and the saints prescribed for him in three subsequent dream visitations the following remedy: 'By declaring that you are wise you have been proven rather a fool; fetch the pack-saddle of an ass and wear it over your pain-ridden shoulders.' He was then to put a large bell around his neck and a horse bit in his mouth and be pulled around the church at midday by one of his servants, shouting: *I am a fool!* The saints do not forget to ask in a fourth dream appearance: 'Tell us where Hippocrates set down the medications for your infirmity? Where does Democritus prescribe anything?' In this farce, I would say that the real punishment was the cure, rather than the illness.

The great figures of Greek medicine and natural science reappear in the *Thaumata*, as human and divine medical knowledge are opposed. A patient 'relieved, went to Cyrus and to John, the fellow-martyr of Cyrus, exponents of divine medicine, not of that one, which made Hippocrates, Galen, and Democritos doctors, who are talked about (only) on the earth' (MCJ43). But Sophronius also had respect for good physicians; he praised the knowledge of Zosimos, chief physician of Byzantium (MCJ52). He extolled the doctor-patient of MCJ55, Theodorus, whom he described as a well-versed and famous physician and who could not cure his own paralysis only because it was caused by magic; however, the remedies he tried, wrote Sophronius, were otherwise useful in cases of non-magical paralysis.

As this example shows, the failure of medical treatments could be an indicator that the cause of illness was not something physical, as it is so often in miraculous healing. KDM47 tells about a sick monk to whom the physicians applied all the supposedly useful treatments of Hippocrates and Galen. The sick physician of the London Codex (CL20) likewise merited the hagiographer's praise when he writes, 'Menas the doctor was an expert in his craft, an honest man, skilled in the art, who knew illnesses by experience.' After trying all his knowledge on himself, Menas turned to Cosmas and Damian, who did not treat him with the least derision or spite. In MCJ13, Sophronius neatly divided the separate spheres of medical and ritual healing. Elias the leper carried his spots as *signs*, the marks of his own wrongdoing ('Ταῦτα φέρων Ἠλίας τὰ στίγματα, τῆς ἁμαρτίας ὑπάρχοντα σύμβολα') and thus neither observing Moses' laws nor the science of Hippocrates and Galen could help him.

In contrast, the miracles of Artemius's later commentator show doctors in a completely different light. 'So, where are the fine-sounding Hippocrates and Galen and the countless other quacks?' — so begins one of his invectives in MA24. The hagiographer, or more probably a later redactor of the corpus, saw physicians as bitter enemies of the saint, maybe even as his rivals. His severe attacks went hand in hand with invectives against Jews and heretics (MA26, 28, 32, 38).

Ridiculing the Doctor's Craft: Mock Cures

Besides castigating doctors as incredibly greedy and heartless, another tool for denigrating medical learning used deliberate mock-cures that were absurd in the eyes of doctors and patients alike. Such mock cures could be performed by the saint himself; Artemius once appears in dream ready to operate in the manner of a butcher, 'holding butchers' tools and a cup [… and] pierced him with a knife in his lower abdomen and took out all his intestines. Then he cleaned them, washed them off, and twisted them with a rod. And the sick man saw him folding them up and making sausages' (MA25). After the cure was accomplished, the (later) hagiographer zealously commented:

> What do you, boastful surgeon, say to me? For if you had gotten hold of one of those who effected the cure, you would no doubt still require the man to name what ancient authority asserts that one cures hernia patients with butcher's tools and where it is enjoined to remove and replace their intestines. But your work contract is revoked and your scalpels are consumed with rust. Your consultation couches are useless and your blunt retractors as well.

When told without such bitterness, as in the miracles of Cosmas and Damian, mock cures were more often a source of laughter, being closer to the entertainment function of the miracles than a reflection of the saints' animosity with physicians. In KDM11, the saints instruct a man with intestinal ailments to drink a potion. This seems like a medical prescription, but the potion turns out to be a poison, hidden in the hippodrome. When the guards catch the patient searching for it there at night, as the saints prescribed, he is brought to the judges on the charge of practising magic. There he told his story, which the judges were unwilling to believe unless the man drank the poison. This he did, and he was cured and released. Moreover — and here is the sense of the mock cure — he was cured of his addiction to horseraces. Candlewick used as medicine, or the jujube berries prescribed as pills, or even the Eucharist to be taken as a pill to cure heresy were the many ways to challenge medical methods. At the same time, these mock cures also confirm the saints' place in the medical realm.

Non-doctors Performing Miracle Cures

Very close to mock cures are the miracles where the healer instructs an unskilled man, emphatically a non-doctor, to perform the cure in his name. Although I discussed this theme briefly in the previous chapter, I consider it worth including here as well, as this motif often includes or contrasts doctors with people without medical knowledge and enriches the healers' repertoire of miraculous cures with a deliberately anti-medical character.

The operation is often contrasted with the failure of reputable physicians in the patient's surroundings. The saints had the power to teach outsiders to work with medical tools, according to valid secular medicine (MA22, KDM19, 22). In a miracle of Cosmas and Damian (KDM19) a stranger performed an operation on a woman with dropsy. Inside the saints' church, he made an incision in her with a razor, telling the sick woman and her relatives that the saints had guided him there. He explained that he would never have dared to carry out such an operation just as the woman would never have entrusted herself to an ignorant stranger had not the divine physicians provided both of them with courage. The same story in the London Codex (CL24) makes it explicit that the stranger's role was to carry out the saints' command to operate according to Christ, showing also that the saints' power needed nothing medical in order to cure.

KDM34 unites the mock-cure theme with a test of faith in the double cure, where two patients were healed miraculously: the butcher with his paralytic hands had to shave a fellow patient in order to become cured, and the man in question had to allow himself to be shaved by the man's trembling hands.

The saints also could involve someone, a non-doctor, in a miraculous healing without the person being conscious of it, in order to work a miracle in an often absurd, non-medical way (MA26, 42, 44; MCJ18, 33, 67). For example, a sick man, seeking a cure from Saint Artemius, was ordered in a dream to go to a certain blacksmith and ask his help. The desperate man obeyed the prescription, but the blacksmith insisted that he had no talent whatsoever to perform a medical cure and became increasingly angry with the sick man's persistent visits. Finally, he struck the man with his hammer, who in turn became healed.

> What do you say to this, o famous Hippocrates? For he [Saint Artemius] ignored your divine consultation and prescriptions since he assessed neither time nor place nor age. Nor as a consequence did a man who had completed his third score of years remain uncured. For anyone who may be your disciple, when he is about to operate on such a swelling of the testicles, receives the scalpel from the patient's hand more despairing than hopeful of effecting the cure [...] if death should follow the operation, a short funeral hymn delivers the patient from your pseudo-knowledge. Where did you hear from time immemorial that a blacksmith raised his

hammer and a man with diseased testicles was relieved of suffering? But the Hammer of all diseases, Christ our God. (MA26)

So runs the comment of the hagiographer-redactor at the end of the miracle story.

The performer of the cure on behalf of the healer could be an animal as well. Just as Asclepius miraculously healed through his sacred snakes and dogs, Thecla also could perform miraculous surgery with the help of an animal, curing a blind child when one of her sacred birds pierced the child's eyeball with its bill, which was analogized to a medical lancet and the plucking to medical skill (MT24). The story of the tame deer in the miracles of Cosmas and Damian, together with the 'veritable zoo' around Thecla's shrine, attest that just like the doctor figures, these animals also had a multitude of roles in the miracles. In addition to being votive gifts, a source of entertainment, or a testimonial to the fame and splendour of the place, they also act as the actual means of the cure and a welcome enrichment in the narrative itself. Similar examples are familiar from the pre-Christian material as well: the dog licking the sore wound, the goose plucking the affected area, or even the friendly snakes at Epidaurus all acted as the god's instruments of a miraculous cure, either as his epiphanies or in their own right.

Doctors Acting Emphatically in a Non-Healing Role or upon the Orders of Saints

Doctors can be depicted in the stories not only as spectators and witnesses of the saints' cure but as active participants, the saints' miraculous agents (KDM20, 28, 32; MT11, 12). Reduced to passivity as doctors but elevated to active agents in the miracle, they acted as intermediaries of the holy healers; willingly admitting their own lack of means, they were not ridiculed or challenged by the saints as helpers. When a father left his sick son in the church of Cosmas and Damian awaiting incubation (KDM20), he left with him one of the family's trusted doctors — not to cure the son, but to give him relief and calm him while he was waiting. The son asked the doctor for some remedy against his pains, and when the physician fell into despair at what to do (since he was in the holy healers' territory), Cosmas and Damian appeared in a dream to him, forbade him to give any medicine to the young man, and assured the doctor that they themselves would take care of his patient. When the young man pressed him for medicine, he told him his dream, which explained his refusal to apply any medical treatment, and the promise of a miraculous cure was soon fulfilled.

In another miracle (KDM28), Cosmas and Damian ordered the doctor of a sick woman (who already lay in the church, waiting for the saints' dream-appearance) to go to her and make an incision on the spot they showed him, in the precise way they prescribed. The physician consented and, taking his scalpel, saw that the woman's breast had already been operated on, and the fresh scars were exactly on the place where the saints had indicated. Elsewhere, the doctors performed the operation in the church, guided by the saints (e.g. KDM5, CL10). Physicians were also the most suitable witnesses. Their expertise in the medical field and their counter-position to the holy doctors made their testimonies the most authentic to miraculous interventions.

Doctors may be described as being left unemployed because of the divine healer's intercession. In MT12, they came with their scalpels, but the patient (the hagiographer) had already been healed by Thecla; he added jokingly that the doctors rejoiced with him, but were probably also disappointed at losing their salary. In a variant form, the saints may involve the patient's physician by dissuading him from performing the operation and make him, the doctor, advise the patient to turn to the saints (KDM32). Such a non-healing doctor was the most striking when it was his own son who had fallen ill, and the father, a chief physician in Constantinople, took his sick son to the church of Artemius — a story that became the opening miracle of the collection (MA1). Turning to physicians always had the potential to be a catalyst in the miracle story for the saints' intervention (e.g. MCJ40, MA22, MA23).

Doctors praised, doctors put to shame and ridiculed, or their competence questioned — this varying attitude towards the medical profession may well reflect a social concern. It is representative of the initial uncertainty in which way medicine and doctors, for so long a bulwark of pagan *paideia*, should be integrated into Christianity's own belief-system. We should not forget that the Greek medical tradition was kept alive among physician-scholars, a circle the least inclined towards Christian faith. They often were not only the repositories of medical lore but men traditionally educated in Greek learning. The great doctor figures of the fourth to fifth centuries — Oribasius, Agapius of Alexandria, Asclepiodotus of Aphrodisias, Jacobus Psychrestus — openly held to their pagan religion.[40] Until as far as the fifth to sixth centuries, groups of pagan intellectuals — doctors, philosophers, professors of rhetoric, sophists, and aristocratic men of letters and scientific learning — gathered around the prominent cult sites of healing, the temples of Asclepius-Isis-Serapis.[41] The other factor that raised suspicion was the connection of doctors with early heretical movements. In Christian hagiography, doctors were sharply attacked for their exorbitant fees, and an additional cause for denigrating them might have been that, among physicians, Jews were in great number. That the Jews were renowned physicians quite early on, called to the bedside by Greeks and Christians alike, was illustrated by John Chrysostom's castigation of

---

40 A wonderful illustration of this is Oribasius, one the greatest Alexandrian physicians and personal doctor to Emperor Julian, who, on the emperor's behalf went to consult the Delphic oracle in 362 and received one of the last oracles of the Pythia; cf. earlier in the paragraph related to note 194.
41 For doctors as representing a stronghold of paganism and heresy, cf. Arnobius, *Adversus Gentes*, II. 5, and Nutton, 'From Galen to Alexander', pp. 6–7.

Christians who turned to Jewish doctors, speaking in Antioch [...] had made it a clear-cut issue, saying, in effect: 'Would you heal your body, even if you thereby lost your soul?'[42]

As is well illustrated by the varieties of involvements of doctors in the healing miracle narratives, attitudes to the medical craft and towards individual doctors were complex. What I tried to emphasize with these diverse examples is that we should not lose sight of the narrative role of doctors — so useful and malleable from the writer's point of view and so familiar for the readers and beneficiaries of the miracles. Their presence against this compositional background is paired with the versatile nature of the medical market and the saints' relationship to them; any kind of relationship, even animosity, strengthened their share of this medical market as healers. The next chapter will continue to expand the social dimension of these miracle narratives, acting more and more as a mirror for our contemporary society and for their views on ethnic or religious diversities.

---

42 PG 48, col. 855, quoted from Starr, *The Jews in the Byzantine Empire*, p. 90.

CHAPTER 10

Mirroring Society and its Beliefs

Sinners, Pagans, Jews, Heretics, Non-Christians in Terms of Illness and Cure

The miracle stories create narrative reference points to contrast and confirm their own message, but they also reflect the actual surrounding social reality.[1] They mirror their audience: the possible future adherents of the cult or its opponents. By extending enquiries about the sick on the basis of information provided by the hagiographer, it is possible to outline the social and private background of the characters, their professions, their personal preoccupations, and their (official or lay) relationship to the cult. Likewise, broader issues can also be explored: What financial or family problems could be caused by the illness? How did generational conflicts manifest themselves in the quest for healing, and in general what sort of value systems were revealed? All these factors together serve to richly characterize everyday life in contemporary Byzantium.[2] Instead of addressing such issues in general terms, I concentrate on their representations in the incubation miracle accounts in the context of illness and healing.

The Byzantine incubation miracle stories strongly reflect upon concepts around illness and illness causation, just as much as they reflect on the spiritual, mental, and theological as well as on the communal-social aspects around healing, often using the repertoire of the physical symptoms of disease and cure. In this way, sometimes openly, sometimes accidentally, these narratives allow us a glimpse into the anxieties of the community. One of such anxieties that is often manifest in the miracles is interpreting disease as a result or punishment of sin, or as *miasma*, pollution. Our healing miracles echo conceptions from Greek Antiquity that consider the cure as a washing

---

1 A major volume that addresses several issues and gives the most updated bibliography on individual topics within the seventh-century Byzantine context: Haldon, *Byzantium in the Seventh Century*, as well as Haldon, ed., *A Social History of Byzantium*; a work with a similar interest on the example of Aelius Aristides and second-century Pergamon: Israelowich, *Society, Medicine and Religion in the Sacred Tales of Aelius Aristides*.
2 Some of the vast research that relies on the miracle collections as well when addressing issues of sociology, private life, history, or urban life: Patlagean, *Pauvreté économique et pauvreté sociale*; her *Structure sociale, famille, chrétienté à Byzance*; and also her Introduction to the volume, edited by herself, *Maladie et société à Byzance*; Seiber, *Urban Saint in Early Byzantine Social History*; Saradi, 'Constantinople and its Saints'; Dagron, 'L'ombre d'un doute'; Hackel, ed., *The Byzantine Saint*.

off of dirt by means of the external cleansing of the body (ablution) or by applying a more unclean material.³ On the other hand, the defiled/diseased body can be cleansed/cured through the healing of the soul, by punishment miracles, or by orders given by the healers; these orders were to confess sin or turn to orthodoxy as a prerequisite of the cure. That diseases, especially skin diseases, originated from pollution and could be washed away by ritual ablution is familiar from Greek ritual healing:

> There is a cave not far from the river at Samikon belonging to Anigros's daughters the nymphs. The traditional law is that anyone who enters it with any kind of leprosy first prays to the nymphs and promises whatever sacrifice it may be, and then wipes off the diseased parts of his body, and when he swims across the river, he leaves his disgrace in its water, and comes out healthy and clear skinned.⁴

Asclepius also applied it, but our testimony from the *Iamata* interestingly places the god's cleansing of the sick man's body into a dream.⁵ Similar to Asclepius, Apollo was also associated with washing away illnesses in his capacity of a healer. As Plato described him in the *Cratylus*:

> For in the first place, purification and purgations used in medicine and in soothsaying, and fumigations with medicinal and magic drugs, and the baths and sprinklings connected with that sort of thing all have the single function of making a man pure in body and soul, do they not? [...] But this is the god who purifies and washes away (ἀπαλοούων) and delivers (ἀπολύων) from such evils, is he not? [...] With reference, then, to his acts of delivering and his washings, as being the physician of such diseases, he might properly be called Apoluon (ἀπαλούων, the washer).⁶

It may well happen that the cleansed spots remain as memorial to the miraculous cure. There is the most extraordinary case when Asclepius used one healed man's marks from his forehead, left imprinted on a cloth, to punish a perjurer by putting the same spots onto the perjurer's head as memorial of the miraculous punishment.⁷

Ablution of marks features in the *Thaumata* as well (MCJ8), where we learn that, after the miraculous cleansing, even the birthmarks left the patient's body. Saint Artemius once used cleansing in the case of an internal disease, in a symbolic washing away of the illness from the internal organ, but not the external symptoms: 'He pierced [the man with testicular disorders] with a knife in his lower abdomen and took out all his intestines. Then he cleaned

---

3   Cf. Douglas, *Purity and Danger*, esp. pp. 6–11, and pp. 136–38.
4   Pausanias, *Guide to Greece*, v. 5. 11.
5   T423.28, Cleinates of Thebes with lice.
6   Plato, *Cratylus* 405a–405c (trans. by Fowler).
7   T423.6–7.

them, washed them off and twisted them with a rod. [...] And arranging them, as it were, in one coil, he put them back again into the sick man's belly' (MA25). In addition to the concept of curing by washing off, this image has other layers as well. It undoubtedly drew on the medical practices of the time. It is a mock operation, and the dream perhaps really originated from the sick man's fear of surgery; picturing Artemius as a butcher folding sausages could well have been also a grin towards medical science. The notions of physical and spiritual purification return in the *sermo* at the end of MA34; its writer spoke in a more metaphorical way, and his account is packed with the imagery of water, spring, water well, baptism, and ablution, including likening Artemius's relics to a spiritual Jordan.

Another archetype of healing diseases caused by pollution is the application of a similarly defiling material to the illness. Thecla advises dirt as medicine (MT18); but more telling is the case of Elias the leper, who was 'carrying his *stigmata* as signs of his error' on his skin and was advised by Cyrus and John to prepare a medicine from camel dung and smear all his body with it (MCJ13) — a remedy that verges on the practice of purifiers and magicians and serves as a test of faith. He did as he was ordered but did not smear it on his face; of course, his body was cleansed of the disease except for his face.

In her *Purity and Danger*, Mary Douglas differentiated between two methods for cancelling pollution: one is ritual, which has no interest in causality and responsibility; the other one is the confession.[8] Together with ritual purification, the public confession of sin and atonement in order to placate that deity who sent the illness as punishment for wrongdoing was by no means a Christian novelty.[9] Besides the testimonies of Greek Antiquity and the thought world of the Old Testament, there is an intermediary group of testimonies, from the second to third centuries AD from Asia Minor.[10] The formulae of the propitiatory inscriptions or confession stelai usually had the following scheme; someone committed a sin (often of a religious nature) and a god inflicted a punishment on the sinner in the form of various illnesses. He or she confessed the sin, made amends, and set up the stelai to placate the god. In several cases, the inscription ends by confirming that the cure has been received. In addition to the story, we often find reliefs depicting the parts of the body and sometimes a reference to the sin.[11]

Naturally, the pattern of incubation narratives is different; nevertheless, the saints and their patients often arrive at a similar conclusion, but it rarely concerns an act of wrongdoing. Instead of focusing on the act itself, it is rather about being in the wrong status. Nemesius the astrologer was said to

---

8 Douglas, *Purity and Danger*, p. 138.
9 Cf. Noorda, 'Illness and Sin, Forgiving and Healing'.
10 Cf. Pettazzoni, *La confessione dei peccati*; his 'Confession of Sins and the Classics'; also Nock, 'Review of Raffaele Pettazzoni, *La confessione dei peccati*'; Varinlioğlu, 'Eine Gruppe von Sühneinschriften'; Chaniotis, 'Illness and Cures'.
11 Van Straten, 'Gifts for the Gods', p. 101.

have merited the deprivation of his eyesight, 'with which he was studying the sky in a distorted way, inspecting the movement of the stars with too much curiosity' (MCJ28). The most common error, the state of sinning against the healers, involves the patient being, in one way or another, on the other side of what the saints represent. Thus, the cause of becoming ill or of being punished by the saints with an illness is a sickness of the soul: that is, being non-Christian, or not a proper Christian.

Both accidental and purposeful reflection on the surrounding social and religious milieu had a twofold aim: as religious propaganda, and as a narrative representation of the various 'others'. Both tendencies coincide in the dynamics of the miracle; it is a narrative as well as a theological necessity that the healers appear also to those who do not believe in their capacities or that they confront them with the authority of another healer who is held to be more efficacious. Propaganda could of course be a matter of rivalry between sanctuaries and not between beliefs. In this case, as Vincent Déroche has pointed out, cult propaganda of a certain sanctuary could not be overtly expressed because the saints, as servants of the same Christ, could not contradict each other.[12] Hence, confirmation of the saints' efficacy can be achieved by representing groups to which the saints (or the hagiographer) could freely oppose. This may account for why pagans remained so long in the miracles when they disappeared from the scenery of Christian Byzantium. At the time of the origin of Thecla's miracles, however, they were socially recognizable figures living around her sanctuary, and their role in the stories was far from symbolic.

However broad the term *pagan* might be, it is not sufficient to incorporate all sorts of non-Christians and their functions in the stories. In the Christian incubation collections, there are several groups of non-Christians to turn to the saints, with different motivations and with different outcomes. The simplest group to define are those about whom we know only that they were 'pagans', that is, they were Hellenes who had not yet been converted to Christianity. A more frequently mentioned set is the learned Greeks: professors, philosophers, sophists, and rhetors who opposed their entire cultural knowledge to the saints' power. They may also be physicians who are thus challenging divine healing as heirs to the Hippocratic and Galenic traditions.[13]

The presence of Jews and the hagiographers' attitude to them probably reflect most closely the ongoing change in their social and theological position in contemporary Byzantium. The examples of the incubation stories demonstrate how surprisingly fast these miracles, with their quite fixed narrative patterns, change to reflect anti-Jewish legislation and social opinion. The most harshly treated group, however, are the heretics: those who turn against the current definition of the saints' (or the hagiographer's) orthodoxy.

12　Déroche, 'Pourquoi écrivait-on des recueils de miracles?', p. 102.
13　Cf. Nutton, 'God, Galen and the Depaganization of Medicine'.

According to the versatility of these groups, the saints' attitude also varies — from nonchalance or attempts at persuasion to anger and violence. The outcome of the confrontation likewise could be various: The healed pagan could return to their fellow believers and tell them about their miraculous recovery, and the pagans thus convert. Turning to the saint may have been the final step in the emerging interest in the new faith on the part of the unbeliever, who may have been already familiar with Christians and Christian rituals. It is not rare that a sick Greek only approached the saints out of extreme necessity, under the pressure of illness alone. Their presence at the cult place was presumably connected to the fact that in some cases the relatively quick Christian replacement of the previous (pagan) healer of the site resulted in the new, Christian saint, the cult place, and the incubation ritual inheriting some of the pilgrims as well, these being those pilgrims who had wanted to turn to the earlier incubation healer. The presence of various non-Christian groups in the stories presupposes that they were still an active part of the collective memory after Christianity conquered the area. Moreover, the narrative role played by these real or fictitious non-Christians served as a model for the target audience, for those hesitant, recalcitrant, or sceptical Christians who did not necessarily number among the 'pagans' of the miracles, yet they represented the theological 'others' — both in the stories and in real life. In what follows, I identify those categories in which non-Christians could play a narrative role in the miracle stories and identify some representations of the underlying social reality.

The Unbeliever as Pagan

That Thecla's hagiographer was the most talented narrator among the other incubation hagiographers is attested (amongst other things) by his most colourful picture of pagans. They are never described plainly, but they are portrayed through social circumstances of contrasting belief-systems. This confrontation might be between generations, spouses, or between lord and servant. What makes the evocation of this context fascinating, beyond the colour it brings to the narrative, is that the adherents of the old faith in this way confront not only the saint but also those near to them. Such was the case with the grandmother in a family where her children were already Christians, and when she turned to Sarpedonius in seeking a cure for her grandchild, Thecla healed the boy as a reward of the parents' faith (MT11). The daughter of a tolerant pagan family was healed and thus her soul was won for Christianity (MT18), and the pagan husband of a devotedly Christian wife was converted in reward for the woman's faith (MT14). Here, as is evident throughout the collections, the events take on the context and terminology of illness. When the wife prayed to Thecla for the conversion of her husband, the conversion was the goal, not a secondary result. Thecla, to achieve this, made the husband ill, that is, she manifested the illness of his soul in bodily pains, and she then healed this illness miraculously.

A Christian servant may also teach a lesson to his master, as so often in the collections the same miracle involves a rich and a poor man together. The rich Maximinus, a sceptical pagan, turned Christian after witnessing the miraculous cure of one of his servants (MT17), while Thecla elsewhere proved her wonder-working capacity to a sceptical Christian by healing his sick horse (MT36). A Christian friend could also familiarize a pagan Greek with the idea of conversion; the stages of such decision-making are described in KDM10, where the pagan man went regularly to pray for a vision or illumination that would eventually bring him to a decision.

It could happen that the Christian ritual experience was viewed by the unbeliever as authentic manifestation of his own faith. Thus, the Sophist rhetor Aretarchos stubbornly interpreted his healing by Thecla as having been performed by Sarpedonius, and the hagiographer, still at home in both worlds, used the vocabulary of initiation into the mysteries when describing how the patient after experiencing a miraculous cure defined himself as a follower of Sarpedonius, 'his supplicant and worshipper and initiate and lover'.[14] For the newly converted, it could also happen that certain Christian rituals seemed reminiscent of old habits. MCJ31 shows the evocative character of the Eucharist as a cult experience that enabled its recipient to attain the highest spiritual knowledge and to enter a state similar to that in which a pagan would have been able to prophesy or perform miracles. It also illustrates the way in which a newly converted Christian might still react in the accustomed way and hesitate between recognizing the significance of the ceremonies of the new faith and their former paganism. According to the miracle story, a certain Theodoros received the Eucharist in the church of Saints Cyrus and John. Immediately after taking the bread, he fell into a peculiar trance and made a terrible noise through his nostrils, an act, the hagiographer says, that is particularly pleasing to the demons.[15] We are dealing here with a pagan magical practice, the exact meaning of which may have faded among the Christians,[16] for, says the hagiographer, they would never have performed this act if they had known its true significance.[17] However, it does not escape the attention of the saints, who immediately strike the man blind.

---

14 'τὴν ἱκετὴν καὶ θιασοτὴν καὶ μυστὴν καὶ ἐραστήν', MT40; cf. *Vie et miracles*, ed. and trans. by Dagron, p. 397, n. 3. I have written about the analogies between the incubation experience and initiation in Csepregi, 'Mysteries for the Uninitiated'.

15 Tertullian describes the same phenomenon in his *Apologeticus* (XXIII. 5): 'Similarly bring forward some one or other of those persons who are supposed to be god-possessed, who by sniffing at altars inhale a divine power in the smell'.

16 For more similar examples, see Barb, 'The Survival of Magic Arts'.

17 For a discussion of the practice, see Bonner, 'A Tarsian Peculiarity'; on its obscenity, see *Sainte Thècle, Saints Côme et Damien*, ed. and trans. by Festugière, p. 236; for further interpretations, see Fernandez Marcos, *Los Thaumata*, pp. 186–87.

The Unbeliever as Heir to Greek Learning

Those Greeks who did not embrace Christianity were not the saints' enemies; on the contrary, they were a challenge, both in the narrative and in the eschatological sense. They often represented the hagiographers' own ideal of manhood: nobility, education, and fidelity to a tradition even if it was fated to decay. In the case of Thecla's hagiographer, this positive attitude is easy to understand. He converted to Christianity but never dreamt of giving up what had made him a man of culture; he rather depicted Saint Thecla as quoting Homer, just as he was quoting Greek authors. More complex was the attitude of Sophronius, who showed himself wildly attacking heretics, the saints' enemies. He was equally fierce with pagans, but occasionally praised Greek knowledge even in non-Christians. What he held as praiseworthy had not changed much over the two centuries that passed between the compilation of Thecla's miracles and the *Thaumata*.

One of Cyrus and John's pagan patients, Isidorus, son of Dionysius of Damascus, was not described as 'a worshipper of idols' or anything similar. He merited instead the highest esteem from Sophronius for being the descendant of the famous philosopher Nicolaus, who once was the teacher of Antonius and Cleopatra's children and all the twelve generations in between that had produced the most excellent and noble philosophers (MCJ54). Where such illustrious personalities were concerned, not even conversion was necessary for them to find a place in the miracle stories: thus, Isocasius could benefit from Thecla's miracle-working power and still refuse to convert to Christianity. Did his visit (even if incredulous) contribute to the fame of Thecla's church? Did the hagiographer want to portray Thecla as learned and tolerant, not withholding her curative powers from anyone? Or was the famous rhetor more important to the rhetor-hagiographer as a figure to be placed next to himself, to be overcome in one aspect, as a believer? In any case, Thecla was happy to have him in her church, no less than the other pagan rhetor Aretarchos, who likewise remained firm about attributing the miraculous cure to Sarpedonius and not to Thecla (and said that Sarpedonius advised him to turn to her). Here, the hagiographer was not sparing in his spite, saying that, however famous they were, the academic achievements of these great professors were as bad as their unbelief.

The Greek Sophist Stephanus, whom we meet in the London Codex, knew the philosophers well, was the author of 'pagan books' (*ethnika biblia*), and was described as a rhetor of Tarsus. However, he was blind in every sense, and after he was healed, he earned praise only when he put his talent to the service of the saints and subsequently wrote a book about them in an act of gratitude (CL10). The other learned pagan of the London Codex, Dioscuros, though he believed himself to be carried to the healing sanctuary of the Dioscuri, recognizing the saints as the new healers, converted and proclaimed the miracle among his pagan friends (CL23). Interestingly enough, his name and his status as a professor are omitted from the KDM9 version of the same story.

Doctors also belong to this category of learned Greek pagans and were often represented in the healing stories. I have treated their narrative role in the miracles in the previous chapter, but here I would like to point out that the hagiography reflected quite sensitively the shifts in physicians' social standing. Kazhdan has observed that after the popularity of the doctor-theme in sixth-/seventh-century hagiography, they disappear from hagiography.[18] When they are reintroduced, it takes some time before they assume the role of the saints' opponent. At the end of the tenth century, the divine and lay medical healers are depicted as enemies, but then the animosity vanished again by the eleventh-century *Life of Lazarus Galesiotes*, which recorded miraculous healing as well.[19] Kazhdan's explanation is as follows:

> After the seventh century the medical profession in Byzantium lost its social standing; in any case the society became lukewarm and negligent towards medical doctors, hagiography ignored them, and intellectuals did not consider them as their peers. The situation began to change, probably at the end of the tenth century: hagiography about *l'an mil* wages a sharp war against secular physicians and scolds the greediness and incompetence of the medical doctor who dares to match the omnipotent healing power of the saint; in other words, the doctor had become too influential to be neglected. But the anti-doctoral attack was no success: by the twelfth century, the physician enters as equal to the establishment of functionaries and literati (one of whom he, indeed, was); he becomes respected, although mocked time and again by a society that started to care for its health more than for its salvation.[20]

A much earlier phenomenon can be traced through the social interpretation of Gesius's story (MCJ30): Rudolf Herzog regarded it as emblematic for the rejection of Alexandrian intellectualism, not so much by Christianity in general, but by Egyptian monks flowing in from the desert who rejected all sorts of learning.[21]

---

18 Together with hagiography, as Ihor Ševčenko pointed out, as there are almost no hagiographical texts from the eighth century; see Ševčenko, 'Hagiography of the Iconoclast Period'.
19 Kazhdan, 'The Image of the Medical Doctor in Byzantine Literature', p. 49; the *Life of Lazarus Galesiotes* is in *BHG* 979, and *AASS* November 3, 563B.
20 Kazhdan, 'The Image of the Medical Doctor in Byzantine Literature', p. 51; see also Ashbrook Harvey, 'Physicians and Ascetics in John of Ephesus', p. 87.
21 Herzog, 'Der Kampf um der Kult von Menuthis', pp. 123–24; cf. ibid. for Neoplatonic philosophers who flirted with Egyptian magic.

Jews in the Miracles

In Thecla's fifth-century collection, Jews appear as part of the community that benefits from the miracles of the saint and emphasize the cultural diversity of the context in which Thecla worked and in which her attention concerned everybody.[22]

> Among the saints there is also the great martyr Thecla, always present, always on the way, incessantly attentive to prayers and unselfishly supporting everyone: healthy and sick people, hopeful and desperate ones, people travelling by land or sea, people in danger or in safety, singles and groups, families, towns, peoples, foreigners and locals, people living here or abroad, men, women, lords and servants, adults and youth, rich and poor, officials, people in the army, at court, in war and in peace. She had often manifested herself to Jews and Greeks and showed them her miraculous power.[23]

In this universality, Thecla's patients also participate. For example, there is the case of Aba from Seleucia, daughter of a pagan Greek family, who we learn was emphatically tolerant towards everyone and was without any aversion to either Jews or Christians (MT18). So when she fell from her mule and broke her leg, she likewise exploited the similarly colourful healing market, turning first to Jews (probably physicians), and then to pagans who made incantations. When these proved to be useless, she tried Sarpedonius, and finally went to Thecla. In this, we see the common practice of sick people who, without any ethnic or religious strains, did the rounds of physicians. Here we have, as often throughout Byzantium, the whole spectrum of the medical market: Jewish physician, faith-healer/magician, the once-powerful local Greek healing hero, and the new occupant of the ritual healing site, a Christian saint.

Jews in Thecla's Isauria are thus represented as not only a culturally and religiously different community, but also through the prominence of Jewish physicians who are represented as persons who offered an alternative (or rivalry) in the healing market.[24] Outside this marked background, however,

---

22 In general, see Simon, *Verus Israel* and more recently Lieu, North, and Rajak, eds, *The Jews among Pagans and Christians in the Roman Empire*, esp. the chapters of Judith Lieu, Fergus Millar, and John North.
23 Prologue, *Vie et miracles*, ed. and trans. by Dagron, pp. 288–89.
24 *Vie et miracles*, ed. and trans. by Dagron, p. 124 ('La société des Miracles'): 'Des minorités ethniques proprement dites, nous n'apprenons presque rien: [...] les Juifs semblent compter beaucoup, bien qu'aucun n'entre en scène: ils sont certainement assez nombreux pour avoir une influence religieuse, que doit favoriser la compétence de quelques médecins. [...] Leur tombes à Korykos sont disséminées dans le cimetière de la ville tandis qu'à Séleucie il y a tout à la fois des tombes individuelles et un παραστατικὸν Ἑβραίων, mais tout donne à penser que la communauté était bien intégrée à la ville. C'est du reste une tradition de la région jusqu'au temps des Croisades.' For testimonies about the religious and medical prominence of Jews, cf. *Vie et miracles*, ed. and trans. by Dagron, p. 93, n. 5: *Monumenta Asiae Minoris*

they did not emerge as individuals in Thecla's corpus. The reason for this might have been the personal position of the hagiographer, a converted and learned Greek, who was more interested in figures similar to him. Judaism appeared once again in the collection as a cultural reference point. When writing about the stylistic marks of the narrative, Dagron called attention to the fact that, among the Old Testament reminiscences, there is a parallel in MT14 between the Christian wife who prayed for her pagan husband's conversion and the biblical Anna who prayed for a child, 'ἰουδαικῆς ἀπειροκαλίας τὸ αἴτημα' — 'demande bien digne de la vulgarité juive'.[25]

The case of another Jewish woman, from the collection of Cosmas and Damian (KDM2), attests to the fact that Jews also turned to the Christian saints when illness compelled them. The wholly sympathetic approach of the miracle reflects the context in which

> Judaism remained an explicitly permitted religion. However, this situation was not only the result of incorporating pre-Christian elements into a Christian code. It was also deliberate Christian policy. Judaism had to be preserved as a living testimony to the Christian interpretation of the scriptures and to the victory of Christianity. Jews were thus sharply distinguished from both pagans and heretics who had no rights and no civil status.[26]

The healing of the soul goes hand in hand with the grace of bodily cure, but the miracles apply the terms 'sick', 'soul', or 'spiritual illness' not only to the theologically different pagans, Jews, and heretics, but likewise to a man who kept a mistress, a fanatic of the circus games, or to the unjustly jealous husband. In the KDM2 story, the Jewish woman with an illness in her breast practised incubation, and the saints, appearing three times, prescribed that she had to eat pork as a remedy. Because of the pains, she ordered her Jewish servants or family members around her (who were also staying in the church) to bring her pork, but they regarded the dream as an illusion and tried to dissuade the woman, emphasizing that the prescription would turn her against the Law of the Old Testament and her ancestral customs. They finally gave in and brought the pork, and when the woman was just about to eat, she noticed her husband coming; frightened, she hid the meat under her dress. Meanwhile, the Lord, thanks to the saints' prayer, made the illness of the woman 'jump' from her breast onto the meat. As soon as she became aware of the miracle,

---

Antiqua, ed. by Keil and Wilhelm, III, nos 23 and 32 for Seleucia; 205, 222, 237, 295, 344, 440, 448, 607, 679 for Corycos; Hicks, 'Inscriptions from Western Cilicia', p. 269, no. 70 for Olba; Jewish inscriptions of Cilica collected: *Corpus Inscriptionum Iudaicarum*, ed. by Frey, II, pp. 39–48 and 124.

25 *Vie et miracles*, ed. and trans. by Dagron, p. 156; in the textual commentary (*Vie et miracles*, p. 327, n. 4) Dagron remarked that the word 'vulgarity' elsewhere (*Vita* 8, 19) received the adjective 'female'.

26 Sharf, *Byzantine Jewry from Justinian to the Fourth Crusade*, p. 20.

she hastened to become baptized. It is worth noting that here the conversion, the confession of the Christian faith, was not a condition of the cure. Even the willingness to convert proved sufficient.[27]

Eating pork was suggested as a remedy in other testimonies of ritual healing. Asclepius also prescribed it, but he was ready to suggest something else when it turned out that pork was a religious taboo for his patient:

> [Domninus, fifth century AD] was not perfect in his manners of life, so to call him a true philosopher. For the Asclepius at Athens revealed the same cure for Plutarch the Athenian and for Domninus the Syrian, of whom the latter continually coughed up blood and had the sickness of this name, the former was ill with some disease, I know not what. The treatment prescribed was to keep [the patient] sated with pork. Plutarch could not abide the health thus acquired although it was not contrary to his ancestral laws, but rising up from the dream and leaning on his elbow on the couch, he looked at the statue of Asclepius (for he happened to be sleeping in the vestibule of the shrine) and said: 'My lord, what would you have prescribed to a Jew suffering this same illness, for certainly you would not bid him to take his fill with pork.' Thus he spoke, and straightway Asclepius spoke from the statue in a very harmonious voice, prescribing another remedy for the illness.[28]

In Lucian, Alexander the false prophet prescribed pork for a man with colic, and although overtly the text mocked only Alexander's poetic capabilities, we may detect some irony also in the remedy: 'The man complained of colic, and Alexander, wishing to direct him to eat a pig's foot cooked with mallow, said: Μάλβακα χοιράων ἱερῇ κυμίνευε σιπύδῳ.'[29]

Whether pork or pig fat were in fact widely recommended in ancient miraculous healing is difficult to say on the basis of scarce evidence.[30] Pork was a remedy also advised by Saints Cyrus and John (MCJ54) to a sick boy's

---

27 Worth comparing with the story of a miraculous conversion of a Jew and his family to Christianity, under the Monophysite patriarch Timothy (518–535), in *The Chronicle of John of Nikiu*, ch. 91, trans. by Charles, pp. 144–45.
28 Suda, s.v. Domninos = T 427. The story continued in a rather surprising way: the privileged patient had preferred obeying the god's command, though he was not compelled to do so, to his ancestral laws. 'But Domninus, trusting the dream, even if it was not in accordance with the law — the ancestral law of the Syrians — and not availing himself of the example of Plutarch, ate of the meat at that time and ever after. It is said somewhere that if he omitted one day, fasting from the meat, the illness unfailingly returned, until he was sated with pork again.'
29 Lucian, *Alexander the False Prophet*, 25 (trans. by Harmon).
30 On the ritual curative use of pork, see Csepregi, 'Pork as a Wonder Drug'; Deubner's references: *De incubatione*, p. 48, n. 1; and the interpretation of the pig in Asclepius's cult and further references: *De incubatione*, p. 40, and Ehrenheim, *Greek Incubation Rituals*, pp. 30–34, 40–43; for how the pig fared in later medieval imagination, cf. Fabre-Vassas, *The Singular Beast*.

mother, who had to anoint her son's body with pig fat, 'because the saints wanted to heal the woman's soul as well', since 'she had an inclination to Greek error and because of the death of Adonis did not eat pork', a fact that she concealed from her family. In the following miracle (MCJ55), pork as a remedy is interesting from two aspects, for it was a doubly magical cure. Here pork is not so much connected with the illness of the sick person (who was doctor), but rather with the one who caused the illness (a Jewish *magos*).[31] Both the cause and the cure of the illness were magical. In a dream, the saints prescribe their doctor-patient to grill a lung of a pig on charcoal, to sprinkle it with wine, and to anoint his aching feet with it. The saints also made the sick man find the object in his house that magically caused his illness, and they identified the agent of the magic who 'was a Jew and as such was not free from the suspicion of magic' ('Εβραῖος δ' ἦν, καὶ τοιαύτης ὑπολήψεως οὐκ ἐλεύθερος').

Fernandez Marcos, analysing the miracle, only saw the pig fat as a magical tool that was efficient against the magic caused by a Jew.[32] However, the encouragement to eat grilled pig lung is also familiar from the prescription of a magical papyrus: 'πολλὰ πίνοντα καὶ μὴ μεθύειν· χοίρεον πνεύμονα ὀπτήσας φάγε' (drink a lot and don't get drunk; eat roasted pig's lung).[33] Medical authors also recommended pork: Pliny the Elder suggested both pork loin and swine marrow for eye complaints (*Natural History*, 28.47), rue 'with nightshade and hogs'-lard for morphew, warts, scrofula, and maladies of a similar nature' (*Natural History*, 20.51), and it fared well later among ancient and Byzantine physicians, from Galen to Oribasius.[34]

Similar to the original miracle of the Jewish woman converting to Christianity through the involvement of pork, I would like to cite another curious miracle about a voluntary conversion of a Jew, which reflects the central motifs of miracles of Cosmas and Damian. In the London Codex of Saints Cosmas and Damian (CL18), recording a cure performed in Constantinople, the saints ordered a blind beggar to take a huge loan to feed himself, while they themselves give surety to the moneylender (otherwise unspecified). In the end, both money and faith and health are miraculously restored. Another mid-seventh-century miracle from Constantinople tells how a Christian merchant suffered shipwreck. Not having his friends' help for a new business, he turned to a Jewish moneylender who was a specialist of financing such voyages (moneylending in Byzantium was by no means a profession practised only by Jews; there was no prohibition to the charging of a reasonable interest, hence such enterprises were underwritten by Christians

---

31 A contemporary example for the Jewish magician is the legend of Theophilus of Adana from the beginning of the seventh century, BHG 1319–22.
32 Fernandez Marcos, *Los Thaumata*, p. 196.
33 Wessely, *Neue Griechische Zauberpapyri*, p. 25; cf. Deubner, *De incubatione*, p. 48.
34 Cf. Rzeźnicka, Kokoszko, and Jagusiak, 'Cured Meats in Ancient and Byzantine Sources'.

and even by Church dignitaries). The man's friends warned him from doing any business with a Jew, yet they refused to give the merchant his necessary surety. However, an icon in a church within the Jewish quarter of Constantinople, the Chalthoprateia, miraculously spoke, stating that it accepted all responsibility. When it became necessary, the surety was abundantly paid and the Jewish moneylender converted to Christianity.[35]

Origen wrote about the important role of dreams producing conversion,[36] a phenomenon that was not unique to the Christian thought-world, as in the *Metamorphoses* of Apuleius, the dream appearance of Isis had the same aim and effect.[37] However, the rabbis did not regard dream as sufficient for converting to Judaism (yet Christian hagiography has a wonderful story, contradicting that, about a monk who in his dreams repeatedly saw the apostles, the saints, and martyrs in a horrible state, while Moses and the prophets were always in their splendour, and this urged him to become a Jew).[38]

Quite different is the picture presented in the collection of Artemius. In the main text of the miracles, we do not encounter pagans, Jews, or heretics. However, there were short sermons that were later added at the end of some miracles, which served as veritable invectives. In these invectives, target-enemies were indiscriminately thrown together: all manner of heretics, Buddha and Mani, Galen and Hippocrates, doctors in general, and Jews in particular. We can find a similar double condemnation of Jewish doctors in the *Life of Symeon Stylite the Younger*, reflecting on the death of Justin I (518–527) who was treated by a Jewish physician.[39] In the case of Artemius's miracle collections, the end of MA38 illustrates the anti-Jewish sentiment:

> What will you say, nation of Jews, you who fashioned a cross for Christ, you who furiously shouted in Pilate's court: 'Kill, kill, crucify him'? The very cross which you have fashioned for destruction, when made by Artemius, itself gives life. How, o brood of vipers, does Christ on account of whom you shouted to Pilate: 'Kill, kill, crucify him' raise up men who are close to death when he himself is invoked by Artemius? How do St John (who baptized Christ) and the wonder-working Artemius along with the gloriously triumphant martyress Febronia reclaim from death those who are held by Hades through the invocation of Christ? Jewish nation,

---

35 Nelson and Starr, 'The Legend of the Divine Surety and the Jewish Moneylender'.
36 Origen, *Contra Celsum*, I. 46.
37 See Nock, *Conversion*, ch. 9, 'The Conversion of Lucius', pp. 138–40; and Stroumsa, 'Dreams and Visions in Early Christian Discourse', p. 193; recent research on this theme, revisiting Nock's ideas: Secher Bøgh, ed., *Conversion and Initiation in Antiquity*.
38 *De monacho qui Hebraeus factus est*, BHG 1448; cf. Dagron, 'Rêver de Dieu et parler de soi', p. 46; and Stroumsa, 'Dreams and Visions in Early Christian Discourse', p. 207, n. 30: 'This is in contradistinction to the thought of the rabbis, for whom the dream of a gentile does not count as a legitimate motive for conversion.'
39 *Vita* of Symeon Stylite the Younger, 208–11 (BHG 1689) = *La vie ancienne de s. Syméon le Jeune*, ed. by van den Ven.

> covered with shame, can you not bear to say? Artemius lays bare your actions and because of your actions he scorns you, he crushes you into the ground, he flogs you with invisible scourges, he wounds you severely and you do not feel it. But let us leave the Jews to groan and return to the miracles of the martyr.

Interestingly, this anti-Judaic outburst is found at the end of a miracle that tells of the miraculous recovery of a boy whose parents were moneylenders (it is not mentioned that they were Jews). When he was around nine years old, he was thoroughly disgusted by that business and turned his back on his parents because he 'recognized their vain and disreputable profiteering and the weighting of scales and their greedy and usurious rate of interest and the unadulterated exorbitance of interest on pawned objects'.[40] He started to visit the church of Saint John, from where he was dragged back home by force, and as a consequence, he fell fatally ill. Thus, his parents brought him back to the same church. At first, all three of them practised incubation, but later only the child did.

John Haldon argues that the violent attacks on Jews and heretics were later interpolations, similar to some other chronologically obvious additions. He identified the social reality behind the outbursts and invectives in the last years of the seventh century, when masses of refugees arrived from the provinces to Constantinople; these harsh and arrogant invectives might serve to attract attention to the saint and his cult place.[41] The narratological disruption also seems to confirm that these sermons were later additions. Haldon has also pointed out that in these outbursts, most visibly the invective at the end of MA41, the attacked heretics appear as if mirroring the heresies condemned in Canon 95 of the Quinisext council, called together by Justinian II in 691.[42]

In addition to what it says of heretics, this council also represented a new tendency towards Jews, forbidding Christians to 'associate' with Jews or to turn to Jewish physicians:

> No one of sacerdotal rank, nor any layman, shall eat the unleavened bread of the Jews, nor associate with them, nor summon them in illness and receive cures from them, nor in any wise bathe with them at the baths. If anyone undertakes to do this, if he is a cleric, he shall be deposed, if a layman, excommunicated.[43]

---

40 MA38.
41 Haldon, 'Supplementary Essay', p. 34.
42 Haldon, 'Supplementary Essay', p. 34.
43 Canon 11, in *The Council of Trullo Revisited*, ed. by Nedungatt and Featherstone, pp. 81–82, with the canons in Greek, Latin, and English; yet we cannot be sure how much effect the canon had.

Like heretics, the shift of emphasis reflects the change of the society's legal and individual attitude towards Jews by the end of the seventh century.[44] Similar to the case of heretics, the same connection may be valid between the eleventh canon of the Quinisext council on Jews and the anti-Jewish outbursts of the miracles. And these miracle stories, with all their established narrative framework, prove to be a sensitive indicator of such a change. In imperial legislation and in theological debates, the Jews both were perceived with more hostility and received an alteration of status. They were grouped together with the heretics who were to be driven back to the only true Catholic faith; as a result, their theological position was also altered. They were no longer the Augustinian testimony to Christianity,[45] in which worldview a Jewish patient cured by a saint might voluntarily embrace the new faith, become a component of a diverse community with mutual consideration and legitimacy (as seen in the corpus of Thecla), and even escape the stereotype 'other' of the mid-seventh-century narratives. To the Jews' gradual loss of legal protection and to the growing impatience and the new eschatology of forced conversions, a new element was added; in late seventh- and eighth-century hagiography, a new character appears who embodies the theologically 'other': the Muslim.[46]

The Unbeliever as Heretic

In the popularization (and reinforcement) of variously defined orthodoxies and dogmas, cult practices and miracle accounts played no small role, sometimes even attributing to the saints a personal view in dogmatic matters. Usually the heretics in the narrative are to be converted to orthodoxy and often punished beforehand. It was quite rare that, in contrast to what happens in pagan miracle cures, the healers contented themselves with the unbelievers acknowledging their power without making a proper confession of a certain creed. The level of tolerance in the stories is a safe indicator of the surrounding theological reality as well as who was the target audience of the various collections.

Thecla's hagiographer was only modestly interested in heretics.[47] The only two miracles that mention them make only indirect references: from two stories (MT10 and 13), along with the credo recited by a newly converted

---

44 For an excellent description, see Déroche, 'La polémique anti-judaïque au VIe et au VIIe siècle', and Dagron and Déroche, 'Juifs et chrétiens dans l'Orient du VIIe siècle', esp. pp. 17–46; as well as Starr, *The Jews in the Byzantine Empire* and Dagron, 'Judaïser'.
45 *De civitate Dei*, XVIII. 46 and *Contra Faustum*, XVI. 21.
46 See Dick, 'La Passion arabe de S. Antoine Ruwah néo-martyr de Damas'; and later in the *Miracles of Saint George*, Mir. 6 in *Sainte Thècle, Saints Côme et Damien*, ed. and trans. by Festugière, pp. 294–307; on this miracle, see Sahas, 'What an Infidel Saw that a Faithful Did Not'.
47 On heresies present in the area of the sanctuary though not mentioned in the miracle accounts, see *Vie et miracles*, ed. and trans. by Dagron, pp. 43–44.

Greek (MT14), we can understand that Thecla's hagiographer believed what became the Chalcedonian creed. There is no heretic protagonist in Thecla's miracles; theologically, the most dubious figure was indeed the hagiographer himself (and we shall never know why exactly he was excommunicated). I analysed earlier the mosaic inscription in Thecla's *martyrion*, 'proclaiming to all people the consubstantiality of the holy and sublime Trinity' (MT10), which Symposius, at that time Arian bishop of Seleucia, wanted to erase, but the worker entrusted with the destruction fell from the ladder due to Thecla's intervention.[48] The hagiographer cautiously attributed Symposius's later conversion to this event: his return to orthodoxy was expressed by his public confession of the dogma inscribed on this very mosaic. The hagiographer's other heretic aside concerns the Monophysites, apropos of a figure loosely connected to the protagonist of MT13, one Saturnilus or Saturninus. The hagiographer angrily attacked the unorthodoxy of a Monophysite priest named Severus, the confidant of the exiled empress Eudocia-Athenais, and the hagiographer portrayed Thecla as protectress of orthodoxy, inasmuch as she repeatedly favoured Saturnilus who, by order of the emperor Theodosius II, had the heretical Severus killed.[49]

Theological standing receives a more marked importance when the heretic stands in the centre of the miracle story, confronting the 'orthodox' saints, as is so often in the collection of Cyrus and John and occasionally in those of Cosmas and Damian. Orthodoxy was defined from various angles that were often contradictory to each other. The hagiography of the popular miracle-working saints was used for theological propaganda, both accidentally and consciously. Moreover, the context of illness and healing facilitated the manifestation of the contrasting credos, since it is a situation when the sick heretic may turn to the 'orthodox' healer saint.

The reasons for which non-Christians and heretics turned to the saints vary within a wide range, as did the results of their consultations: one might find his way to the saint through Christian friends or family members, another out of an intellectual curiosity, or else they might turn to the healers only in despair over their illness. As a consequence of his cure, the healed and converted suppliant may return to his co-religionists, and after he narrates his own experience, the story may end with the conversion of the entire group. In special circumstances, giving up their former pagan or sectarian beliefs, they might become members of a lay community centred on the cult: at times, official church personnel, priests, wardens, deacons, or even (as it happened to Thecla's protégé) the saint's hagiographer.

Cosmas and Damian also had a hagiographer who was a heretic, and they remained so. As the curious story of KDM26 attests, a man who was a

---

48 Symposius became orthodox in 381; Basil of Caesarea in his *Letter* 190, written in 374, mentioned Symposius and referred to their debate over the Eucharist.
49 On Severus and his death, cf. *Vie et miracles*, ed. and trans. by Dagron, p. 17 and p. 323, n. 3.

member of an unspecified heretical sect, although he was not sick, went to the Saturday night vigil of the saints and underwent a strange test of faith upon falling asleep there. According to the miracle writer, the fundamental characteristic of heretics is their lack of belief, and thus Cosmas and Damian appeared to the man not to convince him to become orthodox (no attempt at this is made at any point in the miracle) but to dispel his incredulity (in the miracle-working capacity of the saints). The healer indicates the remedy for a sick noblewoman lying nearby, and thereupon the heretic was doubly tried: as to whether he believed the repeated dreams, and whether he had the courage to approach the lady and repeat the saints' instructions to her. After all that came to pass, the saints vouchsafed the heretic an oracle, saying that he would become the head of the sect. Meanwhile, the heretic had become a regular visitor of the saints' church, and when the oracle came true in the time indicated, he set himself the task of writing the saints' miracles. He considered collecting the miracles as a vehicle to approach orthodoxy, but he never became openly Chalcedonian.

Yet soon simple conversion was not enough; with the radicalization of Christological debates, the healer might require the confession of a particular credo, as Thecla does in MT14, when she appears in her real form in daylight to a blaspheming Greek nobleman, addressing him with the following words:

> Hence, now that you have understood who I am, and have paid a fitting price for your incredulity, stand up, go, get baptised, approach the mysteries, prostrate yourself, confess the Father, the Son, the Holy Spirit, the uncreated and consubstantial Trinity who is the creator of all things, intelligible and sensible, visible and invisible, who carries and directs all, governs and rules all; in addition to these, confess the real presence through the flesh, the advent and coming of the Only-Begotten (I mean the Incarnation and the birth from Mary the virgin, the *Theotokos*), confess his cross and his death, his Resurrection and Ascension; then both your body and your soul will become healthy, and happily you will inhabit this earth, happily you will live, and happily you will go to heaven, where you will live with great surety with Christ the Lord.

This is a clear summary of everything that a person newly converted to Christianity, specifically orthodox Cyrillian Christianity, had to believe and perform. Here, the taking of the Eucharist is an intermediate element of the act of confession, which follows baptism, together with the confession of the credo. The taking of the Eucharist acquired a central role in numerous miracles of incubation healing: it is important to stress that it figured exclusively in connection with pagans, Jews, or heretics and became the most elaborate symbol of what the saint or his hagiographer defined as orthodox.[50]

---

50   I developed this theme in my article 'Mysteries for the Uninitiated'.

A more subtle definition of orthodoxy is expressed in a miracle of Saints Cosmas and Damian (KDM7), where a mute and deaf woman was healed while singing the Trisagion,[51] the liturgical exponent of Trinitarian theology, in line with the Nicaean and Chalcedonian creed. This is a unique example because anti-heretical propaganda was usually sharper and the definition of orthodoxy was more complex.

Among the miracles of Cosmas and Damian (KDM17), we read a story about an Arian, called an Exakionite.[52] The narrative begins with a short prologue about how magnanimous the saints are and that they heal not only the believers of the right faith, but also the enemies of orthodoxy. The sick man, arriving at the church, did not dare to undergo incubation together with the rest of the patients, precisely because he was well aware that he was considered a heretic. Thus, he awaited the curative dream in an external hall. During the first visit of the saints, he witnessed in his dream how they sought to dissuade each other from saving him, saying, 'let him wait, if he is slow to convert', the orthodox patients have priority. In the second dream, the dialogue is similar, but finally one of the saints urges the other to heal the heretic as quickly as he can, 'so that he would not occupy the place of the orthodox'. After a miraculous intervention, they order him to leave the sanctuary, 'because we hate you for your heresy'.

From the perspective of the saints, the hagiographer and his readers' orthodoxy in this miracle referred to the credo established by the Council of Nicaea (325), and which was confirmed by the Councils of Ephesus (431) and Chalcedon (451), in the centre of which stood the definition of Christ's double nature: at once divine and human. At Nicaea, they condemned Arius, who taught that Christ the Son was subject to the Father, and not of the same nature with him. At Ephesus, they condemned Nestorius who emphasized Christ's human nature; as Mary gave birth to the human Jesus, he denied her the epithet *Theotokos*, the Bearer of God. The theological response to the teachings of Nestorius was the Monophysite movement, which proclaimed the one, exclusively divine nature of Christ: a teaching that, from the fifth century onwards, was supported by a decisive majority in Asia Minor, Syria, Persia, and in Egypt (and with time became an independent church).[53] At Chalcedon, with the support of the emperor Marcian and Pope Leo, the Dyophysites triumphed, those who believed in the two natures and their consubstantiality. At the same time, by reinforcing ecclesiastical authority

---

51 For an interesting parallel to the therapeutic use of singing in Asclepius's cult, see Cali, 'La meloterapia come strumento taumaturgico nel culto di Asclepio'; and West, 'The Singing of Hexameters'.

52 Arians were called Exakionites in Constantinople during the reign of Theodosius I (379–395), because their meeting place was in the Exakionion quarter; cf. Festugière's references to Sozomen and Theodoret, *Sainte Thècle, Saints Côme et Damien*, pp. 134–35, n. 71.

53 For an overview, see Frend, *The Rise of the Monophysite Movement*.

through the political leadership of Constantinople, they made their credo the cornerstone of orthodoxy.

In the London Codex version of the same miracle (CL21), the Arian heretic becomes one 'who had two illnesses: one was the grave physical illness, [...] the other, a spiritual one: the heresy of the Dyophysites'. All the details of the story are identical: the patient did not dare to sleep inside the church, 'knowing well, that he is of a creed contrary to that of the saints', and the saints sent him away with the same words, signalling the priority that the 'orthodox' patients should enjoy. Except here, the orthodoxies are reversed: the Dyophysite Chalcedonian is the heretic, and Monophysites are numbered as orthodox.

The same theological message is conveyed in the nineteenth miracle of the London Codex, the protagonist of which is 'a Nestorian man, who also accepted the latter sect's hateful teachings, separating Christ after the Incarnation into two natures and never admitting his Mother to be the Bearer of God. He fell ill with a horrendous disease.' Since his life was in peril because of an abscess on his chest, he wanted to see his daughter for the last time, who lived as a nun in the monastery next to the church of Saints Cosmas and Damian:

> While the heretic was lying there and invoking the saints, somebody appeared to him and very angrily demanded that he should bow and say: 'In the beginning was the Word and the Word was with God and the Word was God', and everything that follows up to the verse 'The Word was made flesh and dwelled among us'. When the man immediately confessed this, the other added, 'Consequently, if the Word is God and the Word was made flesh and dwelled among men, then he is in no way divided, but is one and his nature is one; and the one who gave birth to him, having given birth to God the Word in the flesh, is the Bearer of God.' Having said this, he vanished.

The saints appeared again to the man and testified that they wanted him to say this confession, and they revealed that bean would be the remedy for his illness. 'The man, having done as he was ordered, quickly found relief from his sickness. And until the end of his life he remained a right confessor of the one, undivided nature of God the Word and that the Virgin Mary is the Bearer of God.' The text is clearly based on an anti-Chalcedonian creed. The error attributed to the 'Nestorian' is that, according to him, Christ exists in two natures after the Incarnation. This is simply the dogma of Chalcedon, which the anti-Chalcedonian author of the miracle calls Nestorian. This miracle must have been dear to the scribe or to those who had commissioned the manuscript, since these two folia that record it are richly decorated in comparison with the simplicity of the rest of the codex. Although initials decorated with plain red or brown lines are not rare in this manuscript, this miracle begins with a beautiful, large initial M; still more significant are the highly elaborated floral decorations at the bottom of the page, which are absolutely unique in the codex.

In the narratives of the London Codex, there are several characteristics that may point to the collection having been written in Egypt, that story-material was known from elsewhere, or the version of the text that served as the basis of the copy subsequently gained a local adaptation. In the background of these features, there is the fact that the major part of Egypt (together with Syria) did not accept the Chalcedonian credo. In light of the side-by-side existence of these two versions of Cosmas and Damian's miracles, the questions naturally suggest themselves: Was the London Codex a Monophysite reworking of a Dyophysite text, written in Egypt for the anti-Chalcedonian adherents of the cult? Did a Monophysite incubation cult exist at the place where the collection was read? Or quite to the contrary: instead of representing a Monophysite reworking, does the Codex attest to a healing cult of originally Monophysite character (the cult actually did originate from Syria)—a cult that, after it reached the capital and became highly popular there, underwent a theological and dogmatic transformation? The phenomenon of the rewriting of hagiographical works because at some previous point their content was considered heretical can be illustrated by the sixth-century *Passio* of Cyrikos and Julitta, the earlier version of which Theodore of Iconium found inauthentic and heretical and which Theodore decided to replace with a 'true' and truly orthodox version.[54]

In the case of Cyrus and John, it was the seventh-century hagiographer Sophronius, the later patriarch of Jerusalem, who gave the cult of Cyrus and John a marked orthodox standing.[55] In an Egypt that was Monophysite, for Sophronius, orthodoxy meant the Dyophysite Chalcedonian credo, and he voiced his faith using the saints themselves as his mouthpiece. Hence, Cyrus and John lecture, in a dream, a heretic who is a follower of Julian of Halicarnassus: 'They talked to [Julian] in doctrinal terms, explaining the truth preached in the Church and in this way they confirmed the teaching about the saving union of Christ, our God' (MCJ12). Just as here, the healers on other occasions as well make the confession of orthodoxy to be the condition of the miraculous cure, and as an outward sign, they usually demand the taking of the Eucharist in the orthodox way. The unorthodox way of Communion is depicted in the miracle of a man who was one 'of those who cut themselves off from the Catholic Church [...] namely he was a heretic, a follower of Julian of Halicarnassus' (MCJ36). In a series of incubation dreams, instead of bringing a cure, the saints first inflict pain upon the man until he promises to take orthodox Communion. To test his state of mind, the saints visit him again in disguise and invite him to receive the Eucharist together with them. The man refuses, and according to the custom of heretics, he asks for oil from the lamp burning on the saints' tomb instead of bread and wine. This miracle

---

54   Rapp, 'Byzantine Hagiographers as Antiquarians', p. 38; the *Passio* itself: 'Sanctorum Cyriaci et Julittae actae graeca sincera nunc primum edita'.
55   For context and comparison, see Allan, *Sophronius of Jerusalem*.

opens a separate unit in the centre of the collection within the miracle corpus of Saints Cyrus and John. Their prominent placement within the corpus attests to the importance that Sophronius as hagiographer attributed to them. These miracles (36, 37, 38, and 39) all describe the saints forcing heretics (Monophysites) to take the Eucharist in the orthodox way and confess the creed of Chalcedon. In the next episode (Miracle 37), Communion is regarded as a cure for spiritual blindness. This fundamental conceptual unity of bodily and spiritual healing is expressed in the patient's double infirmity: the blindness of his heresy (he is a follower of Theodosius and Severus, that is, a Monophysite from the Chalcedonian point of view, and a subdeacon of the community), of which the blindness of his eyes is rather an outward symbol. For more than a year, he waits in the church for a cure but refuses to take Communion. In a dream, he sees himself praying for health at the tomb of the saints, who appear and lead him to the altar, offering him bread. All of them, the saints and the patient, receive it and drink wine afterwards; finally, the saints advise him to do the same when he awakes. In the morning, he quickly carries out this order, and on the third day, his eyesight returns together with the illumination of his soul. He soon relapses because he must take the post of his dead father, who was the head of a Severian community. Saints Cyrus and John appear in front of him on his way home, give him a slap, and take away his regained sight. When he understands why this has happened he repents, and after a period of incubation lasting three days and nights, he is visited by a dream referring to the miracles of Jesus. He wakes up cured and becomes a monk, the servant of the martyrs.

The protagonist of the next miracle (MCJ38) suffers from the same diseases: blindness and heresy. After he endures four months of fruitless waiting, the saints appear in a dream dressed as monks and invite him to the sacristy, where they offer him bread with the image of the cross impressed upon it. Three times Cyrus hands the man the bread; three times the man drops it involuntarily. Cyrus sighs and sadly regrets that the man never came to receive the Eucharist, and hence they cannot grant his wish. When awake, the patient hurries to Communion:

> He hastened to the Communion of the Catholic Church, and after partaking in her mysteries his eyesight was restored. Because of this, even his servant has become one of the faithful sheep of the Saviour, considering it clear madness, although a Barbarian, to fight against God, the saints, the Catholic Church, and the orthodox faith.

But when the heretic is asked by his servant whether at home they will also retain this new habit of taking the orthodox Communion, he answers thus: 'While we are here, we do what the saints order. When we leave, we keep our own doctrines as before and the faith transmitted by our fathers.' It is unsurprising that divine punishment strikes him again with pains and restores his former blindness. When the saints reveal to him the cause, a more elaborated initiation, a real *mystagogia* is necessary. The man receives the sacraments directly from the hands of a beautiful maiden in bright garments, Ecclesia herself, the Bride of Christ.

The protagonist of another miracle from this set of forced Eucharist stories (MCJ39) was Peter, prior of an Egyptian Monophysite group; this group, like many others, refused to accept the Council of Chalcedon. Peter is seeking a cure in the church of Saints Cyrus and John when he hears that the condition of the cure would be the taking of orthodox Communion. He states that it is a bad idea, and he curses the Chalcedonian synod, 'because', says the hagiographer,

> out of irrationality and barbaric feeling the Egyptians show a great hatred against this sacred council, just like they did once against the people of Israel, who were their relatives and parents. Hence Peter said that neither wanted to obtain health, nor consented to what was brought together at the synod of Chalcedon.

The saints repeatedly confess their Chalcedonian faith and urge Peter to take Communion.

> While he was still hesitating whether to partake in the mysteries, they said: 'Is it not sufficient for you, o Peter, to believe as we do and to join us in the matter of faith?' But he dared to answer them again in the following way: 'Is this true? You, the great servants of Christ, also believe like the council of Chalcedon?' And the saints affirmed that they agree with the sacred multitude of the holy men and that they believed according to the faith of the council of Chalcedon. They also declared that the definition of the aforementioned council constitutes the correct faith and God-inspired preaching.

The personal conviction of the hagiographer, the Chalcedonian Sophronius, contests what was considered orthodox in the surroundings of the cult by most of the pilgrims. Through their hagiographer, the saints become orthodox in a way contrary to both their cult place and their suppliants. The majority of the miracle collections that I have dealt with share in reinforcing the Chalcedonian propaganda of Sophronius: attacking the teachings of Arius, Nestorius, Theodosius, Severus, and Julian of Halicarnassus. However, the Monophysite London Codex's definition of orthodoxy allows a glimpse into the variety of orthodoxies and the changing definition of it, a phenomenon that points to the shifts of emphasis that the rivalling healing cults underwent and to changes of theological climate within the same cult itself. The laudable skill of all these hagiographers in their theological propaganda is that they exploited the particular form of incubation narratives by picturing the healer's recitation of a creed as a recipe, and presenting the orthodox Eucharist and other gestures of confession as thaumaturgic remedies (functioning in the same way as prescribed herbs or exercises).

The Finality of the Recording

Religious propaganda was openly one of the key elements of writing and disseminating miracle narratives.[56] While performing their cures, the saints advised on everyday moral conduct.[57] Sometimes this was embedded into the remedy, or their miracle stories served simply to strengthen faith in general or enforce a certain theological truth in particular.

The aims of preserving, writing, and 'using' the saints' miracle collections may be set against the larger background of the purpose of hagiography in general. In the recent re-evaluations of hagiographic literature, van Uytfanghe has emphasized its cultic and commemorative function,[58] while Felice Lifshitz challenged Delehaye's definition that hagiography would serve to promote a cult, and Lifshitz cited examples where *Lives of the Saints* existed independently or even without their cult place and feasts. On this basis, Lifshitz connected hagiography to historiography and argued that hagiographic documents often represented a historic legitimization for a community.[59]

When we come to the stories of incubation miracles, and to the circumstances of their actual reading/listening, we discover in them two other important purposes: their entertainment function, and, along with this, miracles that aim at improving the morale of the ailing patients and at offering therapeutic advice at the same time. The instances of stories that direct our gaze to their own mise-en-scène help us to form an idea about the informality of this sort of performance and how it was integrated into the habitual practices of the cult place (or even into the liturgy).[60] That these stories are not to be interpreted exclusively in a theological context is visible not just from the multiplicity of the purposes for which they were recorded but already from their pre-Christian precedents. Werner has emphasized the parallel development of the profane or entertaining aretalogy and religious aretalogy in the ancient Greek and Hellenistic context.[61] Vincenzo Longo sought to determine the origin of aretalogic topoi and located it in part in the ψεῦδος, the narrative invention.[62]

---

56 Déroche, 'Pourquoi écrivait-on des recueils de miracles?'.
57 For example, in KDM6 that he should stop swearing and eating meat in Lent, or stop frequenting the hippodrome (KDM11).
58 Van Uytfanghe, 'L'hagiografie', p. 174.
59 'Biographies of saints provided communities and institutions with written traditions; they defended the independence of communities and institutions against those who wished to subject them; they defended property rights and territorial endowments; they fuelled episcopal rivalries; they conveyed political and theological stances; they propagated an individual author's, or group's notion of 'the holy'; they served, in short, for manifold purposes.' Lifshitz, 'Beyond Positivism and Genre', p. 97, n. 7.
60 Cf. Connor, *Art and Miracles in Medieval Byzantium*, p. 100.
61 Werner, 'Zum Λούκιος ἢ ὄνος', p. 239 ff.
62 Longo, *Aretalogie nel mondo Greco*, p. 20: 'pensò anziché ad una trasformazione avvenuta nel mondo greco-romano della seconda nella prima, ad una fusione dei due tipi attraverso un punto di contatto dall'oggetto comune della narrazione, ossia il ψεῦδος. Dalla necessità di far

An element common to both the cultic and profane miracle narratives is the *incredible* and all those narrative elements that arise from that. Thus, from the very beginning, miracle narratives (ritual or not) had an 'entertaining, because incredible' feature.[63] This entertainment function in Christian hagiography had other aspects and sources. Michel de Certeau called one such aspect the 'vacation function' and illustrated it by citing the fifth-century *Life of Melanie*, in which once, when

> she was 'sated' with canonical books and collections of homilies, 'she went through the lives of the Fathers as though she were eating desserts'. Tales of the saints' life bring a festive element to the community. They are situated on the side of relaxation and leisure. They correspond to a free time, a place set aside, a spiritual and contemplative respite; they do not belong in the realm of instruction, pedagogical norms, or dogma. They 'divert'. Unlike texts that must be practiced or believed, the saints' Lives oscillate between the believable and the marvellous, advocating what one is at liberty to think or do. From both points of view they create an area of 'vacation' and of new conditions outside of everyday time and rule.[64]

There was an entertainment factor that might have been particularly related to the incubation context, which I earlier called therapeutic, that includes the following factors: the framework of the illness itself, the presence of pain, the often long-term staying of sick people in desperation, and their shame concerning their physical symptoms and fears about the healing intervention. In this atmosphere, it was essential to 'divert', to include in the stories not just something funny, but also the ridiculous and grotesque, or the violent and harsh.[65] Saint Thecla quoting Homer was probably aiming to amuse, but the numerous descriptions of the saints' physical violence in the *Thaumata* or the apparently blasphemous prescriptions in dreams are rather shocking. As we are in the context of illness and healing, the means of cures and the way or remedy leading to the cure were the main source of humour. When Cosmas and Damian wanted to give a lesson to an irascible old man who fulminated against them, they appear to operate on him with a huge sword instead of a scalpel, threatening as they go, one saying one the other: 'Give him a nice incision! Why he is so insolent, being as old as he is?' (KDM1). They could even be malicious; when a visitor in their church protested at how disgusting it was to swallow the wax mixed with oil, Cosmas and Damian quickly inflicted her with some illness and not only made her swallow the *kerote* but also forced

---

accettare la "menzogna", ossia l'invenzione fantastica (ma l'aretalogia religiosa pretende di essere documentazione!), sarebbero nati dei τόποι'.

63 This type of miracle narrative found its way into the ancient novel, just as, in turn, miracle stories also acquired novelistic elements. Longo, *Aretalogie nel mondo Greco*, p. 33.
64 De Certeau, 'A Variant: Hagio-Grafical Edification', pp. 273–74.
65 Cf. Harpham, *On the Grotesque*; for an example in Byzantine hagiography, cf. Cox Miller, 'Is There a Harlot in this Text?'.

a candlewick into her nose (KDM16). Another bad joke evokes what could probably happen in a real hospital: Cosmas and Damian tried to operate on a man who was shouting and kicking and protesting in all ways against it, and thus they inserted the man's kicking legs into some railings and raised the scalpel in spite of his howling. The more absurd the prescription was, the more the saints' power was manifested: poison became a medicine (KDM11), slaps given by a poor man to the face of the rich one made them both healthy (KDM39), or the curative power of shaving by the paralysed hands of a butcher (KDM34). Why would Saint Artemius appear as a depressed stranger in the latrines (MA35), as a butcher operating with butcher's tools (MA25), or as a man in the bath complaining about his towels (MA11), and why would he create three testicles for a man if not to make his patients laugh in their despair? Those recipes that involve something apparently blasphemous or make the patient perform a complex series of actions involving bystanders had strong characteristics of a tale. A miracle by Cosmas and Damian includes a jealous husband, a faithful wife, and a blind man, all staying in the church; for the healing of the blind man, the intervention of a chaste woman was needed, thus, the blind man's healing was almost just a tool for convincing the jealous husband about his wife's truthfulness. Somehow, the curing of his jealousy appears to be the real miracle.

    The theological grotesque is not just an absurd means of cure, but it makes the reader laugh. Paul, who had a horrible headache, received from Cyrus and John the instruction that when he wakes up in the morning, he should leave the church through the gate leading to the sea and give a slap to the first man that he meets on his way. The passer-by, of course, happens to be a soldier with a stick in his hand, and when he receives the slap, gives a terrible blow on the man's head — which thus opened and the worms that tortured the patient could come out (MCJ18). At the same time, the story still has a moral, showing that reliance on the healer's advice must be uncompromising. If not, the result is also something laughable.

    The theological grotesque also arose from turning upside down the existent social realities. What the saints' cult represented in theory, namely that the grace of healing was available for everyone with no respect of social difference, and what the ritual itself required in a practice, that the incubants, illustrious or poor, would sleep in the same space next to each other, was also expressed in the narrative level of such stories, as in the case of the already quoted miracle KDM24, which ends with the marriage of the once mute noblewoman and the poor paralytic.

    The event of reading aloud and listening to the miracle stories formed the audience-community by the communal experience of 'consuming' the miracles. Reading the miracles was a public event, not a solitary act, and there are great examples of this, not only from Byzantium but from the medieval West, such as the miracle collection chained to the tomb with the relics.⁶⁶ In the various characters of the stories, everyone could find some figure to whom they could relate. The communal event of telling the miracles not just recalled but also evoked other miracles to happen. In MA35, we see a man who was waiting in vain for his cure give a farewell lunch; when they sadly gathered together, the priests stared comforting him with the telling of miracles, especially those when Artemius healed the patient on his journey back home. Moreover, a miraculous cure could happen in the midst of listening to the previous stories, as in the monastery of the ninth-century saint Peter of Atroa, particularly on his feast day, when a communal reading of his *Life* took place as a part of the public festivities. The saint's hagiographer, a monk called Sabas, records the miracle that happened to him during the reading of the saint's *Life*, which he himself authored. Thus while listening his own work, he became beneficiary of a miracle he would record in his revised version of the saint's miracles:

> It happened that I was there at the monastery one day for the commemoration of the saint; kissing the slab covering his tomb — the slab was thin and without a trace of humidity — I awaited the gushing forth as of another Siloam. And here, during Orthros, as the marvellous *Life* of the saint was being read to all the assembled crowd, suddenly a flow gushed forth, and the crowd, sensing the [saint's] presence, anointed their faces fervently. And I was among them when the wound I had on one of my legs was healed after I had anointed it.⁶⁷

---

66 Cf. the twelfth century tomb of Gerard of Angers, Carrasco, 'Spirituality and Historicity', p. 4.
67 Laurent, *La vie merveilleuse de S. Pierre d'Atroa*, p. 148. Sabas was a rather unique hagiographer, as he revised and enlarged his own text, with some ten years' distance: Laurent, *La vita retractata et les Miracles posthumes de saint Pierre d'Atroa*; cf. Connor, *Art and Miracles in Medieval Byzantium*, p. 100.

Conclusion

The history of Byzantine incubation is that of an organic development and a voluntarily embraced continuity. It was a transmission of the cult, the formation of the source material, and the way of recording the narrative pattern as well. This transmission from the pagan practice to the Christian incubation ritual concerned the elements of the cult: the cult place, the cult function (healing), and the technique of healing as well as the ritual (temple sleep) and the medium (dream). It is common to both pagan and Christian incubation practice that the sacred place was more important than the figure of the healer. Sleeping there, at the specific sacred precinct, is essential to the ritual itself, even if it means that somebody other than the patient has to go as a substitute. Even in the Christian context, this centrality of the cult site generated rivalries between different cult places of the same healer, adding a particular feature to the otherwise universal character of Christ's power and the constant presence of his grace as manifest through the saints. The key role of the place has various other consequences for the ritual and for the narrative. It explains the importance of invitation dreams and the lack of cures at a distance, which are mostly limited to miracles on the way to and from the sanctuary. It explains why the Byzantine incubation saint acts as the master of a house, inhabiting his specific 'home', something which was a holdover of the Greek concept of the deities/heroes dwelling inside their shrines.[1] It may even be related to the visual observation of the saints in dreams circulating easily within their 'house'. Like anyone else, the saints have their favourite spots. Furthermore, both pagan miracle stories and Christian collections celebrated the sacred space and the fame of the sanctuary, not so much the healer in general.[2]

---

1 Origen, *Contra Celsum*, III. 34. 'He [Celsus] next imagines that, "in worshipping him who" as he says, "was taken prisoner and put to death, we are acting like the Getae who worship Zamolxis, and the Cilicians who worship Mopsus, and the Acarnanians who pay divine honours to Amphilochus, and like the Thebans who do the same to Amphiaraus, and the Lebadians to Trophonius." Now in these instances we shall prove that he has compared us to the foregoing without good grounds. For these different tribes erected temples and statues to those individuals above enumerated, whereas we have refrained from offering to the Divinity honour by any such means (seeing they are adapted rather to demons, which are somehow fixed in a certain place which they prefer to any other, or which take up their dwelling, as it were, after being removed (from one place to another) by certain rites and incantations).' Trans. by F. Crombie, in *Ante-Nicene Fathers*, ed. by Roberts, Donaldson, and Coxe, vol. IV; apart from Zamolxis, a chthonic healer, the others mentioned here operated through incubation; their cults are analysed in detail by Ustinova, 'Either a Daimon, or a Hero, or Perhaps a God'.

2 Dorati, 'Funzioni e motivi', p. 97: 'la centralità del santuario, tanto nella pratica quanto nella rappresentazione dei miracoli: Nelle raccolte pagane — come in quelle cristiane — i prodigi interessano in quanto legati a un determinato luogo: non tanto le *aretai* di Asclepio, quanto

Menouthis is an extreme example of how the place called for inventing and accommodating its new Christian occupants who gained all their importance solely as the new masters of the healing place. The relics of the Christian saints complemented the thaumaturgic quality of the place and added the idea to the pagan concept of the sanctuary as the god's (and his cult statue's) abode that it was the housing of the remains of the holy healers. Menouthis is also a case in point for how much the cult practice, the ritual itself, was linked to the place and shows that it was not enough to establish new Christian occupants with the same cult function (healing); it was necessary to accommodate the rite of temple sleep as well.

The healing technique of the Christian incubation saints has a much closer resemblance to the healing gestures and techniques of Asclepius than to those of Christ. Van Cangh established the outline of the two healing techniques, and a glance will suffice to determine which paradigm the incubation saints followed:[3]

1. In Epidaurus, healing in sleep, in dream, with incubation, inside the temple, at its most sacred, specific space. Jesus healed, during daytime, patients who were wide awake, outdoors, without sacred place.
2. Several miracle cures in Epidaurus verge on the extraordinary; the means of the cures display the miraculous. There is nothing like that in the Gospels. Jesus healed with his word, sometimes accompanied with a simple gesture, without performing wonders.
3. In addition to surgical interventions, Asclepius often applied complex treatments that echo (however miraculously) contemporary medicine. Nothing of this sort with Jesus, who heals with the word or with the laying-on of his hands or with his saliva.
4. In Epidaurus, priests of the deity also took part in the cure: they explain the dream, help with the prescribed cure. Jesus acts alone.
5. The Asclepieian sanctuaries were richly appointed, in contrast to the free healing of Jesus.
6. According to Van Cangh, Asclepius expected faith in his thaumaturgical powers and severely punished the sceptical while Jesus also healed the incredulous.

Although some of his statements (surely the last two) are open to challenge, it is useful to keep in mind these differences, especially when it comes to a

---

le *aretai* dello stesso Epidauro, non i miracoli di Cosma e Damiano, ma i loro miracoli nella chiesa di Constantinopoli. [...] ad emerger è dunque la gloria del sanctuario ancor prima di quella della divinità.'

3 Van Cangh, 'Santé et salut dans les miracles d'Epidaure, d'Apollonius de Tyane et de Nouveau Testament'.

closer analysis of the healing techniques of the incubation saints. In addition, the healing gestures of the incubation saints differ not only from the paradigm set by Christ but also from the contemporary model of other Byzantine saints (living saints, stylites, ascetics, or cults centred on the relics).

The Christian acceptance of the dream as medium of the cure also acted as a structuring principle both in the cult experience (the visual encounter and dialogue with the healers and in their capacity to act in a way otherwise unimaginable) as well as in the story pattern of the miracles.[4] I agree with G. Stroumsa that 'in a sense, however, the place of dreams in the medieval imaginaire seems paradoxically closer to their place in pagan antiquity than to the place they occupied in the Christian psyche.'[5] Similarly, the development and handling of the sources of the incubation experience were also analogous in the pagan and Christian context. The order of formation of the sources is chronologically consecutive: votive objects, oral tales, miracle narratives. This logical succession of stages that led from the religious experience to the literarily shaped miracle stories and then to structured miracle collections was in part accidental because when Christianity took over the pagan cult, the channels of cult experience naturally survived. However, the continuity of recorded testimonies and the passage from the cure to the miracle collections were purposeful acts. The Christian recorders of dream cures voluntarily adhered to the ancient model of transmission. This voluntary aspect is attested by the fact that not only did the Christian hagiographers use the same naturally developing oral and material sources, but the miracle stories established a network of references to these sources as part of the narrative pattern. The inclusion of the votive testimonies of the miracle as well as the representation of the telling of the miracles within the stories not only attested to their presence but also generated them and perpetuated their integrity to the cult experience. I found it revealing to examine the 'reality' of these references. They may be actual testimonies of objects, votives, or proofs of the cure; they might be references to the oral source or indicators of the context for the transmission of the miracle. Or they can be fictitious, at times just hints to produce a reality-effect or add colour to the story. But in all cases, they are part of the narrative: of the rules of how to tell/write an incubation miracle story. Studying the formation of these miracles and their close adherence to the practice they recorded, I reached the conclusion that

---

4 'In addition to having a structural role, the dream account is a simple compositional technique whereby authors can introduce a dialogue between God and a human being. This oneiric dialogue may have some concrete end and be the opportunity for a direct intervention on the part of God in the evolution of the dreamer [...]. But this dialogue may also be the form chosen in order to develop some aspect of teaching or for theological reflection [...] provides the setting for a real debate [...] or the opportunity to underline certain theological principles at the key point in the story.' Husser, *Dreams and Dream Narratives*, p. 104.

5 Stroumsa, 'Dreams and Visions in Early Christian Discourse', p. 191.

the scheme of incubation miracle narrative was a specifically strong pattern; we may say that it was a narrative form, but it was a form which could be filled only with one content. My analysis of the compositional structures of the miracle stories inquired what constituted the incubation narrative pattern, with what elements it was built up, and how much this construction was influenced by the personality and literary aim of the writers. But it was not only the hagiographer who composed these stories; the saints, the patients, the dream-imagery of individuals with their community, and the milieu of the cult place also contributed, just as the rules of the incubation story itself shaped its own formation. I could follow how a way of telling a cult experience was so intimately linked to the practice itself, and the Christian takeover of both cult and the way of recording it brought in elements of late antique Christian hagiography that was often foreign to Byzantine miracles. The tenacity of the incubation story-scheme can be ascertained not just by its resistance over centuries and despite major changes in religious climate, but also by evidence that it affected non-incubational hagiography as well. The appearance of Cosmas and Damian in the legend of Saint Dometius brought along both the mention of incubation and its integration into the saint's *Life* and into his cult.[6] Something more happened in the *Vita* of Saint Theodore of Sykeon; the figures of Cosmas and Damian provided the story with an incubatory narrative framework probably well known to Theodore's hagiographer, with elements identical to the miracle scheme that the saints habitually applied.[7] The event took place not only in the saints' church, but in Theodore's 'home', in his monastery. While the sleep was involuntary and the saints were not invoked, at several points the narrative coincides with the incubation pattern, even at points that are secondary to Theodore's miracle:

> After the Saint had returned to his monastery, it happened that he fell so ill of a desperate sickness that he saw the holy angels coming down upon him; and he began to weep and to be sorely-troubled. Now above him there stood an icon of the wonder-working saints Cosmas and Damian. These saints were seen by him looking just as they did in that sacred icon and they came close to him, as doctors usually do.

The story starts as if we were reading the beginning of an incubation rite; Theodore fell ill, and maybe had a vision or fell asleep, seeing the well-known healing saints Cosmas and Damian. The saints appear in their form familiar from their icon and act as usually, turning to the sick man in their quality of doctors. The narration continues with the gestures frequent in the incubation experience, with the saints' medical round, and their making a diagnosis after questioning the sick man with the usual doctor–patient dialogue:

---

6 The presence of incubation could similarly evoke the figures of Cosmas and Damian as well.
7 *Life of Theodore of Sykeon*, ch. 39, in *Three Byzantine Saints*, ed. and trans. by Dawes and Baynes.

> They felt his pulse and said to each other that he was in a desperate state as his strength had failed and the angels had come down from heaven to him. And they began to question him saying: 'Why are you weeping and are sore troubled, brother?' He answered them, 'Because I am unrepentant, sirs, and also because of this little flock which is only newly-instructed and is not yet stabilised and requires much care.' They asked him, 'Do you want us to go and plead for you to be allowed to live for a while longer?' He answered, 'If you do, you would do me a great service, by gaining for me time for repentance, and you shall win the reward of my repentance and my work from henceforth.' Then the saints turned to the angels and begged them to grant him a little more time while they went to implore the King on his behalf.

They succeed in postponing Theodore's imminent death, and the closure of the miracle is also reminiscent of the incubation corpora:

> The Saints, Cosmas and Damian, said to the Saint: 'Rise up, brother, and look to thyself and to thy flock; for our merciful Master Who readily yields to supplication has received our petition on your behalf and grants you life to labour for "the meat which perisheth not, but endureth to everlasting life" and to care for many souls.' With these words they too, vanished. Theodore immediately regained his health and strength; the sickness left him, and glorifying God he resumed his life of abstinence and the regular recital of the psalms with still greater zeal and diligence.

This story preserves the customary patterns attached to these well-known incubation saints and uses its narrative frame to the extreme. Strictly speaking, it is not an incubation miracle, and even the healing part is stretched into averting death, Cosmas and Damian are not mere healers but interceded for more years for Theodore to live. It is a wonderful illustration of how strongly the incubation scheme was attached to Cosmas and Damian and how this was used as a narrative pattern even in a slightly different hagiographical context.

The miracles of Byzantine incubation reflect parallel principles of faith, often challenging each other, and they show clearly the anxieties, expectations, and power struggles of given communities. The narratives reach their reader in a way that, even if theological redaction permeates the sources to such a great extent, the basic layer of the miracle stories is that of personal experience. Hence the reader/listener may witness real internal struggles, such as when a patient is to measure what compromise he is to make as a price of healing; whether he can implore the saints as a heretic; what is the risk of breaking away from his or her family and fellows, or on the contrary, how to stand up for them. The fact that these stories of miraculous healing are at the same time *miroirs des corps* and *miroirs des âmes* means that they not only shed light upon man's relationship to illness, the sacred, conviction, or sin, but they also highlight those human situations where the personal voice overcomes the impersonal theological message, which at the end called them to life.

Works Cited

Primary Sources

Acta Apostolorum Apochrypha, ed. by R. A. Lipsius and M. Bonnet, 3 vols (repr. Hildesheim: G. Olms, 1959)

Aelius Aristides, *Aelius Aristides: The Complete Works*, ed. and trans. by Charles Allison Behr, 2 vols (Leiden: Brill, 1981)

Ante-Nicene Fathers, ed. by Alexander Roberts, James Donaldson, and A. Cleveland Coxe, 10 vols (Buffalo, NY: Christian Literature Publishing, 1885)

Apa Mena: A Selection of Coptic Texts Relating to St. Menas, ed. trans., and comm. by James Drescher (Cairo: Publications de la Société d'archéologie Copte, 1946)

Artemidorus, *Oneirocritica*, ed. by Roger Pack (Leipzig: B. G. Teubner, 1963)

——, *The Interpretation of Dreams*, trans. by Robert J. White (Park Ridge, NJ: Noyes Press, 1975)

——[Artemidoro], *Il libro dei sogni*, trans. and introd. by Dario Del Corno (Milan: Adelphi, 1975)

Asclepius: A Collection of the Testimonies, ed. and trans. by Emma J. Edelstein and Ludwig Edelstein, 2 vols, 2nd edn (Baltimore: Johns Hopkins University Press, 1998)

Chiesa, Paolo, *Le versioni latine della Passio Sanctae Febroniae: Storia, metodo, modelli di due traduzioni agiografiche altomedievali*, Biblioteca di Medioevo latino (Spoleto: CISAM, 1990)

Corpus Inscriptionum Graecarum, ed. by A. Böckh and B. G. Niebhur (Berlin: 1825–1859)

Corpus Inscriptionum Iudaicarum, ed. by Jean-Baptiste Frey, 2 vols (Vatican City: Pontifical Institute of Christian Arcaeology, 1939–1951)

Cosmae et Damiani sanctorum medicorum vita et miracula e codice Londoniensi, ed. by Ernst Rupprecht, Neue Deutsche Forschungen, 20 (Berlin: Junker und Dünnhaupt, 1935)

The Council of Trullo Revisited, ed. by George Nedungatt and Michael Featherstone (Rome: Pontifico Istituto Orientale, 1995)

Delehaye, Hippolyte, 'Synaxarium et miracula S. Isaiae prophetae', *Analecta Bollandiana*, 42 (1924), 257–65

Diodorus Siculus, *The Library of History*, trans. by Ch. H. Oldfather, Loeb Classical Library (Cambridge, MA: Harvard University Press, 1933)

Euagrius Scholasticus, *Historia Ecclesiastica*, ed. and trans. by Joseph Bidez and Léon Parmentier (Amsterdam: Hakkert, 1964)

Girone, Maria, *Iamata: Guarigioni miracolose di Asclepio in testi epigrafici* (Bari: Levante, 1998)

Graecorum de re onirocritica reliquiae, ed. by Dario Del Corno, Testi e documenti per lo studio dell'antiquità, 26 (Milan: Istituto editoriale cisalpino, 1969)

Gregory of Nyssa, *On the Making of Man*, in *Nicene and Post-Nicene Fathers, Second Series*, vol. v, ed. by Philip Schaff and Henry Wace (Buffalo, NY: Christian Literature Publishing Co., 1893), pp. 526–85

Gregory of Tours, *Glory of the Martyrs*, trans. by Raymond Van Dam (Liverpool: Liverpool University Press, 1988)

Herzog, Rudolf, *Die Wunderheilungen von Epidauros: Ein Beitrag zur Geschichte der Medizin und der Religion*, Philologus Supplementum, 22.3 (Leipzig, 1931)

Hesychius, *Origines Constantinopolitanae*, in *Scriptores Originum Constantinopolitanarum*, ed. by Theodor Preger (Leipzig: Teubner, 1901; repr. New York: Arno Press, 1975), fasc. 1, pp. 1–18

Hicks, Edward Lee, 'Inscriptions from Western Cilicia', *Journal of Hellenic Studies*, 12 (1891), 225–73

Hippocrates, *On Dreams [Regimen IV]*, trans. by H. S. Jones, Loeb Classical Library, 150 (Cambridge, MA: Harvard University Press, 1959), pp. 420–47

Holy Women of the Syrian Orient, ed. by Sebastian P. Brock and Susan Ashbrook Harvey (Berkeley: University of California Press, 1987)

Honey, Linda, 'Thekla: Text and Context with a First English Translation of the Miracles' (unpublished doctoral dissertation, University of Calgary, 2011)

Inscriptiones Graecae, IV, *Inscriptiones Argolidis*, fasc. 1, *Inscriptiones Epidauri*, ed. by Friderich Hiller von Gaertringen, 2nd edn (Berlin: de Gruyter, 1929)

John of Nikiu, *The Chronicle of John of Nikiu*, trans. by Robert H. Charles (London: Texts and Translations Society, 1916)

Julian, *The Works of the Emperor Julian*, trans. by Wilmer Cave Wright, Loeb Classical Library, 3 vols (London: Heinemann, 1923)

Kavvadias, Panagis, *Fouilles d'Épidaure*, vol. I (Athens: Vlastos, 1891); the subsequent reports were published in the *Ephémerié Archailogiké* in 1883, 1885, 1918; online at <http://digi.ub.uni-heidelberg.de/diglit/kabbadias1891bd1/0021>

Libanius, *Selected Letters of Libanius: From the Age of Constantius and Julian*, ed. and trans. by Scott Bradbury, Translated Texts for Historians, 41 (Liverpool: Liverpool University Press, 2004)

——, *Selected Works*, trans. by Albert Francis Norman, Loeb Classical Library (Cambridge, MA: Harvard University Press, 1977)

LiDonnici, Lynn R., *The Epidaurian Miracle Inscriptions: Text, Translation and Commentary* (Atlanta: Scholars Press, 1995)

——, 'Tale and Dream: The Text and Compositional History of the Corpus of Epidaurian Miracle Cures' (unpublished doctoral dissertation, University of Pennsylvania, 1989)

Life of Irene, Abbess of Chrysobalantion, ed. and trans. by J. O. Rosenqvist (Uppsala: Acta Univeritatis Upsaliensis, 1986)

Lucian, *Alexander the False Prophet*, trans. by Austin Morris Harmon, Loeb Classical Library, 162 (London: Heinemann 1925), pp. 173–253

Malalas, John, *The 'Chronicle' of John Malalas*, trans. by Elisabeth Jeffreys, Michael Jeffreys, and Roger Scott (Melbourne: Australian Association for Byzantine Studies, 1986)

Mansi, Giovanni Domenico, *Sacrorum Conciliorum Nova et Amplissima Collectio*, cujus Johannes Dominicus Mansi et post ipsius mortem Florentius et Venetianus editores ab anno 1758 ad annum 1798 priores triginta unum tomos ediderunt, nunc autem continuatat et absoluta; online at <http://www.documentacatholicaomnia.eu/01_50_1692-1769-_Mansi_JD.html>

Miracle Tales from Byzantium, trans. by Alice-Mary Talbot and Scott F. Johnson (Cambridge, MA: Harvard University Press, 2012)

Les Miracles d'Artémios, ed. by Vincent Déroche, Le monde Byzantin (Paris: CNRS, forthcoming)

'Les miracles de Saint Ptolémée', ed. and trans. by L. Leroy, *Patrologia Orientalis*, 5 (1910), 789–803

The Miracles of St Artemius: A Collection of Miracle Stories by an Anonymous Author of Seventh-Century Byzantium, ed. and trans. by Virgil S. Crisafulli and John W. Nesbitt (Leiden: Brill, 1997)

Monumenta Asiae Minoris Antiqua, ed. by Josef Keil and Adolf Wilhelm (Manchester: Manchester University Press, 1931)

Pachomian Koinonia: The Life of Saint Pachomius and his Disciples, trans. and introd. by Armand Vielleux, 3 vols (Kalamazoo: Cistercian Publications, 1980)

Pausanias, *Guide to Greece*, trans. by Paul Levi, 2 vols (Suffolk: Penguin, 1971)

Philostratus, *The Life of Apollonius of Tyana*, trans. by Frederick Cornwallis Conybeare, 2 vols (Cambridge, MA: Harvard University Press, 1989)

Pindar, *The Olympian and Pythian Odes*, trans. by Basil L. Gildersleeve (New York: Harper and Brothers, 1885)

Plato, *Plato in Twelve Volumes*, vol. XII, trans. by Harold N. Fowler (Cambridge, MA: Harvard University Press, 1921)

Les plus anciens recueils des miracles de saint Démétrius, ed. and trans. by Paul Lemerle, 2 vols (Paris: CNRS, 1979) [BHG 499–523]

Procopius, *On Buildings*, trans. by Henry Bronson Dewing, Loeb Classical Library, 343 (Cambridge, MA: Harvard University Press, 1940)

Pseudo-Gelasius, *Decretum de libris recipiendis et non recipiendis*, ed. by Ernst von Dobschütz (Leipzig: Pries, 1912)

Sainte Thècle, Saints Côme et Damien, Saints Cyr et Jean (extraits), Saint Georges, ed. and trans. by André-Jean Festugière (Paris: Edition A. et J. Picard, 1971)

'Sanctorum Cyriaci et Julittae actae graeca sincera nunc primum edita', *Analecta Bollandiana*, 1 (1882), 201–07

Sappho, *Poetic Fragments*, trans. by D. W. Myatt (self-pub., Lulu Press, 2010)

Sofronius, *Sophrone de Jerusalem: Miracles des Saints Cyr et Jean (BHG I 477–79)*, ed. and trans. by Jean Gascou (Paris: De Boccard, 2006)

St Kosmas und Damian: Texte und Einleitung, ed. by Ludwig Deubner (Leipzig: L. Deubner, 1907)

Strabo, *Geography*, trans. by H. L. Jones, 8 vols, Loeb Classical Library, 49, 50, 182, 196, 211, 223, 241, 267 (Cambridge, MA: Harvard University Press, 1917–1932)

Suda (Suidas): <http://www.stoa.org/sol/>

Sulaimân, Yūhannā, *Tuḥfat az-zamān fī sīrat-al-farīsain Quzmān wa Damyān* (Cairo, 1926, non vidi)

Theodosius, *Theodosii Meliteni qui fertur Chronographia*, ed. by Gottlieb Lukas Friedrich Tafel (Monachii, 1859)

Three Byzantine Saints: Contemporary Biographies of St. Daniel the Stylite, St. Theodore of Sykeon, and St. John the Almsgiver, ed. and trans. by Elisabeth S. Dawes and Norman H. Baynes (Oxford: Blackwell, 1948)

Vidman, Ladislav, *Syllogae inscriptionum religionis Isiacae et Sarapicae*, Religionsgeschichte Versuche und Vorarbaiten, 28 (Berlin: de Gruyter, 1969)

La vie ancienne de s. Syméon le Jeune, ed. by P. van den Ven, 2 vols (Brussels, 1962–1970) [BHG 1689]

Vie et miracles de sainte Thècle: Texte grec, traduction et commentaire, ed. and trans. by Gilbert Dagron (Brussels: Société des Bollandistes, 1978)

Wessely, Carl, *Neue Griechische Zauberpapyri* (Vienna: F. Tempsky, 1893)

Zacharias Scholasticus, *Vita Severi*, ed. by M. A. Kugener, *Patrologia Orientalis*, vol. II (Turnhout: Brepols, 1903), pp. 7–115

Zonaras, *The History of Zonaras*, ed. and trans. by Thomas Banchich and Eugene N. Lane (London: Routledge, 2009)

Secondary Literature

Abel, Ernest L., 'The Psychology of Memory and Rumor Transmission and their Bearing on Theories of Oral Transmission in Early Christianity', *Journal of Religion*, 51 (1971), 270–81

Achteimer, Paul, 'Jesus and the Disciples as Miracle Workers in the Apocryphal New Testament', in *Aspects of Religious Propaganda in Judaism and Early Christianity*, ed. by E. Schüssler Fiorenza (Notre Dame: University of Notre Dame Press, 1976), pp. 149–77

Agosti, Gianfranco, 'Le brume di Omero: Sofronio dinanzi alla *paideia* classica', in *Il calamo della memoria: Riuso di testi e mestiere letterario nella tarda antichità IV*, ed. by Lucio Cristante and Simona Ravalico (Trieste: Edizioni Università di Trieste, 2011), pp. 33–50

Aleshire, Sara Babousett, *The Athenian Asclepieion: Their People, their Dedications, and their Inventories* (Amsterdam: Gieben, 1989)

Allan, Pauline, 'The Definition and Enforcement of Orthodoxy', in *Cambridge Ancient History*, XIV: *Late Antiquity: Empire and Successors, A.D. 425–600*, ed. by Averil Cameron, Brian Ward-Perkins, and Michael Whitby (Cambridge: Cambridge University Press, 2000), pp. 811–34

——, *Sophronius of Jerusalem and Seventh Century Heresy: The Synodical Letter and Other Documents* (Oxford: Oxford University Press, 2009)

Allport, Gordon W., and Leo Postman, *The Psychology of Rumour* (New York: Henry Holt, 1947)

Amelineau, Émile, *Contes e romans de l'Égypte chrétienne* (París: E. Leroux, 1888)

Amory, Ann, 'The Gates of Horn and Ivory', in *Yale Classical Studies*, XX: *Homeric Studies*, ed. by Geoffrey Stephen Kirk and Adam Parry (New Haven, CT: Yale University Press, 1966), pp. 3–57

Amundsen, Darrel W., 'Medicine and Faith in Early Christianity', *Bulletin of the History of Medicine*, 56 (1982), 326–50

——, *Medicine, Society and Faith in the Ancient and Medieval Worlds* (Baltimore: John Hopkins University Press, 1996)

Anrich, Gustav, *Hagios Nikolaos, der Heilige Nikolaos in der griechischen Kirche*, 2 vols (Leipzig: Teubner, 1913–1917)

Arbesmann, Robert, 'The Concept of "Christus medicus" in St Augustin', *Traditio*, 10 (1954), 1–128

Arnold, Charles John, *The Footprints of Michael the Archangel: The Formation and Diffusion of a Saintly Cult, c. 300–c. 800* (New York: Palgrave, 2013)

Aronen, Jaakko, 'La soppravinvenza dei culti pagani e la topografia cristiana dell'area di Giuturna e delle sue adiacenze', in *Lacus Iuturnae*, ed. by Margareta Steinby (Rome: De Luca, 1989), I, pp. 148–74

Artelt, Walter, *Kosmas und Damian: Die Schutzpatrone der Ärzte u. Apotheker. Eine Bildfolge* (Darmstadt: Merck, 1954)

Artelt, Wolfgang, *Lexicon der christlichen Ikonographie*, ed. by Wolfgang Braunfels, vol. VII (Rome: Herder, 1974)

Ashbrook Harvey, Susan, 'Physicians and Ascetics in John of Ephesus: An Expedient Alliance', in *Symposium on Byzantine Medicine*, ed. by John Scarborough, special issue, *Dumbarton Oaks Papers*, 38 (1984), 87–93

Auzépy, Marie-France, 'La carrière d'André de Créte', *Byzantinische Zeitschrift*, 88 (1995), 1–12

——, 'L'évolution de l'attitude face au miracle á Byzance (VII–IX. siècle)', in *Miracles, Prodiges et Merveilles au Moyen Age: XXXV. Congrès de la S. H. M. E. S. Orleans, juin 1994* (Paris: Publications de la Sorbonne, 1995), pp. 31–46

Baldwin, Barry, 'Beyond the House Call: Doctors in Early Byzantine History and Politics', in *Symposium on Byzantine Medicine*, ed. by John Scarborough, special issue, *Dumbarton Oaks Papers*, 38 (1984), 15–20

Bar, Shaul, 'Incubation and Traces of Incubation in the Biblical Narrative', *Old Testament Essays*, 28.2 (2015), 243–56

Barb, Alphons Augustinus, 'The Survival of Magic Arts', in *Paganism and Christianity in the Fourth Century*, ed. by Arnaldo Momigliano (Oxford: Oxford University Press, 1963), pp. 100–125

Barber, Charles, *Figure and Likeness: On the Limits of Representation in Byzantine Iconoclasm* (Princeton, NJ: Princeton University Press, 2002)

Barnard, Leslie William, *The Graeco-Roman and Oriental Background of the Iconoclastic Controversy* (Leiden: Brill, 1974)

Barthes, Roland, 'L'effet de réel', *Communications*, 11 (1968), 84–89

——, 'Structural Analysis of Narratives', in *Image, Music, Text* (London: Fontana Press, 1977), pp. 79–124

Bayliss, Richard, *Provincial Cilicia and the Archaeology of Temple Conversion* (Oxford: Archeopress, 2004)

Bearman, Peri, and others, eds, *The Encyclopaedia of Islam*, 2nd edn (Leiden: Brill, 1950–2005)

Beck, Hans-Georg, *Kirche und theologische Literatur im byzantinischen Reich* (Munich: Beck, 1959)

Bees, Nikos A., 'Weiteres zum Kult des heiligen Artemios', *Byzantinisch-Neugriechishe Jahrbücher*, 1 (1920), 384–85

Behr, Charles Allison, *Aelius Aristeides and the Sacred Tales* (Amsterdam: Hakkert, 1968)
Belting, Hans, *Likeness and Presence: A History of the Image before the Era of Art*, trans. by Edmund Jephcott (Chicago: University of Chicago Press, 1994); originally published as *Bild und Kult: Eine Geschichte des Bildes vor dem Zeitalter der Kunst* (Munich: Beck, 1990)
Belting-Ihm, Christa, 'Mediomagische Praktiken und die Reaktion der Kirche', in *Salute e guarigione nella tarda antiquità: Atti della giornata tematica dei seminari di archeologia cristiana, Roma - 20 maggio 2004*, ed. by Hugo Brandenburg, Stefan Heid, and Christoph Markschies (Vatican City: Pontifico Istituto di archeologia Cristiana, 2007), pp. 199–226
Benardete, Seth, *Herodotean Inquiries* (The Hague: Martinus Nijhoff, 1969)
Berardino, Angelo di, 'Guarigioni nel contesto della traslazione delle reliquie di S. Stefano al tempo di S. Agostino', in *Salute e guarigione nella tarda antichità: Atti della giornata tematica dei seminari di archeologia cristiana, Roma - 20 maggio 2004*, ed. by Hugo Brandenburg, Stefan Heid, and Christoph Markschies (Vatican City: Pontifico Istituto di archeologia Cristiana, 2007), pp. 226–29
Bernand, André, *Le Delta égyptien d'après les textes grecs*, I: *Les confines libyques*, Mémoires de l'Institut français d'archéologie orientale du Caire, 91 (Le Caire: Presses de l'Institut français d'archéologie orientale du Caire, 1970)
Bernard, Jean-Louis, *Apollonius de Tyane et Jésus* (Paris: Laffont, 1977)
Bernard, Martin, *The Healing Ministry in the Church* (Richmond, VA: Knox, 1960)
Besnier, Maurice, *L'Île Tibérine dans l'Antiquité* (Paris: Ancienne Librairie Thorin et Fils, 1902)
Bevan, Edwyn, *Hellenism and Christianity* (London: Allen and Unwin, 1921)
Blockley, Roger C., 'Doctors as Diplomats in the Sixth Century AD', *Florilegium*, 2 (1980), 89–100
Boesch Gajano, Sofia, 'Verità e pubblicità: I racconti di miracoli nel libro XXII del *De Civitate Dei*', in *Il De Civitate Dei: L'opera, l'interpretationi, l'influsso*, ed. by Elena Cavalcanti (Rome: Herder, 1996), pp. 368–88
Boesch Gajano, Sofia, and Lucetta Scaraffia, eds, *Luoghi sacri e spazi della santità* (Turin: Rosenberg & Sellier, 1990)
Bonner, Carl, 'A Tarsian Peculiarity', *Harvard Theological Review*, 35 (1942), 1–11
——, 'Traces of Thaumaturgic Techniques in the Miracles', *Harvard Theological Review*, 20 (1927), 171–81
Bookidis, Nancy, 'Ritual Dining at Corinth', in *Greek Sanctuaries: New Approaches*, ed. by Robin Hägg and Nanno Marinatos (London: Routledge, 1993), pp. 34–50
Booth, Phil, *Crisis of Empire: Doctrine and Dissent at the End of Late Antiquity* (Berkeley: University of California Press, 2014)
Booth, Wayne C., *The Rhetoric of Fiction* (Chicago: Chicago University Press, 1961)
Bozóky, Edina, 'Le miracle et la maison du saint', *Hortus Artium Mediaevalium*, 9 (2003), 247–52
Brandenburg, Hugo, 'Esculapio e S. Bartolomeo nell'Isola Tiberina: La fine dei sacrari pagani e il problema della continuità del culto in veste Cristiana nella tarda antiquità e nell'altomedioevo', in *Salute e guarigione nella tarda antichità: Atti della giornata tematica dei seminari di archeologia cristiana, Roma - 20 maggio*

2004, ed. by Hugo Brandenburg, Stefan Heid, and Christoph Markschies (Vatican City: Pontifico Istituto di archeologia Cristiana, 2007), pp. 13–51

Brazzale, Felice M., *La dottrina del miracolo in S. Agostino* (Rome: Edizioni Marianum, 1964)

Brelich, Angelo, 'The Place of Dreams in the Religious World Concept of the Greeks', in *The Dream and Human Societies*, ed. by G. E. von Grunebaum and Roger Caillois (Berkeley: University of California Press, 1966), pp. 293–301

Bremmer, Jan M., 'How Old Is the Ideal of Holiness (of Mind) in the Epidaurian Temple Inscription and the Hippocratic Oath?', *Zeitschrift für Papyrologie und Epigraphik*, no. 141 (2002), 106–08

Brenk, Beat, 'Da Galeno a Cosma a Damiano: Considerazioni attorno all'introduzione del culto dei SS. Cosma e Damiano a Roma', in *Salute e guarigione nella tarda antichità: Atti della giornata tematica dei seminari di archeologia cristiana, Roma - 20 maggio 2004*, ed. by Hugo Brandenburg, Stefan Heid, and Christoph Markschies (Vatican City: Pontifico Istituto di archeologia Cristiana, 2007), pp. 79–92

Brillante, Carlo, 'Metamorfosi di un'immagine: Le statuette animate in sogno', in *Il sogno in Grecia*, ed. by Giulio Guidorizzi (Rome: Laterza, 1988), pp. 17–33

Brocker, Heinrich, 'Der heilige Thalelaius, Texte und Untersuchungen' (unpublished doctoral dissertation, University of Münster, 1976)

Brown, Peter, *The Cult of the Saints: Its Rise and Function in Latin Christianity* (London: CSM Press, 1983)

——, *Religion and Society in the Age of St Augustine* (London: Faber and Faber, 1972)

Brunet de Presle, Wladimir, 'Mémoire sur le Sérapeum de Memphis', *Mémoires présentés par divers savants à l'Académie des Inscriptions et Belles-Lettres de l'Institut de France*, 2 (1852), 552–76

Bryer, Andrew, and Judith Herrin, eds, *Iconoclasm* (Birmingham: Centre for Byzantine Studies, University of Birmingham, 1977)

Budge, Ernest Alfred Wallis, *Texts Relating to Saint Mêna of Egypt and Canons of Nicaea in Nubian Dialect, with Facsimile* (London: The British Museum, 1909)

Bultmann, Rudolf Karl, *Die Geschichte der synoptischen Tradition* (Gottingen: Vandenhoed, 1931)

Burkert, Walter, *Greek Religion*, trans. by John Raffan (Cambridge, MA: Harvard University Press, 1998)

Burrus, Virginia, *Chastity as Autonomy: Women in the Stories of the Apocryphal Acts*, Studies in Women and Religion, 23 (Lewiston: Edwin Mellen Press, 1987)

Busine, Aude, ed., *Religious Practices and Christianization of the Late Antique City (4th–7th cent.)*, Religions in the Graeco-Roman World (Leiden: Brill, 2021)

Cali, Valentina, 'La meloterapia come strumento taumaturgico nel culto di Asclepio', in *Cristo e Asclepio: Culti terapeutici e taumaturgici nel mondo mediterraneo antico fra cristiani e pagani. Atti del Convegno Internazionale, Accademia di Studi Mediterranei, Agrigento, 20–21 novembre 2006*, ed. by Enrico Dal Covolo and Giulia Sfameni Gasparro (Rome: LAS, 2008), pp. 73–89

Cameron, Averil, *Christianity and the Rhetoric of Empire: The Development of Christian Discourse* (Berkeley: University of California Press, 1991)

——, 'Images of Authority: Elites and Icons in Sixth-Century Byzantium', *Past and Present*, 84 (1979), 3–35

——, 'The Language of Images: The Rise of Icons and Christian Representation', in *The Church and the Arts*, ed. by Diana Wood, Studies in Church History, 28 (Oxford: Blackwell, 1992), pp. 1–42; repr. in *Changing Cultures on Early Byzantium* (Aldershot: Variorum Reprints, 1996), no. XII

——, 'The Theotokos in Sixth-Century Constantinople: A City Finds its Symbol', *Journal of Theological Studies*, 29 (1978), 79–108; repr. in Averil Cameron, *Continuity and Change in Sixth Century Byzantium* (London: Variorum Reprint, 1981), no. 14

Caquot, André, *Les Songes et leur Interprétation*, Sources Orientales (Paris: Editions du Seuil, 1959)

Carrasco, Magdalena Elisabeth, 'Spirituality and Historicity in Pictorial Hagiography: Two Miracles of St. Albinus of Angers', *Art History*, 12 (1989), 1–22

Case, Shirley Jackson, 'The Art of Healing in Early Christian Times', *Journal of Religion*, 3 (1923), 238–55

Cataudella, Quinto, *Critica e estetica nella litteratura greca cristiana* (Turin: Fr. Bocca, 1928)

Caton, Robert, *The Temples and Ritual of Asklepios at Epidauros and Athens* (London: Clay, 1900)

Cavarero, Adriana, *Relating Narratives: Storytelling and Selfhood*, trans. by P. E. Kottman (London: Routledge, 2000)

Certeau, Michel de, 'A Variant: Hagio-Grafical Edification', in *The Writing of History*, trans. by Tom Conley (New York: Columbia University Press, 1988), pp. 269–84

Chabon, Michael, 'The Game's Afoot', *The New York Review of Books*, February 24, 2005, p. 14

Chandrasekaran, Sujanda, and Anna Kouremenos, eds, *Continuity and Destruction in Alexander's East: The Transformation of Monumental Space from the Hellenistic Period to Late Antiquity* (Oxford: British Archaeological Reports, 2015)

Chaniotis, Angelos, 'Illness and Cures in the Greek Propitiatory Inscriptions and Dedications of Lydia and Phrygia', in *Ancient Medicine in its Socio-Cultural Context*, ed. by Philip J. Van der Eijk, Manfred H. F. J. Horstmansdorff, and Petrus Hermanus Schijvers, 2 vols (Amsterdam: Rodopi, 1995), II, pp. 323–44

Collingwood, Robin George, *The Idea of History* (Oxford: Clarendon Press, 1946)

Connor, Caroline L., *Art and Miracles in Medieval Byzantium: The Crypt at Hosios Loukas and its Frescoes* (Princeton, NJ: Princeton University Press, 1991)

——, 'The Setting and Function of a Byzantine Miracle Cult', in *Abstracts and Program Statements for the 1990 Annual Conference of the College Art Association* (New York, 1990), pp. 69–70

Constantelos, Demetrios J., *Byzantine Philanthropy and Social Welfare* (New Brunswick, NJ: Rutgers University Press, 1968)

——, 'Physician-Priests in the Medieval Greek Church', *Greek Orthodox Theological Review*, 12 (1966–1967), 141–53

Coquin, René-George, *Livre de la consécration du Sanctuaire de Benjamin* (Cairo: Institute français d'Archéologie Orientale, 1975)

Cormack, Robin S., *Writing in Gold: Byzantine Society and its Icons* (London: Philip, 1985)
Cox, Patricia, *Biography in Late Antiquity: Quest for the Holy Man* (Berkeley: University of California Press, 1983)
Cox Miller, Patricia, *Dreams in Late Antiquity: Studies in the Imagination of a Culture* (Princeton, NJ: Princeton University Press, 1994)
——, 'Is There a Harlot in this Text? Hagiography and the Grotesque', *Journal of Medieval and Early Modern Studies*, 33.3 (2003), 419–35
Cozzolino, Ciro, *Origine del culto ai santi martiri Ciro e Giovanni in Oriente e in Occidente* (Jerusalem: Franciscan Printing Press, 1976)
Crapanzano, Vincenzo, 'Saints, Jnūn, and Dreams: An Essay in Moroccan Ethnopsychology', *Psychiatry*, 38 (1975), 145–59
Cristante, Lucio, and Simona Ravalico, eds, *Il calamo della memoria: Riuso di testi e mestiere letterario nella tarda antichità IV* (Trieste: Edizioni Università di Trieste, 2011)
Crum, Walter Ewing, 'Place-Names in Deubner's Kosmas und Damian', *Proceedings of the Society of Biblical Archeology*, 30 (1908), 45–52
Csepregi, Ildikó, 'Changes in Dream Patterns between Antiquity and Byzantium: The Impact of Medical Learning on Dream Healing', in *Ritual Healing: Magic, Ritual and Medical Therapy from Antiquity until the Early Modern Period*, ed. by Ildikó Csepregi and Charles Burnett, Micrologus Library, 48 (Florence: SISMEL, Edizioni del Galluzzo, 2012), pp. 131–45
——, 'Disease, Death, Destiny: The Healer as *Soter* in Miraculous Cures', in *On Old Age: Approaching Death in Antiquity and the Middle Ages*, ed. by Christian Krötzl and Katariina Mustakallio, The History of Daily Life, 2 (Turnhout: Brepols, 2011), pp. 245–67
——, 'Mysteries for the Uninitiated: The Role and Symbolism of the Eucharist in Miraculous Dream Healing', in *The Eucharist in Theology and Philosophy: Issues of Doctrinal History in East and West from the Patristic Age to the Reformation*, ed. by István Perczel, Réka Forrai, and György Geréby (Leuven: Leuven University Press, 2006), pp. 97–130
——, 'Pork as a Wonder Drug, or Religious Taboo as Magical Medicine', in *The Magical and Sacred Medical World*, ed. by Éva Pócs (Cambridge: Cambridge Scholars Publishing, 2019), pp. 435–47
——, 'The Theological Other: Religious and Narrative Identity in Fifth to Seventh Century Byzantine Miracle Collections', in *Identity and Alterity in Hagiography and the Cult of Saints*, ed. by Ana Marinković and Trpimir Vedriš (Zagreb: Hagiotheca, 2010), pp. 59–72
——, 'Who Is behind Incubation Stories? The Hagiographers of Byzantine Dream Healing Miracles', in *Dreams, Healing, and Medicine in Greece: From Antiquity to the Present*, ed. by Steven M. Oberhelman (Farnham: Ashgate, 2013), pp. 161–88
Dagron, Gilbert, 'L'auteur des Actes et des Miracles de Sainte Thècle', *Analecta Bollandiana*, 92 (1974), 5–11
——, 'Holy Images and Likeness', *Dumbarton Oaks Papers*, 45 (1991), 23–33
——, 'Judaïser', in *Travaux et Mémoires*, vol. XI (Paris: De Boccard, 1991), pp. 359–80

―――, 'L'ombre d'un doute: L'hagiographie en question, VIᵉ–XIᵉ siècle', *Dumbarton Oaks Papers*, 46 (1992), 59–69

―――, 'Rêver de Dieu et parler de soi: Le rêve et son interprétation d'après les sources byzantines', in *I sogni nel medioevo*, ed. by Tullio Gregory (Rome: Edizioni dell'Ateneo, 1985), pp. 37–55

Dagron, Gilbert, and Vincent Déroche, 'Juifs et chrétiens dans l'Orient du VIIᵉ siècle', in *Travaux et Mémoires*, vol. XI (Paris: De Boccard, 1991), pp. 17–273

Dalton, Ormonde Maddock, 'A Coptic Wall Painting from Wadi Sarga', *Journal of Egyptian Archeology*, 3 (1916), 35–37

Dauphin, Claude, 'From Apollo and Asclepius to Christ: Pilgrimage and Healing at the Temple and Episcopal Basilica of Dor', *Liber Annus*, 49 (1999), 379–430

David, Joseph, 'L'église Sainte-Marie-Antique dans son état originaire: Étude liturgique et hagiographique, suivie d'un catalogue raisonné des saints de cette église', in *Saint-Marie-Antique*, ed. by Wladimir de Grüneisen (Rome: M. Bretschneider, 1911), pp. 449–559

David-Danel, Marie-Louise, *Iconographie des Saints Côme et Damien* (Lille: Morel & Corduant, 1958)

Davis, Stephen J., *The Cult of Saint Thecla: A Tradition of Women's Piety in Late Antiquity* (Oxford: Oxford University Press, 2001)

―――, 'Pilgrimage and the Cult of Saint Thecla in Late Antique Egypt', in *Pilgrimage and Holy Space in Late Antique Egypt*, ed. by David Frankfurter (Leiden: Brill, 1998), pp. 303–39

Del Corno, Dario, 'Ricerche sull' oniricritica greca', *Rendiconti dell' Isituto Lombardo*, 96 (1962), 334–66

―――, 'I sogni e la loro interpretazione nell'età dell'Impero', in *ANRW*, II: Principat XVI.2, pp. 1605–18

Delehaye, Hippolyte, *L'ancienne hagiographie byzantine: Les sources, les premiers modèles, la formation des genres. Conférences prononcées au Collège de France en 1935*, ed. by Bernand Joassart and Xavier Lequeux, preface written by Gilbert Dagron (Brussels: Société des Bollandistes, 1991)

―――, 'Castor et Pollux dans les légendes hagiographiques', *Analecta Bollandiana*, 23 (1904), 427–32

―――, *Les légendes grecques des saints militaries* (Paris: Libraire A. Picard, 1909)

―――, *The Legends of the Saints: An Introduction to Hagiography* (London: Longmans, 1907)

―――, *Les passions des martyrs et les genres littéraires*, 2nd edn (Brussels: Société des Bollandistes, 1966)

―――, 'Les premiers "Libelli Miraculorum"', *Analecta Bollandiana*, 29 (1910), 427–34

―――, 'Les recueils antiques de miracles des saints', *Analecta Bollandiana*, 43 (1925), 1–85, 305–25

―――, 'Les Saints d'Aboukir', *Analecta Bollandiana*, 30 (1911), 448–50

Delierneux, Nathalie, 'L'exploitation des topoi hagiographiques: Du cliché figé à la réalité codée', *Byzantion*, 70 (2000), 57–90

Déroche, Vincent, 'La polémique anti-judaïque au VIᵉ et au VIIᵉ siècle: Un memento inédit, Les *Képhala*', in *Travaux et Mémoires*, vol. XI (Paris: De Boccard, 1991), pp. 275–311

———, 'Pourquoi écrivait-on des recueils de miracles? L'example des miracles de Saint Artémios', in *Les saints et leur sanctuaire à Byzance*, ed. by Catherine Jolivet-Lévy, Michel Kaplan, and Jean-Pierre Sodini (Paris: Centre National de la Recherche Scientifique, 1993), pp. 95–116

———, 'Tensions and contradictions dans les recueils de miracles de la première époque Byzantine', in *Miracle et Kārama*, ed. by Denise Aigle, Sciences Religieuses, 109, Hagiographies médiévales compares, 2 (Turnhout: Bibliothèque de l'École des Hautes Études, 2000), pp. 145–66

———, 'Vraiment anargyres? Don et contredon dans les recueils de miracles protobyzantine', in *Pèlerinage et lieux saints dans l'antiquité et le moyen âge: Mélanges offerts à Pierre Maraval*, ed. by Béatrice Caseau-Chevallier, Jean-Claude Cheynet, Pierre Maraval, and Vincent Déroche (Paris: Association des amis du Centre d'histoire et civilisation de Byzance, 2006), pp. 153–58

Derouet, Jean-Louis, 'Les possibilités d'interprétation sémiologique des textes hagiographiques', *Revue d'histoire de l'Eglise de France*, 62 (1976), 153–62

Deubner, Ludwig, *De incubatione capita quattuor* (Leipzig: Teubner, 1900)

Devereux, George, *Dreams in Greek Tragedy* (Oxford: Blackwell, 1979)

Devos, Paul, 'Le Juif et le Chrétien, un miracle de Saint Ménas', *Analecta Bollandiana*, 78 (1960), 275–308

———, 'Les Miracles De St. Ménas En Éthiopien', in *Atti del Convegno Internazionale di Studi Etiopici, Roma 2–4 aprile 1959* (Rome: Accademia nazionale dei Lincei, 1960), pp. 335–43

———, 'Un récit des Miracles de S. Ménas en Copte et en éthiopien', *Analecta Bollandiana*, 77 (1959), 451–63; 78 (1959), 154–60

Dibelius, Martin, *A Fresh Approach to the New Testament and Early Christian Literature* (Hertford: Nicholson and Watson, 1936)

Dick, Ignace, 'La Passion arabe de S. Antoine Ruwah néo-martyr de Damas († 25 déc, 799)', *Le Muséon*, 74 (1961), 109–33

Dickie, Matthew W., 'Narrative Patterns in Christian Hagiography', *Greek, Roman and Byzantine Studies*, 40 (1999), 83–98

Dillon, Matthew P. J., 'The Didactic Nature of the Epidaurian Iamata', *Zeitschrift für Papyrologie und Epigraphik*, no. 101 (1994), 239–60

———, *Pilgrims and Pilgrimage in Ancient Greece* (London: Routledge, 1997)

Dinkler, Erich, *Christus und Asklepios: Zum Christustypus der polychromen Platten im Museo nazionale romano*, Sitzungsberichte Heidelberger Akademie der Wissenschaften, 2 (Heidelberg: Winter, 1980)

D'Irsay, Stephen, 'Christian Medicine and Science in the Third Century', *Journal of Religion*, 10 (1930), 515–44

———, 'Patristic Medicine', *Annals of Medical History*, 9 (1927), 364–78

Dodds, Eric R., *The Greeks and the Irrational* (Berkeley: University of California Press, 1951)

Dols, Michel W., *Majnūn: The Madman in Medieval Islamic Society* (Oxford: Clarendon Press, 1992)

Dorati, Marco, 'Funzioni e motivi nelle stele di Epidauro e nelle raccolte cristiane di miracoli incubatori', Συγγραφή, 3 (2001), 91–118

Dorati, Marco, and Giulio Guidorizzi, 'La letteratura incubatoria', in *La letteratura di consumo nel mondo greco-latino*, ed. by Oronzo Pecere and Antonio Stramaglia (Cassino: Università degli Studi di Cassino, 1996), pp. 345–71

Douglas, Mary, *Purity and Danger: An Analysis of the Concepts of Pollution and Taboo* (London: Routledge, 1996)

Doutté, Edmond, *Magie et religion dans l'Afrique du Nord* (Algiers: Jourdan, 1909)

Dörnemann, Michael, 'Einer ist Arzt, Christus: Medizinales Verständnis von Erlösung in der Theologie der griechischen Kirchenväter des zweiten bis vierten Jahrhunderts', *Zeitschrift für Antikes Christentum*, 17.1 (2013), 102–24

——, *Krankheit und Heilung in der Theologie der frühen Kirchenväter*, Studien und Texte zu Antike und Christentum, 20 (Tübingen: Mohr, 2003)

Draycott, Jane, and Emma-Jayne Graham, eds, *Bodies of Evidence: Ancient Anatomical Votives Past, Present and Future* (London: Routledge, 2017)

Duchesne, Louis, 'Le sanctuaire d'Aboukir', *Bulletin de la Société d'archéologie d'Alexandrie*, 12 (1910), 3–14

Duffin, Jacalyn, *Medical Saints: Cosmas and Damian in a Postmodern World* (Oxford: Oxford University Press, 2013)

Duffy, John, 'Byzantine Medicine in the Sixth and Seventh Centuries: Aspects of Teaching and Practice', in *Symposium on Byzantine Medicine*, ed. by John Scarborough, special issue, *Dumbarton Oaks Papers*, 38 (1984), 21–27

——, 'Observations on Sophronius' Miracles of Cyrus and John', *Journal of Theological Studies*, 35 (1984), 71–90

Dumeige, Gerais, 'Le Christ médecin dans la littérature chrétienne des premiers siècles', *Rivista di archeologia Cristiana*, 47 (1972), 115–41

Dummer, Jürgen, 'Fl. Artemius dux Aegypt', *Archiv für Papyrusforschung und verwandte Gebiete*, 21 (1971), 121–44

Duprez, André, *Jésus et les dieux guérisseurs: À propos de Jean V* (Paris: J. Gabalda, 1970)

Dzielska, Maria, *Hypatia of Alexandria* (Cambridge, MA: Harvard University Press, 1995)

Ebersolt, Jean, *Sanctuaires de Byzance: Recherches sur les anciens trésors des églises de Constantinople* (Paris: Edition Ernest Leroux, 1921)

Edelstein, Ludwig, 'Greek Medicine and its Relation to Religion and Magic', in *Ancient Medicine: Selected Papers of Ludwig Edelstein*, ed. by Oswei Temlin and Lilian C. Temkin (Baltimore: Johns Hopkins University Press, 1967), pp. 205–46

Efthymiadis, Stephanos M., ed., *Ashgate Research Companion to Byzantine Hagiography*, I: *Periods and Places*, Ashgate Research Companions (Farnham: Ashgate, 2011), and II: *Genres and Contexts* (Farnham: Ashgate, 2014)

——, 'The Byzantine Hagiographer and his Audience in the Ninth and Tenth Centuries', in *Metaphrasis: Redactions and Audiences in Middle Byzantine Hagiography*, ed. by Christian Høgel (Oslo: Research Council of Norway, 1996), pp. 59–80

——, 'A Day and Ten Months in the Life of a Lonely Bachelor: The Other Byzantium in Miracula S. Artemii 18 and 22', *Dumbarton Oaks Papers*, 58 (2004), 1–26

——, 'Greek Byzantine Collections of Miracles: A Chronological and Bibliographical Survey', *Symbolae Osloenses*, 74 (1999), 195–218

Ehrenheim, Hedvig von, *Greek Incubation Rituals in Classical and Hellenistic Times* (Liège: Kernos Supplement, 2015)

——, 'Identifying Incubation Areas in Pagan and Early Christian Times', *Proceedings of the Danish Institute at Athens*, 6 (2009), 237–76

Ehrhardt, Albert, 'Forschungen zur Hagiographie der griechischen Kirche', *Römische Quartalschriften*, 11 (1897), 67–206

Ehrlich, Ernst Ludwig, *Der Traum in Alten Testament* (Berlin: Töpelmann, 1953)

Eijk, Philip J. van der, 'Aristotle on "Distinguished Physicians" and the Medical Significance of Dreams', in *Ancient Medicine in its Socio-Cultural Context*, ed. by Philip J. Van der Eijk, Manfred H. F. J. Horstmansdorff, and Petrus Hermanus Schijvers, 2 vols (Amsterdam: Rodopi, 1995), II, pp. 447–59

——, 'Divination, Prognosis and Prophylaxis: The Hippocratic Work "On Dreams" (*De Victu* 4) and its Near Eastern Background', in *Magic and Rationality in Ancient Near Eastern and Graeco-Roman Medicine*, ed. by Manfred H. F. J. Horstmanshoff and Marten Stol (Leiden: Brill, 2004), pp. 187–218

Esbroeck, Michael van, 'La diffusion orientale de la légende des saints Cosme et Damien', in *Hagiographie, cultures et sociétés IVe–XIIe siècles: Actes du Colloque organisé à Nanterre et à Paris (2–5 mai 1979)*, ed. by Evelyn Patlagean and Pierre Riché (Paris: Études Augustiniennes, 1981), pp. 61–77

Fabre-Vassas, Claudine, *The Singular Beast: Jews, Christians, and the Pig*, trans. by Carol Volk (New York: Columbia University Press, 1997)

Farnell, Lewis R., *Greek Hero Cults and Ideas of Immortality* (Oxford: Clarendon Press, 1921)

Fernandez Marcos, Natalio, *Los Thaumata de Sofronio: Contribucion al estudio de la incubatio cristiana*, ed. and trans. by (Madrid: Instituto Antonio de Nebrija, 1975)

Ferngren, Gary B., 'Early Christianity as a Religion of Healing', *Bulletin of the History of Medicine*, 66 (1992), 1–15

——, *Medicine and Health Care in Early Christianity* (Baltimore: Johns Hopkins University Press, 2009)

Festugière, André-Jean, *L'idéal religieux des Grecs et l'Évangile* (Paris: Les Belles Lettres, 1932)

——, 'Lieux communs littéraires et thèmes de folk-lore dans l'Hagiographie primitive', *Wiener Studien*, 73 (1960), 123–52

——, *Personal Religion among the Greeks* (Berkeley: University of California Press, 1960)

——, 'Les Proscynemes de Philiae', *Revue des Études Grecques*, 83 (1970), 175–97

——, *La révélation d'Hermès Trismégiste*, 3rd edn (Paris: Les Belles Lettres, 1989)

——, 'Types épidauriennes de miracles dans la vie de Syméon Stylite le Jeune', *Journal of Hellenic Studies*, 43 (1973), 70–73

Finnegan, Ruth, *Oral Poetry: Its Nature, Significance and Social Context* (Cambridge: Cambridge University Press, 1977)

Foucart, Paul Francois, *Mémoire sur les ruines et l'histoire de Delphes* (Paris: Archives des Missions scientifiques, 1865)

Fournet, Jean-Luc, 'Omero e i Cristiani in Egitto secondo due testi agiografici (Panegirico di Macario di Tkôw e Sofrone di Gerusalemme, Miracoli di Ciro e Giovanni)', in *Il calamo della memoria: Riuso di testi e mestiere letterario nella tarda antichità IV*, ed. by Lucio Cristante and Simona Ravalico (Trieste: Edizioni Università di Trieste, 2011), pp. 19–31

Franchi de' Cavalieri, Pio, 'I SS. Gervasio e Protasio sono un imitazione di Castore e Polluce?', *Nuovo Bullettino di Archeologia Cristiana*, 9 (1903) 109–26

Frankfurter, David, *Religion in Roman Egypt: Assimilation and Resistance* (Princeton, NJ: Princeton University Press, 1998)

Frantz, Alison, 'From Paganism to Christianity in the Temples of Athens', *Dumbarton Oaks Papers*, 19 (1965), 187–207

Frend, William H. C., *The Rise of the Monophysite Movement* (Cambridge: Cambridge University Press, 1972)

Frendo, Joseph D., 'The Miracles of St Demetrius and the Capture of Thessaloniki', *Byzantinoslavica*, 58.2 (1997), 205–24

Funk, Robert W., 'The Form of the New Testament Healing Miracle Story', *Semeia*, 12 (1978), 57–96

Fusco, Roberto, 'La cura del corpo nella tradizione monastica bizantina tra V e VII secolo', in *Cultura e Promozione umana: La cura del corpo e dello spirito nell'antichità classica e nei primi secoli Cristiani*, ed. by Enrico Dal Covolo and Isidoro Giannetto (Troina: Oasi, 1998), pp. 377–418

Gascou, Jean, 'Les origines du culte des saints Cyr et Jean', *Analecta Bollandiana*, 125 (2007), 241–81

Gerdhardson, Birgit, *Memory and Manuscript: Oral Tradition and Written Transmission in Rabbinic Judaism and Early Christianity*, trans. by Eric John Sharpe (Lund: Gleerup, 1964)

——, *Tradition and Transmission in Early Christianity* (Lund: Gleerup, 1964)

Gil, Luis, *Therapeia: La medicina popular en el mundo clássico* (Madrid: Ediciones Guadarrama, 1969)

Goodich, Michael, 'Filiation and Form in Late Medieval Miracle Story', *Hagiographica*, 3 (1996), 1–18

Grabar, André, *L'iconoclasm byzantine: Dossier archéologique* (Paris: Collège de France, 1957)

Graf, Fritz, *Roman Festivals in the Greek East: From the Early Empire to the Middle Byzantine Era* (Cambridge: Cambridge University Press, 2015)

Grégoire, Reginald, *Manuale di agiologia: Introduzione alla letteratura agiografica*, 2nd edn (Fabriano: Monastero S. Silvestro, 1996)

Gregory, Timothy E., 'The Christian Asclepieion at Athens', *Byzantine Studies Conference*, 9 (1983), 39–40

——, 'The Survival of Paganism in Christian Greece', *American Journal of Philology*, 107 (1986), 229–42

Grosdidier de Matons, Jean, 'Les *Miracula Sancti Artemii*: Note sur quelques questions de vocabulaire', in *Mémorial André-Jean Festugière: Antiquité, Païenne et Chrétienne*, ed. by E. Lucchesi and H. D. Saffrey (Geneva: P. Cramer, 1984), pp. 263–66

Grossmann, Peter, *Abû Mînâ: A Guide to the Ancient Pilgrimage Center* (Cairo: Fotiadis & Co. Press, 1986)

——, 'Late Antique Christian Incubation Centres in Egypt', in *Salute e guarigione nella tarda antichità: Atti della giornata tematica dei seminari di archeologia cristiana, Roma - 20 maggio 2004*, ed. by Hugo Brandenburg, Stefan Heid, and Christoph Markschies (Vatican City: Pontifico Istituto di archeologia Cristiana, 2007), pp. 125–40

——, 'The Pilgrimage Center of Abû Mînâ', in *Pilgrimage and Holy Space in Late Antique Egypt*, ed. by David Frankfurter (Leiden: Brill, 1998), pp. 281–302

——, 'Zur Gründung des Heilungszentrums der Hl. Kyros und Johannes bei Menouthis', in *Timelines: Studies in Honour of Manfred Bietak*, ed. by E. Czerny and others, 3 vols (Leuven: Peeters, 2006), III, pp. 203–12

Guidorizzi, Giulio, 'Motivi fiabesche nella agiografia bizantina', in *Studi Bizantini e neogreci*, ed. by Pietro Luigi Leone (Galatina: Congedo Editore, 1983), pp. 457–67

Güttemanns, Erhardt, *Candid Questions Concerning Gospel Form Criticism: A Methodological Sketch of the Fundamental Problematics of Form and Redaction Criticism*, trans. by William G. Doty (Pittsburg: Pickwick Press, 1979)

Hackel, Sergey, ed., *The Byzantine Saint: Fourteenth Spring Symposium of Byzantine Studies* (Birmingham: University of Birmingham, 1981)

Hahn, Cynthia, 'Picturing the Text: Narrative in the Life of the Saints', *Art History*, 13.1 (1990), 1–33

Hahn, István, *Traumdeutung und gesellschaftliche Wirklichkeit: Artemidorus Daldianus als sozailgeschichtliche Quelle* (Konstanz: Xenia, 27, 1992; originally published Budapest: Akadémiai Kiadó: 1982)

Hahn, Johannes, Stephen Emmel, and Ulrich Gotter, eds, *From Temple to Church: Destruction and Renewal of Local Cultic Topography in Late Antiquity* (Leiden: Brill, 2008)

Haldon, John F., *Byzantium in the Seventh Century* (Cambridge: Cambridge University Press, 1990; repr. 1993)

——, ed., *A Social History of Byzantium* (Chichester: Wiley – Blackwell, 2009)

——, 'Supplementary Essay: The Miracles of Artemius and Contemporary Attitudes: Context and Significance', in *The Miracles of St Artemius: A Collection of Miracle Stories by an Anonymous Author of Seventh-Century Byzantium*, ed. by Virgil S. Crisafulli and John W. Nesbitt (Leiden: Brill, 1997), pp. 33–73

——, 'Tortured by my Conscience: The Laudatio Therapontis. A Neglected Source of the Later Seventh or Early Eighth Century', in *From Rome to Constantinople: Studies in Honour of Averil Cameron*, ed. by Hagit Amirav and Bar ter Haar Romeney (Leuven: Peeters, 2007), pp. 263–78

Halkin, François, ed., *Euphémie de Chalcédonié: Légendes byzantines publiées* (Brussels: Société des Bollandistes, 1965)

——, 'La Passion greque des Saintes Libyè, Eutropie et Léonis, martyres à Nisibe', *Analecta Bollandiana*, 76 (1958), 293–315

——, 'Publications récentes de textes hagiographiques grecs. II. Part', *Analecta Bollandiana*, 53 (1935), 366–81

Halliday, W. Robert, 'Some Notes on the Treatment of Disease in Antiquity', in *Greek Poetry and Life: Essays Presented for Gilbert Murray on his Seventieth Birthday* (Oxford: Clarendon Press, 1936), pp. 277–94

Hamarneh, Sami Kh., 'Cosma and Damian in the Near East: Earliest Extant Monument', *Pharmacy in History*, 27 (1985), 78–83

Hamilton, Mary, *Incubation: The Cure of Disease in Pagan Temples and Christian Churches* (London: W. C. Henderson, 1906)

Hanson, John S., 'Dreams and Visions in the Graeco-Roman World and Early Christianity', in *ANRW*, II: Principat, XXIII.2, pp. 1395–1427

Hardon, John A., 'The Concept of Miracle from St Augustine to Modern Apologetics', *Theological Studies*, 15 (1954), 229–57

——, 'The Miracle Narratives in the Acts of the Apostles', *Catholic Biblical Quarterly*, 16 (1954), 303–18

Harnack, Adolf, *The Expansion of Christianity in the First Three Centuries*, trans. and ed. by James Moffatt, 3 vols (New York: G. P. Putnam's Sons, 1940)

——, 'Medicinischen aus der altesten Kirchen geschichte', in his *Texte Untersuchungen zur geschichte dre altchristlichen Literatur* (Leipzig: Hinrich, 1892), pp. 35–152

Harpham, Geoffrey Galt, *On the Grotesque: Strategies of Contradiction in Art and Literature* (Princeton, NJ: Princeton University Press, 1982)

Harris, Randall J., *The Cult of the Heavenly Twins* (Cambridge: Cambridge University Press, 1906)

Harris, William V., *Dreams and Experience in Classical Antiquity* (Cambridge, MA: Harvard University Press, 2009)

Harris, William V., and Brooke Holmes, eds, *Aelius Aristides between Greece, Rome and the Gods*, Columbia Studies in the Classical Tradition, 32 (Leiden: Brill, 2008)

Hartog, Francois, *Le miroir d'Hérodote: Essai sur la représentation de l'autre* (Paris: Gallimard, 1980)

Hauck, Karl, 'Gott als Arzt', in *Text und Bild: Zwei Aspekte des Zusammenwischens zweier Künste im Mittelalter und früher Neuzeit*, ed. by Christel Meier and Uwe Ruberg (Wiesbaden: L. Reichert, 1980), pp. 19–62

Hausmann, Ute, *Kunst und Heiligtum: Untersuchungen zu den griechiechen Asklepiosreliefs* (Potsdam: Stichnote, 1948)

Havelock, Eric A., *The Muse Learns to Write: Reflections on Orality and Literacy from Antiquity to the Present* (New Haven, CT: Yale University Press, 1986)

Heijer, Jan den, 'Miraculous Icons and their Historical Background', in *Coptic Art and Culture: The Netherlands Institute for Archaeology and Arabic Studies in Cairo*, ed. by Hans Hondelink (Cairo: Shouhdy Publishing House, 1990), pp. 89–100

Herzfeld, Ernst, and Samuel Guyer, *Meramlik und Korykos* (Manchester: Manchester University Press, 1930)

Herzog, Rudolf, 'Der Kampf um der Kult von Menuthis', in *Pisciculi. Studien zur Religion und Kultur des Altertums: Franz Joseph Dölger zum sechzigsten Geburtstage dargeboten von Freunden, Vererhren und Schülern*, ed. by Theodor Klauser and Adolf Rücker (Münster: Aschendorff, 1939), pp. 117–24

Hinterberger, Martin, 'Autobiography and Hagiography in Byzantium', *Symbolae Osloenses*, 75 (2000), 139–64

Høgel, Chistian, 'Literary Aspects of Greek Byzantine Hagiography: A Bibliographical Survey', *Symbolae Osloenses*, 72 (1997), 164–71

Holowchak, Mark Andrew, 'Interpreting Dreams for Corrective Regimen: Diagnostic Dreams in Greco-Roman Medicine', *Journal of the History of Medicine and Allied Sciences*, 56 (2001), 382–99

Honey, Linda, Review of Scott Johnson's *The 'Life and Miracles of Thekla': A Literary Study*: Bryn Mawr Classical Review, 19 August 2006, <http://ccat.sas.upenn.edu/bmcr/2006/2006-08-19.html>

Horden, Peregrine, 'Saints and Doctors in the Early Byzantine Empire: The Case of Theodore of Sykeon', *Studies in Church History*, 19 (1982) 1–13

Horstmanshoff, Manfred H. F. J., 'Asclepius and Temple Medicine in Aelius Aristides' *Sacred Tales*', in *Magic and Rationality in Ancient Near Eastern and Graeco-Roman Medicine*, ed. by Manfred H. F. J. Horstmanshoff and Marten Stol (Leiden: Brill, 2004), pp. 325–41

Husser, Jean-Marie, *Dreams and Dream Narratives in the Biblical World*, trans. by Jill M. Munro (Sheffield: Sheffield Academic Press, 1999)

——, *Le songe et la parole: Étude sur le rêve et sa fonction dans l'ancien Israël* (Berlin: de Gruyter, 1994)

Israelowich, Ido, *Society, Medicine and Religion in the Sacred Tales of Aelius Aristides* (Leiden: Brill, 2012)

James, Montague Rhodes, *The Apocryphal New Testament* (Oxford: Clarendon Press, 1924)

Janin, Raymond, *La Géographie Ecclésiastique de l'Empire Byzantine*, III: *Les Églises et les Monastères*, 2nd edn (Paris: Centre National de la Recherche Scientifique, 1969)

——, 'Les sanctuaires byzantins de saint Michel', *Echos d'Orient*, 33 (1934), 28–52

Jaritz, Felicitas, *Die Arabischen Quellen zum Heiligen Menas* (Heidelberg: Orientverlag, 1993)

Jayne, Walter Addison, *The Healing Gods of Ancient Civilizations* (New Haven, CT: Yale University Press, 1925)

Johnson, Scott F., *The 'Life and Miracles of Thekla': A Literary Study* (Washington, DC: Center for Hellenic Studies, 2006)

Julien, Pierre, François Ledermann, and Alain Touwaide, *Cosma e Damiano: Dal culto popolare alla protezione di chirurgi, medici e farmacisti. Aspetti e immagini* (Milan: Antea, 1993)

Kantorowicz, Ernst H., *Laudes Regiae* (Berkeley: University of California Press, 1946)

Kaplan, Michel, 'Le miracle est-il nécessaire au saint byzantin?', in *Miracle et Kārama*, ed. by Denise Aigle, Sciences Religieuses, 109, Hagiographies médiévales comparées, 2 (Turnhout: Bibliothèque de l'École des Hautes Études, 2000), pp. 167–96

Kazhdan, Alexander, *Authors and Texts in Byzantium* (London: Variorum Reprints, 1979)

——, 'Holy and Unholy Miracle Workers', in *Byzantine Magic*, ed. by Henry Maguire (Washington, DC: Dumbarton Oaks Research Library and Collection, 1995), pp. 73–82

——, 'The Image of the Medical Doctor in Byzantine Literature of the Tenth to Twelfth Centuries', in *Symposium on Byzantine Medicine*, ed. John Scarborough, special issue, *Dumbarton Oaks Papers*, 38 (1984), 43–51

Kazhdan, Alexander, and Henry Maguire, 'Byzantine Hagiographical Texts as Sources on Art', *Dumbarton Oaks Papers*, 45 (1991), 1–22

Kee, Howard Clark, 'Aretalogy and Gospel', *Journal of Biblical Literature*, 92 (1973), 402–22

——, *Medicine, Miracles and Magic in New Testament Times* (Cambridge: Cambridge University Press, 1986)

——, *Miracle in the Early Christian World: A Study in Sociohistorical Method* (New Haven, CT: Yale University Press, 1983)

Kelber, Werner H., *The Oral and Written Gospel: The Hermeneutics of Speaking and Writing in the Synoptic Tradition, Mark, Paul and Q* (Philadelphia: Fortress Press, 1983)

Kelsey, Morton T., *God, Dreams, and Revelation: A Christian Interpretation of Dreams* (Minneapolis: Augsburg, 1991)

——, *Healing and Christianity in the Ancient Thought and Modern Times* (New York: Harper and Row, 1976)

Kennedy, George Alexander, *Progymnasmata: Greek Textbooks of Prose Composition and Rhetoric. Writings from the Greco-Roman World* (Atlanta: Society of Biblical Literature, 2003)

Kerényi, Károly, *Asklepios: Archetypal Image of the Physician's Existence*, trans. by Ralph Manheim, Bollingen Series, 65.3 (New York: Pantheon, 1959)

——, 'Telesphoros: Zum Verstundes Etruskischer, griechischer, and keltisch Germanischer Damongestalten', *Egyetemes Philologiai Közlöny*, 57 (1933), 156–64

Kessels, Antonius Hendrik Maria, *Studies on the Dream in Greek Literature* (Utrecht: HES Publishers, 1978)

King, Helen, 'Comparative Perspectives on Medicine and Religion in the Ancient World', in *Religion, Health and Suffering*, ed. by John R. Hinnells and Roy Porter (London: Kegan Paul, 1999), pp. 276–94

——, ed., *Health in Antiquity* (London: Routledge: 2005)

Kitzinger, Ernst, 'The Cult of Images in the Age before the Iconoclasm', *Dumbarton Oaks Papers*, 8 (1954), 83–151

Kleinman, Arthur, 'Concepts and a Model for the Comparison of Medical Systems as Cultural Systems', *Social Science & Medicine. Part B: Medical Anthropology*, 12 (1978), 85–93

——, *Patients and Healers in the Context of Culture* (Berkeley: University of California Press, 1989)

Knipp, David, 'The Chapel of Physicians at Santa Maria Antiqua', *Dumbarton Oaks Papers*, 56 (2002), 1–23

Kötting, Bernhard, *Peregrinatio religiosa: Wallfahrten in der Antike und das Pilgerwesen in der alten Kirche* (Münster: Regensberg, 1950)

Krueger, Derek, 'Early Byzantine Historiography and Hagiography as Different Modes of Christian Practice', in *Writing 'True Stories': Historians and Hagiographers in the Late Antique and Mediaeval Near East*, ed. by Arietta Papaconstantinou, Muriel Debié, and Hugh Kennedy, Cultural Encounters in Late Antiquity and the Middle Ages, 9 (Turnhout: Brepols, 2010), pp. 13–20

——, *Writing and Holyness: The Practice of Authorship in the Early Christian East* (Philadelphia: University of Pennsylvania Press, 2004)

Krug, Antje, *Heilkunst und Heilkult: Medizin in der Antike* (Munich: C. H. Beck, 1985)

Kruger, Steven F., *Dreaming in the Middle Ages* (Cambridge: Cambridge University Press, 1992)

Lang, Mabel, *Cure and Cult in Ancient Corinth* (Princeton, NJ: American School of Classical Studies at Athens, 1977)

Laurent, J., 'Sur la date des églises Saint Démétrius et Sainte-Sophie à Thessalonique', *Byzantinische Zeitschrift*, 4 (1895), 420–34

Laurent, Vitalien, *La vie merveilleuse de S. Pierre d'Atroa* (Brussels: Société des Bollandistes, 1956)

——, *La vita retractata et les Miracles posthumes de saint Pierre d'Atroa* (Brussels: Société des Bollandistes, 1958)

Le Goff, Jacques, 'Le christianisme et les rêves (IIe–VIIe siècle)', in *L'imaginaire médiéval* (Paris: Gallimard, 1985), pp. 265–316

——, 'Les rêves dans la culture et la psychologie collective de l'Occident médiéval', in *Pour un autre Moyen Age: Temps, travail et culture en Occident. 18 essais* (Paris: Gallimard, 1977), pp. 299–306

Lecos, E. P., and Gerasimos E. Pentogalos, 'Early and Late Asclepieia', in *Ancient and Popular Healing: Symposium on Ancient Medicine, Athens, 4–10 October, 1986*, ed. by Paavo Castren (Athens: Finnish Institute at Athens, 1989), pp. 13–25

Lehmann, Karl, 'Ein Reliefbild des Heiligen Artemios in Konstaninopel', *Byzantinisch-Neugriechishe Jahrbücher*, 1 (1920), 381–84

Lévy, Edmond, 'Le rêve homérique', *Ktema*, 7 (1982), 23–42

Lieshout, R. G. A. van, *Greeks on Dreams* (Utrecht: HES Publishers, 1980)

Lieu, Judith, John North, and Tessa Rajak, eds, *The Jews among Pagans and Christians in the Roman Empire* (London: Kegan Paul, 1992)

Lieu, Samuel N. C., 'From Villain to Saint and Martyr – Flavius Artemius Dux Aegypti', *Byzantine and Modern Greek Studies*, 20 (1996), 56–76

Lifshitz, Felice, 'Beyond Positivism and Genre: Hagiographical Texts as Historical Narrative', *Viator*, 25 (1994), 95–113

Ligota, Charles R., 'This Story Is Not True: Fact and Fiction in Antiquity', *Journal of the Warburg and Courtauld Institutes*, 45 (1982), 1–13

Longo, Vincenzo, *Aretalogie nel mondo Greco*, I: *Epigrafi e papiri* (Genova: Istituto di Filologia Classica e Medioevale, 1969)

Loos, Hendrik van der, *The Miracles of Jesus*, trans. by Trevor S. Preston (Leiden: Brill, 1965)

Lopez Salva, Mercedes, 'Afecciones orquíticas y curaciones oníricas en el templo del Precursor de Oxeia: Contribución a la historia de la medicina', *Erytheia: Revista de estudios bizantinos y neogriegos*, 17 (1996), 21–40

——, 'Observaciones lexicales a los "Thaumata" de Artemio y de Cosma e Damián', *Cuadernos de Filología Clásica*, 8 (1975), 303–20

——, 'El sueño incubatorio en el cristianismo oriental', *Cuadernos de Filología Clásica*, 10 (1976), 147–88

Lord, Albert B., *The Singer of Tales*, 2nd edn (Cambridge, MA: Harvard University Press, 2000)

Lucius, Ernst, *Die Anfänge des Heiligenkults in der christlichen Kirche* (Tübingen: J. C. B. Mohr, 1904); in French as *Les origines du culte des saints* (Paris, 1908)

Luongo, Gennaro, 'Il *dossier* agiografico dei Santi Cosma e Damiano', offprint from *Sant' Eufemia d'Aspromonte: Atti del convegno*, ed. by Sandro Leanza (Catanzaro: Soveria Manelli, 1997)

Maas, Paul, 'Artemioskult in Konstantinopel', *Byzantinisch-Neugriechishe Jahrbücher*, 1 (1920), 377–80

——, 'Review of Ludwig Deubner's Kosmas und Damian', *Byzantinishe Zeitschrift*, 17 (1908), 602–09

Magdalino, Paul, 'What We Heard in the Lives of the Saints We Have Seen with our Own Eyes: The Holy Man as Literary Text in Tenth-Century Constantinople', in *The Cult of Saints in Late Antiquity and the Early Middle Ages: Essays on the Contribution of Peter Brown*, ed. by James Howard-Johnston and Paul A. Hayward (Oxford: Oxford University Press, 1999), pp. 83–112

Magoulias, Harry J., 'The Lives of the Saints as Sources of Data for the History of Byzantine Medicine in the Sixth and Seventh Centuries', *Byzantinische Zeitschrift*, 57 (1964), 127–50

——, 'The Lives of the Saints as Sources of Data for the History of Magic in the Sixth and Seventh Centuries A.D.: Sorcery, Relics and Icons', *Byzantion*, 37 (1967), 228–69

Maguire, Henry, 'Magic and Christian Image', in *Byzantine Magic*, ed. by Henry Maguire (Washington, DC: Dumbarton Oaks Research Library and Collection, 1995), pp. 51–72

Mallardo, Domenico, 'L'incubatione nella cristianità medievale napoletana', *Analecta Bollandiana*, 67 (1949), 465–98

Mango, Cyril, *The Art of the Byzantine Empire: Sources and Documents in the History of Art* (Englewood Cliffs, NJ: Prentice-Hall, 1972)

——, 'A Byzantine Hagiographer at Work: Leontinos of Neapolis', in *Byzanz und der Westen: Studien zur Kunst des europäischen Mittelalters*, ed. by Irmgard Hutter and Herbert Hunger (Vienna: Österreichische Akademie der Wissenschaften, 1984), pp. 25–41

——, 'On the History of the *Templon* and the Martyrion of St Artemios at Constantinople', *Zograf*, 10 (1979), 40–43

Maraval, Pierre, 'Fonction pédagogique de la littérature hagiographique d'un lieu de pèlerinage: L'exemple des Miracles de Cyr et Jean', in *Hagiographie, cultures et sociétés IV*^{e}*–XII*^{e} *siècles: Actes du Colloque organisé à Nanterre et à Paris (2–5 mai 1979)*, ed. by Evelyn Patlagean and Pierre Riché (Paris: Études Augustiniennes, 1981), pp. 383–97

——, 'Songes et visions comme mode d'invention des reliques', in *Sogni, visioni e profezie nell'antico cristianesimo: XVII Incontro di studiosi dell' Antiquità cristiana, Roma 5–7 Maggio, 1987*, special issue, *Augustinianum*, 29 (1989), 583–99

Mathews, Thomas F., *The Clash of Gods: A Reinterpretation of Early Christian Art* (Princeton, NJ: Princeton University Press, 1993)

Maury, M. Alfred, 'Du temple appelé Sosthenium, qui existait avant Constantin au lieu appelé Hestiae, pres de Constantinople et de sa conversion en une église consacrée a saint Michel', *Revue Archeologique*, 6 (1849), 144–63

Mazzini, Innocenzo, 'La malattia e metafora del peccato nel mondo antico, pagano e cristiano' in *Cultura e Promozione umana: La cura del corpo e dello spirito nell'antichità classica e nei primi secoli Cristiani*, ed. by Enrico Dal Covolo and Isidoro Giannetto (Troina: Oasi, 1998), pp. 159–72

McCasland, Vernon, 'The Asclepios Cult in Palestine', *Journal of Biblical Literature*, 58 (1939), 221–28

McKenzie, Judith, *The Architecture of Alexandria and Egypt, c. 300 B.C. to A.D. 700* (New Haven, CT: Yale University Press, 2007)

Meier, Carl A., 'The Dream in Ancient Greece and its Use in Temple Cures (Incubation)', in *The Dream and Human Societies*, ed. by G. E. von Grunebaum and Roger Caillois (Berkeley: University of California Press, 1966), pp. 303–19

——, *Healing Dream and Ritual: Ancient Incubation and Modern Psychotherapy* (Switzerland: Daimon Verlag, 1918; repr. 1989)

Menze, Volker, *Justinian and the Making of the Syrian Orthodox Church*, Oxford Early Christian Studies (Oxford: Oxford University Press, 2008)

Merola, Nicola, and Caterina Verbaro, eds., *Il sogno raccontato* (Vibo Valentia: Monteleone, 2017)

Messer, William Stuart, *The Dream in Homer and Greek Tragedy* (New York: Columbia University Press, 1918)

Meyerhof, Max, *Von Alexandrien nach Bagdad: Ein beitrag zur Geschichte des Philosophischen und Medizinischen Unterrichts bei den Arabern* (Berlin: Verlag der Akademie der Wissenschaften in Kommission bei Walter de Gruyter, 1930)

Miller, S. Timothy, *The Birth of the Hospital in the Byzantine Empire* (Baltimore: Johns Hopkins University Press, 1985)

——, 'Byzantine Hospitals', in *Symposium on Byzantine Medicine*, ed. by John Scarborough, special issue, *Dumbarton Oaks Papers*, 38 (1984), 53–63

Misset-van de Weg, Magda, 'Magic, Miracle and Miracle Workers in the Acts of Thecla', in *Women and Miracle Stories: A Multidisciplinary Exploration*, ed. by Anne-Maria Körte (Leiden: Brill, 2000), pp. 29–52

Mittermaier, Amira, *Dreams That Matter: Egyptian Landscapes of the Imagination* (Berkeley: University of California Press, 2011)

Montserrat, Dominic, 'Pilgrimage to the Shrine of SS Cyrus and John at Menouthis in Late Antiquity', in *Pilgrimage and Holy Space in Late Antique Egypt*, ed. by David Frankfurter (Leiden: Brill, 1998), pp. 257–79

Moulinier, Louis, *Le pur et l'impur dans la pensée des Grecs d'Homère a Aristote* (Paris: Librairie C. Klinksiech, 1952)

Murray, Oswyn, 'Herodotus and Oral History', in *The Historian's Craft in the Age of Herodotus*, ed. by Nino Luraghi (Oxford: Oxford University Press, 2001), pp. 16–44

Musurillo, Herbert A., 'The Pagan Acts of the Martyrs', *Theological Studies*, 10 (1949), 555–64

Nelson, N. Benjamin, and Joshua Starr, 'The Legend of the Divine Surety and the Jewish Moneylender', *Annuaire de l'Institute de Philologie et d'Histoire Orientales et Slaves*, 7 (1939–1944), 289–338

Neyrey, H. Jerome, 'Miracles, in Other Words: Social Science Perspectives on Healings', in *Miracles in Jewish and Christian Antiquity: Imagining Truth*, ed. by John C. Cavadini (Notre Dame: University of Notre Dame Press, 1999), pp. 19–56

Nissen, Theodorus, 'De SS. Cyri et Johannis Vitae formis', *Analecta Bollandiana*, 57 (1939), 65–71

Nock, Arthur Darby, *Conversion: The Old and New in Religion from Alexander the Great to Augustine of Hippo* (Oxford: Clarendon Press, 1933)

——, 'Review of Raffaele Pettazoni, *La confessione dei peccati*, Vol. 1–3', *Gnomon*, 15 (1939), 18–23

——, 'Soter and Euergetes', in *Essays on Religion and the Ancient World*, ed. by Zeph Stewart (Cambridge, MA: Harvard University Press, 1972), II, pp. 722–35

Noorda, Sijbolt, 'Illness and Sin, Forgiving and Healing', in *Studies in Hellenistic Religions*, ed. by Maarten Jozef Vermarsen (Leiden: Brill, 1979), pp. 215–24

Nutton, Vivian, *Ancient Medicine* (London: Routledge, 2004)

——, 'From Galen to Alexander: Aspects of Medicine and Medical Practice in Late Antiquity', in *Symposium on Byzantine Medicine*, ed. John Scarborough, special issue, *Dumbarton Oaks Papers*, 38 (1984), 1–14

——, 'God, Galen and the Depaganization of Medicine', in *Religion and Medicine in the Middle Ages*, ed. by Peter Biller and Joseph Ziegler (York: York Medieval Press, 2001), pp. 17–32

Oberhelman, Steven M., 'Dreams in Graeco-Roman Medicine', in *ANRW*, II: Principat XXXVII.1, pp. 121–56

——, 'The Interpretation of Prescriptive Dreams in Ancient Greek Medicine', *Journal of the History of Medicine and Allied Sciences*, 36 (1981), 416–24

Oppenheim, Leo, 'The Interpretation of Dreams in the Ancient Near East', *Transactions of the American Philosophical Society*, 46.3 (1956), 179–373

Osborn, John, 'The Atrium of S. Maria Antiqua, Rome: A History in Art', *Papers of the British School at Rome*, 55 (1987), 186–223

Otranto, Giorgio, and Carlo Carletti, *Il Santuario di S. Michele Arcangelo sul Gargano dalle origini al X secolo* (Bari: Edipuglia, 1990)

Papaconstantinou, Arietta, *Le culte des saints en Égypte des Byzantins aux Abbasides: L'apport des inscriptions et des papyrus grecs et coptes* (Paris: CNRS, 2001)

Papadopoulos-Kerameus, A., *Varia Graeca Sacra* (St. Petersburg: At the University, 1909; repr. Leipzig, 1975)

Parker, Robert, *Miasma: Pollution and Purification in Early Greek Religion* (Oxford: Clarendon Press, 1983)

Parmentier, Mark, 'Incubatie in de antike hagiografie', in *De heiligenverering in de eerste eeuwen van het christendom*, ed. by Antonius Hilhorst (Nijmegen: Dekker & van de Vegt, 1988), pp. 27–40

Parry, Milman, 'Project for a Study of Jugoslavian Popular Oral Poetry' (typewritten reports from Parry, Milman Parry Collection, Harvard, Widener Library), repr. in Albert B. Lord, *The Singer of Tales*, 2nd edn (Cambridge, MA: Harvard University Press, 2000)

Patlagean, Evelyne, 'Ancienne hagiographie byzantine et histoire sociale', *Annales E.S.C.*, 23 (1968), 106–26

——, 'Discours écrit, discours parlé: Niveaux de culture à Byzance aux VIIIe–XIe siècles (Note critique)', *Annales E.S.C.*, 34 (1979), 264–78

——, ed., *Maladie et société à Byzance* (Spoleto: Centro italiano di studi sull'alto Medioevo, 1993)

——, *Pauvreté économique et pauvreté sociale à Byzance 4–7 siècles* (Paris: La Haye, 1977)

——, *Structure sociale, famille, chrétienté à Byzance: IVe–XIe siècles* (London: Variorum Reprints, 1981)

Peabody, Berkley, *The Winged Word: A Study in the Technique of Ancient Greek Oral Composition as Seen Principally through Hesiod's Works and Days* (Albany: State University of New York Press, 1975)

Peace, Arthur Stanley, 'Medical Allusions in the Works of St Jerome', *Harvard Studies in Classical Philology*, 25 (1914), 73–86

Peeters, Paul, 'S. Dometios le martyr et S. Dometios le médecin', *Analecta Bollandiana*, 57 (1939), 72–104

Petsalis-Diomidis, Alexia, 'Between the Body and the Divine: Healing Votives from Classical and Hellenistic Greece', in *Ex Voto: Votive Giving Across Cultures*, ed. by Ittai Weinryb (New York: Bard Graduate Center, 2016), pp. 49–75

——, 'Sacred Writing, Sacred Reading: The Function of Aelius Aristides' Self-Presentation as Author in the "Sacred Tales"', in *The Limits of Ancient Biography*, ed. by J. Mossman and B. McGing (Swansea: Classical Press of Wales, 2006), pp. 193–211

——, *'Truly Beyond Wonders': Aelius Aristides and the Cult of Asklepios* (Oxford: Oxford University Press, 2010)

Pettazzoni, Raffaele, 'Confession of Sins and the Classics', *Harvard Theological Review*, 30 (1937), 1–14

——, *La confessione dei peccati*, 3 vols (Bologna: N. Zanichelli, 1936)

Pilch, J. John, 'Insights and Models for Understanding the Healing Activity of the Historical Jesus', in *Society of Biblical Literature Seminar Papers: 1993* (Atlanta: Scholars Press, 1994), pp. 154–77

——, 'Understanding Biblical Healing: Selecting the Appropriate Model', *Biblical Theology Bulletin*, 18 (1988), 60–66

——, 'Understanding Healing in the Social World of Early Christianity', *Biblical Theology Bulletin*, 22 (1992), 26–33

Pizarro, Joaquin Martinez, *A Rhetoric of the Scene: Dramatic Narrative in the Early Middle Ages* (Toronto: University of Toronto Press, 1989)

Pratsch, Thomas, 'Exploring the Jungle: Hagiographical Literature between Fact and Fiction', in *Fifty Years of Prosopography: The Later Roman Empire, Byzantium and Beyond*, ed. by Averil Cameron, Proceedings of the British Academy, 118 (Oxford: Oxford University Press, 2003), pp. 59–72

——, *Der hagiographische Topos: Griechische Heiligenviten in mittelbyzantinischer Zeit* (Berlin: de Gruyter, 2005)

——, 'Rhetorik in der byzantinischen Hagiographie: Die Prooimia der Heiligenviten', in *Theatron: Rhetorische Kultur in Spätantike und Mittelalter / Rhetorical Culture in Late Antiquity and the Middle Ages*, ed by. Michael Grünbart, Millennium-Studien, 13 (Berlin: de Gruyter, 2007), pp. 377–408

Price, Richard M., *Cyril of Scythopolis: The Lives of the Monks of Palestine*, Cistercian Studies, 114 (Kalamazoo: Medieval Institute Publications, 1991)

Privitera, G. Aurelio, ed., *Paideia Cristiana: Studi in onore di Mario Naldini* (Rome: Gruppo Editoriale Internazionale, 1994)

Propp, Vladimir, *Morphology of the Folktale*, trans. by Laurence Scott, 2nd edn (Austin: University of Texas Press, 1968)

Rademacher, Ludwig, 'Die Wunder Theklas', in *Hippolytus und Thekla: Studien zur Geschichte von Legende und Kultus* (Vienna: A. Hölden, 1916), pp. 121–26

Rapp, Claudia, 'Byzantine Hagiographers as Antiquarians, Seventh to Tenth Centuries', in *Bosphorus: Essays in Honour of Cyril Mango*, ed. by Stephanos Efthymiadis, Claudia Rapp, and Dimitris Tsougarakis (Amsterdam: Hakkert, 1995), pp. 31–44

——, 'For Next to God, You Are my Salvation: Reflections on the Rise of the Holy Man in Late Antiquity', in *The Cult of Saints in Late Antiquity and the Middle Ages: Essays on the Contribution of Peter Brown*, ed. by James Howard-Johnston and Paul A. Hayward (Oxford: Oxford University Press, 1999), pp. 63–81

——, 'The Origins of Hagiography and the Literature of Early Monasticism: Between Invention and Tradition', in *Unclassical Traditions*, I: *Alternatives to the Classical Past in Late Antiquity*, ed. by Christopher Kelly, Richard Flower, and Michael Stuart Williams, Proceedings of the Cambridge Philological Society, Suppl. 34 (Cambridge: Cambridge Philological Society, 2010), pp. 119–30

Reinach, Salomon, 'Les Arétalogues dans l'Antiquité', *Bulletin de correspondense hellénique*, 9 (1885), 257–65

Reitzenstein, Richard, *Hellenistische Wundererzählungen* (Leipzig: Teubner, 1906)

Remus, Harold, *Jesus as Healer* (Cambridge: Cambridge University Press, 1997)

——, *Pagan–Christian Conflict over Miracle in the Second Century* (Philadelphia: Philadelphia Patristic Foundation, 1983)

Renberg, Gil, *Where Dreams May Come: Incubation Sanctuaries in the Greco-Roman World*, 2 vols (Leiden: Brill, 2017)

Riethmüller, Jürgen W., *Asklepios: Heiligtümer und Kulte*, 2 vols, Studien zu Antiken Heiligtümern (Heidelberg: Verlag Archäologie und Geschichte, 2005)

Robert, Louis, 'De Cilicie à Messine et à Plymouth, avec deux inscriptions grecques errantes', *Journal des savants*, 3 (1973), 161–211

Rohde, Erwin, *Psiche: Culto delle anime e fede nell'immortalità pressi I Greci* (Rome: Laterza, 2006); originally published, *Psyche: Seelencult und Unsterblichkeitsglaube der Griechen*, 2 vols (Freiburg, 1894)

Rosenqvist, Jan Olof, 'Miracles and Medical Learning: The Case of St Eugenios of Trebizond', *Byzantinoslavica*, 56.2 (1995), 461–69

Rouse, William Henry Denham, *Greek Votive Offerings: An Essay in the History of Greek Religion* (Cambridge: Cambridge University Press, 1902)

Rousselle, Alaine, *Croire et guérir: La foi en Gaule dans l'Antiquité tardive* (Paris: Fayard, 1990)

Rustafjaell, Robert de, *The Light of Egypt from Recently Discovered Predynastic and Early Christian Records* (London: Kegan Paul, 1909)

Rüttimann, René Joseph, 'Asclepius and Jesus: The Form, Character and Status of the Asclepius Cult in the Second Century CE and its Influence on Early Christianity' (unpublished doctoral dissertation, Harvard University, 1986)

Rydén, Lennart, 'Kyrkan som sjukhus: Om den helige Artemius' mirakler', *Religion och Bibel*, 44 (1985), 3–16

——, 'New Forms of Hagiography: Heroes and Saints', in *The 17th International Byzantine Congress: Major Papers, Dumbarton Oaks/Georgetown University, Washington, D.C., August 3–8, 1986* (New Rochelle, NY: Aristide D. Caratzas, 1986), pp. 534–54

——, 'Ueberlegungen zum literarischen Wert oder Unwert hagiographischer Texte', *Eranos*, 91 (1993), 47–60

Rzeźnicka, Zofia, Maciej Kokoszko, and Krzysztof Jagusiak, 'Cured Meats in Ancient and Byzantine Sources: Ham, Bacon and Tuccetum', *Studia Ceranea*, 4 (2014), 245–59

Sahas, J., 'What an Infidel Saw that a Faithful Did Not: Gregory Dekapolites (d. 842) and Islam', *Greek Orthodox Theological Review*, 31.1–2 (1986), 47–67

Saintyves, Pierre, *Les saints successeurs des dieux* (Paris: E. Nowrry, 1907)

Sansterre, Jean-Marie, 'Apparitions et miracles à Menouthis: De l'incubation païenne à l'incubation chrétienne', in *Apparitions et Miracles*, ed. by Alain Dierkens (Brussels: Éditions de l'Université de Brussels, 1991), pp. 69–83

Saradi, Helen, 'Constantinople and its Saints (IV–VI c.): The Image of the City and Social Considerations', *Studi Medievali*, 36.1 (1995), 87–110

Saxer, Victor, 'Jalons pour servir à l'histoire du culte de l'archange Saint Michel en orient jusqu'à l'Iconoclasme', in *Noscere Sancta: Miscellanea in memoria di Agostino Amore OFM*, ed. by Isaac Vázquez Janeiro OFM (Rome: Pontificium Athenaeum Antonianum, 1985), I, pp. 357–426

Scarborough, John, 'Symposium on Byzantine Medicine: Introduction', in *Symposium on Byzantine Medicine*, ed. by John Scarborough, special issue, *Dumbarton Oaks Papers*, 38 (1984)

Schadewaldt, Hans, 'Die Apologie der Heilkunst bei den Kirchenvätern', *Veroeffentlichungen ger internationalen Gelleschaft für Geschichte der Pharmazie*, 26 (1965), 115–30

Schipperges, Heinrich, 'Zur tradition des "Christus Medicus" im früchen Christentum und in der älteren Heilkunde', *Arzt und Christ*, 11 (1965), 12–20

Schlumberger, Gustave, 'Amulettes byzantines anciens à combattre les maléfices et maladies', *Revue des Études Grecques*, 5 (1892), 73–93

Schouten, Jan, *The Rod and the Serpent of Asklepios: Symbol of Medicine* (Amsterdam: Elsevier, 1967)

Schönborn, Christoph von, 'Sophrone de Jérusalem (Saint)', in *Dictionnaire de spiritualité ascétique et mystique, doctrine et histoire* (Paris: Beauchesne, 1988), fasc. 91, pp. 1066–73

——, *Sophrone de Jérusalem: Vie monastique et confession dogmatique* (Paris: Beauchesne, 1972)

Secher Bøgh, Birgitte, ed., *Conversion and Initiation in Antiquity: Shifting Identities – Creating Change. Papers Originally Presented at a Conference Held in Ebeltoft, Denmark, December 1st–4th, 2012, at Aarhus University*, Early Christianity in the Context of Antiquity, 16 (Frankfurt am Main: Lang, 2014)

Seiber, Julia, *Urban Saint in Early Byzantine Social History*, British Archaeological Reports, Suppl. Ser., 37 (Oxford: British Archaeological Reports, 1977)

Ševčenko, Ihor, 'La agiografia bizantina dal IV al IX secolo', in *La civiltà bizantina dal IV al IX secolo*, ed. by André Guillou (Bari: L'Erma di Bretschneider, 1977), pp. 87–173

——, 'Hagiography of the Iconoclast Period', in *Iconoclasm*, ed. by Anthony Bryer and Judith Herrin (Birmingham: Centre for Byzantine Studies, University of Birmingham, 1977), pp. 113–31; repr. in *Ideology, Letters and Culture in the Byzantine World* (London: Variorum Reprints, 1982)

——, 'Levels of Style in Byzantine Prose', *Jahrbuch der Osterreichischen Byzantinistik*, 31 (1981), 289–312; repr. in *Ideology, Letters and Culture in the Byzantine World* (London: Variorum Reprints, 1982)

——, 'A Shadow Outline of Virtue: The Classical Heritage of Greek Christian Literature (Second to Seventh Century)', in *Age of Spirituality: A Symposium*, ed. by Kurt Weitzmann (New York: Metropolitan Museum of Art, 1980), pp. 53–73

Sharf, Andrew, *Byzantine Jewry from Justinian to the Fourth Crusade* (London: Routledge and Kegan Paul, 1971)

Siebenthal, Wolf von, *Krankheit als Folge der Sünde* (Hannover, 1950)

Simon, Jean, 'Note sur l'original de la Passion de Sainte Fébronie', *Analecta Bollandiana*, 42 (1924), 69–76

Simon, Marcel, *Verus Israel: Étude sur les relations entre chrétiens et juifs dans l'empire romaine (135–425)* (Paris: E. de Boccard, 1964); in English as *Verus Israel: A Study of the Relations between Christians and Jews in the Roman Empire, 135–425*, trans. by Henry McKeating (Oxford: Oxford University Press, 1986)

Sigal, Pierre-André, *L'homme et le miracle dans la France médiéval (XI–XII siècle)* (Paris: Édition du Cerf, 1985)

Skrobucha, Heinz, *Kosmas und Damian*, Iconographia ecclesiae orientalis (Reckinghausen: A. Bongers, 1965); in English as *The Patrons of Doctors*, Pictorial Library of Eastern Church Art, 7 (Reckinghausen: A. Bongers, 1967)

Smith, Dennis Edwin, *From Symposium to Eucharist: The Banquet in the Early Christian World* (Minneapolis, 2003)

Smith, Morton, *Jesus the Magician* (San Francisco: Harper and Row, 1978)

——, 'Prolegomena to a Discussion of Aretalogies, Divine Men, the Gospels, and Jesus', *Journal of Biblical Literature*, 90 (1971), 174–99

Sodini, Jean-Pierre, 'Les cryptes d'autel: Essai de classification', *Travaux et Mémoires du Centre de Recherche d'Histoire et Civilisation de Byzance*, 8 (1981), 437–58

Speck, Paul, 'Wunderheilige und Bilder: Zur Frage des Beginns der Bilderverehrung', *POIKILA BYZANTINA*, 11 (1991), 163–247

Spieser, Jean-Michel, 'La christianisation des sanctuaires païens en Grèce', in *Neue Forschungen in griechischen Heiligtümern*, ed. by Ulf Jantzen (Tübingen: Wasmuth, 1976), pp. 309–20

Starr, Joshua, *The Jews in the Byzantine Empire, 641–1204* (Athens: Verlag der Byzaninisch–Neugriechischen Jahrbücher, 1939)

Steger, Florian, *Asklepiosmedizin: Medizinischer Alltag in der römischen Kaiserzeit* (Stuttgart: Franz Steiner Verlag, 2004)

Stewart, Charles, 'Ritual Dreams and Historical Orders: Incubation between Paganism and Christianity', in *Greek Ritual Poetics*, ed. by Dimitrios Yatromanolakis and Panagiotis Roilos (Washington, DC: Center for Hellenic Studies, 2004), pp. 338–55

Straten, Folkert van, 'Daikrates' Dream: A Votive Relief from Kos, and Some Other Kat'Onar Dedications', *Bulletin antike Beschaving*, 5l (1976), 1–38

——, 'Gifts for the Gods', in *Faith, Hope and Worship: Aspects of Religious Mentality in the Ancient World*, ed. by Henk Simon Versnel (Leiden: Brill, 1981), pp. 65–151

Stroumsa, G. Guy, 'Dreams and Visions in Early Christian Discourse', in *Dream Cultures: Explorations in the Comparative History of Dreaming*, ed. by David Shulman and Guy G. Stroumsa (Oxford: Oxford University Press, 1999), pp. 189–212

Taffin, André, 'Comment on rêvait dans le temple d'Aesculape', *Bulletin de l'Association G. Budé*, 1960, 325–66

Takács, Sarolta, 'The Magic of Isis Replaced or Cyril of Alexandria's Attempt at Redirecting Religious Devotion', *POIKILA BYZANTINA*, 13 (1994), 489–507

Talbert, Charles H., 'Biographies of Philosophers and Rulers as Instruments of Religious Propaganda in Mediterranean Antiquity', in *ANRW*, II: Principat XVI.2, pp. 1619–51

Talbot, Alice-Marie, 'Healing Shrines in Late Byzantine Constantinople', in her *Women and Religious Life in Byzantium* (Aldershot: Ashgate, 2001), pp. 1–24

——, 'Metaphrasis in the Early Palaiologan Period: The Miracula of Kosmas and Damian by Maximos the Deacon', in *The Heroes of the Orthodox Church: The New Saints, 8th–16th Centuries*, ed. by Eleonora Kountoura-Galake (Athens: Institute for Byzantine Research, 2004), pp. 227–37

——, 'Two Accounts of Miracles at the Pege Shrine in Constantinople', in *Travaux et Mémoires*, XIV: *Mélanges Gilbert Dagron* (Paris: Association des Amis du Centre d'Histoire et Civilisation de Byzance, 2002), pp. 605–15

Tea, Eva, *La basilica di Santa Maria Antiqua* (Milan: Universita Cattolica di Sacro Cuore, 1937)

Temkin, Oswei, *Hippocrates in the World of Pagans and Christians* (Baltimore: Johns Hopkins University Press, 1991)

Temkin, Oswei, and Lilian C. Temkin, eds, *Ancient Medicine: Selected Papers of Ludwig Edelstein* (Baltimore: Johns Hopkins University Press, 1967)

Theissen, Gerd, 'Itinerant Radicalism: The Tradition of Jesus Sayings from the Perspective of the Sociology of Literature', *Radical Religion*, 2 (1976), 84–93

——, *The Miracle Stories of the Early Christian Tradition*, trans. by F. McDonagh (Philadelphia: Fortress Press, 1983)

Thompson, Edward Arthur, 'The Last Delphic Oracle', *Classical Quarterly*, 40.1 (1946), 35–36

Thrämer, Eduard, 'Health and Gods of Healing (Greek)', in *Encyclopedia of Religion and Ethics*, ed. by J. Hastings (New York: Ch. Scribner's Sons, 1914), VI, pp. 540–53

Tinker, George E., 'Medicine and Miracle: A Comparison of Two Healing Types in the Late Hellenistic World' (unpublished doctoral dissertation, Graduate Theological Union, 1983)

Turner, Victor, and Edith Turner, *Image and Pilgrimage in Christian Culture: Anthropological Perspectives* (Oxford: Blackwell, 1978)

Ustinova, Yulia, 'Either a Daimon, or a Hero, or Perhaps a God: Mythical Residents of Subterranean Chambers', *Kernos*, 15 (2002), 267–88

Uytfanghe, Mark van, 'La controverse biblique et patristique autour du miracle et ses répercussions sur l'hagiographie dans l'Antiquité tardive et le haut Moyen Âge latin', in *Hagiographie, cultures et sociétés IVe–XIIe siècles: Actes du Colloque organisé à Nanterre et à Paris (2–5 mai 1979)*, ed. by Evelyn Patlagean and Pierre Riché (Paris: Études Augustiniennes, 1981), pp. 205–33

——, 'L'hagiografie: Un "genre" chrétien ou antique tardif?', *Analecta Bollandiana*, 111 (1993), 135–88

Vailhé, Siméon, 'Sophrone le sophiste et Sophrone le patriarche', *Revue d'Orient Chrétien*, 7 (1902), 361–85; 8 (1903), 32–69, 356–87

Van Cangh, Jean Marie, 'Santé et salut dans les miracles d'Epidaure, d'Apollonius de Tyane et de Nouveau Testament', in *Gnosticisme et monde hellénistique*, ed. by Julien Ries and others (Louvain: Université Catholique de Louvain, 1982), pp. 263–77

Vanderlinden, S., 'Revelatio Sancti Stephani (BHG 7850-6)', *Revue des études byzantines*, 4 (1946), 178–217

Vansina, Jan, *Oral Tradition as History* (Madison: University of Wisconsin Press, 1985)

Varinlioğlu, Ender, 'Eine Gruppe von Sühneinschriften aus dem Museum von Usak', *Epigraphica Anatolica*, 13 (1989), 37–50

Velmans, Tania, 'L'image de la Déisis dans les églises de Géorgie et dans celles d'autres régions du monde byzantine', *Cahiers archéologiques*, 29 (1980–1981), 47–102

Versnel, Henk Simon, 'Religious Mentality in Ancient Prayer', in *Faith, Hope and Worship: Aspects of Religious Mentality in the Ancient World*, ed. by Henk Simon Versnel (Leiden: Brill, 1981), pp. 1–64

——, 'What Did Ancient Man See When He Saw a God? Some Reflections on Greco-Roman Epiphany', in *Effigies Dei: Essays on the History of Religions*, ed. by Dirk van der Plas (Leiden: Brill, 1987), pp. 42–55

Vidman, Ladislav, *Isis und Sarapis bei den Griechen und Römern: Epigraphische Studien zu den Trägern des ägytpischen Kulte* (Berlin: de Gruyter, 1970)

Vikan, Gary, 'Art, Medicine and Magic in Early Byzantium', *Dumbarton Oaks Papers*, 38 (1984), 65–86

——, *Byzantine Pilgrimage Art* (Washington, DC: Dumbarton Oaks, 1982); rev. edn as *Early Byzantine Pilgrimage Art*, Dumbarton Oaks Collection Publications, 5 (Washington, DC: Dumbarton Oaks, 2011)

Vooght, Paul de, 'La notion philosophique du miracle chez saint Augustin dans le "De Trinitate" et le "De Genesi ad litteram"', *Recherches de théologie ancienne et médiévale*, 10 (1938), 317–43

Wacht, Manfred, 'Inkubation', in *Reallexikon für Antike und Christentum*, ed. by Ernst Dassmann (Stuttgart: Hiersemann, 1997), XVIII, cols 179–265

Walde, Christine, *Die Traumdarstellungen in der griechisch-römischen Dichtung* (Munich: K. G. Saur, 2001)

Weinreich, Otto, *Antike Heilungswunder*, Religiongeschichte Versuche und Vorarbeiten, 8.1 (Giessen: Alfred Töpelmann, 1909; 2nd edn, 1969)

Werner, Herzog, 'Zum Λούκιος ἢ ὄνος', *Hermes*, 53 (1918), 225–61

West, Martin L., 'The Singing of Hexameters: Evidence from Epidaurus', *Zeitschrift für Papyrologie und Epigraphik*, 63 (1986), 39–46

Westerink, Leendert Gerrit, 'Philosophy and Medicine in Late Antiquity', *Janus*, 51 (1964), 169–77; repr. in his *Texts and Studies in Neoplatonism and Byzantine Literature* (Amsterdam: Hakkert, 1980), pp. 83–91

Weyh, Wilhelm, *Die syrische Kosmas – und Damian-Legende* (Schweinfurt: Druck der Reichardt'schen, 1910)

Wilkinson, John, *Egeria's Travels*, 3rd edn (Warminster: Aris and Phillips, 1999)

——, *Jerusalem Pilgrims before the Crusades*, 2nd edn (Warminster: Aris and Phillips, 2002)

Wipszycka, Eva, 'La Christianisation de Égypte aux IV–VI siècles: Aspects sociaux et ethniques', *Aegyptus*, 68 (1988), 117–65

——, 'Les confréries dans la via religieuse de l'Égypte chrétienne', in *Proceedings of the Twelfth International Congress of Papyrology*, ed. by Deborah H. Samuel, American Studies in Papyrology, 7 (Toronto: A. M. Hakkert, 1970), pp. 511–24

Wiśniewski, Robert, *The Beginnings of the Cult of Relics* (Oxford: Oxford University Press, 2019)

——, *Christian Divination in Late Antiquity* (Amsterdam: Amsterdam University Press, 2020)

——, 'Looking for Dreams and Talking with Martyrs: Internal Roots of Christian Incubation', *Studia Patristica*, 63 (2013), 203–08

Wittmann, Annalise, *Kosmas und Damian* (Berlin: E. Schmidt, 1967)

Zeppezauer, Dorothea, 'Warum wirken Wunder? Die Sprache der Ärzte im Traum', *Zeitschrift für Antikes Christentum*, 17.1 (2013), 143–59

Ziegler, Robert, 'Aigeai, der Asklepioskult, das Kaiserhaus der Decier und das Christentum', *Tyche*, 9 (1984), 187–212

Zimmermann, Kees W., *One Leg in the Grave: The Miracle of the Transplantation of the Black Leg by the Saints Cosmas and Damian* (Maarsen: Elsevier/Bunge, 1998)

Zipser, Barbara, ed., *Medical Books in the Byzantine World* (Bologna: Eikasmos, 2013)

——, 'Medicine, Byzantine', in *Encyclopedia of Medieval Philosophy*, ed. by Henrik Lagerlund (Dordrecht: Springer, 2011), pp. 746–48

Index

abaton: 27, 113
Acta Theclae (also Acta Pauli et Theclae): 57–59, 63
Aegae: 43, 50, 58, 61–70, 102, 151
Aelian: 44, 110
Aelius Aristides: 26–27, 29, 31, 44, 49–50, 126, 169, 213, 224, 251, 263
Alexandria, Alexandrian: 31, 36, 39, 58, 70, 80–90, 100–01, 118, 130, 163, 179–80, 186, 189, 195, 209–10, 212, 217, 247, 249, 253, 256
Amphiaraus: 22, 40, 112–14, 212, 289
amulet: 92, 119–20, 119
anargyroi: 37, 68, 75, 79–80, 98
Apollo (Phoebus, Loxias): 23–25, 30, 38, 60, 65, 66, 88, 113, 151, 224, 264
archive (of miracle records): 14, 31, 48–51, 109, 143–44, 178–79
aretalogy: 14, 44–45, 179, 193, 226, 285
Arian, Arius, Arianism: 88–90, 135, 195, 254, 278, 280–81, 284
Artemis: 23, 24, 234
Asclepieion
　of Aegae: 61, 64–67
　of Alexandria: 83
　of Athens: 37, 51, 98, 109-110
　of Corinth: 36
　of Cos: 111
　of Epidaurus: 25–28, 40, 51, 34, 94, 194
　of Pergamon: 36, 49-50
　of Piraeus: 37
　of Rome, near the Bath of Traian: 49
　of Troizen: 51
Asia Minor: 11, 48, 57–58, 68, 265, 280
Athena: 61–62, 152, 224, 231, 234
Athens: 37, 61, 98, 108–09, 112, 146, 273
Augustine, Saint: 35, 51, 210, 247

Blachernai (quarter of Constantinople): 58, 76, 95–96

Chalcedonian (synod, credo): 56, 87, 129, 189, 209–10, 212, 235, 278–84
Cheiron: 23, 30
Christ (Jesus), as healer: 13, 22, 32–34, 36, 54, 65, 120, 127–30, 133, 151, 225, 227, 234, 247–49, 252, 283, 290–91
chthonic: 23, 27, 60, 289
cleaning (ritual cleansing, ablution): 247, 264–65
confession stelai see stelai
conversion: 130, 135, 194, 202, 253, 267–69, 272–75, 277–79
Coronis: 23–24
Cos: 30, 65, 107, 111
cult statues, appearing in dream: 28, 126–27, 224
Cyril of Alexandria: 80–85, 170
Cyril of Scythopolis: 223
Cyrrhus: 67, 69–71, 79, 98–99, 204

326   INDEX

Delphoi, Delphic 24–25, 50, 65, 80, 150, 261
Demetrius, Saint: 55, 99–100, 114
Dioscuri (Castor, Pollux): 73–74, 154, 206, 219, 269
Diocletian: 49, 67–68, 90
Dyophysite:186, 280–82
disguise (healers appearing in): 28, 97, 122, 127, 186, 232, 235, 282–83
divination: 12, 22, 34–35, 49, 224, 243
    oracles, oracular: 12, 21–22, 29, 49–50, 58, 60, 62, 65–66, 151, 178, 224, 243, 279
Dometius, Saint: 98–99, 292
Dor, Doura: 38
drugs, use of 21, 29–30, 80, 264

encomium: 79, 213–15
Epidaurus: 23–28, 30, 32, 40, 48, 50–51, 65, 107, 112, 136, 151, 213, 219, 228, 232, 241, 260, 290
epiphany: 12, 21, 24, 28, 48–49, 101, 108, 115, 143, 220, 242, 250, 260
Eucharist (communion), seen in a dream or as part of a miracle: 189, 212, 226, 235, 258, 268, 278–79, 282–84
eulogies, *eulogia*: 13, 27, 111, 120, 132–33, 146

Febronia, Saint: 90, 92, 275
Felix IV, Pope 72
folk motifs, folklore: 17, 141, 168, 176, 219–20

Galen, Galenic: 30–31, 33, 246, 248, 257–58, 266, 274–75
genre, hagiography 14, 43–48, 55–56, 79, 176, 198, 254, 285
George of Picida 248
Gesius: 163, 211, 256–57, 270
Gospel: 14, 16, 54, 142, 170

Herodotus: 47–48, 137, 143–44, 150, 152, 156, 180,189, 193, 195–96
heroes: 12, 22– 24, 40, 52–53, 60, 109, 151, 271
Hippocrates, Hippocratic medicine: 12, 30–31, 35, 80, 224, 246, 248, 251, 257, 259, 266, 275
Homer, Homeric: 21, 24, 47, 60, 139,158, 185–86, 189, 196, 225, 237, 269, 286
hospitals: 38, 91,180, 187, 248–49, 252, 254, 287

Iamata (healing narratives) *see* stelai
icons, healing: 121–26, 128–32
initiation, initiate: 241, 268, 283
Isaiah, prophet as incubation healer: 35, 82, 96
Iseion, temple of Isis: 80, 81, 261
Isis: 22, 35, 50, 52, 80–82, 84, 127, 151, 215, 242, 245, 275
Isocasius: 63,163, 195, 269
Iulius Apellas: 169

Jerome: 39, 82, 248
Jerusalem: 39, 54–55, 59, 84–86, 90, 96, 110, 179, 212, 248–49, 282
John Moschus: 69, 86, 180, 186, 215
John the Almsgiver: 86,180, 189, 195, 215
Julian, Empreror: 41, 65–67, 82, 88–89, 261
Julian of Halicarnassus: 130, 282, 284

lamp-oil, wax, kerote, as miraculous medicine: 53, 92, 95, 116, 118, 120, 123–25, 146–47, 198, 231, 286
Lebadea: 22, 289
Lebena: 108–09, 114, 169, 219, 242

Libanius: 66–67
libelli miraculorum: 14, 51, 210

Maxentius, basilica of: 72–73
Menas, Saint: 52, 57, 78, 80, 100–01, 103, 115, 118, 121, 156, 212, 215, 239, 257
Menouthis (Abukyr): 54, 80–85, 87, 101, 118, 131, 164, 169, 172–73, 180, 211, 233, 290
Michael (archangel), as incubation healer: 79, 97–98
Monophysite: 58, 79, 82, 87, 99, 101, 186, 189, 209–10, 212, 273, 278, 280, 282–84
Moses: 40, 241, 257, 275
Muslim (Islam) incubation: 11–12

Neilos of Ancyra: 249
Nestorius, Nestorian: 99, 280–81, 284
New Testament, miracles in: 18, 36, 53, 220
New Testament studies: 16, 140–42, 171

offering (thanksgiving gift): 44, 75, 108, 110, 115–16, 120, 133, 143, 147–48, 233–34
Old Testament: 141, 169, 238, 245–46, 265, 272
Oribasius: 65, 261, 274
Oropos: 22, 108, 112
Orthodox
Oxeia, quarter of Constantinople: 90–91, 165, 168, 172, 195

paideia: 17, 63, 84, 189, 196, 261
pannychis (all-night vigil): 92–94, 116, 145–48, 155, 157–58, 165, 187–89, 195, 279
Paul, Saint: 40, 57, 72, 120, 195

Pergamon: 27–28, 30–31, 36, 50, 64–65, 151, 169, 251, 263
Pheremma: 68–70, 79, 203–04
philoponoi: 163, 207
Ploutos, of Aristophanes: 26, 252.
pollution, miasma: 247, 263–65
propaganda, theological: 15, 17–18, 87, 93, 140, 177, 234, 266, 278, 280, 284–85
psychosomatic: 26, 35
purity, purification (ritual): 11, 26–27, 34, 264–65

Romanos the Melodist: 146

sacrifice: 11, 26–27, 39, 64, 110, 233, 264
salvation: 54, 207, 245, 249, 256, 270
Santa Maria Antiqua (church in Rome): 73, 85, 92, 193
Sarpedonius: 50, 60–63, 143, 151, 201–02, 267–69, 271
Seleucia: 57–59, 61–63, 135, 144, 153, 172–73, 179, 180, 182–83, 189–95, 200, 202, 225, 271–72, 278
Serapis, Serapeion: 22, 36, 39, 44, 48, 50, 70, 80–81, 87, 98, 178, 215, 241, 261
Soter, Saviour: 25, 32–33, 36, 61, 64–65, 98, 130, 247, 256, 283
stelai
  confession stelai: 48, 113–14, 265
  of Epidaurus (incl. *Iamata*): 25–26, 28, 43, 48–49, 51, 107, 109–10, 112–14, 117, 120, 135–36, 140, 142, 169, 171, 193–94, 232, 264
surgery, in miracles: 29–30, 127, 249, 254, 256, 260, 265
Symeon Stylite the Younger, Saint: 27, 123, 132–33, 230, 275

Theodore of Sykeon, Saint: 126, 132, 249, 292
Theodoret (of Cyrrhus): 70, 88, 99, 111, 189, 280
Theophilus (patriarch of Alexandria): 81, 83
Therapon, Saint: 55, 94–95, 114, 187
Tiber Island: 29, 38, 43, 109, 169
tomb of Asclepius: 40
Tricca: 24
Trophonius: 22, 24, 27, 40, 179, 289

votives, ex votos: 15, 22, 25, 31, 43–44, 48–50, 88, 92, 107–18, 121, 133, 135–36, 147, 150, 161, 171, 209, 211, 213, 229, 260, 291
    anatomical: 108–09, 111–12
    commemorative: 133–34, 136, 161
    invocational: 110–11, 120, 133

Zeus: 24, 33, 39, 113, 151